Places in Motion

PLACES IN MOTION

The Fluid Identities of Temples, Images, and Pilgrims

JACOB N. KINNARD

OXFORD
UNIVERSITY PRESS

OXFORD
UNIVERSITY PRESS

Oxford University Press is a department of the University of Oxford.
It furthers the University's objective of excellence in research, scholarship,
and education by publishing worldwide.

Oxford New York
Auckland Cape Town Dar es Salaam Hong Kong Karachi
Kuala Lumpur Madrid Melbourne Mexico City Nairobi
New Delhi Shanghai Taipei Toronto

With offices in
Argentina Austria Brazil Chile Czech Republic France Greece
Guatemala Hungary Italy Japan Poland Portugal Singapore
South Korea Switzerland Thailand Turkey Ukraine Vietnam

Published in the United States of America by
Oxford University Press
198 Madison Avenue, New York, NY 10016

Library of Congress Cataloging-in-Publication Data

Cataloging in Publication data is on file with the Library of Congress

ISBN 978–0–19–935965–3 (hbk.); 978–0–19–935966–0 (pbk.)

1 3 5 7 9 8 6 4 2
Printed in the United States of America
on acid-free paper

For Megan

Contents

Preface: The Questions of Places ix

Acknowledgments xxi

1. Place, Contestation, and the Complexities of Agency 1

2. Power Fallen from the Sky 27

3. The Polyvalent *Pādas* of Viṣṇu and the Buddha 56

4. The Drama of Viṣṇu and the Buddha at Bodhgayā 80

5. Bodhgayā, UNESCO, and the Ambiguities of Preservation 117

6. The Power and the Politics of Emplacement 145

7. Public Space or Sacred Place? 169

8. Fences and Walls: A Not-So-Final Reflection on Preservations, Prohibitions, and Places in Motion 187

Notes 193

Bibliography 237

Index 261

Preface: The Questions of Places

> *This is a call, then, for attention to religious messiness, to multiplicities, to seeing religious spaces as always, inevitably, and profoundly intersected by things brought into them from outside, things that bear their own histories, complexities, meanings different from those offered within the religious space.*
>
> —ROBERT ORSI[1]

> *The same place at the same moment will be experienced differently by different people; the same place, at different moments, will be experienced differently by the same person; the same person may even, at a given moment, hold conflicting feelings about a place. When, in addition, one considers the variable effects of historical and cultural particularity, the permutations on how people interact with place and landscape are almost unending, and the possibilities for disagreement about, and contest over, landscape are equally so.*
>
> —BARBARA BENDER[2]

ON A BLAZING morning in June of 1995, I boarded a small regional bus in Bodhgayā, in the north Indian state of Bihar, for a two-hour ride to Rājgīr. I was finishing research on a project on medieval Buddhist art and was stopping in Rājgīr on my way to see the ruins of Nālaṇḍā, which is the site of what was one of the largest and most important Buddhist monasteries in medieval India. Rājgīr is a famous Buddhist site as well: in the Pāli Canon, it is mentioned as the place where the Buddha, after attaining enlightenment at Bodhgayā, spent several months meditating and teaching—he is said to have delivered the "Heart Sutra" in Rājgīr, at "Vulture's Peak." He also is said to have converted King Bimbisara, one of the first royal patrons of Buddhism, at Rājgīr. It is also the site of the First Buddhist Council. Although it is not certain when it became a significant pilgrimage place for Buddhists, the Chinese pilgrim Faxian saw it as important enough that he visited the site in the fourth century C.E. as part of his grand tour of Buddhist sites in India. Here is his description:

> Entering the valley, and keeping along the mountains on the south-east, after ascending fifteen le, (the travellers) came to mount Gridhra-kuta. Three le before you reach the top, there is a cavern in the rocks, facing the south, in which Buddha sat in meditation. Thirty paces to the north-west there is another, where Ananda was sitting in meditation, when the deva Mara Pisuna, having assumed the form of a large vulture, took his place in front of the cavern, and frightened the disciple. Then Buddha, by his mysterious, supernatural power, made a cleft in the rock, introduced his hand, and stroked Ananda's shoulder, so that his fear immediately died. The footprints of the bird and the cleft for (Buddha's) hand are still there, and hence comes the name of "The Hill of the Vulture Cavern."[3]

One of the images on which I was working at the time was the *Aṣṭamahāpratiharya*, the depiction of the eight great pilgrimage places associated with the life of the Buddha that seem to have presented a kind of virtual pilgrimage route of many of the places that Faxian visited;[4] although most Buddhists could not practically visit all of these sites, which would have required months, if not years, of grueling and dangerous travel, they could experience them via the sculptural representation of the group. All of these places are located in northeastern and north central India, and I had hoped to visit each one during my research (Bodhgayā and Nālaṇdā are both included). In the sculptural depiction of Rājgīr, it is the place where the Buddha tames the wild elephant Nilagiri, who has been unleashed to trample the Buddha by the schismatic monk Devadatta.

Despite its importance in Buddhist literature and art, there was not much to the town, as I remember—a scattering of stalls for the pilgrims and tourists. With some difficulty I was able to discern the way to Vulture's Peak and set out to climb it. It was very hot and very dry, the monsoons having not yet begun, and I remember feeling that I was crazy for setting out. It was also not pilgrimage season, for good reason, given the pounding heat. As I climbed, there wasn't another person in sight, a rare thing in India, and I felt rather anxious, worried that I was climbing the wrong hill, since the directions I was able to get consisted of a vague wave in the direction of a rocky hill. I was perhaps half way up when the trail suddenly became crowded with young men on their way down. They were all wearing loose white pants and shirts, and each had an identical red scarf wrapped around his shoulders with images of Śiva on it. After passing dozens of these young men, who were staring at me as if I were some sort of alien creature, I finally stopped one of them and asked what they were doing there. "We have come to visit Buddha!" he shouted, and then loudly bellowed "Jai Śiva! Śankar! Jai Māhadev!" which was then echoed up and down the trail as his fellow pilgrims returned the call.

What were these Śaiva pilgrims doing there? Why were they visiting a Buddhist site? I had seen Vaiṣṇava pilgrims at Bodhgayā, certainly, but the presence of these Śaivas puzzled me. Rājgīr is a pilgrimage town, and pilgrims from a number of different strands of Hinduism, as well as Buddhists and sometimes Muslims, visit the seven peaks and the various temples located in the area. This much I knew before my trip, but I had assumed that pilgrims would visit the places specifically associated with their own religious tradition—Hindus to the Hindu sites, Jains to the Jain sites, and so on. What I didn't understand was why Śaivas would have any interest in a Buddhist place.

Looking back, I am a little embarrassed at my surprise at seeing these young Śaiva pilgrims on Vulture's Peak. Not because I didn't realize that Śaivas visited the site, which was an acceptable kind of ignorance—and I must admit that I still do not know if they were visiting as part of a standard pilgrimage route, or if they had simply made a slight detour for some other reason (such as simple curiosity). There is often an ad hoc aspect to pilgrimage in India, as there is elsewhere. Individual pilgrims make little side trips, sometimes for what we might label "religious" reasons, sometimes for what seems more like tourism. No, I am not chagrined by my ignorance of the details here, but rather by my surprise at thinking these Śaivas didn't belong, that they were, essentially, trespassing on Buddhist ground. It is this kind of World Religions view of what people should and should not do that troubles me still, a discomfort with the fact that even after years of studying comparative religions, I could so easily fall into such an essentialist division of the religious world.

Weeks after my climb up Vulture's Peak, I returned to Bodhgayā and stayed for several more weeks. I had essentially finished my work there but stayed in part because I now found myself looking at the people who milled around the great Mahābodhi temple with very different eyes. During my prior visits to Bodhgayā, I had had this idea that there were three sorts of people who traveled there: Buddhists, Hindus, and foreign tourists. However, the more time I spent there actually paying attention to who these people actually were and what they were doing in the temple's environs, the more I realized how wrongheaded this neat division was. First, there were the Buddhists. Although I am not an anthropologist and was doing archaeological and art historical research at Bodhgayā, I had spent enough time there that it was obvious to me, just on the surface, that not all Buddhist pilgrims were the same. There were Tibetans, Burmese, Japanese, Sri Lankas, and others. There was also a sizeable Ambedkar, or Dalit, Buddhist presence at Bodhgayā. These are the formerly untouchable Hindus who, following the example of A. K. Ambedkar—one of the drafters of the Indian Constitution and the country's first Law Minister, who became a Buddhist in 1956 to protest the harsh caste divisions in India—have converted to Buddhism. The Hindu pilgrims, likewise, were not uniform: I had earlier assumed that they were Vaiṣṇavas who had come to the region to visit Gayā, but I began to notice a sizeable number of Śaivas at Bodhgayā as well. There were also many Indians who seemed simply to be on holiday, visiting this significant archaeological site as tourists. And then there were the Western tourists, some of whom had come on tour buses, some of whom were backpackers, and some of whom were clearly Buddhists and had come as pilgrims, and so were not really tourists at all.

I had, over the course of several years, probably spent a total of two months in Bodhgayā, but now, having had something of an epiphany on Vulture's Peak in Rājgīr, I was struck by the fact that I had been paying attention to almost nothing other than Buddhist iconography. I realized that I'd barely noticed the Hindus at Bodhgayā, nor paid any sort of attention to what they actually did there. After my trip to Rājgīr, it was clear to me that my understanding of Bodhgayā as a religious place, and my assumptions about the sorts of religious people who visited it, needed serious revisions. So once I finished my book on Buddhist art, I turned my attention to the complex social history of Bodhgayā, and in particular to the colonial construction of it as the center of the Buddhist world—largely to the exclusion of the Hindus who also claimed it as a pilgrimage place. Several of the chapters that make up this book are the result of that research.

The more I worked on Bodhgayā, though, the more I became convinced that I needed to address a larger issue in the study of religions: namely, the easy assumptions that we—academics and non-academics alike—adopt about the singular, static identities of religious people, religious objects, and religiously significant places. When a person we identify as a Vaiṣṇava Hindu goes to a place we identify as a Buddhist temple and performs an act we identify as a Hindu ritual that is directed toward an object that we identify as a Buddhist image, what is going on? And what about when, a few moments later, a Buddhist performs a different ritual act before the very same image? Or what about when a Hindu goes to a Muslim tomb to pray to a Sufi saint? Or when a Christian in South India prays before an image of Kṛṣṇa? Who is the "we" doing the identifying here, and what sorts of political and social complexities are masked by the labels we affix to people and places? What are the power dynamics in the affixing of such labels?

These are complicated questions, certainly, and I offer up no simple answers in the pages that follow. Rather, it is the questions themselves that I find most interesting, and in the chapters that make up this book I explore specific instances of what I see as the vibrant messiness of religious practice, the multivocality of religious objects, the fluid and hybrid dynamics of religious places, and the shifting and tangled identities of religious actors. When I first began to teach comparative religions, these issues seemed far less complicated to me than they do now. Indeed, the more I know about the religions on which I write and about which I teach, the more I think that many of the ways we talk and write about such matters are simply wrongheaded, and do not line up with the ways in which religions have played out on the ground. For instance, in my introductory classes—inevitably some variation of "World Religions"—I had long been of the habit of beginning each section on each individual religion with a basic question: What are the minimal conditions to be a Hindu, or a Buddhist, or a Christian? This struck me as a good way to think about identity and belonging, to think about the beliefs or practices that all members of a particular religion held in common.

When I took up my current position at Iliff School of Theology, after having spent a decade teaching in liberal arts colleges, I was immediately confronted with the fallaciousness of my thinking. "What are the minimal conditions for being a Christian?" I asked on my first day of teaching. I expected my students—liberal Protestants, mostly—to give the usual answer: belief and faith that Christ is who Christians say he is. I was met, however, with puzzled looks and wrinkled noses. Silence. So I offered up a possibility: "How about belief that Jesus Christ died for your sins? That faith in him guarantees salvation? Or how about baptism—you're dipped and you're in." Someone snickered, "Seriously?" A student in the back shouted, "I don't believe that!" A cacophony of dissent, which was followed by a long discussion—lesson plan scrapped—about what it means to be a Christian *and* a liberal, or *and* a lesbian, or *and* a gay black man, or—and this one still intrigues and puzzles and challenges me—a Christian *and* an atheist. For my students, there could be no minimal conditions for religious identity: Christian identity for them is fluid and contextual and highly subjective, all the way down.

The Śaiva pilgrims I encountered on Vulture's Peak were certainly Hindus, and they were certainly Śaivas. Visiting what is labeled a Buddhist place did not change that. Hindus who perform *pūjās* to what was originally constructed as an image of the Buddha do not change that original identity. However, for the practitioner the identity of the image or the temple is, at least temporarily, changed. It is, for the Hindu, an image of Viṣṇu. And it is also an image of the Buddha. This is complicated. I am reminded of this each day as I drive home from my office: I pass a condominium building that was until a few years ago a Methodist church. It still looks like a church, but it is clearly no longer a church, having been converted into two very expensive condominiums. I wonder about the space, about how "churchy" it still feels inside; I wonder about the people who live there, and whether is it important to them that they live in what used to be a church; I wonder if it feels like a different sort of living space than, say, a tract house on a cul-de-sac in the suburbs, and what, really, the difference is.

I have found it very useful to think with a rather large grouping of theorists while writing this book. Some I have engaged quite explicitly, and they appear throughout these chapters; others have informed my thinking in significant ways but make only cameo appearances in the text, and some do not appear at all except in the bibliography. I think of all of these theorists, and really everyone I have read in relationship to writing this book, as part of the conversation. It is, to my mind, a more interesting and engaging conversation because there are so many people talking, but I recognize that some readers will find this sort of methodological eclecticism frustrating, wishing that I had, instead, relied more heavily and consistently on only one or two theorists.

In this regard, I am in agreement with Edward Soja, himself one of the most influential recent writers on space and place—and very much one of the people I have thought with while writing this book—who takes an intentionally interdisciplinary and trans-theoretical approach in his work, and who is quite explicit about his use of other theorists. Soja urges us to "set aside the demands to make an either/or choice and contemplate instead the possibility of a both/and also logic, one that not only permits but encourages a creative combination of postmodernist and modernist perspectives, even when a specific form of postmodernism is being highlighted...."[5] Borrowing from Henri Lefebvre, Soja uses the term transdisciplinary to describe his methodology, by which he means the interplay of historicality, sociality, and spatiality. This is Soja's rewording of Lefebvre, who describes his own methodology as *un dialectique de triplicitè*, a "triple dialectic." I do not claim to be anywhere near as sophisticated a thinker as Soja (or Lefebvre!) but my own multidisciplinary approach has been an intentional and really unavoidable move on my part. This is simply how I think through the issues in which I am interested. I also believe that we better understand the kinds of places that I discuss when we approach them from multiple directions. Indeed, much as we see and experience a temple or a church differently when we approach it from the front or the back, or sit in the center or the side, so too do I think we understand these places better when we engage a variety of interpretive and analytical positions.

The various places that I discuss here are what we might call, borrowing Soja's terminology—which he in turn explicitly borrows from Lefebvre—Firstplaces. That is, they are physical places, places that are made up of material—buildings and walkways and trees and dirt. John Berquist has called these "geophysical realities... the concrete materiality of spatial forms... things that can be empirically mapped."[6] But through human use these places become what Soja calls Thirdspace—they exist not only in the physical realm, but also in practice and ideology. A great deal has been written on Soja's notion of Thirdspace; it is a complex, slippery, and often frustrating concept. That said, I have very much had the idea in my head as I have written these chapters. In Thirdspace, Soja posits, things come together and interact, intertwine, and tangle: "subjectivity and objectivity, the abstract and the concrete, the real and the imagined, the knowable and the unimaginable, the repetitive and the differential, structure and agency, mind and body, consciousness and the unconscious, the disciplined and the transdisciplinary, everyday life and unending history."[7] Another way to put this is that religiously significant places—Ayodhya, Bodhgayā, Mato Tipila, Karbala, and so on—become overdetermined through use and association, and thus are freighted with all sorts of social and political and mythological and theological significances.

These places also can be understood as what Soja calls Secondspace, by which he means imagined space, or "ideas about space, . . . thoughtful re-presentations of human spatiality in mental or cognitive forms."[8] Soja's Secondspace is the Bodhgayā in Edwin Arnold's imagination, the idealized version of this elemental Buddhist place that I discuss in Chapter 4, a Buddhist Jerusalem that Arnold had formed through reading Buddhist texts in his study in London, an imagined place that very much clashed, when he finally made his pilgrimage, with the messy, lived Thirdspace—and Firstspace as well—reality that he encountered in India. Karbala could also be understood as Secondspace, for as will become evident in Chapter 6, Karbala is both a physical place—a Firstspace—as well as a highly charged idea, a kind of orienting virtual place that is at the very core of Shi'a Muslim identity. Karbala is also very much a Thirdspace in Soja's sense. Likewise, the area in lower Manhattan known as Ground Zero after the attacks on September 11, 2001, which is the topic of Chapter 2, has come to occupy a metaphorical place in American discourse and imagination, and so it too could be understood to be Secondspace (as well, again, as Firstspace, and Thirdspace). What all of this highlights, I think, is that places are very much not limited to their physical dimensions, to the stone and steel with which they are constructed. They become embedded in our individual and collective imaginations, and as such become part of the ongoing formation of our identities. The early nineteenth-century house I lived in for the first seven years of my life may no longer physically exist—this I do not know, actually—but it is very much present in my imagination and a part of my sense of myself.

Although it may not always seem to be the case, I have actually tried to downplay the theoretical in these chapters, have tried to resist the academic urge to inject theory into every paragraph. This is not a book about Soja, nor is it an extended application of his theoretical position (or, more properly, positions). It is my hope that more theoretically inclined readers will hear Soja and Lefebvre and Foucault and Heidegger and many others with whom I have thought at critical junctures, but hear them as part of, and not as dominating, the conversation.

This is very much intended to be an inter- and intra-disciplinary book, and as I have said, a theoretically eclectic one. Indeed, in the second volume of his trilogy on space and place, *Thirdspace: Journeys to Los Angeles and Other Real-and-Imagined Places*, Soja makes what I think is an elegant defense of this sort of methodological and theoretical promiscuity (as it has sometimes been derisively called). What he describes as his "creative combination of postmodernist and modernist perspectives" is intended to be a methodological invitation—and not, I think, a dogmatically prescribed method or theory:

> It is instead an efficient invitation to enter a space of extraordinary openness, a place of critical exchange where the geographical imagination can be expanded to encompass a multiplicity of perspectives that have heretofore been considered by the epistemological referees to be incompatible, uncombinable.[9]

One of my own teachers, Wendy Doniger, has used the image of the bricoleur—which she in turn has borrowed, as have many others, from Claude Lévi-Strauss—to describe what she thinks is the most appropriate methodological stance for the scholar of religion: we are jacks-of-all-trades, using whatever tools we have at our disposal to get the job done.[10]

The job, in this case, is comparison. Jonathan Z. Smith, who along with Pierre Bourdieu often dominates my particular scholarly conversation, has emphasized throughout his work that comparison is a matter of difference:

> As Lévi-Strauss, among others, has convincingly demonstrated, when we confront difference we do not encounter irrationality or bad faith but rather the very essence of thought. Meaning is made possible by difference. Yet thought seeks to bring together what thought necessarily takes apart by means of a dynamic process of disassemblage and reassemblage, which results in an object no longer natural but rather social, no longer factual but rather intellectual. Relations are discovered and reconstituted through projects of differentiation.[11]

Difference is where the interest lies, as I find I must frequently remind my students, who tend to want to stop at surface similarities. Although they often wish to see Christianity in Buddhism, to see the Buddha or Kṛṣṇa as a Christ figure, it is in the differences between the two traditions or figures where the conversation gets interesting. Again, for anyone who has read Smith, this is the foundation upon which all of his work is based.

That said, Smith has also pointed out that comparison begins with some sense of similarity—otherwise there would be no conversation. So what is the logic of comparing the places that I discuss in the following chapters? All of these places are religiously significant; they are what many people call sacred places. This commonality is what gets the conversation going: in what way sacred, though? sacred for whom? sacred why? I will have significantly more to say about the sacred later in the book, but I want to emphasize at the outset that these places are conceived as sacred by someone. As Rob Shields puts it, "Sites are never simply locations. Rather, they are sites for someone, and of something."[12] My point is perhaps too obvious, but I shall make it nonetheless: sacred is a designation, an argument to be made. Individuals and communities make places sacred. I am paraphrasing Smith here, but I want to push this, and ask, bluntly and basically: what do we get, in the end, by comparing these places, by thinking of these places—and the objects that are placed in and at them which make them sacred—in relation to one another? What sort of relation are we talking about?

Thinking about the various theoretical discussions of space that are out there—and theorizing about space has, since Lefebrve and then Soja's work on place and space, become its own academic cottage industry—it is tempting to offer up a general theory of the places I discuss, a theory that would in some way unify my discussion, and neatly answer my questions.[13] I find it difficult to imagine what such a theory might look like, though—these are all Thirdspaces...they are messy, conflicted, inconsistent...and that is the nature of such places. But that is not a theory—that is simply a fact. I am not sure that a theory would be possible here, precisely because these places are in motion and are constantly changing in relation to the complex agents who make and use and transform them. In this sense, Soja's Thirdspace is a good orienting point for me, but again, I am not sure that it is so much a theory as a descriptive and analytical category: "Thirdspace is a purposefully tentative and flexible term that attempts to capture what is actually a constantly shifting and changing milieu of ideas, events, appearances, and meanings."[14] As such, it is an appropriate way to think about what I call places in motion. Thus what I strive for here is the application of theories as they are useful, as they help us understand these places. I thus align myself with Shields, when he writes at the beginning of his own ruminations on space and place: "This is an exploratory work, a book of reappraisals and rereadings of the taken-for-granted, which sets out to cover a great deal of terrain and to produce a workable mapping of the cultural importance of the spatial."[15] This is an iteration that I must say I wish I had come up with on my own.

Thus a way to think about how the different places I discuss relate to each other is that they are places on a conceptual map, a map that I have constructed, a map that is not a reflection of the way things actually are (as if any map is ever that). I have in mind here a kind of thematic map, or the kind of map I can conjure up on the GPS in my car, one that locates, say, gas stations or hospitals or state parks. The map itself is what puts these places in relation to one another. Put another way, contested conceptions of religiously significant places and objects is what brings these various examples together. With a different map there would be a different organizational, or relational, logic. What do the shrines of John the Baptist and Hussein's heads at the Great Mosque of Damascus have to do with, say, Ground Zero or Ayodhya or Mato Tipila? They are all religiously charged places of contestation. Sometimes it is sacredness itself that is contested: one group simply does not recognize or accept the claim of sacredness (as is the case at Mato Tipila and, to a degree, Ground Zero). More typically, though, sacrality is claimed by more than one group, and so it is not so much the place's sacrality itself that is at issue, but what sort of sacrality it is. Whose sacred is it?

It is this question that makes me often go back to that encounter with the Śaiva pilgrims on Vulture's Peak; I am struck, still, by how very little I know about why they were there and what they did. Did they perform a *pūjā* to the image of the Buddha? Did they see the image as an image from another religion, or did they see it as a *mūrti* of Viṣṇu, as an embodiment of the god on earth? What sites had they visited before their climb, and where were they going next?

When I returned to Bodhgayā after my time in Rajgir, I spent a great deal of time talking with pilgrims, particularly Hindu pilgrims. "Why are you worshipping this image?" I would ask. Retrospectively it was at the very least a decidedly unsubtle question: did they see the image as an image, or as a *mūrti*, as a living god? "Is it the Buddha, or Viṣṇu?" Again, wrong question, because I assumed at the time that it had to be one or the other. Open any World Religions textbook, and there will be a chapter on Hinduism, followed by a chapter on Buddhism. Some will explain that Buddhism grew out of, or broke away from Hinduism.

They are separate religions—chapter four, and then chapter five. But is that in fact how people have experienced these traditions, on the ground? Is that how the places associated with these traditions have been experienced? So many questions. In the end, it is these questions, and so many others, that have informed my study of religions. "What's going on here?" This is the first question I bring to each of the places I discuss in this book.

Acknowledgments

THIS BOOK IS very much the product of what has seemed a long, sometimes meandering conversation with a great many people. I am, first of all, grateful to my students at both Iliff School of Theology and the University of Denver who have read early iterations of several of these chapters in my Comparative Religions seminars. In particular, I'd like to thank Mary Ragan, Kit Lim, Katherine Rousseau, Donnie Featherstone, Patrick Soch, Wendy Felese, Christa Schwind, and Sophia Shafi (who later became a colleague and offered many suggestions for Chapter Six) for their very thoughtful comments and suggestions. Catherine Orsborn worked with me on editing these chapters and compiling the bibliography, and I thank her for her diligence and care. Michael Hemenway has been both a great conversation partner about a wide range of topics relevant to this project and a technological guru. I am also grateful to my colleagues at Iliff for their careful readings of some of these chapters, particularly Ted Vial, Sheila Devaney, and Edward Antonio—I thank them for confirming the true value of comparative thinking. Mark George, with whom I have co-taught a seminar on Space and Place several times, has pushed me in vital ways and helped me think through and refine my own position on place. I had many conversations with Pam Eisenbaum about things I was thinking through for Chapter Six, and she pointed me to an article by Robert Markham that, in turn, pointed me in a number of useful directions. I am also grateful for the feedback and critique I have been given in the various forums where I have presented this work: colleagues too numerous to mention at the AAR, SAR, AAS, and SSSR, and those who participated in the Material Objects and Performance Events conference at the North Carolina Center for South Asia Studies. I benefited tremendously from the conversations about related matters at the three Iconic Books Seminars, sponsored by the Ray Smith Symposium of the College of Arts and Sciences at Syracuse University; thank you, especially, James

Watts, for inviting me and for leading these discussions. I presented a version of Chapter Five at the Meaningful Space conference in Zurich, and am grateful to Mark George and Daria Pezzoli-Olgiati for inviting me, and to the various participants who offered insightful critiques of that early draft. At Oxford University Press, Cynthia Read has been a wise and wry counsel and has guided this project with a deft and firm hand. Also at Oxford Charlotte Steinhardt has been a model of attentiveness and efficiency. I am also very grateful to the three anonymous readers for Oxford University Press, and their careful readings of the manuscript and their insightful suggestions.

In all of my academic work I have been consistently mindful of two of my teachers: John Holt, who introduced me to South Asia and who first pointed me toward the Turners as a freshman at Bowdoin College and who has been a consistently helpful critical voice in my ear; and Frank Reynolds, who taught me how to be a scholar and a colleague, in the broadest sense, when I was at the University of Chicago and for whom I think I am always, fundamentally, writing.

Finally, I want to thank my family for putting up with me as I at times wrestled with this book. I dedicate this to Megan Ring, for giving me the space and encouragement I have needed, and without whom, well, this never would have been.

Places in Motion

1

Place, Contestation, and the Complexities of Agency

1.1 Communitas, *Conflict, and Context*

Pilgrimage, then, offers liberation from profane social structures that are symbiotic with a specific religious system, but they do this only in order to intensify the pilgrim's attachment to his own religion, often in fanatical opposition to other religions.

—VICTOR AND EDITH TURNER[1]

Instead of choosing between starkly opposed instrumentalist and primordialist accounts, however, students of South Asia's Hindu-Muslim conflicts of ethnic mobilization, of nationalism, indeed of contentious politics in general can adopt a third alternative: they can recognize the conversational character of contention. They can examine such a conversation's location in continuously negotiated interchanges among specific interlocutors, its constraint and mediation by historically accumulated understandings concerning identities and relations of the parties, its incessant modification of those identities and relations, hence its crucial causal contribution to interactions that instrumentalists explain on the basis of individual or collective interests and primordialists explain on the basis of deeply grounded individual or collective sentiments.

—CHARLES TILLY[2]

[A]gents are ceaselessly occupied in the negotiation of their own identity.

—PIERRE BOURDIEU[3]

IT SEEMS ALMOST self-evident to say that religiously charged places and spaces, as well as the images that are associated with them, become powerful because they are made powerful. That is to say that there is nothing inherently sacred about any place or space or physical object; human agents give them power and maintain that power. As Jonathan Z. Smith reminds us, "Human beings are placed, they bring place into being."[4] Durkheim really said as much over a century ago, although many scholars working in the field of religious studies seem to have forgotten—or, more likely, ignored—this basic point, and still seem under the haze of a kind of Eliadian hangover that makes the sacred seem like some sort of timeless essence.[5] We have to recognize, however, that there is also nothing simple about the dynamics of the power of places, nor about the complex sorts of agents who are involved with this power. So-called sacred places and spaces, and any power that they might possess, exist in and are the products of history—specific, complex, messy historical processes. As David Chidester and Edward T. Linenthal put it, "Against all the efforts of religious actors, sacred space is involuntarily entangled with the entrepreneurial, the social, the political, and other 'profane' forces."[6] Although I agree with their basic point, and their critique of the essentializing project of Eliade et al., I think the preposition "against" is incorrect here; indeed, I argue in the chapters that follow that it is precisely the competing conceptions and motivations of the various actors involved in a particular place—religious as well as secular, if that distinction has any purchase at all—that constitute it. In other words, it is not "against" at all, but "because of" such forces, messy as they are, that places are what they are. As George Marcus puts it, talking specifically about anthropology, "The idea is that any cultural identity or activity is constructed by multiple agents in varying contexts, or places," and we must develop methodologies that are "strategically conceived to represent this sort of multiplicity and to specify both intended and unintended consequences in the network of complex connections within a system of places."[7]

What places are, however, is a matter that needs some clarification at the outset. Those working in religious studies and anthropology (perhaps less so) typically employ the language of the sacred, labeling the sorts of places and spaces I discuss in this book as "sacred." I am, however, reluctant to use the language of the sacred here, in part because it is so very laden with murky and essentialist connotations, and in part because I am not at all convinced that these places are sacred, or, if they are, whether their sacrality is what is most significant (and interesting) about them. Chidester and Linenthal provide a useful review of some of the ways in which "sacred space" has been discussed by scholars of religion, including Emile Durkheim, Rudolph Otto, Gerardus van der Leeuw, Mircea Eliade, and others. They propose that we think of the sacred in two different ways, as "substantial" (Eliade, say) and as "situational" (Durkheim, say). This is a useful distinction, certainly, in the sense of thinking about the ways scholars have discussed the sacred, but I reject the notion that spaces can be sacred in any but a situational sense. Indeed, I will, when possible, avoid the term altogether and side with Claude Lévi-Strauss, who quips that the sacred "is a value of indeterminate signification, in itself empty of meaning and therefore susceptible to the reception of any meaning whatsoever."[8]

It is with the dynamics of such "reception" that I am concerned here, and the chapters that make up this book are an attempt to untangle some of the historical messiness of certain religiously charged places, and to look specifically at the dynamics of such discourse and the real consequences—including, all too frequently, violence—such discourses and practices entail. These chapters examine several shared and contested religiously charged places in the Indian subcontinent and elsewhere, and ask of each a set of broad questions: What and who has made them important, and why? How are they shared? How and why are they contested? What is at stake in their contestation? How are the particular identities of place and space established? How is individual and collective identity intertwined with space and place? In this regard, I am very much in agreement with Roger Friedland and Richard D. Hecht, who, in their discussion of the contested Temple Mount in Jerusalem, point out that sacred space is "socially constructed. Its meaning is made, and that making has implications for the doctrines which motivate those who claim it as their own." Thus the violence that is often associated with such places "cannot be understood as simply the irrational acts of desperate men.... These are not simply acts of violence. They are symbolic discourses about the status of a symbolic place."[9]

Thus one thing I need to make clear at the outset is that the battles over place and space, and the objects connected with them, are rarely simply about who controls the physical monuments or images or spaces or who has access to them, and rarely about what we conventionally call religion. Indeed, it is precisely because of the over-determined, highly charged nature of such spaces and places that they become more than physical: they are caught up in a tangle of symbolic discourse and often become markers and constituters of identity as well. Indeed, for a particular group to lay claim to such a place—to possess it, if that is possible—is to wield a great deal of symbolic capital and power. The places that I analyze here are all in some sense pilgrimage places, and as the quotation from the Turners with which I begin this chapter duly notes, pilgrimages and pilgrimage places are intimately entwined with religious identity, both personal and collective. Such places and spaces serve as indexes of religious identity, certainly, but they are also entangled in the very construction and maintenance of such identities, and this construction and maintenance is very often oppositional. In many cases, an inimical other who makes a claim on the place is constructed against whom the individual and collective self is dynamically defined. What is more, none of this is in any sense static: the identities of spaces and places, as well as the people who claim them, are fluid, shifting, and decidedly slippery phenomena. Indeed, one of the things that I will argue throughout this book is that although the western Orientalists who have studied space and place in India, in particular, have gone to great lengths to fix their identities, to demonstrate their origins, and thus to constitute them, discursively and physically, as singular and thus fundamentally monosemic, the spaces themselves, and very often the identities of the various people who lay claim to them, are inherently polysemic, dynamic, and, as I have said, fluid. These are places in motion.

It is perhaps not so difficult to imagine that the identities of temples or images might be fluid; images move about, space is often "converted" from one religion to another, building material is reused to construct different structures, and so on.[10] One might well ask, however, how an individual's identity, particularly his or her religious identity, can be fluid. Given the primacy and exclusivity of religious identity in the West, such an idea seems on its face contradictory—although on the ground this sort of fluidity is common enough, even in the West, where there are Buddhist Jews and Sufi Methodists aplenty.[11] A complex illustration of this are the Dalit Buddhist communities in India, the formerly untouchable Hindus who have converted to Buddhism and who, as we will see in Chapter 4, have relatively recently been involved in the conflict centering on the status and control of Bodhgayā. There has been and continues to be much tension and debate about their identities and the whole issue of conversion in the more general Indian political context; anti-conversion laws are periodically debated—and sometimes passed—that are in part intended to "fix" their identity as Hindu.[12]

This invocation of the fluidity of identities is not simply a modern phenomenon, nor simply is it a post-modern conceit; as Daniel Boyarin has meticulously documented in his discussion of the "border" between Judaism and nascent Christianity in the first few centuries of the first millennium, "Christian" and "Jew" were identities that emerged through a long process of contestation. He thus argues that "identities were much less sure than they have appeared to us until now, in which the very terms of identity were being worked on and worked out."[13] Boyarin is specifically concerned with the emergence of "Christian" and "Jew"—or "Christianity" and "Judaism"—but he makes a more broadly applicable point, drawing on Homi Bhabha's articulation of hybridity, and argues that religions "are not natural kinds that have somehow split off from each other or been born of each other but are distinctions produced (and resisted) for particular purposes by particular people."[14]

This, then, points to one of the major contentions of this book: religious identity, of places and of people, is very often not fixed, not singular, and not static. Indeed, as much as World Religions textbooks teach us to divide up the world into neatly defined religious groups with singular labels—Hindu, Buddhist, Muslim, etc.—and exclusive beliefs and practices, the groups and individuals that actually are the objects of these labels are very much messier and more complex than this. It would be foolish to maintain that all religious groups and individuals are characterized by hybridity,[15] but I argue here that such hybridity (or fluidity, as I will also call it) is very much in play in a great many instances in the Indian subcontinent and elsewhere. I think it is important to point out, furthermore, that even this hybridity is fluid and contested; at times people and groups—often labeled "fundamentalists"—actively resist any notion of hybrid or fluid identity. My focus in the chapters that make up this book is more specifically on the fluidity of the identity, and identifications, of places and spaces and images, but as I argue here, this fluidity is inextricably intertwined with the issue of the religious identity (or identities) of those who participate in such places and spaces and images.

All of the places that I discuss in this book are pilgrimage places of some sort, and each of them, in very particular ways, is what we might call a "dual usage" place. By that I mean a place that is used and claimed as significant by more than one group. I begin in this first chapter with a very specific pilgrimage place in northern India, the much-analyzed pilgrimage town of Ayodhya, and I view it, fundamentally, as a charged and fluid field—a physical, symbolic, and discursive space—of contestation, and a complex locus and marker of social and religious identity. In other words, although Ayodhya is indeed a physical space, a place on a map, a city, it is also significantly more than just a place or a physically delineable space. I want to use Ayodhya, specifically, as an entrée into the ways in which different claims, contested claims, on a single place function to create the power of that place, power that is very much not naturally given—in other words, not inherently sacred. I also use Ayodhya as a kind of lens through which we might begin to see and think about the ways in which this sort of contestation over place instantiates religious identities.

1.2 The Dynamics of Communitas and the Limits of Liminality

[C]ommunitas has something "magical" about it. Subjectively there is in it the feeling of endless power.

—VICTOR TURNER[16]

The dominant mode of analysis in the study of pilgrimage places for the last forty or so years has been the imposition of the twin concepts of liminality and communitas offered up by Victor and Edith Turner. Since Victor Turner's early work on pilgrimage in the 1960s, it has been very difficult to read or to write or even to think about the subject without the residual influence of his conceptions of liminality and communitas.[17] Whether in the context of Malcolm X's journey to Mecca or Rajasthani pilgrims at Puri, the key hermeneutic concepts offered up by the Turners—the breakdown of barriers, the abandonment of social strictures and hierarchies, and the spontaneously joyful identification with one's fellow humans—have frequently emerged as the essential elements of pilgrimage and pilgrimage places. Certainly, this essentially utopian vision of humanity is not without attraction; indeed, there is something quite seductive about it. In so focusing on this peculiarly agentless formation of a value-free group identity, though, scholars who have used Turner's categories have tended to overlook another, rather obvious, component of pilgrimage and, particularly, of pilgrimage places: namely, the formulation of communal identity vis-à-vis another group, a real or created "collective other." After all, pilgrimage and pilgrimage places present opportunities not just for what Turner frequently refers to as "ludic communitas"—and here may lay the real "magic"—but also for open confrontation and physical violence.

No doubt the most prominent contemporary example of this more contested form of pilgrimage and religiously charged space is Jerusalem, where on the ground the last thing that seems evident is communitas of any sort.[18] In a different geographical and religious context, the north Indian town of Ayodhya—the mythical birthplace of the Hindu god Rāma (Hindi, Rām), and until very recently the location of an important mosque that was said to have been built by the medieval Moghul ruler Babar on the site of the "original" Hindu temple—has emerged as a pilgrimage place where there is very little evidence of such communitas, ludic or otherwise. Instead, Ayodhya has been the site of violent confrontations between the Hindus and Muslims who both claim the site as their own. In the process, Ayodhya—the overdetermined symbol and the discursive signifier as much as the physical place—has become a bellwether in the rise of what is typically called "Hindu Nationalism," and has been used as a powerful instrument in shaping the character of contemporary Hinduism itself, a character that is very much tied to both a national geography and a collective—but also necessarily exclusive—national identity.

In late 1992 and early 1993, there was an outburst of communal violence centered at Ayodhya, and over two thousand people were killed.[19] Among the crucial circumstances that led to these riots, two factors stand out that are particularly relevant here. First, there was a general attempt to forge a pan-Indian identity.[20] It might seem, at first blush, that what was intended in this process was a kind of communitas predicated on liminality—a leveling and obscuring of individual identity and difference, and a forging of a new, collective identity. To the contrary, however, this new identity, despite overtly inclusive and non-sectarian language, was often predicated on the exclusion of non-Hindu Indians, particularly Muslims. Furthermore, in the immediate years leading up to the riots a massive pilgrimage was organized—the *Rām śila pūjā*—to gather bricks from all over India. This pilgrimage, although it was consciously begun as a non-sectarian, non-caste, non-locative event—and thus explicitly and consciously intended to forge both liminality and communitas—was also intended to provoke a clash with the Muslims at Ayodhya.

The limitations of the Turnerian thesis here are glaring. First, and perhaps most basically, it emphasizes the dissolution of individual identity and the subsequent assumption of a group identity without fully considering the mechanisms and implications of this process. In other words, as much as the pilgrimage experience, broadly understood, may create and highlight a leveled kind of collective identity, it also, inherently, highlights difference. In their many works on pilgrimage, the Turners do not consider—or only consider in passing—the many cases where pilgrimage is contested, where different groups have very different claims to the same place, where place and space are situated in a highly charged political field. Indeed, in so emphasizing the formation of shared group identity, the Turners tend to overlook the fact that communitas, or for that matter any sort of shared identity, is often only possible when there is an "other" against whom the group can identify itself.[21] To be fair, part of the problem here is not with the Turners, but with the ways their work has been appropriated: so much of Victor Turner's work, in particular, is focused on the Ndembu tribe of Zambia, and thus specific to that very particular context, a context in which pilgrimage was generally not contested but was a cultural given, a highly scripted and controlled rite of passage. Nonetheless, the Turners do, especially in later works, frequently invoke other contexts—modern and premodern, industrial and agrarian—and it is in this work that the Turnerian thesis becomes particularly problematic, rather crudely universalizing, idealistic, and utopian.

It is worth asking: Why bring the Turners into the discussion at all? The Turnerian thesis has been severely critiqued from a number of angles in recent years, and given the serious flaws in its theoretical position, one might well wonder if the Turners' understanding of pilgrimage, place, and space has not had a long enough corner on the pilgrimage market, and if it is not now simply time to move on. There are certainly many other theoretical positions that prove more fruitful for understanding the dynamics of pilgrimage places, and in the chapters that follow I will put some of them to use. So, again, why bother with the Turners at all? Part of the answer is precisely because it has been so hard to see pilgrimage and pilgrimage places without the Turners. Thus it is important not merely to demonstrate that it is time to move on, but to demonstrate why. We should ask some basic questions: Is the Turnerian thesis applicable, or even useful, in contexts that do not easily fit their utopian tendencies? Is communitas possible where there is violence? Can we introduce intentionality and forethought into the equation without reducing communitas to mere wishful thinking?

In the first part of this chapter, then, I want to identify and analyze these apparent shortcomings within their context in the Turners' *oeuvre*, and I want to suggest that although there are serious flaws and substantial shortcomings in their theoretical approach, there has also been a tendency in recent years to sell the Turners short, to dismiss them rather too easily. Liminality and communitas are unquestionably romantic notions, a rather blatant exercise in wishful thinking—what we often get is a utopian vision, literally a vision of a "no place." However, on closer look the Turners' articulation of communitas, their understanding of the kinds of group and individual identities, and the dynamics through which they are formed, are both nuanced and complex, and a careful application of their analysis can still serve as a useful lens through which to view the dynamics of places like Ayodhya, in particular, as well as the other shared and contested places I will consider in subsequent chapters. Let me say at the outset, however, that I by no means consider myself a Turnerian; rather, I simply think they still are useful tools to have in one's methodological toolbox.

Let me begin, then, by teasing out of Victor Turner's own work his understanding and articulation of communitas. First, though, I think it is important to point out that he does not always appear to be consistent in his definition or application of communitas, a fact that should neither surprise nor alarm us, given both the breadth and depth of Turner's writings and his frequent (sometimes unmarked) revisions and reformulations of earlier ideas, and also given his own consistent emphasis on flux, fluidity, and process. On the most basic level, communitas is "a spontaneously generated relationship between leveled and equal total and individuated human beings, stripped of structural attributes."[22] It is, thus, a "relational quality of full unmediated communication, even communion, between definite and determinate identities."[23] We can see that communitas fundamentally is the formation of a shared identity, a bonding in which normally prominent (and divisive) characteristics such as race, class, gender, politics, etc., are broken down (or at least suspended), and replaced by a mutual identity, a shared sense of self. This is no ordinary camaraderie, however, because unlike the bonds of normal life, according to Turner, communitas cuts across, reverses, and ignores structure. As such, the "bonds of communitas are anti-structural in the sense that they are undifferentiated, egalitarian, direct, extant, nonrational, existential, I-Thou (in Buber's sense) relationships. Communitas is spontaneous, immediate, concrete—it is not shaped by norms, it is not institutionalized, it is not abstract.... Communitas does not merge identities; it liberates them from conformity to general norms."[24] Turner freights communitas with a great deal here, and there is much that could be said about just this iteration of the concept. It is the last part that I would like to unpack here, though, since so frequently communitas is taken by those who adopt the concept to be the loss of individual identity and the formation of a collective sense of self; what Turner seems to mean here, however, is rather more subtle. For him, communitas entails a truly dialectic dynamic, a breakdown in the normal structure of society that allows individuals to come together to form a new communal identity while, at the same time, remaining fully themselves.[25] Thus, Turner emphasizes that communitas must, by necessity, be transient—the individuals must re-emerge from this state, and return to normal, although this "normal" will, necessarily, be different, altered by the experience of communitas. If this sounds fuzzy, that is because in Turner's work it is fuzzy.

In *The Ritual Process*, a relatively early work, Turner nuances his conception of communitas by distinguishing between three different types: existential, normative, and ideological.[26] Briefly, existential communitas is that which is most immediate and spontaneous, most absorbing and, thus, most fleeting. This is, as it were, the classic iteration of communitas, an experience that Turner describes, as we have seen, as being very similar to Martin Buber's theologically charged "I-Thou" relationship. "This relationship is always a 'happening,' something that arises in instant mutuality, when each person fully experiences the being of the other."[27] This sort of communitas, Turner adds, "can never be adequately expressed in structural form, but it may arise unpredictably at any time between human beings who are institutionally reckoned or defined as members of any or all kinds of social groupings, or of none."[28] Normative communitas arises to replace existential communitas; it is a kind of routinization of existential communitas, whereby it is "organized into a perduring social system,"[29] the very structure that Turner insists communitas subverts. However, once normative communitas is established, there is a need—an urge? a desire? a trend toward? (it is difficult to pin Turner down here)—to return to the more immediate and more powerful existential form of communitas. It is ideological communitas, however, that is most elusive and also that most interests me here.

Ideological communitas, like the normative variety, differs from existential communitas in that it is, paradoxically, caught up in structure. And, rather than being immediate and spontaneous, it seems in some way to be intentionally orchestrated. The Turners note that ideological communitas's "most distinctive feature is the way in which it polarizes the general and particular, the universal and the local."[30] What they mean by this, I think, is that a particular symbol within a ritual context in which communitas arises, the Rām chariot, say, at once conveys the "Great Tradition" (this is Turner's usage, not my own)—here classical Hindu myth and ritual—and at the same time the local, "Little Tradition"—here the village temple, the local variants on the myth, particular ritual practices, and so on. This dual symbolic valence allows, then, for the individual to connect personally to the specific object and also collectively to the larger cause. In *Image and Pilgrimage in Christian Culture*,[31] the Turners discuss the medieval Irish pilgrimage to Lough Derg:

> At Lough Derg, it is entirely probable that Catholic ideas and doctrines become impregnated with Irish experiences, not only personal experiences but communitas experiences in an Irish landscape and culture setting, while the specific symbols and ideas of Irishness, including that of being a persecuted people, are correspondingly Catholicized, "elevated to the altars of the Church," so to speak, where Ireland becomes "the martyr nation." In other words, Irishness is raised to a more abstract plane of generalization and normativeness. Hence the generation of a dual loyalty to Pope and people. Pilgrimage symbology provides a clue to the dynamic interaction of the emotion-laden particular with the cognitive general.[32]

There are several points that stand out here, not the least of which is the sheer murkiness of the analysis. Perhaps most glaring, to my mind at any rate, is the apparent lack of agency or intentionality in all of this.

As the Turners say over and over again, communitas is spontaneous, and seems to arise (and dissipate) entirely on its own accord, without conscious manipulation on the part of those who become absorbed into it. Even when they talk of normative communitas, they do not, really, spell out the mechanism by and through which existential communitas is made structural, is "organized into a perduring social system." Clearly, Lough Derg (the place and the process) was engaged by real people on the ground, real people who had real intentions and motivations. As such, then, it cannot possibly have arisen spontaneously, without some intentionality, without some real goals and motivations—although, as we shall see, frequently what does arise differs from what might have been intended. We see this peculiar lack of agency later in the same piece when the Turners note that, far "from being an opiate for the people, Lough Derg and other pilgrimage shrines in Ireland—as in Mexico, Poland, and elsewhere—may have kept alive the cultural basis for national political struggle, providing it with its root paradigm: that martyrdom should be embraced, if necessary, for the good of the people."[33] The critical point is that such things are "kept alive" and "embraced" by real people, and these real people very often position and define themselves in opposition to other real people; thus although there may often be a disjunction between the motivations and the results—I shall have more to say on this in a moment when I turn to the specific case of Ayodhya, and later in this book when I discuss Karbala—there are still motivations and intentions that must be examined.

Significantly, in *The Ritual Process* Turner seems to have anticipated this very criticism, but while he recognizes it, he also seems to wish to evade it. Indeed, he makes a pointed distinction between his own conception of communitas and Durkheim's articulation of solidarity, noting that the latter "depends upon an in-group/out-group contrast."[34] This is important, for clearly what Turner is most interested in is the bonds that form only between members of the same community, and he believes that these bonds form not in contrast or opposition to other relationships or structures, but as a kind of disruption and disjunction, something pure and autonomous and spontaneous that emerges out of the moment, and, as the invocation of Buber indicates, something existentially transcendent. Later, however, the Turners seem to recognize the idealism (and romanticism) of such a notion, although it is, to be sure, a grudging acknowledgment: they lament that in instances where pilgrimage involves struggle, "the purity of existential communitas has now become polluted by the seven deadly sins of social structure, against which the Ten Commandments were directed. 'Our' community becomes a structured cell opposed to 'their' community, and the sentiment of human kindness at the heart of communitas vanishes as though it had never been."[35] Here, then, we see that the Turners very much recognize the contention, the our/their opposition that is so frequently part of the flux of the pilgrimage process—and, for that matter, all of what they call "social dramas"—but they see this conflict as a violation of communitas's basic character. In short, it is apparent that the Turners really want (and perhaps also believe) communitas to exist as something pure and good, despite the fact—which they acknowledge—that in actual practice it does not.

Caroline Bynum has suggested that one of the weaknesses in Victor Turner's articulation of liminality and communitas is that when extended beyond the premodern, agrarian context—exemplified by his extremely detailed and careful work on the Ndembu—the theory proves problematic, and the universality that Turner claims (and desires) is just not there, in part because, as Bynum notes, "the modern examples are often tossed in without the care or elaboration necessary to make the analysis convincing."[36] I think there is more, though. The Ndembu ritual world about which Turner so frequently writes early in his career and from which he builds the foundations of his theoretical position is one of a high degree of structure, repetition, and predictability (or at least that is how he represents it); indeed, even the emergence of communitas in the rites of passage rituals in the Ndembu context can be seen to be expected. Furthermore, the tripartite movement that Turner adopts from Arnold van Gennep—separation, liminality, reintegration—and later applies to a broad range of contexts is obviously highly structured and predictable, even if a fundamental element of the liminal phase is the abandonment of all structural relationships and identities (resulting, of course, in communitas). But even if we grant that structure is a necessary, defining characteristic of ritual—as virtually everyone who has written on the topic over the past century agrees—we also must recognize that ritual is also surprisingly unpredictable, with all manner of ad hoc consequences. It is certainly true, as Jonathan Z. Smith has most prominently articulated, that ritual is at least in principal about ordering that which is fundamentally disorderly;[37] in practice ritual is often disorderly, improvisational, and unpredictable in its outcomes if not in its practices.[38] Furthermore, as much as communitas can be said to be spontaneous, I want to suggest that there are also instances where it is a decidedly intentional, planned consequence.

1.3 Ayodhya in 1992: Communitas or Chaos?

[T]he eruption of a riot is always expected and yet takes everyone by surprise.

—SUDHIR KAKAR[39]

The communal violence that erupted in the small north Indian pilgrimage town of Ayodhya in late 1992 and early 1993 has been exceedingly well documented and analyzed,[40] so it is not my intent here to produce an exhaustive account of it. Rather, I wish to attempt to view the events leading up to the riots, as well as the riots themselves, through a kind of Turnerian lens—to, essentially, apply Turner's formulation of the dynamics of communitas to this context. This may on its face seem odd, given that what transpired at Ayodhya and throughout much of India during this period was intensely non-ludic—an outburst not of undifferentiated love, but of atrocious violence. Nonetheless, I think this is a particularly good test case for the applicability of the Turners' thesis. The Turners, as I have noted, thought that the liminality/communitas thesis could be applied universally, to any number of pilgrimage processes and places, and Ayodhya would seem to fit the bill, in that many of the dynamics about which the Turners write are present.

What I want to argue, though, is that the dynamics at Ayodhya move in an almost opposite direction to what the Turnerian thesis suggests. In his early formulations, Victor Turner adopts van Gennep's tripartite movement and pays particular attention to the liminal phase as the culmination of communitas; the third phase, integration, involves the return to structure, the formulation of normative or ideological communitas, which, as we have seen, the Turners see as a lesser sort of experience, but the only way that the immediacy of communitas can last. I want to suggest that Ayodhya begins with a very conscious, very deliberate articulation of communitas, what the Turners would perhaps deem ideological communitas, through the intentional harnessing of a variety of potent symbols and rituals, most notably pilgrimage, and it is only in the eventual eruption of violence in late 1992 and early 1993 that we see anything like the spontaneous power of the Turners' existential communitas. Although it may at first blush seem that I am forcing the Turners into a context in which they do not fruitfully or logically apply, seeing Ayodhya through the Turnerian lens actually highlights some very important elements of this complex set of events that might otherwise go unnoticed and, at the same time, brings to the foreground some of the important weaknesses of the Turners' work.

In the years since the violence associated with Ayodhya, scores of scholars have attempted to understand its causes. Some have suggested that Ayodhya—the name of the place has become, essentially, synonymous with the violence there, much as, say, one need only use "Jonestown" or "Waco" to evoke, synecdochely, the full process of the events that took place in those towns—was the result of a popular mass movement and the violence that transpired was the spontaneous venting of emotions that had been building for months and years. Others have argued that in fact Ayodhya was the boiling over of a long-simmering enmity between Hindus and Muslims that reaches back at least as far as the sixteenth century. Still others have seen Ayodhya as decidedly post-colonial event, with origins in the divisive nineteenth-century social and political structure imposed by the British. And still others have posited the existence of an elaborately orchestrated elite conspiracy that opportunistically exploited Ayodhya for its own economic and political gains. Although each of these orientations has its own validity, there is also in each an overly neat reductionism. David Ludden has critiqued, for instance, the positing of an ancient enmity between Hindus and Muslims, which draws "from an old storehouse of imagery that identifies the religions we have seen in the headlines with those that define Indian civilization and also implies that the conflict at Ayodhya dramatizes the very religious traditionalism and irrationality that describe and explain India's poverty and backwardness,"[41] when in fact the very formulation of some fundamental opposition and separation between Hindu and Muslim is as much a creation of the colonial administration as it ever was a matter of fact. Furthermore, as the authors of one account of the roots of the conflict at Ayodhya have pointed out, the "frequent representations of Hindutva as a spontaneous mass movement in search of Hindu identity naturalizes and suppresses a whole history of meticulously organized efforts towards a Hindu Rashtra."[42] I want to suggest, then, that it was the complex coalescence of these various factors that led to Ayodhya, and that as much as there was real agency and intentionality at play, with specific actors attempting to orchestrate specific outcomes, there was also something highly unpredictable and spontaneous as well.

Any account of the contested history of Ayodhya must, it seems, begin with the construction of the Babri Masjid itself, the mosque that became the focus of a great push of Hindu activism in the late 1980s. The site on which the mosque was built had been a contested spot probably since the founder of the Moghul empire, Babar, had it built in the sixteenth century. The town of Ayodhya itself is the legendary birthplace of the god Rāma and one of the most important Hindu pilgrimage places in India, and whatever the actual dynamics of its construction, it seems likely that placing the mosque in Ayodhya was an act of aggression—as we shall see, this building of a significant religious structure on the site where another had stood is a common enough occurrence—although there is no clear historical evidence to demonstrate that Hindus and Muslims clashed at the site until the nineteenth century. The contemporary history of Ayodhya begins, really, in the 1850s, when, in 1855, a group of Sunni Muslims claimed that the small Hanuman temple—Hanuman is Rāma's simian general, the embodiment of both strength and devotion in Hindu ideology—that stands near the Babri Masjid was actually built on the site of another mosque that had been destroyed to build the Hindu temple. This group (accounts are not specific on the number) of Muslims set out to reclaim the temple, but were confronted by a group of Hindu warrior-ascetics;[43] the Muslims, it would seem, got the worst of the encounter and retreated, and the immediate tensions were defused. Two years later, however, while much of the country was reeling from the violence that marked the so-called Mutiny of 1857, the Mahant ("Abbott") of the Hanuman temple responded to the Muslim claims on the temple by erecting a platform in the courtyard of the mosque complex, claiming that it marked the exact spot of Rāma's birth (*janmabhūmi*).[44] There were, predictably, complaints from the Muslim community, but the matter seems to have simply festered at this point (or at least there is no clear record of further conflict).

Nearly thirty years later, though, the Hanuman temple's Mahant, wishing to build a larger, permanent temple to mark the space where the platform had been placed, sued for the space within the mosque complex. The suit was denied, and things at Ayodhya remained relatively quiet until the 1940s; in 1949, a newly-emerged Hindu group, the All-India Ramayan Assembly (Akhil Bharatiya Ramayana Mahasabha) began a new round of protests at the mosque. They staged a nine-day, round-the-clock recitation of the *Rāmayāna*—the Hindu epic that recounts the great deeds of Rāma and lauds his character as an ideal earthly ruler—outside of the mosque, which attracted large crowds. Apparently inspired by this performance, a group broke into the Babri Masjid and therein installed a small image of Rāma; the appearance of the image was celebrated as a miracle, the Rāma *avatāra* descended to earth to restore dharma. This was an obviously charged situation, and the whole town of Ayodhya, as well as the outlying area, became very tense—Jawarhalal Nehru himself intervened in an attempt to defuse the situation. The case then went back to court, and the courts eventually ruled that the Rāma image could remain in the mosque, a stunningly misguided sort of compromise. The effect of this last bit of wrangling was a pyrrhic victory of sorts for the Hindus, since the mosque was closed because of the simmering conflict, effectively ending both Muslim and Hindu worship at the site.

Given the obvious tensions, it is perhaps surprising that it was not until the early 1980s that things at Ayodhya once again heated up, when the Vishva Hindu Parishad (VHP)—a kind of religious/political umbrella group that had been formed in 1964 in order to unite a variety of Hindu figures and factions—intentionally brought the issue back to the boiling point. In 1983, the VHP launched the first of a series of campaigns that it called the "*ekamata yajña*," the "sacrifice for unanimity," at once yoking the central Hindu motifs of sacrifice and pilgrimage to, perhaps ironically, a post-independence conception of a non-sectarian secular India. This campaign consisted of three simultaneous pilgrimage processions with trucks carrying large brass pots of Ganges water that was distributed in villages throughout the country—and then replaced with water from local temples—in order to create what Richard Davis has called a "pan-Indian reservoir of holy water."[45]

This procession was clearly intended to create a sense of Hindu unity and community that extended beyond the geographical, linguistic, sectarian, and caste distinctions that are so much a part of the fabric of India, but as Davis notes, "to define and mobilize a Hindu community of faith, the VHP had decided, it would be important to identify an enemy."[46] Thus the next year, the VHP launched another, more ambitious campaign—the *Rām śila pūjā*, or "veneration of the bricks of Rāma"—this time intended not simply as a gesture of Hindu unity, but as a "liberation" of important northern temples from their Muslim captors,[47] and "the temple liberation project indissolubly linked this Hindu unity with an active anti-Muslim rhetoric.... Far more widespread in their influence than the Christians of the northeast, Muslims would be cast as violators of the sacred homeland."[48] The *Rām śila pūjā* was started in the autumn of 1984 and consisted of a pan-Indian pilgrimage to gather bricks—locally consecrated and inscribed with the words, in Devanagari script, "*Śrī Rāma*"—to build (or rebuild, as the activists would have it) a temple on the site of Rāma's mythical birthplace in Ayodhya.

This was very much a process intended to forge a kind of *communitas*: Hindus from all over India, with different sectarian identities, of different castes, of different social and economic positions, all would contribute to the building of this temple. As such, it was a unique event in the history of India, for as Davis has pointed out,

> no Hindu temple has ever been built with such a heterogeneous assortment of building materials, nor has the sponsor of a temple ever so explicitly involved the public at large in the building scheme. From the VHP perspective, the project allowed it to conduct a "mass contact" campaign as well as to keep up a continuous moral pressure, in the physical form of brick processions converging on Ayodhya, on the site and on government authorities.[49]

Additionally, a more diffuse campaign was quietly and surreptitiously begun by the VHP, one that involved the appearance in various public places of stickers, banners, and painted *oṃs*, in which the organizers intentionally "allowed them to appear as if they represented a spontaneous popular upsurge in Hindu devotional productivity."[50] The BJP—the Bharata Janata Parishad, the political party that has close ties to the VHP—actually went so far as to send out "video *ratras*," which included deified politicians as well as "throngs of ordinary men and women joining in the Ram janmabhoomi movement," thus projecting not only the size of the procession, but its unity, blending all levels of Hindu society.[51]

This is, I think, an extremely important point, since all of these actions—the processions, the pilgrimages, the co-opting of religious rituals and images, the appearance of religious paraphernalia—were carefully planned and orchestrated, but they very often produced something immediate and spontaneous nonetheless, something very much like what Turner depicts as communitas. Indeed, much of this looks very much like ritual—planned, structured activity intended to create a particular result, a result that appears in context to emerge on its own, organically, and with its own internal energy and power: "A planned coordination that deliberately organized a phased self-multiplication, was presented as spontaneous participation by new ranks of Hindus, the mutual conjoining of society and organization. The movement thus appeared as rooted in an unmediated social will rather than in the directive of an organization."[52]

This point is particularly evident in the next major act of this drama. Having been energized by the success of the *Rām śila pūjā*, the BJP, led by its former president and most visible member, L. K. Advani, organized another, larger procession, called the *Rath Yātrā* (literally, "car procession") in September of 1990, one that prominently involved the chariot of Rāma (with Advani, bow in hand, dressed as the god) and that would traverse northern India, beginning in the west, in Gujarat,[53] and eventually ending in Ayodhya. This was a highly orchestrated, planned event from its outset, involving politicians in mythical garb, tens of thousands of pilgrims (mostly drawn from the lower classes), and intense media coverage.[54] Despite the highly orchestrated, scripted nature of the *Rath Yātrā*, however, it was, on the ground, also uncontrolled and uncontrollable, and the "procession quickly took on a ceremonial life of its own, often outside the control of the BJP leadership."[55] This is even more evident in the final culmination of all of these actions at Ayodhya.

A particularly conspicuous constituency in the *Rath Yātrā* was the Bajrang Dal, a group that first entered the Ayodhya fray in December 1985; it is the Bajrang Dal, in fact, that was generally blamed for the actual destruction of the Babri Masjid. The Bajrang Dal was founded in 1984 and consisted of a large, loosely organized force of mostly disenfranchised, uneducated or unemployed young men who were brought together "to implement the policies of the VHP."[56] They vowed to protect Hinduism, essentially: to fight for the protection of cows,[57] to protect the purity of Hindu mothers and sisters, and to prevent foreigners from "infiltrating" the country, and so on. These young men went through a brief initiation ceremony, which included the recitation of a short religious text called the *Hanuman Calisa*, which is associated with the *Rāmayāna* itself. They were also trained to fight.[58] These young men acted essentially as the Turners' idealized pilgrims act—they were initiated before they journeyed out from their homes, an initiation that involved a significant dissolution of their normal identities and the adoption of a new identity (the fact that they wore the garb of Śaivas despite their Vaṣṇava religious affiliations is significant). Furthermore, their own self-designation, as "Hanuman's troops," is an indication of their adoption of a self-consciously low, servile position (but one with great power as well), precisely what the Turners describe in their articulation of the formation of communitas in the pilgrimage process.

This emphasis on lowliness was in fact a consistent element in the entire campaign; the BJP (and VHP as well) intentionally tapped into a broad, grass-roots sort of populism, what they referred to as "people power," or *lok śākti*, which they explicitly contrasted with "royal power," or *rāj śākti*, which was associated with not only the ruling power in New Delhi, but the elites of India in general.[59] Be that as it may, though, there was a simultaneous attempt, at a kind of meta level, to create a single unified Hindu community, one that carefully brought together such groups and was "achieved through a controlled pluralism, through a single organizational cluster that allows yet coordinates a large range of sacred events."[60]

It was during the *Rath Yātrā* campaign as well that a new, particularly powerful element emerged in the movement, one that played on the elemental Hindu image of sacrifice and which, simultaneously, co-opted a key element in Muslim discourse: martyrdom. In October of 1990, a group of about three hundred VHP activists—many of them members of the Bajrang Dal—attempted to storm the heavily guarded Babri Masjid in Ayodhya. Tension had been building for months prior to this, and riots had already broken out in the wake of Advani's *Rath Yātrā*, most notably in the western state of Rajasthan. It was observed that these riots were not, in fact, spontaneous: "'The riots did not happen, they were made to happen,' was the refrain of many."[61] As Ashis Nandy and his collaborators have charged, as is usual with riots in contemporary India, the Jaipur riot was methodically planned and professionally executed.[62]

In the meantime, activists (*karsevaks*) had begun to congregate in Ayodhya itself. Then, on October 30 things came to a head, as the *karsevaks* themselves, and local citizens who had until then been mostly uninvolved in the agitation, all "got carried away by the excitement and the religious fervour in the air and poured onto the streets."[63] Although much planning had gone into this agitation, events took on a kind of life of their own, and, as one eyewitness put it, "there was no one and nothing to stop the *karsevaks*.... The more excited they became, the more violent their words" and actions became.[64] Although the *karsevaks* were unsuccessful in gaining control of the mosque, they did manage to place several saffron flags on the domes of the mosque. By the end, the immediate eruption of violence had given way to a kind of ludic celebration in the streets of Ayodhya, a joyful—despite the obvious threat of violence still hanging in the air—commingling of the various Hindu groups, many of them up to this point antagonistic toward one another: "A carnival-like atmosphere prevailed in Ayodhya following the attack on the mosque.... Policemen, who till just a little while ago looked tense and wary, were also seen celebrating."[65] Without the violence that preceded it, this bears a striking resemblance to the Turners' communitas.

The fact was, however, that there was violence in Ayodhya in October of 1990, and in a perverse sort of way it only heightened the sense of communitas. The police, who had mostly been overrun by the crowds and who, during the assault on the mosque, had been relegated to bystanders, finally intervened, and eventually opened fire on what had become an angry crowd of several thousand young men, in the process killing more than fifty of the activists. "This direct confrontation with the state government, headed by what the BJP called a 'pro-Muslim pseudo secularist' (Mulayam Singh), created a heroic legend of kar seva martyrdom in Ayodhya and provided the optimal habitat of confrontation and clear frontiers in the ensuing campaigns" to liberate the temple.[66] The BJP and VHP seized this highly symbolic image, publishing booklets and distributing videos of the martyrs' mutilated bodies and circulating their ashes, while at the same time greatly inflating the death toll. This would be an image that they would repeatedly use, creating what Thomas Blom Hansen refers to as an "almost epic atmosphere of sacrifice and honor that the BJP propaganda machine worked hard to generate."[67]

Given the decade of building tensions, it would be hard to say that the end result of this drama was surprising to anyone. The Babri Masjid was destroyed on December 6, 1992. In October of that year, yet another *pūjā*—focused on the veneration of thousands of copies of Rāma's sandals—was organized by the VHP. This one, however, was considerably smaller and attracted much less attention than the *Rām śila pūjā* had four years earlier.[68] Nonetheless, by early December some 200,000 activists had gathered at Ayodhya. On the morning of December 6, a group of young men—apparently well organized and well armed for the task—began to attack the mosque.[69] They were unhindered by the few police officers guarding the site (speculation was that they were under the BJP's control). The mosque was razed. There can be little question that the destruction of the Babri Masjid was a deliberately planned event, the culmination of decades of carefully orchestrated agitation on the part of the VHP, RSS, and, to a degree, the BJP, despite their expressed disavowal of any intentionality in the event.[70]

1.4 The Absence of Agency

It is by uttering the same cry, pronouncing the same word,
or performing the same gesture in regard to some object
that they become and feel themselves to be in unison.

—ÉMILE DURKHEIM[71]

What, in the end, do we gain from looking at Ayodhya through a Turnerian lens? On the most basic level, there is the obvious highlighting of the whole issue of pilgrimage. As in the Turners' many discussions on the topic, the pilgrims involved in the various Ayodhya *yātrās* journeyed out, making a physical and a symbolic break from home, from "normal" life. In the process, a new identity was forged for the participants—one caught up in the general notion of Hindutva—that was born out of the liminality of the journey: " 'We are all Hindus, we are all the same,' every spokesman of each organization recited at the beginning of their exposition. All of them reduced differences and practices to personal idiosyncrasies."[72] One essential element of this journey, specifically the liminal element within it, is that it was fundamentally transgressive. It was not just that people came together in the various pilgrimages, but that this coming together was a kind of release, a venting of pent up anger and aggression and fear, and it brought with it real danger, as Turner, directly borrowing from van

Gennep, duly notes: "During the novitiate, the young people can steal and pillage at will or feed and adorn themselves at the expense of the community."[73] Turner then goes on to elaborate that these unruly youths are "temporarily undefined, beyond the normative social structure."[74] This is anti-structure in essence, the heart of the liminal, a rupture when not only the danger, but also the creativity of ritual truly emerges. This is the "interfacial region or, to change the metaphor, an interval, however brief, of *margin* or *limen*, when the past is momentarily negated, suspended, or abrogated, and the future has not yet begun, an instant of pure potentiality when everything, as it were, trembles in the balance."[75]

This is, I think, a useful way to understand the Bajrang Dal movement, and, particularly, their seemingly spontaneous destruction of the Babri Masjid. Like Turner's initiands, the Bajrang Dal were young men, from the lower classes, men who were initiated, who were marked as different (they wore distinctive clothing, for instance, and often carried tridents), and who, as a group, were disruptive and unruly, transgressive of the normal social rules. As such, they were both powerful and dangerous.

After the initial rupture of the destruction of the mosque, we see a more diffuse, collective kind of rupture—an extension of this liminal zone that was, in the immediacy of Ayodhya, initially occupied by the Bajrang Dal mobs, much the same as that which had been witnessed after the rioting in October 1990. Hansen has described the period after the destruction of the Babri Masjid as a "Hindutva wave," a "wave of untrammeled pride in Hindu strength, a wave of revenge vis-à-vis the Muslim community, a new jingoist self-confidence among broad sections of Hindus—middle and lower class, rural and urban."[76] Significantly, Hansen describes this in distinctively Turnerian language, as "a sort of collective *jouissance* organized around transgressing the norms of public utterances, around saying the 'unsayable'—sensing the 'real' communal hatred and fascination floating freely. If not before, the idea of Hindu rashtra—as a sense of common 'flow' of Hindu *communitas*—lived transiently in these short days and weeks."[77]

Of course we do not necessarily need the Turners here. Sudhir Kakar, for instance, turns to Freud in his discussion of Ayodhya and mob violence (although it is not at all clear that this is any more useful). The collective characterization of the Muslim other as the enemy can be seen, Kakar suggest, as analogous to what the child does in externalizing hostile emotions toward those upon whom it depends, first onto inanimate objects and then to people in other groups. The Muslim, then, becomes an "emotionally charged target of externalization" for the Hindu's own " 'bad' representations and angry feelings," and this is coupled with an assimilation of the "in" group's self perception, so that on an individual level, the Hindu comes "to resemble them more and more," while increasing his or her own "emotional investment in the group's shared symbols and traditions."[78] Kakar continues: "Since the enemy is also a reservoir of our own unwanted selves and negative feelings, it is important it be kept at a psychological distance. Consciously, the enemy should never be like us. Even minor differences between 'us' and 'them' are therefore exaggerated as unbridgeable chasms in what Freud called the 'narcissism of minor differences.' "[79] This then builds to a crisis point—the moment of collective violence, in which the "individual is practically wrapped up in the crowd and gets continuous sensual pounding through all the avenues that one's body can afford. The consequence is a blurring of the body image and of the ego, a kind of self-transcendence that is reacted to by panic or exhilaration as individuality disappears and the 'integrity,' 'autonomy,' and 'independence' of the ego seem to be wishful illusions and mere hypothetical constructs."[80]

In the crowd, in the mob, then, the individual is lost, essentially, and becomes the crowd. In none of this, however, is there anything like agency. People are swept up—they transcend themselves—as if by some primal force. Certainly, it may be the case that this kind of agentless-frenzy is at work, but without all of the very specific, often very intentional, acts and actors leading up to it none of it would even happen.

The Turners certainly did recognize that ritual in general, and pilgrimage in particular, could serve as a form of social critique, a means of political change. David Kertzer, for instance, has drawn attention to the "powerful way of looking at the political role of ritual" that we find in Turner's work, noting that he drew our attention away from Durkheim's focus on the solidarity created by ritual, and toward the degree to which "ritual symbols can be the symbols of change, indeed of revolution."[81] Ritual presents a means by which the status quo is, however transiently, ruptured, in which structure breaks down. Turner was quite explicit about this late in his career, here writing with his wife, Edith: "Like certain other liminoid genres of symbolic action elaborated in the leisure time of modern society, pilgrimage has become an implicit critique of the life-style characteristic of the encompassing social structure."[82] But as much as Turner helps us refocus our vision, helps us move away from understanding ritual as a static repetition of the status quo and toward a dynamic and creative force of change, we also see in his discussions of ritual a consistent lack of agency. Pilgrims are swept up, awash in liminality, but only rarely does anything like agency or historical or social specificity come to the surface; the degree to which individuals and institutions manipulate the ritual process is, for the most part, obfuscated. After all, as much as we can say that the participants in the destruction of the Babri Masjid were swept away by a wave of emotion that created a kind of communitas, we must also, as I have argued here, recognize that this was a highly orchestrated event. Indeed, as the authors of *Khaki Shorts* point out, "The Hindutva of today constitutes a major departure from previous phases of Hindu communal mobilization in one crucial respect. Unlike earlier periods of acute communal tensions (in the 1890s, the 1920s, 1940s, or 1960s) it is inseparably identified with a concrete organizational complex."[83]

Late in his career, Turner was particularly attracted to the language of theater, and for good reason; ritual, as Turner maintained throughout his career, is drama, performance, and like theater, it is a highly structured, planned event. He refers to social dramas as "units of aharmonic or disharmonic social process, arising in conflict situations,"[84] and describes ritual as "a kind of meta-theater, that is, a dramaturgical language about the language of ordinary role-playing and the status-maintenance which constitutes communication in the quotidian social process."[85] Indeed, in his last major work Turner acknowledges the "postmodern turn," and says that by rethinking our understanding of ritual as drama, our focus would be on "the very flaws, hesitations, personal factors, incomplete, elliptical, context-dependent, situational components of performance," and we would then see the "freedom of the performance situation . . . what Durkheim (in his best moment) called the social 'effervescence,' exemplified for him in the generation of new symbols and meanings by the public actions, the 'performances'."[86]

In adopting the language of theater to understand ritual, and particularly politically charged ritual, Turner was attempting to get at the complexity of the relationship between structure and anti-structure, between that which is planned and manipulated, on the one hand, and the spontaneity of the collective moment on the other. This last, late turn may have been too little too late; it has been largely overlooked by those who adopt the Turners' mode of analysis. Certainly others have used the language of theater to get at some of the complexity of ritual. Pierre Bourdieu talks of *habitus* as systems of "durable, transposable *dispositions*" that are, nonetheless, always in a state of flux, allowing "agents to cope with unforeseen and ever-changing situations" in ways that are never entirely conscious nor unconscious, planned nor spontaneous,[87] very much as actors in a play respond to, but do not absolutely follow, a script. Charles Tilly, likewise, picks up the language of drama, and notes that, in fact

> identities remain unclear until participants dramatize them. All people have multiple identities at their disposal, each one attached to a somewhat different set of social relations: neighbor, spouse, farmer, customer, tenant, schoolmate, lover, or citizen. Some available identities appear in public only intermittently, as is the case with many varieties of party affiliation, association membership, and adhesion to social movements. In these circumstances, participants in contentious conversation regularly make a point of the capacities in which they are interacting, of the identities they are activating.[88]

In a similar vein, Nandy and company refer to the rituals and the violence that they gave rise to as an "omnibus expression for a variety of conflicts...the violence served as a rubric under which many diverse motives could find place. These motives ranged from the eagerness to settle personal scores or oust one's tenants to open greed and plunder."[89]

If, then, ritual, and particularly what Turner calls "the pilgrimage process," can be seen as a drama, it is a very, very unpredictable sort of drama. For when—if I may stretch the metaphor—the play is actually performed, the script, the director—here the collective officials of the VHP and BJP—the set, the audience, and the actors themselves, all become absorbed in the power and spontaneity of the moment, the performance. In such moments, even though everything is planned, quite literally scripted, there is a point at which the actors are outside of the play, and the moment itself obfuscates, even dissolves, agency. The one, however—the communitas (or just chaos)—cannot exist without the other—the specific intentional, embedded lead-up. To return to the basic point with which I began this chapter: sacred places are made sacred, by actors, agents, by real people engaged in real processes. It is our task to examine the process, not simply to describe the outcome.

In the next chapter, I move from the Indian subcontinent to the United States, to the highly charged discussion of what is known in popular discourse as "Ground Zero." What sort of place is this? It is obvious that it has been understood as sacred space, a pilgrimage place, even, but what constitutes its sacrality, and what does the articulation of a discourse of sacredness vis-à-vis this particular place actually entail? Some of the same issues at play at Ayodhya are also present there. In particular, I wish to analyze the rancor over the Park 51 project—the so-called "Ground Zero Mosque"—and the fight over not only the identity of the space itself, but also the people who participate in this space.

2

Power Fallen from the Sky

2.1 The Seats of the Goddess

Sites are never simply locations. Rather, they are sites for someone, and of something. The cultural context of images and myths adds a socially constructed level of meaning to the genus loci, the classics' "unique sense of place," said to derive from the forms of the physical environment in a given site.

—ROB SHIELDS[1]

IT WOULD HARDLY be an exaggeration to say that the most discussed, debated, and analyzed place in the United States for the first decade of the twenty-first century has been the site where the World Trade Center towers had stood until September 11, 2001. For many Americans, this is hallowed ground, a most charged and sacred place, but swirling about the site is an array of questions concerning the space it actually occupies and the precise terms of its sacredness. What sort of place is this? What constitutes its sacrality? Where does its sacredness begin, and where does it end? Who has access to, or can participate in, this sacrality—and, perhaps more to the point, who cannot? This is a most complex place, a messy and ambiguous physical area that embodies a range of contested meanings.

Places that are regarded as sacred, such as Ayodhya, or Jerusalem, or the site where the World Trade Center towers once stood, become sacred because of something that happened there, or something that mythically took place there, or because of something that is located there. But such myths and etiologies and histories tell only part of the story. There is also the human use of and discussion about such places. There are often competing versions of the significance of a site, such as in the case of Ayodhya; or the same physical object that lends power to the site is regarded quite differently by different groups, such as the footprints at Bodhgayā and Gayā, which I will discuss in subsequent chapters, that are alternately regarded as belonging to either the Buddha or Viṣṇu (or, for some, both the Buddha and Viṣṇu).

Before I turn to the contested place where the Twin Towers once stood, I wish to go on a bit of a tangent, but what I think is a relevant tangent. In the small town of Tarapur, three hundred miles north of Calcutta, in the Indian state of West Bengal, there is a temple dedicated to the Hindu goddess Tārā. People come to the temple to make offerings to her, so that they can receive some of her awesome power; they ask her for boons, for protection, for fertility. Tārāpīṭh, the temple, is a mostly local place visited by local Hindus, although despite its remote location and relatively small size it is also an important national pilgrimage place.[2] There are several stories that relate the temple's significance. One holds that this is where Satī's third eye, her eye of insight, fell.[3] Tārāpīṭh, according to this version of its origins, is one of dozens of temples known as *śākta pīṭhas*, places—literally "seats"—that are thought to embody the power of the goddess, her *śākti*. Some of these places are quite well known, such as the famous Kalighat temple in Calcutta, while others, such as Tārāpīṭh, are rather obscure and located in very remote places. There are often said to be fifty-one of these *pīṭhas*, although some sources put the number at over one hundred.[4] Each is in some way related to a well-known myth involving Śiva and Satī. Although the myth has several variations, here is the basic outline of this story: The god Dakṣa once held a great sacrifice and invited all of the inhabitants of the heavens. He excluded his daughter Satī, however, and her husband, Śiva, because he disapproved of their union: Śiva was an inappropriate partner for his daughter; he lived in cremation grounds, with the ghosts and the ghouls, and he smeared his naked body with ash and spent all of his time in meditation; furthermore, he was an ascetic, celibate, and thus could hardly be counted on to produce sons. Although Śiva himself was unaffected by this slight—why would a renouncer care about such mundane matters?—Satī was quite upset. She went to the sacrifice and became so angry, in fact, that she generated a tremendous amount of heat, *tapas*, and she self-immolated. Śiva, when he learned of what had happened, became enraged and engulfed in grief. He wreaked havoc on the whole affair, destroyed the sacrifice and lopped off Dakṣa's head, and then flew about the heavens with Satī's body, screaming in grief.

Śiva's wailing was so loud that it blocked out all other sounds – including the Vedic verses chanted in ritual in the universe- and order, dharma, broke down. Chaos, adharma, engulfed the cosmos, and in some versions of the story the universe went dark. The other gods did not know what to do, until Viṣṇu—in his typical role as restorer of dharma—then took his cosmic weapon, the *sudharśana cakra*, and used it to cut Satī's body to pieces, which eventually caused Śiva to forget his grief and cease the adharmic din he had been creating. The pieces fell to earth, and the places where they landed became the *śākta pīṭha*s.

This myth is about many things—devotion, asceticism, Śiva's power—but at its core it is an etiology, explaining and substantiating the religious power of the sites. The power of these places is constituted both by the corporeal remains of the goddess, which may or may not be actually thought to be located at the sites, and the association of the place with the myth. Although it is often said that the goddess is everywhere, and that she is fully embodied in any of her thousands of temples,[5] it is at these special places where the power of the goddess is most condensed, where it is particularly charged. In a similar manner, the god Śiva's power is universally available, but it is thought to be most concentrated in the city of Banaras, which is understood to be the special abode of Śiva; millions of pilgrims visit the city because it is there that Śiva is thought to be most present.[6] Likewise, pilgrims and devotees go to the *śākta pīṭha*s in order to partake in that power; devotion directed to the goddess is thought to be more effective at these sites.

This is not the only story of how Tārāpīṭh came to be a sacred place. Another is connected to one of the distinct iconographic forms of Tārā at the temple—she is depicted as a loving mother, holding Śiva on her lap nursing him. This myth, which seems to be part of the local, oral history of the temple, involves the Buddha and the Hindu sage Vaśiṣṭha. Vaśiṣṭha had been engaged in ascetic practices for ten thousand years, but failed to gain any power from his practices. He then went to the god Brahmā for help, and Brahmā explained to him that it is through Tārā's power that he creates the world, and through Tārā's power that Viṣṇu maintains it and Śiva destroys it.[7] Brahmā told Vaśiṣṭha to recite the Tārā mantra, which he did, and then worshipped her for one thousand years. Again he gained no power, and became angry. At this point Tārā appeared to him, and told him he did not know or understand her, and thus his worship was futile: "only Viṣṇu in the form of Buddha knows my form of worship, and to learn this kind of worship you have to go to China."[8]

Vaśiṣṭha then went to Tibet, where he had a vision of the Buddha, intoxicated, surrounded by beautiful, naked girls. Vaśiṣṭha was understandably shocked, and refused to join in this behavior, until a voice from the sky told him that this was the best way to worship Tārā. Confused, he went to the Buddha—who was really Viṣṇu—and asked what he should do. The Buddha/Viṣṇu gave him a special form of tantric *sādhanā*, or practice, along with a basic primer in tantric practice and instructions. He performed the rituals as instructed, and then went to Tārāpur where the Tārāpiṭha temple is now located. According to Alan Morinis, the "stone image of Ugratārā which was seen by Vasiṣṭha had actually existed before that time. The eye of Satī (some say the third or spiritual eye) which fell to earth at Tārāpiṭh turned to stone and sprang up in the form of the image which Vasiṣṭha saw."[9]

This is a rather more complicated etiology than the myth about Śiva and Satī, in part because it presupposes that myth—that is why Tārāpiṭh is regarded as powerful in the first place, because it is where Tārā's eye fell—and then adds another etiological layer, explaining how the particular image of Tārā, suckling Śiva, got there. In this instance, these layers add depth to the Hindu identity of the site. This is not unusual, of course; we have already encountered this at Ayodhya. What is at play in such instances is a kind of palimpsest quality that in part constitutes the sacrality of places, in which stories and myths and histories and building materials are layered one upon another—although, really, it is more dynamic than this, more of a tangle than a layering. I borrow this notion of the palimpsest from Andreas Huyssen, who begins his complex discussion of memory and history and architecture, *Present Pasts: Urban Palimpsests and the Politics of Memory*, by pointing out—it actually seems like a lament—that historical memory is not what it used to be, and that the boundary between past and present has become rather more porous than it once was. "Untold recent and not so recent pasts impinge upon the present through modern media of reproduction like photography, film, recorded music, and the Internet, as well as through the explosion of historical scholarship and an ever more voracious museal culture."[10] Huyssen intentionally overstates his case, and although there may be real truth that what we are seeing in the contemporary world is something new, and that history and the past have taken on a new meaning, I am not convinced that this has not always, to some degree, been part of collective memory and orientation;

the mythical, historical, political, and personal intersect, conflict, overlap, and become entangled and confused in praxis. Just as physical structures such as temples are built, altered, destroyed, rebuilt, converted, and so on, so go the histories of those buildings and places.[11]

What I think is useful about Huyssen's use of palimpsest is that it gets at something of the dynamic character of religiously charged places. Part of what makes them charged in the first place may be a kind of collective mimetic desire, to invoke René Girard, in which what leads one group to make a claim on a place is precisely that some other group has already made a claim to the place.[12] Certainly something like that seems to have been in play at Ayodhya. In this regard, the figure of Tārā, and the places where she is worshipped, where she is embodied, provide a significant contrast to many of the places and objects I discuss here. For Tārā is shared by both traditions, Hindu and Buddhist, but that sharing is rarely contested and, really, rarely sharing at all. It is, rather, more like there are two female deities who share a name and have some overlapping characteristics, but who otherwise are so distinct as to be, for lack of a better term, unthreatening. In other words, they are other, but not inimical.

Whereas in most Hindu contexts Tārā is a fierce figure, haunting the cremation grounds, at Tārāpiṭh she is benign; the central image presents Tārā nursing Śiva, and her devotees treat her as a domesticated woman, a benign mother who bestows favors and cares for her worshippers. In this regard, she resembles the Buddhist Tārā, although at the temple she also receives blood offerings. Despite the presence of the Buddha in this myth, however, and despite Tārā's more benign, and perhaps more Buddhist, character, Tārāpiṭh is unambiguously a Hindu temple. This, then, is a largely monothetic sort of religious place, one that is not contested. Given the presence of Buddhist motifs and Buddhist figures in this etiology, it would be reasonable to expect that some Buddhists might visit the site, or claim it as their own, but in my experience the site is rarely ever visited by Buddhists, no doubt in part because there are virtually no Buddhists in this remote part of the subcontinent.

Although the primary focus of this chapter is the very recent dispute over the Muslim Community Center—known as Park51 or, to its detractors, the Ground Zero Mosque—that has been proposed to be built in Lower Manhattan, near the site of the destroyed World Trade Center, I began this chapter with this brief discussion of the *śākta pīṭhas* because one of the larger issues I address throughout this book is the question of how and why particular places become freighted with religious significance, and why that religious significance sometimes leads to conflict (the question of why, in most instances, it does not lead to conflict is decidedly more difficult to analyze). In India, many sites that Western scholars typically call sacred are the places where some significant event has happened (or is alleged to have happened): the Buddha attained enlightenment there, say, or Śiva slayed a demon there, or Kṛṣṇa was born there, or some saint performed a miracle there. In other instances, sites are significant because of what is located there: in the case of the *śākta pīṭhas*, it is the power of the goddess; across Rajasthan, in northwestern India, there are tombs where Sufi saints are buried; in Sri Lanka, at the Dalaga Maligawa in Kandy, the Buddha's tooth is enshrined, and so on.

To say that sites such as the *śākta pīṭhas* became significant because of their association with the myth of Śiva and Satī only tells part of the story, however; left out are the personal dynamics, the political machinations, the physical work, and so on, that make up the dense history, or more properly histories, of the sites. Furthermore, as we have seen in the last chapter, places, like people, often have shifting, dynamic, and contradictory identities. They are in motion.

It is useful here to return to Charles Tilly who, in writing about the vexing question of social identity, has suggested that a conversational model of analysis might offer a way out of the impasse of instrumentalist (identity is constructed) versus primordialist or essentialist (identity is a given) approaches to religious conflict.[13] He says that we could instead "recognize the conversational character of contention" and "examine such a conversation's location in continuously negotiated interchanges among specific interlocutors."[14] This is, I think, a useful way to think about contested religious sites, as places that are continuously negotiated; in other words, as much as one side or the other might wish to fix the identity and character of the site, the dynamics of the contestation subvert this. Tilly points out, however, that it is not a matter simply of a kind of free-form, anything-goes struggle for control. Rather, adopting the language of performance—and thus echoing, in a sense, the Turners—he suggests the notion of "contentious repertoires," in which the "pair of interlocutors has available to it a limited number of previously created performances within which the people involved can make claims."[15] These repertoires are not unlike Bourdieu's habitus, in the sense that there is a kind of limiting structure amidst, or underlying, the fluidity. Thus the history of the place, the usage, the ownership, the physical structures, all are, in a sense, limiting, in the same way, say, that legal rules and the specific evidence presented limit what goes on in a courtroom, or the way a script limits a dramatic performance. But they are only partially limiting, precisely because of the interpretive, performative dynamics of the sites and the people who claim them.

To return briefly to the question of why some sites are contested and others are not, we might adopt Tilly's notion of the conversational character of contestation, and say that in the case of non-contested sites, such as Tārapiṭh, there is no conversation. That is not to say that people do not talk about the site; rather, it is to say that they do not talk—although such talk may well emerge at some point in the future—about what sort of site it is, or what it really represents, or what deity is really present there. There is no contestation here—it is what it is. But of course that is not the case at all sites. Indeed, for many religiously significant sites, such an iteration is precluded by the more pressing question: What is it? and for whom? This has been at the heart of the contested discussion about how to mark the sacredness of what is called Ground Zero and the fierce debate that erupted in the American media in 2010 over the Muslim community center, the Park51 project that was proposed for the site of the damaged Burlington Coat Factory in Lower Manhattan.

2.2 *Consecrating a Void*

Basically, though, we don't want to live in a memorial.
—Battery Park Resident[16]

One of the important conceptions of the sacred space of Ground Zero has been the image of the towers' footprints. As the various designs for the memorial were publicly vetted, analyzed, critiqued, rejected, and revised over the course of several years in the early and mid-2000s, the footprints where the towers had stood became central; thus as Marita Sturken puts it, "the footprints of the building are asked to give the vanished dead a home, a place where they are imagined to be, where one can imagine visiting them, to make them present in the absence of their remains. And it is, above all, the absence of remains that haunts this site."[17] The final design for the memorial at Ground Zero—Michael Arad's "Reflecting Absence"—prominently features the footprints: the central memorial consists of two block-length squares, where the original bases of the towers were, with two square fountains cascading down the sides of each of the footprints into two 350,000-gallon reflecting pools thirty feet below surface level. The chair of the Lower Manhattan Development Committee (LMDC) jury that selected Arad's design said that his memorial had the capacity to "make the gaping voids left by the Towers' destruction the primary symbol of loss."[18]

The sacrality of Ground Zero itself is complicated and complex, as I noted at the outset of this chapter; Arad's memorial in an important sense reduces and limits this sacrality by making it primarily about loss. As Sturken puts it:

> The idea that the towers should be mourned as lost buildings is so taken for granted in the debate over how to rethink Ground Zero that few have attempted to question it. This means that lower Manhattan is constantly conceived as a space of absence, not only where the dead are lost but as a place that will always seem to be lacking the towers no matter what is built in their place (and whatever is built will always be seen as having been built *in their place*).[19]

Jay Winter, in his *Sites of Memory, Sites of Mourning*, calls such spaces an "embodiment of nothingness."[20]

There is indeed something profoundly powerful about the footprint as an image of absence; it is a space, an empty space, whose emptiness is constituted precisely by a presence that no longer is. A footprint marks a place where a person has been but is no longer. It is perhaps understandable, then, that the concept of the towers' footprints became so central to the conception of the planning of the memorial. As early as 2002, Governor George Pataki talked of the footprints of the towers as an inviolable space. Sturken points out that during the process of planning the memorial, there was

> very little questioning (and almost none initially) of the constant reemphasis of the footprints and reassertion of the twin towers in these designs. The discourse of sacredness has inscribed the footprints of the towers with a particularly charged meaning, and in relation to that the repetition of the towers in these designs, either as absence or presence, is remarkable. This underscores the way this reenactment has functioned as a kind of mourning and a compulsive repetition, one that has constituted both stasis, with architectural imaginings caught in the moment of trauma, but also mourning."[21]

This intertwining of absence and presence was visually captured in one of the first formal memorials associated with the World Trade Center site—although there were of course dozens of impromptu memorials on the streets of New York in the days and months after the attack on the towers—the Tribute in Light in March of 2002.

Created by the artists Paul Myoda and Julian LaVerdier, this temporary memorial, which has been repeated on each anniversary of the attack, consisted of two huge beams of blue light projected into the night sky, from where the towers had stood. There is something ghostly about this (they originally called the project "Phantom Towers"), the lights creating a kind of chimera of the towers. Sturken notes that in many of the artistic images of Ground Zero, the towers had been "a constant refrain, constantly reemerging in the space as if they cannot be erased from people's artistic imaginations of the skyline."[22] Much like Jacques Derrida's—via Martin Heidegger—notion of writing *sous rature*, "under erasure," the towers are crossed out, as it were, absent, but also present, a presence that is perhaps made all the more powerful by the iconicity of their absence. Hence the power of the footprints. When the *New York Times* published the September 23, 2001 edition of the *Sunday Magazine*—less than two weeks after the attacks, after all—it focused on the destruction of the towers, not surprisingly, and featured an article titled "To Rebuild or Not: Architects Respond." The husband and wife team, Elizabeth Diller and Ricardo Scofidio, responded this way, seeming to channel Derrida in what now seems to be a most ironic way: "What's most poignant now is that the identity of the skyline has been lost. We would say, Let's not build something that would mend the skyline, it is more powerful to leave it void. We believe it would be tragic to erase the erasure."[23]

Presence and absence comingle in Arad's memorial design, not just with the prominence of the footprints of the buildings, but also with the inscribed names of the dead on the inner walls of the subterranean space of the footprints and the inclusion of parcels of the remains of the dead, deposited in small bags, interned within the memorial. Like relics in other contexts, all of this serves both to remind us that there is loss, and thus absence here, but also presence. David Simpson has called the central motif of the memorial a "double void."[24] This goes to the core of at least one aspect of Ground Zero's sacrality: it is a graveyard. When George Pataki famously declared, in a speech at a gathering of victims' families in February of 2002, that nothing could be built where the towers had stood, calling the area "hallowed ground," he was invoking the sense that the place was a graveyard, in part, and also tapping into the patriotic—if not xenophobic—symbolism of the sacrifice of the "heroes" of 9/11. It was a projection of a kind of sacredness on the site, and Pataki invoked, in that speech, the importance of the footprints: "They will always be a permanent and lasting memorial to those we lost." Many have since pointed out the rather ironic clash of the imputed, or imposed, sacredness of the site and the commercial interests of the owners of the parcel, but it is not insignificant that this tension was noted immediately after Pataki's speech by Bruce S. Fowle, who was the senior principal at Fox & Fowle Architects, the firm that had helped to produce an early report on possible configurations and uses of Ground Zero: "You can't even find the footprints right now because everything has been taken away. To think of it as sacred ground is purely symbolic. And once you're in symbolic mode, you have to ask whether there are other alternatives you could consider that might be better."[25]

When the towers collapsed, they came down with almost unimaginable violence, and the destructive power was almost total. The towers, and everything in them, were effectively reduced to dust and rubble. As a firefighter in the documentary *9/11* said, "You have two 110-story office buildings. You don't find a desk, you don't find a chair, you don't find a computer. The biggest piece of telephone I found was a keypad and it was this big. The building collapsed to dust. How are we supposed to find anybody in this stuff? There's nothing left of the building."[26] Patricia Yaeger and Sturken have each written extensively and incisively about this dust,[27] and both have noted its peculiar and alarming ambiguity; it was both dirt, refuse, a dangerous pollutant that needed to be removed as quickly as possible—it is this dust that is suspected of sickening many of those who worked at the Ground Zero site in the months after the attack—and it was also the comminuted bodily remains of those who died in the towers and the planes that crashed into them.

Much of this dust—and I must point out here that in fact it was not really dust at all, or at least not all dust, but over one million tons of rubble—and all but a few large structural pieces of the towers and the damaged building near them, was removed to Fresh Kills landfill, where forensic scientists would eventually spend thousands of hours combing through the debris searching for recognizable corporeal remains on which they could conduct DNA tests. They eventually recovered nearly 3,000 body parts. Some of the dust was also collected only a few weeks after the attacks, in steel drums—standard fifty-five gallon oil drums—at

Fresh Kills and given police escort back into the city. There, on October 14, 2001, this dust was ceremoniously scooped into four thousand urns, which were then distributed to those families that wanted one. Thus the dust had been, through this ritual act, transformed—same material, but the status of that material is largely determined by the context in which it is situated. One is reminded here of Jonathan Z. Smith's quip that in the field we talk of soil, but in the house it is dirt.[28]

The imputed sacrality of the site where the Twin Towers stood is, in part, constituted by the attack on the towers, by the deaths of over 2,000 people there, and by the continued presence of the remains of those who died there. Indeed, even with the meticulous search for the remains of the dead, and the removal of the rubble and dirt and dust from the site, the remains of the dead are still very much present at Ground Zero and, really, across much of Lower Manhattan. Small pieces of human remains continued to be found near where the towers stood years after the attack and, of course, the dust scattered and then settled across the region. In a dubious note in the March 24, 2007 edition of the *Daily Observer*, a worker for the Department of Sanitation claimed that the city had used some of the debris from Fresh Kills to fill potholes in the city: "I observed the New York City Department of Sanitation taking these fines [building material] from the conveyor belts of our machines, loading it onto tractors and using it to pave roads and fill potholes, dips, and ruts."[29]

The World Trade Center occupied sixteen acres of land: "And as the smoke cleared in those very early days, those sixteen acres downtown were being asked to do the impossible: to makes sense of the senseless; to extol the dead even as they were being exhumed; to transform victims into heroes and heroes into gods; to find meaning in the squalor or real-time mass murder."[30] Larry Silverstein, the developer who had leased the World Trade Center only months before it was destroyed, was a vocal advocate for rebuilding, for quickly restoring the thousands of square feet of office space that had been lost; to him, the site was commercial to the core. Many others strongly disagreed, but Silverstein said that it would be "the tragedy of tragedies not to rebuild this part of New York," since, to him, not restoring the financial vitality of the area would "give the terrorists the victory they seek."[31] In the long, contentious debate about rebuilding, about what to rebuild and whether to rebuild at all, it became clear that not all of those sixteen acres were going to be a memorial—despite Mayor Rudolph Giuliani's opinion that nothing mundane nor commercial should be built on the site, and Pataki's early sentiment, echoed by many of the victims' family members, that nothing at all should be built there—the commercial development of the site was virtually a given. But if the site was sacred, as it had been deemed, then how would or could this sacredness be preserved and marked? Part of the definition of the sacred is, after all, that it is restricted, separate, not sullied by the mundane.

By as early as 2002, this question had become important in the discussions about the memorialization and development of the site. In November of that year, the LMDC produced a formal development document, "The Blueprint of the Future of Lower Manhattan," that presented fifteen guiding points for the development of the site, one of which was to "reserve an area of the site for one or more permanent memorials." Although various groups representing the victims were opposed to any commercialization of the site, eventually a "memorial quadrant" was proposed, an area that was centered on the towers' footprints, and that space covered about two acres. Given the competing memorial and commercial conceptions and functions of the area, many felt the need to separate and preserve the sacred, to create a clearly demarcated boundary between the mundane space of Manhattan and the sacred zone of the memorial. That space, however, would contract and expand; by 2005 the actual bounded area of Ground Zero itself had tripled in size to 6.5 acres. Eventually the LMDC fixed the memorial quadrant as a 4.7 acre space—although in the final iteration of the memorial it has grown to 8 acres—that would be bound by Fulton, Greenwich, Liberty, and West Streets. Stefan Pryor, the president of the Corporation, used religious language to describe this quadrant, saying that it was "special; indeed, sacrosanct."[32] This is an interesting moment in the discussion of Ground Zero, because it seemed to be a point at which the geographical parameters of sacredness were, finally, after years of debate, established. The sacred space of Ground Zero, however, could not be so easily bound.

Indeed, when plans to build an Islamic cultural center in Lower Manhattan were first reported in 2009—a project that became for several months a ubiquitous topic of conversation and debate in the national popular media—a phrase that was heard and read over and over again, attaining a kind of iconic status, was "in the shadow of Ground Zero." The phrase "Ground Zero" had been used to designate the site where the towers had stood just hours after the attacks;[33] although the phrase has been critiqued, certainly, as a striking instance of American exceptionalism—there are any number of places around the world, including Auschwitz, Hiroshima, Dresden, Darfur, or Baghdad, to which this label could equally apply—"Ground Zero" is used largely without further thought or qualification to refer to the place where the World Trade Centers stood.[34] The phrase "in the shadow of Ground Zero," likewise, came to be used so frequently in the media in the spring and summer of 2010 that it goes utterly unmarked as a figure of speech, and has become a kind of rhetorical fetish or totem, a metonymically charged iteration that essentially speaks for itself, that makes an entire argument in six words, in the process expanding, symbolically and physically, the resonance of "Ground Zero." But where did this phrase come from, and how has it become so charged?

The first usage I have found occurred in the *New York Times* just six days after the planes crashed into the towers, in a report on the displaced residents of Battery Park: "Gus Ouranitsas, the resident manager of 200 Rector Place, has been sleeping in the lobby for almost a week—a sentinel at one of the evacuated apartment buildings in Battery Park City, a 92-acre complex in the shadow of the ruined World Trade Center."[35] It appeared again six days later, in an article by the critic Michiko Kakutani, who writes about the strange and uneasy continuance of the mundane amidst the chaos and rubble and trauma of Lower Manhattan: "Still, it would take awhile. In what used to be the shadow of the World Trade Center, a couple of children played catch, their faces obscured by dust masks."[36] These two usages are, significantly, different: in the first, it is the ruins of the towers and the other buildings that cast the shadow, a kind of absent shadow, after all, in that it would be a shadow of a shadow; in the second, Kakutani actually uses the past tense, marking the absence of the buildings and, thus, the shadows that they would have cast.

The rhetoric of the shadow of Ground Zero seems to reflect a desire, conscious or not, to preserve the towers somehow, while at the same time it seems to be a way of marking their absence. There is something decidedly mournful about the phrase, and, indeed, mourning and loss have, as Sturken and others have noted, been a consistent theme in discussions of the place.[37] A shadow is constituted by a presence, of course; something that is not there cannot cast a shadow. But a shadow is also not the object itself. Clearly, "in the shadow of Ground Zero" is connected to the towers themselves, to the physical shadows that they once cast; these shadows, the actual shadows cast by the actual buildings, were not, importantly, static, but moved with the course of the sun, both on a daily basis and with the changing angle of the sun over the course of the seasons. The phrase, though, in this context is even more complex: How can an absence have a shadow? How can something that is not there extend... well, to where? How is it that this non-existent shadow, this chimera shadow, has come, for some, to delimit—physically and conceptually—the sacrality of Ground Zero?

2.3 *Polluting the Shadow of Ground Zero*

The Cordoba House is a 16-storey middle finger to America.

—Editorial on *Atlas Shrugged* Website[38]

Religion has nothing to do with this.

—RICK LAZIO[39]

When the second plane—United Flight 175—tore into the south tower of the World Trade Center on September 11, 2001, it was a scene that tens of millions of Americans, and millions living elsewhere, witnessed on live television, and hundreds of millions would eventually see videos of the event; the image was on the cover of both *Newsweek* and *Time*, and countless other magazines and newspapers as well. It continues to be shown over and over again. In some ways, the image of the plane hitting the tower became an image of the nation's collective trauma, a synechdochally charged image, and a video icon, one that could be played over and over again, and this experience and sense of trauma certainly has contributed to the perceived sacrality of Ground Zero.

A far less noted and noticed scene occurred at virtually the same moment, only a few blocks away, and was directly linked to this iconic image and the event itself. A large part of the plane's landing gear tore off when it hit the tower and hurled through the sky at tremendous speed. It crashed through the roof of the Burlington Coat factory, at 45 Park Place; the store was not open at the time, although a few workers were inside having breakfast. No one was injured there, but there was considerable damage to the building. Given the tremendous destruction caused by the impact of the two planes, and the subsequent collapse of the towers themselves, it is little wonder that initially no one really noticed the debris that crashed into the Burlington Coat Factory. Such violent intrusions occurred across a wide swath of Lower Manhattan; Setha Low writes, for instance, of a woman who returned to her apartment weeks after the attacks, only to find a filing cabinet that had fallen from one of the towers in her living room.[40] Gradually, the pieces of the planes that had rained down were gathered and taken away as evidence; the debris and dust was eventually gathered as well, much of it taken to Fresh Kills. The partially destroyed building at 45 Park Place remained locked and empty, a gaping hole in its roof where the rain and snow and sunlight poured in.

In the fall of 2009, some of Lower Manhattan's sizeable Muslim community began to gather in the empty space for Friday prayers; they had a permit issued by the City of New York, as well as the permission of the building's owners. The space was used as an overflow space for the Al Farah mosque, at 245 West Broadway. Perhaps some New Yorkers saw this as a kind of sacrilege, Muslims praying on the site of this great trauma that was, for many, caused by Islam. Mostly, though, these gatherings went unnoticed. For many of the Muslims praying there, it was a kind of act of defiance aimed at the radicals who had flown into the towers; as Feisal Abdul Rauf, the imam at Al Farah, put it at the time: "We want to push back against the extremists."[41]

A few years after the attacks, the owners of the damaged building that had housed the Burlington Coat Factory building, Kukiko Mitani and Stephen Pomerantz, attempted to sell it, but were unsuccessful; the area in Lower Manhattan around what had been the World Trade Center remained for years a chaotic place, at once a site of broad destruction and frenetic building, and the larger commercial real estate market had been badly affected by the housing downturn and subsequent recession that began in 2005. Eventually, the real estate investment group Soho Properties purchased the property in July of 2009 for $4.85 million, considerably less than the original $18 million asking price. The chairman of the Soho group, Sharif El-Gamal, said at the time that the space would "provide a place of peace, a place of services and solutions for the community which is always looking for interfaith dialogue."[42] One of the investors in the site was the Cordoba Initiative, an interfaith group that was founded by Imam Feisal in 2004, as well as another group he is associated with, the American Society for Muslim Advancement.

The Cordoba Initiative is "a multi-national, multi-faith organization dedicated to improving understanding and building trust among people of all cultures and faith traditions," named after the city in Spain that, under Muslim rule from the eighth to the eleventh centuries, has come for some to symbolize the possibility of inter-religious coexistence. [43] As Daisy Khan, Imam Feisal's wife and herself an active voice in the interreligious dialogue movement, has put it, the proposed center, initially called Cordoba House and later changed to Park51, "is a symbol... that will give voice to the silent majority of Muslims who suffer at the hands of extremists. A center will show that Muslims will be part of rebuilding Lower Manhattan."[44] Initially, El-Gamal had bought the property to develop it as a commercial project, intending to build a condominium on the site. It was Rauf and Khan who convinced him to build a cultural center instead, intended to be a kind of Muslim version of a Jewish Community Center or YMCA—specifically they had in mind the model of the Jewish-run 92nd Street Y—but with an expressed intent to foster interreligious dialogue and understanding. The initial vision of the project was a 13-storey cultural center that would include a 500-seat performing arts space, a cooking school, a restaurant, exhibition space, a swimming pool and gym and basketball court, a library, and an art studio. There would also be ample space for prayer. "We insist on calling it a prayer space and not a mosque," Khan noted, "because you can use a prayer space for activities apart from prayer. You can't stop anyone who is a Muslim despite his religious ideology from entering the mosque and staying there. With a prayer space, we can control who gets to use it."[45] This last remark seemed particularly directed at those, such as Robert Spencer, who have condemned all mosques as breeding grounds for radical Islam.

Despite their intentions to foster dialogue and understanding at Cordoba House/Park51, Rauf and Khan were well aware of the potential controversy the proposed center might stir. As Rauf put it: "I have been part of this community for 30 years. Members of my congregation died on 9/11. That attack was carried out by extremist terrorists in the name of my faith. There is a war going on within Islam between a violent, extremist minority and a moderate majority that condemns terrorism. The center for me is a way to amplify our condemnation of that atrocity and to amplify the moderate voices that reject terrorism and seek mutual understanding and respect with all faiths."[46]

An initial hearing was held with a local community board, at which the issues discussed were mostly logistical; however, this meeting came only a few days after the arrest of Faisal Shahzad, a disgruntled and perhaps also mentally ill Pakistani American who had attempted to detonate a car bomb in Times Square on May 1, and the atmosphere in New York was again highly charged with anti-Islam feelings. The community board was immediately inundated with calls and emails, some of them threatening. A second hearing was held on May 25 before Community Board No. 1—which is an advisory board for Tribeca, Battery Park City, City Hall, South Street Seaport, the Financial District, and Civic Center in Manhattan that makes recommendations to the city government—to debate the project. The hearing was only advisory, but it was tense and contested, with some in attendance voicing their adamant support of the right to free speech and worship, and the power of such a place to heal the wounds of 9/11, and others decrying the project as an affront to those who died in the attacks. The Board voted 29-1, with 10 abstentions, in favor of the project.[47] The New York Landmarks Preservation Commission would later vote on the project, with a 9-0 vote backing the proposal.

The Lower Manhattan community, including prominent Christian and Jewish leaders, largely embraced the project, viewing it as a significant peace initiative and a financial boon to the area, which was still struggling to financially and socially recover from the attacks on the World Trade Center. As soon as the project entered the national public consciousness, though, the tone changed dramatically. One of the first national figures to seize upon the issue was Mark Williams, a Tea Party figure who, in a paroxysm of religious confusion—and a telling example of the way in which the Muslim other was a kind of magnet for other sorts of otherness—denounced the project on his website, declaring that "The monument would consist of a Mosque for the worship of the terrorists' monkey-god."[48]

It was at this point that things became particularly rancorous, and the issue moved from a mostly local one to the national stage. Pataki passionately defended the project, citing the U.S. Constitution; congressman Rick Lazio, who was running to replace Pataki, was equally passionate in his denouncements of it. For the next several months, Park51 was hotly debated in the U.S. media; there were protest marches both against and in favor of the project. Although the most vocal national opponents of the project were associated with the Tea Party and other conservative political organizations, more mainstream politicians denounced the project as part of their campaigns, and a wide variety of religious groups, from conservative Christian organizations to moderate Jewish groups, including the Anti-Defamation League, joined in the fray. President Barack Obama publicly supported the project, as strongly as Sarah Palin and other conservative figures denounced it. The issue became part of the campaigns of any number of politicians.

The mayor of New York City, Michael Bloomberg, was a vocal supporter of the project, and, in response to the increasingly vocal critics of the proposal after the vote to allow the project to move forward, gave an emotional speech on the subject at Governors Island on August 3, 2010, in which he cited the First Amendment of the U.S. Constitution as well as

New York's long history of racial and religious tolerance: "Let us not forget that Muslims were among those murdered on 9/11, and that our Muslim neighbors grieved with us as New Yorkers and as Americans. We would betray our values and play into our enemies' hands if we were to treat Muslims differently than anyone else. In fact, to cave to popular sentiment would be to hand a victory to the terrorists, and we should not stand for that."[49] The issue would soon include not just the center itself, but the sanctity of the Ground Zero site, the status of Muslims—and really all immigrants—in the country, and, in the end, the very legitimacy of Islam as a religion. There were protests across the country, including a threat by an obscure evangelical pastor in Florida, Terry Jones, to publicly burn the Koran; these plans were aborted after international and national pressure, including direct pleas from both Secretary of State Hillary Rodham Clinton and General David H. Petraeus.[50]

2.4 *The Muslim Other and the Indeterminate Sacrality of Ground Zero*

81% of US Mosques Promote Jihad

—Widely Used Headline Responding to M. KEDAR AND D. YERUSHALMI's Study of Violent Images and Literature in American Mosques[51]

We can perceive the collapse of the WTC towers as the climactic conclusion of twentieth-century art's "passion for the Real"—the "terrorists" themselves did not do it primarily to provoke real material damage but for the spectacular effect of it.

—SLOVOJ ZIZEK[52]

On the morning of the attacks on the World Trade Center and the Pentagon, I was home writing and had taken a break to read the *New York Times* online; I vividly remember seeing the "Breaking News" headline scroll across the homepage of the *Times*, reporting that a plane had crashed into one of the World Trade Center towers. I turned on the television to see if I could find more information about what was happening, and spent much of the remainder of the day, as did millions of people across the country and world, watching the events unfold in real time and talking with friends and my family on the phone. I was worried and frightened.

I had many friends in New York, some of whom worked in the towers, and my mother was in the city, about to fly back to her home in Warsaw. The day is a blur in my memory, but I know that at some point I went to pick up my young son at preschool. Partly it was an act of protection; we were in Virginia, less than two hours from the Pentagon, and I felt, somehow, that he would be safer at home. I also simply wanted him near me, for my own sake and, I thought, for his. Although the events in New York and Washington and Pennsylvania began to become clear as the day wore on, no one knew who was behind the attacks, why they had happened, nor whether this was the end or the beginning of the violence. I am not sure if I slept that night, glued to the television and the Internet, trying, like so many millions across the world, to gain some understanding of what had happened. It is difficult to remember that virtually nothing was certain in the hours and days after the attacks. Speculation was everywhere, but little else.

I was scheduled to teach my Hinduism class the next morning, and my college decided, in an attempt to maintain a degree of normalcy in that chaotic and confusing time, to hold classes as usual. I could not see how I could possibly stick to my planned lesson, and so I simply went into the classroom, sat down with my students, and asked them what they would like to discuss. There initially was silence, my students looking exhausted and dazed, until one young woman half-raised her hand and asked, holding back tears, "Why do they hate us so much?" It was a chilling moment, a sentiment that was echoed across the nation, an expression of fear and shock and bewilderment. As I looked at this young woman, tears now streaming down her face, and scanned the tear-streaked faces of my other students, I was deeply struck by how frightened these students were.

This fear was palpable, and this was understandable: many of my students, I knew, had parents and siblings living in Washington, and I knew that some of them also had parents and relatives working in the military, some of them at the Pentagon. But what was most striking to me was the wording of the question: "they," "us," and "hate." Although none of us knew anything of the attackers or their motives at this early time, the immediate sentiment in the United States after the attacks on September 11 was that this was the work of terrorists, and that those terrorists were Muslim;[53] for many, this was seen as the first salvo in a cosmic war between us and them, between the benign forces of western Modernity and Christianity and the other as conceived of as the evil forces of Islam.[54]

All of this points to an important aspect of the constitution of sacred places: the discursive process through which a threatening, inimical other is constituted, an other—like the Muslims who were seen as polluting the sacrality of not only Ayodhya, but by extension all of India—whose intent is to usurp such a place. I use "discursive" here not to imply that such an other is never physically threatening or dangerous, which they often are, but rather to highlight the fact that the perception of otherness, and the threat it poses, often precedes the kinds of on-the-ground conflicts that often become violent.[55]

This is a complex topic, and there is a vast body of philosophical literature on otherness and alterity; I am hesitant to wade into these waters here for fear of drowning my specific discussion in their depths. That said, however, it is really impossible to understand the dynamics of a place such as Park51 and the controversy it has created without giving some attention to the way otherness comes into play in the discourse. Judith Butler, in her provocative *Giving an Account of Oneself*, draws on Nietzsche, Levinas, and Foucault, among others, in emphasizing the centrality of the encounter with the other, and the pain and injury and, yes, fear that such an encounter can entail. Nietzsche, Butler points out, "remarks that we become conscious of ourselves only after certain injuries have been inflicted."[56] The injury, the pain and trauma, forces a self-reflection and self-evaluation, what amounts to, really, self-recognition for Butler: "[W]e become reflective upon ourselves, accordingly, through fear and terror. Indeed, we become morally accountable as a consequence of fear and terror."[57] I will leave it to others to apply Butler's ethical excursus to post-September 11 American identity—this is, I must say, fertile ground for analysis—but her point is important here in that it points to the way in which the controversy over the Park51 project, and its intimate relation to the perceived sacredness of Ground Zero, has been a collective assertion of self over and against a perceived Muslim other.[58]

Muslims have long been the other in Europe, of course, but before the attacks on the World Trade Center and the Pentagon, America had other others. Furthermore, anti-Muslim sentiment in the United States did not begin on September 11, 2001; there were waves of such sentiment during the oil crisis of the 1970s, for instance, or immediately after the first bombing of the World Trade Center in 1993, or in connection with the ongoing conflict between Israel and Palestine. The broad influence of Samuel Huntington's divisive "clash of civilizations" thesis, which he first articulated in a lecture in 1992, is telling here, in that there was a receptive audience already in place for such a binary view of Islam and the West.[59] However, since the attacks in 2001 there has been a rising tide of Islamophobia in the United States,[60] the high water mark of which seemed to have been reached with the vitriolic response to the Park51 project. This discourse has born a marked similarity to the anti-Muslim sentiment that preceded and followed the destruction of the Babri Masjiid in India that I discussed in the preceding chapter, in which the Muslim other was intimately related to an understanding, on the part of some extreme Hindu nationalists, of an India that is exclusively Hindu and cannot include any foreigners.

Pamela Geller and Robert Spencer, and their organization, Stop Islamization of America (SIOA) have been perhaps the most visible proponents of this popular discourse, issuing proclamations on an almost daily basis. Spencer has long been one of the most prominent voices of anti-Muslim sentiment in the United States, running the inflammatory website www.jihadwatch.org, speaking on any number of conservative talk shows, and producing a string of books beginning with *Islam Unveiled: Disturbing Questions About the World's Fastest Growing Faith* in 2002 and including *The Truth About Muhammad, Founder of the World's Most Intolerant Religion* which spent time on the *New York Times* bestseller list in 2009, and others denigrating Islam and Muslims. Geller, for her part, rose to prominence largely because of her relentless attacks on the Park51 project in her blog, *Atlas Shrugged*, and, like Spencer, has been a ubiquitous figure on conservative talk shows.

When she was presented with an award by the conservative activist David Horowitz in November of 2010, Geller used her acceptance speech to once again denounce the Park51 project:

> You have to understand that we're in a war. We are at war now. It's not coming. It's not around the corner. We're at war now. The GZM is the second wave of the 9/11 attack.... We are under attack. Obviously, the violent jihad, the academic jihad, the sociological jihad, the cultural jihad, the academic jihad, we have been infiltrated at the senior level of the DOD.... This is not a conventional war. Each one of you must fight this war...you're each activated.... We have not yet recovered the bodies from 9/11 and we're under attack with ground zero mega mosque. And make no mistake, Cordoba, iconic of Islam's conquering of the West, it's quite deliberate.... It's a triumphal mosque. Because one shmuck in New York

says "it's a mosque of healing" doesn't make it so. It's ridiculous, it's insulting.[61]

The SIOA went on, in early 2011, to produce an inflammatory documentary on the Park51 project, *The Ground Zero Mosque: The Second Wave of the 9/11 Attacks*, that picked up and extended Geller's rhetoric.[62] In a press release, Geller called the film a "teaching tool." "This film," she said, "is perfect for showing your skeptical friends and family what we're really up against, and explaining to them how and why we must fight back. It is the first accurate reportage of the number one national and international news story that became national news without the mainstream media."[63]

Geller and Spencer are certainly extremists, but their anti-Islam rhetoric has been echoed across the country, and the Park51 project has very much been at the center of the storm. A substantial element in this discourse is the widely held opinion that Islam is a violent, predatory religion, and that mosques—any mosque, all mosques—are breeding grounds for extremists and the launching points of a new, global *jihad*. There have been calls from media pundits and political figures and religious leaders to curtail all mosque building in the country; hence Bryan Fischer, the director of the American Family Association—a prominent conservative organization with ties to such political figures as Michele Bachman, Mitch McConnell, and Newt Gingrich—pronounced, "Permits should not be granted to build even one more mosque in the United States of America, let alone the monstrosity planned for Ground Zero. This is for one simple reason: each Islamic mosque is dedicated to the overthrow of the American government."[64]

The question of what could and could not, or rather should and should not, be located in the sixteen acres that had been the World Trade Center was, as we have seen, an important topic during the debates about how to memorialize the site—recall Guiliani's insistence that there should be nothing mundane located in that space. Many of these debates were confined to the actual sixteen acres of the space, but there were all sorts of questions about what sort of buildings and institutions would be appropriate in the immediate vicinity of the site. Pataki, for his part, did not go so far as to publicly denounce those proposals that he found inappropriate—tacky, commercial, kitschy, trite, or simply insensitive—but he did say that "I view that memorial site as sacred grounds, akin to the beaches of Normandy or Pearl Harbor, and we will not tolerate anything on that site that denigrates America, denigrates

New York or freedom, or denigrates the sacrifice or courage that the heroes showed on Sept. 11."[65] Pataki was talking specifically about the sixteen acres, but the perceived sacredness of Ground Zero did not end there; it extended, it seems, outward, like the shadows of the buildings that were no longer standing, and, like those shadows, it seemed to be constantly shifting.

When the plans for Park51 entered the public discourse, those who denounced them initially did so on the basis of a conception of the sacrality of where the towers had stood; it was a grave, a place of deep loss and trauma, and to place anything that was inappropriate in its immediate vicinity was construed as sacrilege. A mosque, as the Park51 project was described in the popular press, was portrayed as an affront, a pollution, a victory monument to the terrorists. That, of course, is precisely the inverse of what Imam Rauf and Daisy Khan and the other planners intended. The irony here is palpable: a center intended to promote tolerance provokes blatant intolerance. But even without this particular irony, there is something deeply ironic about the perceived sacrality that radiates out from Ground Zero, because there are all sorts of elements located in Ground Zero's diffuse sacred space, in its shadow, that in another context might be seen as pollutants: bars, strip clubs, fast food joints, and betting parlors. As long as such things are not located within the memorial quadrant, though, they seem to be tolerable, seem not to impinge on the site's sacrality. It is Islam's proposed presence in the form of Park51 that most violates Ground Zero's presumed sacredness.

From a comparative perspective, the contestation over Park51 is somewhat different from that of a place such as the Babri Masjid, in that both Muslims and Hindus see that site as sacred space and claim it as their own, and their competing conceptions of sacredness do not mesh. The Temple Mount in Jerusalem is similarly contested: Jews, Christians, and Muslims all claim the site as sacred to their religion, and theirs alone. By contrast, the planners of Park51 have repeatedly stated that it is not a sacred space at all but a community center surrounded by similarly secular buildings. As Imam Rauf has put it, "It is absolutely disingenuous, as many have said, that that block is hallowed ground."[66] His point is clear enough: the block that runs from 47 to 51 Park Avenue is and has for a very long time been a commercial district. However, he—and he is certainly not alone here—has also missed something of the complexity of the conception of sacredness with which Ground Zero is infused. This is not, in the end, a static sense of the sacred, one that is bounded or fixed, but a strikingly fluid conception, one that is in part physical and in part amorphous. Certainly it is about place, but that sense of place extends beyond the physical and the locative, to the point that the whole of the United States could be understood to be Ground Zero, and thus sacred.[67]

I have, up to this point, avoided defining what I mean by sacred as it applies to Ground Zero, because as I noted in the last chapter, "sacred" as a static, normative category has little purchase. Durkheim famously defined the sacred in instrumental terms, and argued that the sacred is a category created by human beings. In other words, things and places and people are made sacred, and part of what constitutes their sacrality is that they are in some way set apart: "The sacred thing is, par excellence, that which the profane must not and cannot touch with impunity. To be sure, this prohibition cannot go so far as to make all communication between the two worlds impossible, for if the profane could in no way enter into relations with the sacred, the sacred would be of no use."[68] In a sense, then, the profane is the sacred's other, necessary for it to exist.

It seems clear enough that the sacredness of Ground Zero has been thrust upon the place, without any clear definition of what makes it sacred. As I noted earlier, for some it is sacred because it is a graveyard, while for others it is the trauma and suffering and violence that took place there that makes it sacred; there are, it would seem, gradations of sacrality at play here. It is as if Ground Zero and its sacredness are a kind of spatial *habitus* that shifts and morphs, depending on who is conceiving of it and in what context and for what purpose, although it is not at all clear that any of this is conscious, or fully conscious, on the part of those who employ the term. As Bourdieu puts it, "*habitus* contains the solution to the paradoxes of objective meaning without subjective intention. It is the source of these strings of 'moves' which are objectively organized as strategies without being the product of a genuine strategic intention."[69] In this sense, there is both a kind of givenness to the sacredness of Ground Zero, but also a field of practice, to use Bourdieu's term, within which there is negotiation and play.

One place this was played out was in the discussion of what sorts of commercial establishments could be located around Ground Zero; another instance was in the protracted debates about the memorial. Although there may have been little debate about the sacredness of the sixteen acres of the actual site, there has been far more ambiguity when it comes to the shadow of Ground Zero. As I have noted, this shadow is not defined, and it is not fixed. It seems that some things can be located in the shadow that might otherwise seem to compromise any conception of purity: betting parlors, strip joints, fast food restaurants.

There is also no consensus on what sort of religious images and structures might be located within Ground Zero's sacred zone. For instance, the two iron girders that formed what for many was a cross and which remained standing after the towers came down were seen by many as sacred and became a kind of pilgrimage site; however, when plans were announced to move the beams to the memorial museum, a group of atheists threatened to sue, invoking the United States' Constitution,[70] and, in a sense, articulating a kind of secular conception of the sacred in which the site's sacrality is conceived as national, not religious.[71] Indeed, for this group the religious image of the cross is seen as a pollution. In contrast, in the summer of 2011, the *New York Times* ran an article about a Greek Orthodox Church, Saint Nicholas, which had been destroyed in the attacks. A movement was afoot to rebuild the church, and the *Times* reported that there had, thus far, been no public criticisms of the plan, despite the fact that the church would be located very much within the shadow of Ground Zero as it is typically conceived. Indeed, Pataki—himself a Greek American—stood alongside the chancellor of the church, Bishop Andonios of Phasiane, in support of the rebuilding. This silence is striking, given the debate and contestation over virtually every structure in the immediate vicinity of Ground Zero. Bishop Andonios noted that the controversy over Park51 had actually aided his cause. "It's unfortunate that it took a controversy over a mosque to bring attention to the church," he said, but the Park51 debate was actually "a silver lining," because it drew attention to the plight of the church and, presumably, made the rebuilding of such a structure seem far less controversial in comparison.[72]

2.5 *On the Power of the Sacred*

> *[T]he sacred, as a kind of behaving, is not merely a number of immediate appearances, but a set of rules—prescriptions, proscriptions, interdictions—that determine the shape of the behavior and whether it is to count as an instance of the category in question.*
>
> —RICHARD COMSTOCK[73]

Why is a Greek Orthodox church not a pollution when a Muslim community center is? Or, alternately, why are two steel beams that form a cross a marker of sacrality for some and for others a pollution? What is the understanding of "sacred" that is at play here? This is how I believe Bourdieu helps us: the sacred is structured by the *habitus*, which, in the case of Ground Zero, is constituted by the events of September 11, the violence and death and ongoing trauma of the place, religious and civic ideals, and a great deal more. But within this structure is a kind of fluidity, what Bourdieu calls a field of practice, in which there is room for manipulation. Thus there is a strategic quality to Ground Zero's sacredness, or at least how this sacredness is discussed and manipulated.

A Greek Orthodox church is not a pollution, in part because there had been such a church at the site; however, there had also been prayer rooms in the Twin Towers, and two mosques in the immediate vicinity of the towers. Masjid Manhattan, on Warren Street, was founded in 1970 and is four blocks from the site; Masjid al-Farah, where Imam Rauf has long been a prayer leader, is about twelve blocks from where the World Trade Center was, and has been in its present location on West Broadway since 1985. It was because of overcrowding at Masjid al-Farah that prayers were being held at the Burlington Coat Factory. Furthermore, the Muslim presence in Lower Manhattan dates to the late nineteenth century, when the area was called "Little Syria"—most of the residents were, in fact, Orthodox Christians, but there was also a substantial Muslim population as well. The neighborhood was demolished during the construction of the Brooklyn-Battery Tunnel in the 1940s. It is not, then, simply that there had been a Greek Orthodox church that should be rebuilt, whereas Park51 represents something new. Rather, it is the fact that Greek Orthodox Christians are not threatening in this context; they may be other, but they are not The Other. Thus their presence is not polluting to Ground Zero's perceived sacredness, whereas the Muslim presence is.

The designation "sacred" in this context thus becomes a discursive means of exclusion, in that the other—The Other, Islam—must be kept out to preserve the sacredness of the place. Concomitantly, this discourse of otherness becomes a means by which the self, individually and collectively, is formulated and fortified; recall Butler's assertion that we come to know ourselves through the trauma of the encounter with the other. Not only the trauma of that encounter, but also, I would argue, the very threat that the other poses to the self. We become a self, in this sense, through the opposition with this other.

Islam is the "they" through which we constitute our sense of "we"; the question my student asked on September 12 was "why do they hate us?" after all. But who was the "us," and who the "they"? Addressing this question has been at the center of what became the national discussion of Park51, and although it may be clear who the "they" are—radical Muslims—it is far less clear who the "we" are. George W. Bush tapped into this dynamic only weeks after September 11, when, announcing that the United States military had begun attacks on purported al Qaeda camps in Afghanistan, he closed his address to the nation on October 7, 2001 with the following: "The battle is now joined on many fronts. We will not waver; we will not tire; we will not falter; and we will not fail. Peace and freedom will prevail. Thank you. May God continue to bless America."[74]

In the many protests and verbal attacks on the Park51 project, there has been a consistent and rather simple logic at play: it was terrorists motivated by radical Islam who attacked America on September 11, 2001, and so Islam, and therefore all Muslims—except, for some, those conceptual "moderate" Muslims that the conservative critics of the Park51 project find so rare—are the enemy. Park51 has been seen as a mosque by its opponents—the Ground Zero Mosque, as it is typically called in this discourse—despite assertions to the contrary by its supporters, and through an easy synecdoche it becomes Islam. All of America, by extension, is understood as Ground Zero, since it was not just New York and Washington that were attacked, but all of America, and the very American way of life; thus any mosque in America, no matter where it is located, is construed as a violation of American sacred space. The sacred, as Durkheim pointed out, seems to be quite contagious indeed.

This fallacious logic has been most consistently articulated by Geller and Spencer, but it has been broadly echoed by diverse individuals and politically conservative media outlets. Their message is consistent: Park51 is "sacrilege on sacred ground," as Sally Regenhard, whose son died on 9/11, put it.[75] "This is a place which is 600 feet from where almost 3,000 people were torn to pieces by Islamic extremists," said Debra Burlingame, the co-founder of the group 9/11 Families for a Safe & Strong America and a vocal opponent, at least initially, of any plans to build on the site.[76] And Newt Gingrich, likewise, prominently remarked that there "should be no mosque near Ground Zero in New York so long as there are no churches or synagogues in Saudi Arabia."[77] No matter that the United States is fundamentally a secular state founded on the principle of religious freedom and tolerance, whereas the kingdom of Saudi Arabia is, constitutionally, an Islamic state, and that the first article of the Saudi constitution makes this unambiguously clear: "The Kingdom of Saudi Arabia is a sovereign Arab Islamic state with Islam as its religion; God's Book and the Sunnah of His Prophet, God's prayers and peace be upon him, are its constitution, Arabic is its language and Riyadh is its capital." Anti-Islamic messages could be seen on the signs carried by protesters at the many anti-Park51 rallies held during the summer of 2010, a sampling of which included: "MUSLIMS INSENSITIVE TO VICTIMS & THEIR FAMILIES WITH MOSQUE 600FT. FROM GROUND ZERO. WE DON'T NEED A MONUMENT TO THOSE WHO ATTACKED OUR COUNTRY AT GROUND ZERO!!!" and "ISLAM IS NO LONGER A LEGITIMATE RELIGION," or, simply, "ISLAM KILLS."

This particular construction of sacred space, one that echoes the Durkheimian sense of the sacred as defined, in part, by exclusion, has seemed, at times, to be the only one in play, but in fact there have been many groups and individuals who have resisted this monolithic, aggressive, and exclusionary sense of the sacred space of Ground Zero. After all, when the plans for the Cordoba House were first vetted, there was in fact widespread support for the center; recall that Community Board No. 1 voted 29-1 in favor of the project, and The New York Landmarks Preservation Commission voted 9-0 in support of the plans.[78] The support for the project has been broad and diverse, and for some has been based on a sense of the inherent plurality of religion in the United States, and for others it has been based on the constitutional protection of the freedom of religion. For many citizens of the United States, Imam Rauf's original vision for Park51—a place of peace and reconciliation and resistance to extremism—remains profoundly compelling.

So why has this not been the dominant discourse here? It seems too easy to say that hate and bigotry simply win, that the zealot's voice is heard simply because he or she shouts louder. The matter is surely more complex than that. Returning to the example of Ayodhya that I discussed in the prior chapter, the enmity between Hindus and Muslims that erupted in 1992 did not come out of nowhere; indeed, as Kakar and others have attempted to demonstrate, there were long simmering and deeply embedded tensions between the two communities; the violence of Ayodhya was only spontaneous in a narrow sense, and was, as I have argued, highly orchestrated, the product of intense and complex manipulation by a range of conscious and unconscious agents.

Ground Zero has been no less complexly manipulated. Although it initially may have been seen as sacred because of the attacks on the World Trade Center and the violence and trauma of that event, the sacredness of the site has never been simply a given, and it has never been static; it is the product of interwoven political and social and commercial and religious discourses. Aspects of this discourse tap into deeply held beliefs for some Americans, as well as deep fears. Extending Butler's discussion of alterity, the discursive formulation of the Muslim other has been a means through which the American self has been defined and recognized. Ground Zero, in this regard, can be seen as the physical manifestation of this encounter, and as such it is intimately connected with a kind of collective American sense of self. As such, Ground Zero has become a synecdochally charged space, a place that is imbued with what Paul Ricoeur might have called a surplus of meaning. It is a place conceived by many as sacred, a place whose sacredness is constituted by particular sorts of absences and presences. The sixteen acres that for some delimit Ground Zero, and the long, long conceptual shadow this space casts, are thus central to a larger cultural debate about the presence of Islam and Muslims in America and the very conception of what it is to be American.

I have argued in this chapter, extending my discussion in Chapter 1, that the sacred is not a static concept, but a decidedly dynamic one that is frequently contested, that is employed not naturally, not as a neutral description. In the case of the debate over Park51, the category "sacred" has been used polemically, as a weapon in a social and political battle, a battle that is about the space of what had been the World Trade Center and what that place should be, but also a battle that extends far beyond the sixteen acres of the site, one that has become not just what should or should not be located there, but what should or should not, and who should and should not, be located in the United States. The shadow of Ground Zero is, indeed, a long one.

As a final note, there is a deep and opprobrious irony at play here that has been too easily lost on those who have so stridently opposed the Park51 project: many Muslims worked in the towers of the World Trade Center, and dozens of those workers lost their lives in the attacks on the towers. Muslim children lost fathers and mothers in the attacks; Muslim husbands and wives lost spouses. If part of what makes Ground Zero sacred is that it is a grave, then the unrecovered remains of these Muslim men and women are scattered about and mixed into the space that is Ground Zero. They are very much part of the site's sacredness.

3

The Polyvalent Pādas *of Viṣṇu and the Buddha**

3.1 *The Fluid Identities of Sacred Objects*

They in no way have the slightest association with Buddha at the time of worshipping it and they never identify it with Buddhism.

—L. P. VIDYARTHI[1]

I TURN IN this chapter away from place *per se* and toward the objects that make a place significant; specifically, my topic is a striking example of the ways in which a particular religiously charged object in India—the footprint, or *pāda* in both Pāli and Sanskrit—has defied attempts to fix it with a single, static identity. My focus here is on sculptural images of footprints at Bodhgayā and Gayā, located in northeastern India, in the modern state of Bihar, images that are caught up in a complex signifying web; for like the Buddha images located there that I will discuss in the next chapter, these footprints are venerated by both Buddhist and Hindu pilgrims, who attach very different identities and significance to the same objects. However, the issue of whose footprint is whose—the Buddha's or Viṣṇu's—seems not to have arisen at all on the ground, among those who actually participate in such images. Rather, identity proves to be a fluid matter depending on both the particular ritual and discursive context in which a given footprint is located, and the particular identity and religious affiliation of the participant in the image. Thus as L. P. Vidyarthi has pointed out, although it is extremely common to see Buddhist images, including footprints, in Hindu temples in and around Gayā, these images "are not identified with Buddha and are worshipped by the important and devoted Hindus as their own gods and goddesses."[2] This fundamentally multivalent potential is, I think, striking, particularly so in the case of footprints, which, as I pointed out in the last chapter in the context of the highly charged "footprints" of the Twin Towers at Ground Zero, possess a special quality as a kind of open symbol, the meaning of which must be, almost literally, filled in by the individual or collective participants in that image in the context in which the image is discursively and ritually located.

The very nature of a footprint is, I want to suggest, both fluid and ambiguous, perhaps more so than any other sort of image in India. On the one hand, a footprint—and here I mean an actual footprint, in contrast to the metaphoric footprints of the twin towers, although there are also similarities at play here—is considered to be the mark left by Viṣṇu or the Buddha while they walked on earth, and thus has been regarded as a kind of corporeal extension, and even an actual embodiment of these beings. On the other hand, however, a footprint is not a foot, but rather the empty mark left by a foot; it is thus a kind of empty signifier, a most graphic marker of an absence, and the identity of the maker must be imaginatively determined by the individual or collective ritual agents who continually respond to these *pādas*.[3] It is in part because of this kind of iconographic open-endedness, I shall argue, that both Buddhists and Hindus have been able to share these images on the ground. But it is also, I want to suggest, in part because of a kind of *conceptual* open-endedness within Buddhist discourse in particular—where there is a kind of ambiguity as to exactly what sort of objects these are, and as to exactly what their "value" is, which is in stark contrast to the Vaiṣṇava Hindu conception of the *pāda*s as the actual abode of Viṣṇu—an openness that allows for the Buddha's footprints to, as it were, do double duty as objects of veneration. I will first examine this categorical fuzziness—and what it implies—before turning to a discussion of the ways in which various scholars have attempted to fix, and therefore a-contextually limit, the footprints' identities through polemically motivated discussions of the origins of the footprint motif in India. I will then turn to some of the footprints themselves, and discuss their specific iconographic polyvalency.

I would not be the first to point out that to see an object of Indian sculpture in a modern museum is to see an image that is decidedly out of place. In a museum, an image—be it of Kṛṣṇa, Kālī, or the Buddha—is stripped of the ritual context that quite literally animates it: the priests, the devotees, the various ritual implements, the sounds and smells.[4] The image is naked, without the garments and garlands that would clothe and adorn it in its temple setting; the stone or metal of which it is made, likewise, is typically almost antiseptically clean, with the layers of colored powders mixed with oils and wax and sometimes paint that would have all but covered it in the temple setting completely removed. Furthermore, the image is bathed in the sharp and invasive light that is peculiar to museums, a light that certainly highlights the aesthetic qualities of a particular piece of sculpture, but which also highlights both its nakedness and, more importantly, its lifelessness. In a very real sense, the modern art museum kills the Indian image.

It is not, however, only the lifelessness of the image in the museum that is so jarring; it is also the almost clinical precision with which images are arranged and labeled. The taxonomic obsessions of early collectors of Indian art has been discussed by Bernard Cohn, who argues that collecting art and artifacts was part of the larger hegemonic colonial program in India. The colonial administrators thus sought to control, and if necessary also to construct, the history of India in part by controlling the physical objects that were the products of that history, and they thus

> defined in an authoritative and effective fashion how the value and meaning of the objects produced or found in India were determined.... [They] determined what was valuable, that which would be preserved as monuments of the past, that which was collected and placed in museums.... Each phase of the European effort to unlock the secret of the Indian past called for more and more collecting, more and more systems of classification, more and more building of repositories for the study of the past and the representation of the European history of India to Indians as well as themselves.[5]

Part of the legacy of this taxonomic drive—and part of the conventions of art display as well—is the way Indian art is arranged and, particularly, how objects are labeled in modern museums.[6] An image's—and, as we shall see in the next two chapters, a temple's as well—identity, its date, and its place of origin are all fixed on the prominently displayed label. Thus not only are Indian sculptures killed in museums, the dynamic and varied lives that they have lived prior to their entombment in the museum is all but erased.

The need to fix the identity and origin of images in the museum setting very much goes against the contextual dynamics of sculptural images in India, for a sculpture "on the ground" in India is an active participant in what Richard Davis has aptly called the "ongoing social life of its communities."[7] A single image may, over the course of its ritual life, move from place to place and participate in several very different communities, and as it does its symbolic and ritual identity changes depending on which context it happens to be participating in at any given time. As Davis puts it: "Even as the images hang on to their distinctive insignia, they may find themselves carried off to new places, where they encounter new audiences, who may not know or appreciate their earlier significance. Or, even staying in their original locations, the images may take on new roles and new meanings in response to the changing world around them."[8] The "life" of an image in the Indian context thus parallels that of discourse (or utterance) as described by Mikhail Bhaktin in *The Dialogic Imagination*, in that once created, an image, like discourse, "enters a dialogically agitated and tension-filled environment," in which its identity "having taken meaning and shape at a particular historical moment in a socially specific environment, cannot fail to brush up against thousands of living dialogic threads, woven by socio-ideological consciousness around the given object.... [I]t cannot fail to become an active participant in social dialogue."[9] We have already seen this sort of contested fluidity at play with both Ayodhya and Ground Zero, and the ways in which Bodhgayā has been understood, as we see in the next two chapters, is also very much dialogically agitated.

This is, in my view, a crucial critical position in attempting to understand the phenomenology of both places and images, particularly in India; far too often, not only have Indian sculptural images been viewed when removed from the contexts in which they originally existed, but even when such contexts have been recreated or reimagined, the images have tended to be confined to a single context, a context in which they appear to have maintained a single, unified, and consistent identity to all who beheld them. As Frederick Asher has pointed out, however, the attempt to fix a single identity to a single image in the Indian context is likely to be misguided, because it is likely to miss the very phenomenology of such images: "It is not just the relativism that is so inherently Indian and permits varying interpretations but the obvious fact that different beholders may read an image differently. This should serve as a warning to those who imagine that we have discovered an absolute truth when we find a text whose description of a deity corresponds precisely with a stone or metal representation. The textual word does not offer an ultimate interpretation."[10]

In some contexts in India, then, images from one tradition have been introduced, albeit in an altered form, into the other: so, for instance, various Hindu deities are depicted attending, in a subservient mode, the Buddha, while the Buddhist goddess Tārā—who is associated with the Bodhisattva Avalokiteśvara as a savior, the embodiment of kindness, compassion, tenderness and guidance—appears in her Hindu guise in an *ugra* form, as a terrifyingly ugly and fierce bloodthirsty goddess akin to Kālī,[11] although as we saw in the last chapter, she can also be a loving mother in the Hindu context. In other contexts, images are simply recycled, transformed from one tradition's figure into the other's, such as the "conversion" of Buddhist *stūpas* (reliquaries) in Bihar to Śiva *liṅgams*.[12] And in still other contexts, a single image is viewed and treated as representing or embodying two very different figures, depending on who is doing the viewing, such as images at Bodhgayā that are the Buddha to Buddhist pilgrims and Viṣṇu to Hindu pilgrims; I will spend much more time on this particular dynamic in the next two chapters.

This is, of course, an issue that is very much at the center of this book: the fluid, shifting, and contested identities of places and the physical objects that make them significant. This shifting landscape of identity in India has been rather puzzling to a great many Western scholars, stretching at least as far back as the early British colonialists who, although they were often perplexed as to the differences between Hinduism and Buddhism, were also—rather paradoxically—intent on emphasizing the separateness of the two religions.[13] Part of this was, to be sure, motivated by the basic Protestant worldview of the British colonialists,[14] and the early British view of Buddhism as the Protestant-like reformation of the decrepitude of Catholic-like Hinduism.[15] But this taxonomic drive was also part of a larger nineteenth-century obsession with origins, an obsession motivated by the basic belief that if one could uncover the origins of a given phenomenon, then one would also uncover the essence of the thing itself,[16] an obsession that has proven hard to shake even today. Such a stance, however, could hardly be less appropriate to the Indian context, where the issue of origins is, quite simply, very often not an issue at all; indeed, a common legitimizing trope is to assert the originless nature of a given discourse or image.

3.2 Blurred Categories

When Aśoka had ascended the throne, he changed his capital and built this town; he enclosed the stone with the impression; and as it was near the royal precinct, he paid it constant personal worship.

—XUANZANG[17]

As a matter of fact, wherever they are set up in a modern Buddhist shrine, they occupy an unimportant place, and may, therefore, be ignored.

—BENIMADHAB BARUA[18]

The footprint of the Buddha is one of the more common and wide-ranging motifs in the Buddhist tradition—and it has long been a favorite trope of Western writers.[19] For those who have championed the theory that there was an early "aniconic" period of Buddhist art, holding that there was originally a prohibition against iconically representing the Buddha, the *pāda* has been of particular importance.[20] Such scholars have seen the footprint—along with the empty throne and the Bodhi tree under which the Buddha attained enlightenment—as a central means of representing the Buddha's presence through his absence: David Snellgrove points out that one of the "most unequivocal signs indicating the Buddha's personal presence are the footprints (*buddhapāda*). . . ."[21] Not only does such a boldly unambiguous characterization simply sidestep the complex and contentious question of the "aniconism" thesis, it also masks the inherent signifying complexity and ambiguity of the Buddha's footprints, both in terms of the ways Buddhists themselves have regarded such objects, but also the ways in which Vaiṣṇava Hindus have invested them with a very different set of significations.

I want first to focus on what might be deemed the *buddhapāda*'s classificatory ambiguity within Buddhism, because although footprints are generally considered to be relics in the Buddhist context, exactly what sort of object the Buddha's footprint is, and what its function is, are not at all clear. Relics are, to be sure, ambiguous and problematic objects in Buddhism; as Gregory Schopen has aptly put it, there is "both a startling precision and a maddening conceptual fuzziness" in what Buddhists have said about relics over the centuries.[22] On the one hand, a relic is a reminder of the Buddha's own human body and the susceptibility of that body to the basic principle of impermanence; on the other hand, the relic is an object of great value that has the ability to effect a sense of the continued physical presence of the Buddha. Thus a relic conveys an essential Buddhist message, as at once a visceral reminder of the impermanence of all things—including the Buddha—and the need to conquer the thirst for existence. At the same time, however, a relic is also a physical object that gives rise to deep emotions—and sometimes attachments—that are in tension with that basic message; indeed, relics are frequently regarded as the living Buddha himself. In this regard, a footprint is a particularly complex sort of relic, a kind of negative signifier, a relic under erasure, as it were, in that it is precisely the empty space that marks the place where the person (the Buddha) is not that constitutes the footprint.

But it is also this emptiness that gives the footprint its particular significance: a footprint is, quite clearly, not a foot, and thus, from the outset appears not quite to fit into the category of bodily relic, but also not quite to fall completely outside of that category. Buddhists do not consider only body parts as relics; garments, begging bowls, sleeping mats, representational images, combs, toothpicks—to name only a few possibilities—are all, in various contexts, considered relics of the Buddha.[23] There are, however, traditionally three categories of relics in the Pāli canonical tradition: corporeal relics (*sārīraka dhātu*), relics of use (*parībhogika dhātu*), and relics of commemoration (*uddeśika dhātu*).[24] Confining my discussion to this early tripartite division, it would seem that a footprint would most logically fall into the *uddeśika* category, as a relic of commemoration (or representation), such as a sculptural image,[25] since the overwhelming majority of footprints in Buddhist contexts are sculpturally-rendered images, often many times the size of an actual footprint of even the largest of humans.[26] But a *buddhapāda* is not exactly an *uddeśika* relic, since the empty indentations that are the footprints are typically regarded not merely as *representations* or models of the Buddha's footprint, but as the genuine traces of what was once the Buddha's physical presence, his actual footprint. It would thus follow that footprints then fall into the category of relics of use or contact (*parībhogika*), in the sense of an object that came into contact with the Buddha when he was alive—here, specifically, the ground or stone upon which he tread. According to the authors of *The Image of the Buddha*, however, footprints are bodily relics (*sārīraka*),[27] an assertion echoed by John Irwin, who refers to the *buddhapāda* as a "symbol for the corporeal Buddha."[28] So, the question remains, what sort of relic is a *buddhapāda*? Let me begin with the *sārīraka* possibility, the degree to which the Buddha's footprint is regarded as an actual bodily relic.

The earliest canonical warrant for relic veneration in Buddhism is generally considered to be the *Mahāparinibbāna Sutta*. This well-known text recounts the Buddha's last days, his death and cremation, and the distribution of his bodily relics. The Buddha himself gives instructions for the treatment of his corporeal remains—including the preparation of his corpse for cremation, the building of a monument to enshrine the remains, and the rationale for the veneration of his relics: "Those who offer there a garland, or scents, or paint, or make a salutation, or feel serene joy in their heart, for a long time that will be to their benefit and well being."[29] There is no mention of the Buddha's footprints in the *Mahāparinibbāna Sutta*, which is not surprising, given that the text is explicitly concerned with the funereal arrangements following the death of the Buddha and it is rather hard to imagine how a footprint could figure into this context. Indeed, despite the pronouncement by the authors of *The Image of the Buddha*, I know of no text that explicitly classifies the footprint as a bodily relic, although as we shall see, there are at least a few references to *pādas* that seem to regard them as an extension, if not an actual part, of the Buddha's body.

The dominant emphasis in early Buddhist texts is on corporeal relics;[30] we see an intimation of this in the *Mahāparinibbāna Sutta* itself. After all the eight portions of the bodily relics have been distributed, the Brahmin Doṇa, who has assisted in the division of the Buddha's bones, is left with no relic portion for himself. He is, however, given the pot in which the bones have been kept as a kind of *de facto* relic—not a bodily relic, but a relic of use (*pāriboghika dhātuyo*).[31] Although it is not explicitly stated in the text, it would seem that this pot is given to Doṇa as at once a recognition of his service, but also as a mark of his lesser (i.e., non-Buddhist) status. Kevin Trainor draws attention to Buddhaghosa's depiction of Doṇa in the *Sumaṅgala Vilāsinī*, the commentary on the *Dīgha Nikāya*, as a rather evil and conniving figure who steals one of the teeth while overseeing the division of the bones; the tooth is returned after the intervention of the god Sakka, and Doṇa is left with just the vessel which, nonetheless, still has, according to Buddhaghosa, at least the "character of a relic" (*dhātu-gatiko*).[32]

In the *Sammohavinodanī*, the commentary on the *Vibhaṇga*, the second of the seven books of the *Abhidhamma Piṭaka*, there is an unusually explicit expression of the superiority of *sāriraka* relics: "[T]he shrine (containing a part) of the body is more important than a shrine (in commemoration) of what was made use of."[33] Significantly, however, in a later version of the division of the relics given in the *Buddhavaṃsa*,[34] the *buddhapāda* is mentioned—not as a bodily relic, though, but rather as a relic of use (*pāribhogika-dhātu*), included with various other objects, such as the Buddha's robes, his alms bowl, his sitting mat, etc. It is unclear from the text why these other relics are added to the original objects, but it may reflect a general expansion of what could be classified as a relic in the centuries immediately following the Buddha's death. Indeed, as Trainor has noted, "By the time of Buddhaghosa in the fifth century, it is clear that nearly every Buddhist monastery had its own *stūpa* enshrining relics. There was a growing demand for new relics with some claim to authenticity."[35] A *stūpa* containing relics was not necessary for the monastery to be a monastery, of course, but seems to have been an essential way to draw lay support, which was necessary for the monastery to survive. Trainor's comment about "new relics" implies objects other than body parts, and no doubt also objects other than those that might have actually come into direct contact with the Buddha.

Footprints are most commonly discussed as if they were *pāribhogika* relics, although most frequently there is in fact no explicit discussion of what category they fall into, which may reflect, in part, the fact that it was simply as relics that the *buddhapādas* were valued, not as a particular kind of relic. Be that as it may, in several discussions of footprints in the commentarial texts, it seems that no particular classification is mentioned because it is unclear to the author (or authors) of the text exactly what sort of relic a footprint is—the *pādas* seem to straddle the line between relics of use and relics of commemoration. In the commentary on the *Majjhimanikāya*, for instance, there is a story about a serpent king to whom the Buddha teaches the *dhamma*. After he has been taught, however, the *nāga* wishes to have something to remember the Buddha by after he is gone: " 'Grant me, Venerable Lord, something to worship,' entreated the *nāga*. The Lord caused a footprint relic to appear on the bank of the Nammadā. Covered by the waves washed up on the bank and revealed as they receded, it became an important place of worship."[36] The text does not elaborate any further, so it is impossible to say what sort of relic this footprint is, and it is also impossible to say what sort of "worship" might have been performed, whether it was worship in the form of *buddhapūjā*, veneration of the Buddha, or whether the footprint was an object on which one could engage in the important meditational practice of *buddha anussati*, "remembrance of the Buddha." What the text does tell us, at least, is that the Buddha's footprint is a physical object that can serve, in some sense, as a substitute for him in his absence, a familiar trope in Buddhist literature, and that the presence of such an object makes a particular place especially significant.[37]

This short story is directly followed in the same text by a similar one also featuring footprints, involving an ascetic named Saccabandha who has been engaged in leading people down paths that end in inauspicious rebirths. Through the power of the *dhamma*, the Buddha causes him to mend his ways, and, like the *nāga*, afterward Saccabandha wants something to remember him by once he is gone: "As for Saccabandha, he asked the Lord for an object of worship. The Teacher created a footprint shrine in the solid rock as if he was making an impression in a mound of fresh mud."[38] Again, there is no discussion of what sort of relic these footprints are: as objects that have come into direct contact with the Buddha himself they most logically fall into the *pāribhogika* category (although these are clearly not objects that the Buddha "used"); however, since they serve to commemorate the Buddha's presence in a particular spot, they could also be considered *uddeśika* relics.

In the commentary on the *Buddhavaṁsa*, the *Madhuratthavilāsinī*, there is another brief discussion of footprints made by the Buddha. He has descended from the heavens into the center of the city of Amara in order to teach the *dhamma* to two brothers, Sambahula and Sumitta, who rule the kingdom. The text states that the Buddha came down "making footprints visible (*padacetiyāni dassetvā*) as though he were treading the surface of the earth by walking on it with the soles of his feet which were adorned with wheels."[39] The text, again, really does not provide any more on the footprints, although it goes on to say that the two brothers, having seen these footprints, follow them to the Buddha, and then learn the *dhamma* from him and subsequently attain Arahatship. Here, the footprints cannot exactly be said to embody the living Buddha, but they do, at any rate, lead to him and his teachings, in much the same way that a sculptural image can be said, as an object of meditation and remembrance of the Buddha, to lead to the Buddha and the *dhamma*.[40]

Certainly, on its face there is nothing exceptional about the fact that the footprints are not usually given a definite classificatory identity, but this apparent ambiguity does, in my view, highlight the fluid nature of the footprint, its status as a kind of floating signifier. In all of these texts, however, the footprints made by the Buddha are described by the term *pādacetiya*; thus although what sort of relic they are is not clear, it does seem clear that they are considered to be at least relic-like objects. The use of the Pāli "*cetiya*" (Sanskrit, *caitya*) here is immediately reminiscent of bodily relics; a *caitya* is typically taken to be a relic shrine.[41] But as Andre Bareau has persuasively argued, on the basis of his reading of the Mahāsāsāghika *Vinaya*, in their earliest usage the two terms Buddhists used for reliquaries, *caitya* and *stūpa*, denoted quite different memorial objects. In short, he argues that if there are relics, the word *stūpa* is used, whereas *caitya* denotes a shrine without relics: "S'il y a des reliques, on le nomme *stūpa*. S'il n'y a pas de reliques, on le nomme *caitya*."[42] According to Bareau, *caitya* would originally have referred to an object that marked or was intended to recall some significant event in the Buddha's life, such as one of the four great places worthy of pilgrimage mentioned in the *Mahāparinibānna Sutta*; later, however, *caitya* and *stūpa* became indistinguishable, such that the two could be used interchangeably as a memorial with or without relics.[43] By the time the Pāli commentaries were written in the fourth and fifth centuries of the Common Era, then, it would seem that the two forms of shrine had coalesced, and thus a phrase such as *padacetiyāni dassetvā*, "making footprints visible," cannot of itself tell us anything specific about what sort of relic a footprint is, although certainly it does seem that these footprints conform to the earlier, non-relic sense of *cetiya*.

In this regard, it is worth briefly considering another instance in which the Buddha creates a relic for remembrance of himself after he is no longer present, an episode in which the self-created relic is specifically a bodily relic, and in which this bodily relic seems to conform to precisely the "living presence of the Buddha" conception of relics.[44] In the commentary on the *Anguttara Nikāya*, there is a story of two merchant brothers, Tapassu and Bhallika, to whom the Buddha preaches the *dhamma*. The brothers then take refuge in the Buddha and the *dhamma*, and as they are about to leave the presence of the Tathāgata, make this by now familiar request: "Good sir, give us a memento of yourself that we can worship."[45] The Buddha then rubs his head and presents the two men with eight handfuls of hair, which they then take back to their home city and erect a *cetiya* to contain the hairs, which are explicitly called in the text "living hair relics" (*jīvakesadhātuyā*). Again, the text is not explicit about what sort of relic we have here, although the fact that these strands of hair came directly from the Buddha's head seems to indicate that they are in some way extensions of the Buddha's body, and thus would be *sāriraka dhātus*. Furthermore, these strands of hair are called "living" hair relics, which seems to indicate that they are relics that conform to Schopen's argument that bodily relics in early Buddhism were not simply signifiers of the Buddha's presence, but in fact effected that presence: "[T]here is no distinction between a living Buddha and a collection of relics—both make the sacred person equally present as an object of worship."[46] The treatment of the footprints in the passages I have cited here do not in fact discuss them in terms of anything like a "living presence"; indeed, these passages create, if anything, the impression that these are objects that are intended to evoke memories of him only.

The question, of course, is what to make of this apparent difference. I would certainly not want to go so far as to suggest that the Buddha's footprints, as Benimadhab Barua has put it, "occupy an unimportant place, and may, therefore, be ignored,"[47] but it does seem that in all of these references there is at least, in addition to the kind of classificatory ambiguity that I have just been discussing, also a certain ambivalence about the status of footprints, if not in fact a sense that if the *buddhapādas* are indeed to be considered as relics, they are a lesser sort of relic in comparison to such things as the Buddha's bones, his alms bowl, robe, or even strands of his hair. It is at least in part this ambivalence, I would suggest, that enables them to be inscribed, as it were, with multiple significance, in the sense that these were not objects that were rhetorically marked as particularly special. Significantly, the footprints *in situ* in and around Bodhgayā were frequently also not indelibly marked as belonging specifically to the Buddha, and thus are open to being seen, and ritually treated, as those of Viṣṇu.

3.3 *Blurred Origins*

> *[T]he history of the conversion of Gayā to Hinduism... leaves no doubt in my mind that it was originally a Buddhist emblem.*
>
> —RAJENDRALALA MITRA[48]

> *On the contrary, it may not be unreasonable to think that, since in all probability the* Viṣṇupāda *at* Gayā *was already in existence during the lifetime of their Master, the Buddhists might have conceived the idea of foot-print worship from the celebrated precedence almost next door to the Tathāgata's place of enlightenment.*
>
> —DEBJANI PAUL[49]

Before I turn to the physical footprints themselves, I wish briefly to consider the question of which tradition, Buddhist or Hindu, can lay claim to the origins of footprint veneration, since it is this, more than any other issue, that has been the basis for most discussions of—and, as we see above, dispute about—the *pādas*. The question of origins has long preoccupied scholars of religion,[50] and so it is perhaps not surprising that at the center of most scholarly discussions of the topic of footprints in

India is the issue of which came first—Buddhist or Hindu—and therefore which is original and which is merely derivative. However, even if it could be proved that the Buddhists did get the idea of footprint veneration from their Vaiṣṇava counterparts, would this really tell us anything, about either Buddhist or Hindu practice, or their interaction? Aside from Rajendralala Mitra, who was clearly himself polemically motivated from the Buddhist point of view, the Buddhist use of the *pāda* motif has been portrayed as merely derivative: "The concept and practice of the Viṣṇupada became such a dominant religious ideology that even the later Buddhists of the Mahāyāna school borrowed this idea and started the worship of the Buddha's foot-prints at Bodhgayā."[51] Perhaps this sheds some light on the polemical position of the scholar who wrote it, but it tells us nothing about the actual contexts—ideological, ritual, artistic—in which such worship was grounded. This is unfortunate for at least two reasons: first, it is in my opinion impossible to demonstrate the origins of footprint worship in India; and second, historical priority, even if it could be proved, would tell us very little about the sorts of ideological and ritual embeddedness of the footprints at Gayā and Bodhgayā, let alone about their mutual interaction.

This said, however, a brief review of this discussion of origins is enlightening, in that it highlights some of the ways in which the identity of an image in general, and the footprints at Gayā and Bodhgayā in particular, is not simply "cast in stone," but is very much a matter of a kind of continual and contested construction, even if this contestation exists at what we might call a secondary level. Again, Bhaktin's analysis of discourse and utterance is useful here: "But no living word relates to its object in a *singular* way: between the word and its object, between the word and the speaking subject, there exists an elastic environment of other, alien words about the same object."[52] Thus we need to be mindful not only of what we might call the multivalent potential—which is another way to say fluidity, of course—of sculptural images such as the *pāda*s in and around Bodhgayā, but also of the degree to which the potentially multiple identities of a single image are, as Bhaktin says, elastic, in a constant state of flux and negotiation.

There is, first, no question that Gayā predates Bodhgayā as a religious place; its status as a center of religious activity had been established long before Śākyamuni arrived there in the fifth century B.C.E. As Barua has pointed out, Gayā had "already been renowned as a place of pilgrimage where bathing in the Gayā tank (*Gayā-pokkharai*) and the Gayā river (*Gayā-nadī*) was believed to have been of special merit as a means of washing away sins and impurities."[53] Although he was initially attracted by the ascetics practicing at Gayā, Śākyamuni eventually abandoned the various ascetics who had settled on the banks of the Phalgu—specifically rejecting their methods as misguided deprivations that gave rise only to more karmic baggage, and thus setting a precedent for tensions between the Hindus at Gayā and the Buddhists at Bodhgayā. He instead took up the solitary meditation in nearby Bodhgayā that led to his enlightenment. The Buddha did, however, return to Gayā on several occasions, most notably to share his teachings with a group of matted-hair ascetics, the Jailas, with whom he had come into contact in the course of his pre-enlightenment ascetic experimentations.

There are several episodes in the Pāli canon and its commentaries in which the Jailas figure,[54] the most significant of which occurs in the *Udāna* and its commentary; here we see a certain contentiousness in the relationship between Hindus and Buddhists in ancient Magadha from the very beginning: "There is no cleanliness by water, or the masses would bathe here; the one in whom there is truth and the Dhamma, he is the one who is clean and who is a brāhmin."[55] Elsewhere, for instance in the *Vatthupāma Sutta* of the *Majjhima Nikāya*, the purifying qualities of the Phalgu at Gayā—and the sacred waters at several other *tīrthā*s—are also derided: "In Bāhukā, at Adhikākka's ghāt, Gayā, Sundārikā, Saraswatī, Bahumatī, Payāga—the fool may bathe and bathe, yet never cleanse his heart.... Why seek Gayā? Your well at home is Gayā."[56] In its early history, Gayā's power and significance is associated with the purity of its water; in none of the early Buddhist texts in which Gayā figures, and in which the religious practices there are critiqued, is there any mention of the veneration, or mention even of the existence, of Viṣṇu's footprint. There are any number of reasons for an absence of discussion of the *viṣṇupāda* in early Buddhist texts, the most obvious and most simple of which is that during the Buddha's lifetime there simply was no *viṣṇupāda* at Gayā to remark on, and that, consequently, whenever it did become the central object of veneration, it was after the advent of Buddhism. This makes a certain amount of sense, intuitively at least; if there had been a prominent *viṣṇupāda* at Gayā, one that was the object of veneration for the many pilgrims who congregated there, one might expect it to be the recipient of the same sort of criticisms that we have already seen directed at the ablutions in the Phalgu, or at the fire sacrifices of the Jailas. Silence, however, despite Sherlock Holmes's famous example of the non-barking dog, proves nothing.[57]

Early Brahmanical texts, on the other hand, are not entirely silent—although they are also not entirely explicit, either—about the sacrality of Viṣṇu's feet and footprints, and a number of scholars have seized on these pre-Buddhist references to the *viṣṇupāda* as incontrovertible evidence that the motif is Hindu in origin. The various lines of argument here are convoluted, reaching back at least to Mitra's 1878 monograph on Bodhgayā, and in perusing them one quickly becomes entangled in a web of polemics, extrapolation, and sheer conjecture. I do not wish myself to become caught up in the details of these arguments, although I do at least want to mention the highlights. The starting point of most of these discussions is the *Vanaparva* section of the *Mahābharata*, which lists the major pilgrimage sites in India, including Gayā: "One should then go to Mount Udyanta, which is clamorous with songs; there one may see the *sāvitra pada*, Oh Bull of the Bharatas."[58] The phrase here that has been seen as a reference to the *viṣṇupāda, sāvitra tu padam*, is perhaps most literally translated as, "the footprint of the rising sun," which seems, at least in the context in which it occurs, to mean simply the top of the hill where the sun first hits it; the next line of the text seems to support such a reading, stating that the devout Brahmin who worships the dawn there receives twelve years worth of merit. Such a simple reading has been typically eschewed, though, and instead this verse has been taken as an unambiguous reference to Viṣṇu's footprint and thus proof that, as Debjani Paul has put it, "the tradition of the *Viṣṇupāda* at Gayā can be traced as far back as pre-Buddhist times."[59] Paul does not stop there, though, but argues that this verse actually refers to the very image of the *viṣṇupāda* currently *in situ* at Gayā: "It is, then, fairly likely that the *Sāvitra-pada* of the epic verse is indeed the *Viṣṇupāda* as it still exists in Gayā."[60]

There are serious flaws with such an unambiguous conclusion. First, there is the dubious methodological move of attempting to trace the origins of a specific physical object—and the various ritual and social practices in which such an object is situated—to what is, surely, a rather oblique textual reference.[61] Second, there is the basic fact that the Viṣṇupāda currently *in situ* at Gayā cannot, by Paul's own admission, be dated any earlier than the tenth century.[62] Third, there is the basic problem of the ambiguity of this textual reference—is this a solar metaphor for a physical place? is it a reference to an actual foot?—an ambiguity that is not unique. In the *Ṛg Veda*, for instance, to which Paul and others ultimately trace the origins not only of the *viṣṇupāda*, but by extension of the *buddhapāda*,[63] there are certainly indirect references to Viṣṇu's feet and footprints, such as the well-known image of his three strides at *Ṛg Veda* I.154. Again, however, it is far from clear that such references are to physical footprints (that is, footprints that actually exist somewhere in the human realm). Indeed, it seems just as likely that the intent of such verbal images is metaphorical—as the multivalent potential of a word such as "*pāda*" certainly allows—in the sense of places where Viṣṇu "touched down" on earth and, in a sense, thus still resides,[64] as is implied later in verse 154: "We wish to go to your dwelling places, where there are untiring, many-horned cattle. There the highest footstep of the wide-stepping bull shines brightly down."[65]

Regardless, however, of whether the intent of such statements is metaphorical, whether *pāda* refers to a physical place, or whether it refers to an actual footprint on the ground, it seems clear that the larger issue here is that in these early texts, "*viṣṇupāda*" refers most broadly to the earthly presence, the abode, of Viṣṇu, and that this becomes the significance of the footprints at Gayā: here is where Viṣṇu is located. This is perhaps no more clearly emphasized than in the *Gayāmahātmya*—a semi-independent part of the larger, relatively late *Vāyupurāṇa*—that contains an etiological myth of the origins of Gayā and the *viṣṇupāda*.[66] Among other things, the *Gayāmahātmya* gives an account of the defeat by Viṣṇu of the *asura* Gayāsura, who had become extremely powerful through the practice of austerities, and who had been tormenting the gods for thousands of years. He is eventually subdued by Viṣṇu when the god places a huge rock (or, given the description of it in the text, perhaps "mountain" would a better translation for "*śilā*") on the *asura*'s head and then whacks it with his mace. Once Gayāsurā is subdued, he asks the gods, including Viṣṇu, to make their earthly abode on the mountain: "As long as the earth, mountains, the Sun, Moon and stars last, may Brahmā, Viṣṇu, Śiva and the other gods remain on the śila / Let this sacred spot be know by my name. Let all tīrthas be centered in the midst of Gayā.... May all the gods remain here in manifest forms (images & c.) and unmanifest forms (such as footprints & c.)!"[67] Here, the *viṣṇupāda* is discussed as, essentially, a *mūrti*, a physical image in which the god is thought to reside, although the special status of the *pāda* as *svayambhū*, a physical mark created by Viṣṇu himself—as opposed to a man-made image in which, through its ritual consecration, the god is invited to dwell—no doubt adds to its sanctity.[68]

Given that I have taken issue with the obsession about origins in the study of religion, I should stop before I descend further into this particular rabbit hole. It should at least be clear, even from this brief discussion, that the *viṣṇupāda* motif is quite ancient, and although it seems entirely plausible that the verbal imagery of the three strides in the *Ṛg Veda* might eventually have been, as it were, "translated" into stone at Gayā and elsewhere,[69] it does not, therefore, follow that the Buddhists, in developing their own verbal and sculptural *pāda* imagery, simply co-opted this motif from the Brahmanical sources. The *pāda* motif most certainly appeared in Buddhist discourse earlier than the rise of the Mahāyāna, and perhaps earlier than its definite mention in the *Mahābharata*;[70] there are, for example, several footprints represented at sites such as Amarāvatī and Bhārhut dating back to the second century B.C.E.[71] It may be, in other words, that the *viṣṇupāda*, rhetorically if not also physically, predates the *buddhapāda*, although based on the extant evidence it may also be just the reverse. What is significant in the end is not the issue of origins, but rather the way in which the footprint motif, and the discursive and ritual practices associated with it, developed in the two traditions; in this regard, I think it abundantly clear that the manner in which the *buddhapāda*s are discussed in Buddhist texts is not simply derivative, as many of the polemical scholars who have discussed the issue have maintained, but rather is part of the evolving Buddhist discourse on the remains of the Buddha and the significance and function of those remains. What is also evident, however, is that regardless of their origins, on the ground, in the context of the ritual function of these footprints, their identities blur and overlap.

3.4 Blurred Identities

> *On the whole the marks on the Buddhapad bear a closer resemblance to Hindu than to Buddhist religion, and I am disposed to accept the authority of the inscription, and to believe that the stone, though popularly called the foot of Buddha (Buddhapad), was put up by the Hindus to convert the place to Hindu worship.*
>
> —RAJENDRALALA MITRA[72]

There are dozens of stone footprints *in situ* in and around Bodhgayā and Gayā, and it is frequently extremely difficult—if not, as I would suggest, impossible—to distinguish between those that are the Buddha's and those that are Viṣṇu's. This is in part due to the fact that many of these images have been moved, sometimes more than once, from Bodhgayā to Gayā or vice versa, as well as moved from one of these sights to a museum or private collection. It is thus frequently impossible to tell what might have been their original ritual and discursive contexts, let alone to tell what might have been their intended identity by those who made them. Furthermore, many of these images are ambiguously marked, inscribed with symbols that are common to both the Buddhist and Vaiṣṇava iconographic lexicons, such as the wheel, lotus, and fish, and what is more, many of these markings have long been obscured by weather and use. None of this, however, has stopped scholars from attempting to assign fixed identities to these objects.

Debjani Paul, for instance, has suggested that the *cakra*, the seemingly ubiquitous motif of the wheel of dharma, is the defining characteristic of the Buddha's footprint: "In any event, it cannot escape an observer's attention as to what constitute the most essential of symbols used in the decoration of the foot-prints of Bodhgayā.... one can safely say that the wheel-incrusted foot-print, *cakrākapādam*, is patently Buddhist."[73] Paul's assertion conforms to any number of descriptions of the Buddha's feet, such as that found in the *Bodhisattvabhūmi*: "Upon the soles of his feet there are thousand-spoked wheels with hubs and ribs, complete in every aspect."[74] A similar description can be found in the *Buddhavaṃsa*, where the Buddha's feet are said to be marked by wheels (along with a flag and an umbrella), and we find the same basic descriptions in Aśvaghosa's *Buddhacarita*, the *Lalitavistara*,[75] and numerous other texts. There are several problems with such an unequivocal statement, and perhaps the most glaring is the assumption that physical images always conform to, or are even informed by, textual descriptions. Indeed, as Mitra pointed out long ago with regard to a particular footprint from Bodhgayā: "The sectarial marks on it comprise, on the right foot, a discus, an umbrella, a flag, a conch-shell, a pitcher, a fish, an elephant-goad, an arc, and a lotus-bud; and on the left foot the same, except the discus, which is replaced by a wheel. These marks do not correspond with any Vaiṣṇava description of Viṣṇu's feet, nor with any Buddhist account of Buddha's foot-mark that I have seen. Nor do they conform to any known canons of palmistry, Hindu or Buddhist, regarding auspicious marks on the sole of the foot."[76] Barua, in his later study of Bodhgayā, also points out that in actual practice early Buddhist artisans, such as the those working at Barhūt, "carved the feet of the Buddha Śākyamuni in utter disregard of this literary description," and that in fact *buddhapāda*s frequently bear entirely different markings than those described in the texts, or, for that matter, none at all.[77] Barua further notes that the footprints of Viṣṇu are also frequently adorned by wheels (in Viṣṇu's case, according to Barua, symbolizing the sun), although the wheel was grouped with the lotus, discus, and mace in the case of Viṣṇu.[78]

Mitra published several line drawings of *pāda*s that were excavated by the Burmese at Bodhgayā, images that were, according to Mitra, "popularly called the foot of Buddha (Buddhapad)," although in his opinion they were in fact originally *viṣṇupāda*s that were "put up by the Hindus to convert the place to Hindu worship."[79] These are particularly interesting images, in that they are inscribed with what appears to be an almost random—at least from the point of view of textual descriptions of either the feet of the Buddha and of Viṣṇu—collection of symbols that are common enough to both traditions that they could easily have been identified with either the Buddha or with Viṣṇu. Whether or not this kind of iconographic overlapping was intentional is impossible to say, but certainly inscribing a *buddhapāda* with a fish (which to a Vaiṣṇava conjures up Viṣṇu in his *matsya avatāra*) or a *viṣṇupāda* with a *dharmacakra* (a ubiquitous Buddhist symbol) heightens the *pāda*s' multivalency potential.

Despite this apparent disregard by both Buddhists and Hindus for textual descriptions of the *pāda*s, and despite the blurring of Buddhist and Vaiṣṇava iconographies, scholars have persisted in attempting to differentiate the one from the other, and thus Barua—even given his own recognition that the artisans who made such images seem to have done so "in utter disregard" of the textually expressed iconographic conventions—also attempts to definitively delineate Viṣṇu's feet from those of the Buddha, and suggests that Viṣṇu's feet can "easily be distinguished from the impression of Buddha's feet by the fact that it is an imprint of just one foot on a circular block of stone," whereas Buddhists always represented the Buddha's feet in pairs.[80] Again, however, the context in which the actual footprints under discussion are or were situated is all but ignored by Barua, as if somehow *where* such an image is located—and, more importantly, how it is regarded by those who actually participate in it—is not of vital importance in discerning *what* the image actually is. As if to emphasize the folly of the whole classification endeavor, Paul later asserts that Barua was absolutely mistaken in his argument: "As we shall see, from Gupta period onwards, a pair of feet rather than a single foot happened to be what the Vaiṣṇavas themselves preferred for installation."[81]

In her larger attempt to prove the temporal primacy of the *viṣṇupāda*, Paul goes to great lengths to distinguish with a kind of generalizable certainty between those footprints that are the Buddha's and those that are Viṣṇu's. For instance, she discusses a quite unusual footprint that is on a stone votive *stūpa* from Bodhgayā, currently located in the Berlin museum, and labeled there as a *viṣṇupāda*. The label, in Paul's opinion, is wrong: first, the image depicts a single footprint, which she argues is a singularly Buddhist motif; second, the lone marking on the image is a wheel, which as we have seen Paul argues is the defining mark of the *buddhapāda*; and third, the footprint on this image is enclosed in what Paul refers to as the "*caitya* window" motif, a motif employed on several votive *stūpas* at Bodhgayā. In Paul's view, this motif, which is made up of an engraved *stūpa* in the center of which is the footprint, not only definitively marks this as a *buddhapāda*, but it also, interestingly, may in her opinion be a concrete example of the "*pādacetiya*" references from various Buddhist texts that I have discussed above.[82] This is certainly an intriguing possibility, and one that would represent a remarkable correlation between a textual reference and an actual image, although without any evidence to indicate that those who made the image were actually influenced by the textual references, this correlation may be merely a superficial one. Even given the unusual iconography of this particular image, in its current location (a museum) it is impossible to know in what ritual or discursive context the image was originally situated—was it originally located in a Buddhist or a Vaiṣṇava temple? did it remain in its original setting? who actually worshiped it and why?—and therefore impossible to know what the intention was of those who were responsible for its creation, let alone how the image was actually regarded by those who participated in it.

Significantly, things get markedly more ambiguous when we consider other, less iconographically specific images from Bodhgayā and Gayā. For instance, Paul discusses a double footprint that is located in front of the Mahābodhi temple at Bodhgayā, an image that Mitra had earlier said is, despite its location, actually a *viṣṇupāda*, based in part on the now obscured inscription on the image,[83] as well as the assortments of symbols etched into the stone—including the mace, conch, fish, etc. (symbols which are now, significantly, so worn as to be invisible). Paul disagrees with Mitra's *viṣṇupāda* label, however, and argues that this must in fact be a *buddhapāda*: first, both feet are inscribed with an image of the wheel; more significantly, however, the symbols inscribed on each foot are identical, which, Paul argues, is "a phenomenon clearly in abayance [*sic*] with textual injunction" about *viṣṇupāda*s, as well, she asserts, as actual depictions in art. "[T]he tradition of decorating one foot as a mirror image of the other is essentially Buddhist."[84] Her evidence is suspect at the very least, and she gives only the anachronistic examples of "early Āndhradeśa" and "late Pagan" to prove her point, as well as several small portable models of the Mahābodhi that have the image of the double footprint at their entrance. Furthermore, Paul does not raise the obvious possibility that this might indeed originally have been made and regarded as a *buddhapāda*, but then "converted" to a *viṣṇupāda*—by the addition of the inscription and additional Vaiṣṇava symbols—when the Mahābodhi temple was occupied by Śaivas and run as a Vaiṣṇava temple, and then converted back, as it were, when the stewardship of the Mahābodhi passed back into Buddhist hands.[85]

3.5 *On Converting Objects and Places*

> *First of all, it is obvious that to primitive mankind the footmarks either of men or animals had a very special significance as the most certain tokens indicative of their presence, albeit the beings to which they belonged had not shown themselves in bodily form. As such the footmark presumably possessed something mysterious and awe inspiring.*
>
> —J. PH. VOGEL[86]

The handful of actual images I have been discussing in this chapter seem to me to highlight the difficulty, if not also the folly, of attempting to pin a single identity onto an image as inherently multivalent as a footprint in the vicinity of Gayā and Bodhgayā; here, identity is very much a fluid concept that depends on a variety of factors, including the particular context in which a given image is situated, who is worshiping the image, and the image itself. Furthermore, as I have argued here, the attempt to fix the identity of an image on the basis of a textual description overlooks the essential dynamics of Indian sculptural images: namely, that they are in constant motion, very often moved from and used in very different contexts than those in which they might initially have been situated.

Significantly, much of the debate about the origins and identities of Gayā and Bodhgayā's many footprints is an academic matter, a product of a nineteenth-century taxonomic drive that was particularly in play in the colonial context of India. This rather obsessive attention to the origins of particular places and the objects that make them religiously significant is a topic I will take up in greater detail in the next chapter, but one of the effects of this fixation has been the static assigning of labels that is one of the hallmarks of the modern art museum. There are many footprints situated in the museums of the West, and they are without exception affixed a singular identity, an identity that is very often the product of precisely the sort of academic debates I have been discussing here: a particular image is Viṣṇu's footprint; it is not, then, and cannot be—at least in the museum setting—also the Buddha's footprint.

However, as I have attempted to demonstrate in my analysis of the categorical fuzziness with which footprints are discussed in Buddhist texts, the *pādas* are inherently open-ended, in part because, at least from a Buddhist perspective, there is a marked uncertainty as to exactly what sort of objects they are and as to what their relative value is, and in part because, by its very nature, a footprint is not an object that projects a specific identity, but one into which identity and specific significance is placed by the viewer. Although the respective importance to their traditions and the proximity of Bodhgayā and Gayā certainly intensify the degree to which their *pāda*s are multivalent, this open signifier quality is not limited to the footprints in this specific region of India. Indeed, perhaps the most famous of all of the Buddha's footprints, located on the top of the mountain in Sri Lanka known to some as Adam's Peak—or, significantly, to others as Śrī Pāda—is claimed by nearly everyone: Buddhists see it as a *buddhapāda*, Hindus regard it as the footprint of Śiva, Muslims claim that it is the footprint of Adam, and Christians lay stake to it as the footprint of St. Thomas the Apostle.[87]

There are, to be sure, polemical issues involved in staking claim to such an image, issues that we see borne out in the dispute over the propriety of Bodhgayā itself which I focus on in the next chapter, but there is no inherent identity of this famous footprint, no definitive sectarian markings, no textual proof of its origins. Rather, its identity, and therefore its significance—like the identity and significance of the footprints of Bodhgayā and Gayā—is supplied by its various viewers.[88] In one of the earliest records we possess outside of the Pāli canon and commentarial literature of a Buddhist's view of an actual footprint on the ground, one that at least implicitly captures the fluidity of the *pāda*'s identity and significance, the fifth-century Chinese pilgrim Faxian remarks on one of the many footprints he encountered in his wanderings throughout India, one near Udyāna: Faxian notes that this *pāda* possessed the miraculous quality of changing size, sometimes appearing long, sometimes short, "according to the thoughtfulness of a man's heart."[89]

There is a final aspect of the *pāda*s of Gayā and Bodhgayā that I wish to raise in closing; namely, the idea of "conversion" to which I have alluded above. It is certainly true that images in India do frequently seem to be converted from one tradition to another: an image of Mahāvira becomes the Buddha, an image of Avalokiteśvara becomes Śiva, an image of Prajñāpāramitā becomes Saraswatī, *stūpa*s become *liṅgams*, and so on. But it is perhaps the case that this very language of conversion misses the point, because in saying that an image is *converted* from one thing to another, one implies somehow that its identity is simply shifted, so that its prior identity is erased and replaced. But as I think should be clear from the examples of the footprints I have been discussing here, such an apparent act of conversion is hardly final; rather, I would suggest, it is frequently the case that the prior identity of the image actually remains, while the new identity is added to it. Thus when a footprint that may have been intended in its original context to be a *buddhapāda* is moved to a Vaiṣṇava context, it does not stop being a *buddhapāda*, but rather becomes both the footprint of Viṣṇu and the footprint of the Buddha.

This is a point, though, that begs further thought, because the dynamics of this "both" are very complex indeed. Again, I return to Huyssen's notion of the palimpsest quality of places—the way in which a place's prior identity is both effaced and erased by new buildings, and at the same time perpetuated. When a Vaiṣṇava pilgrim visits Bodhgayā and performs a pūjā before an image of a footprint, to whom or what is she making an offering? The obvious answer is, no doubt, to Viṣṇu. But this assumes that she does not know that the image in question is identified as a Buddhapāda, or that she does not know that Bodhgayā is identified as a Buddhist place, or that most of her fellow worshippers are Buddhists. But what if she is intimately aware of these things, as I found many such Hindus at Bodhgayā to be. The image, for her, is an image of Viṣṇu—or, more properly in such a ritual context, it is Viṣṇu—but it is also an image of the Buddha, even if it is not the Buddha that she is worshipping. As I found in speaking with many such pilgrims at Bodhgayā over the years, the answer to the question "Is this Viṣṇu's footprint?" is almost always yes. But the answer to the question "Is this the Buddha's footprint?" is also yes. Same person, same image, with two interwoven, or overlapping, identities. Indeed, the fact that it is both Viṣṇu's and the Buddha's footprint—and the same holds true for the Buddha images at Bodhgayā—seems, if anything, to imbue the object, and the place it is located, with greater power and significance.

Why limit oneself to one or the other, when one can have both? Indeed, I often have found, when asking pilgrims questions about the identity of images at Bodhgayā that the most typical response I would get is a smile and a head wag, that ubiquitously ambiguous Indian yes-no-maybe response. Such a response frustrates a great many Western visitors to India, particularly those seeking directions. But in this case, it may be a far more precise response than it seems.

4

*The Drama of Viṣṇu and the Buddha at Bodhgayā**

4.1 Prelude: Covering a Dispute with a Façade of Harmony

How do images accrue values that seem so out of proportion to their real importance?

—W. J. T. MITCHELL[1]

The focus of the present chapter—as well as that which follows—is Bodhgayā, the place where Siddhārtha Gautama attained enlightenment in the fifth century B.C.E. This is the place where he became the Buddha. Despite its considerable significance in Buddhist literature and iconography, Bodhgayā is not, and never has been, only a Buddhist place; Hindus have been visiting Bodhgayā since at least the Buddha's own lifetime, and beginning in the fifteenth century and extending into the twentieth, the site was actually maintained by a lineage of Śaiva priests. Thus Hindus and Buddhists both have claimed Bodhgayā as their own, and, consequently, revolving around Bodhgayā are a number of especially volatile issues not unlike those we have seen with Ayodhya and Park51—the tangled dynamics of religious conflict, the effects of colonial and post-colonial discourses on religious practices, the role of so-called sacred space and place in the formation and definition of religious identities. That said, though, Bodhgayā also stands in sharp contrast to a place such as Ayodhya, in that the sort of conflict that has been centered on Bodhgayā has had a very different sort of outcome, and Hindus and Buddhists have ultimately negotiated a means through which they share the site.

Why is this? Why in this instance are two different religious communities able to share the same place in relative peace, while at places such as Ayodhya or Jerusalem or Mato Tipila—the ultimate outcome of the dispute over Park51 remains to be seen—the different parties seem far more entrenched, far more antagonistic, and far more "other." There are no easy answers here, since each of these places is embedded in very particular histories and very particular social and political contexts. In the specific case of Bodhgayā, the colonial construction of the place in the nineteenth century—which was both a physical and a discursive construction—is essential to its present identity. Thus in this chapter I explore the history of this construction, with a particular focus on how it is that Bodhgayā, for some at least, came to be conceived of as an exclusively Buddhist place, and how it is that this exclusive conception of identity did not, in the end, entirely prevail. In the next chapter, I turn to the contemporary reconception and reconstruction of Bodhgayā as a UNESCO World Heritage Site.

Although Hindus and Buddhists had each long been worshipping at Bodhgayā, the conflict there did not begin until the late nineteenth century. At the very center of the conflict stands the Buddha image, because the dispute was not just about the question of who were the rightful proprietors of the site, but also about the question of who was entitled to worship the image of the Buddha at Bodhgayā, and, perhaps most importantly, what sorts of worship were appropriate and what sorts were not. Significantly, however, the answers to these questions—and indeed the questions themselves—were largely informed not, as might perhaps be expected, by long-standing on-the-ground conceptions of and disagreements about what is and what is not appropriate worship. Indeed, not only had Buddhists and Hindus shared the space of Bodhgayā for many centuries, but they had also shared the image of the Buddha, as well as the Buddha and Viṣṇu's footprints, as we have seen in the preceding chapter. So the debate over control of Bodhgayā was not a debate initiated by Buddhists and Hindus who had conflicting claims to the image of the Buddha.

Rather, the whole issue of who ought to have proprietary control over Bodhgayā was informed, and in significant ways actually created, by the opinions of a select group of mostly British Orientalists who were engaged in a prolonged and diffuse anti-Hindu polemic. One particularly significant component of this discourse was an attack on the syncretic tendencies of the Hindus, the purported—or imputed—tendency of Hinduism simply to swallow whatever was in its path, including the image of the Buddha.

Thus although this chapter is specifically about Bodhgayā, it is also about how we think about religions and religious identities—a central concern of this book—because for the Orientalists who wrote about Bodhgayā and other religious sites in India, a place, like a person, could only belong to one religion. If Bodhgayā was Buddhist, then it could not be Hindu, just as a person could not be both a Hindu and Buddhist. This stance, however, is not simply a given, an assertion of fact, but is itself a position, an argument to be made, and one that is often polemically charged. As Amartya Sen has pointed out, echoing the point I made in Chapter 1, we need to recognize that "identities are robustly plural and that the importance of one identity need not obliterate the importance of others."[2] Again, this is a complex subject, and Sen's point, although a good one, is perhaps too naively argued. It nonetheless calls into question many of the ways religions are portrayed, and again raises basic questions in the specific context of Bodhgayā—can a place be both Buddhist and Hindu? can a person be both Hindu and Buddhist?—and a range of broader questions relevant to the study of religions, questions that cut across the many sub-disciplines of Religious Studies.

On May 28, 1953, a ceremony was held at Bodhgayā marking the formal transfer of control of the Mahābodhi Temple, regarded as the actual site of Śākyamuni's enlightenment, from the Śaiva Mahant, Harihar Giri—whose lineage of *sannyāsins* had overseen the temple complex for nearly four hundred years—to the Mahābodhi Temple Management Committee. Assembled together on that day were Buddhist monks from Sri Lanka, Burma, Cambodia, Tibet, and India; Śaiva *sannyāsins* from Bodhgayā's *math;* the nine members of the Committee itself (four Buddhists, five Hindus); various government officials, foreign dignitaries, and influential Hindu and Buddhist lay people; and a sizable crowd of local Hindus and Muslims.[3] During the ceremony, Sanskrit verses were recited by one of the *math*'s brahmin priests; a *bhikkhu* from the Mahābodhi society recited the *tiratana* in Pāli; a popular Indian singer performed two *bhajans* (in Hindi) in praise of Viṣṇu; felicitations from Jawaharlal Nehru, the Sri Lankan prime minister, the Mahārāja of Sikkhim, and others, were read aloud; and, finally, an employee of the Bihar Education Department read passages from Edwin Arnold's epic poem, *The Light of Asia*.

On the surface, this was a stunningly ecumenical moment, bringing together not only individuals and groups with different and, at least up to this point, competing interests and conceptions of Bodhgayā—Śaivas, Buddhists, Vaiṣṇavas, government officials—but also very different factions within the Buddhist world. The obvious question, then, is how did this apparent moment of *communitas* come about after what had been many years of acrimony at Bodhgayā? And, perhaps more importantly, what did this coming together signify? Was this indeed the realization of Arnold's vision of Bodhgayā as the place where, as he put it, "a million oriental congregations" would come together?[4]

The answers to such questions are, predictably, complex, but one thing that can be said at the outset is that this apparent moment of unity seems to bear little resemblance to the *communitas* described by Victor Turner, the "spontaneously generated relationship between leveled and equal total and individuated human beings, stripped of structural attributes."[5] Certainly, the group gathered to mark the transfer of control of Bodhgayā could be said to represent a single community, a pan-Asian religious community with its roots in India: in this they would appear to be both "leveled" and "equal," and the very fact that they were gathered together seems to indicate a certain "stripping" of their individual identities and the formation of what Turner describes as a "comity of comrades and not a structure of hierarchically arrayed positions."[6] However, there was virtually nothing spontaneous about the relationships between the individuals who seemed to constitute the single community represented that day at Bodhgayā. Rather, this was a highly orchestrated and tensely negotiated single moment, and it must be seen not so much as a conclusion but as simply one act in an ongoing drama that continues to be played out at Bodhgayā, a long process of intentionally constructed definitions and redefinitions of the different communities that each had a stake in the place.

Furthermore, when we look beyond the single moment, at the actual process of communal definition that led up to it, one thing that becomes clear is that the definition of a religious community is not merely a matter of how that particular community constitutes itself, internally—as I think is implicit in Turner's discussions of liminality and *communitas* in the context of pilgrimage—but also of how it is conceived of and constituted by those who do not belong to it. What we see played out at Bodhgayā over the last one hundred years conforms to what Vasudha Dalmia and Heinrich von Stietencron have called, describing specifically the construction of Hindu identity in India, "a growing tendency towards ingroup-outgroup polarization," which "has resulted in most communities in a negative projection of the 'Other' against which the self is set off and defined."[7] Thus although there was in the last quarter of the nineteenth century the construction of a new understanding of the Buddhist community centered on Bodhgayā, one that was both international and non-sectarian, this new communal vision was not a wholly internal matter, but was in part constituted by various Orientalist conceptions of Buddhism, and, in part, constituted by this very community's sometimes vitriolic rejection of Hinduism.[8] Likewise, we see the Hindu community at Bodhgayā redefining itself, in part influenced by how it was portrayed by the Buddhists and colonial administrators during the protracted legal wrangling over control of the temple, during which the courts on a number of occasions defined, delineated, and divided Hinduism. Finally, we see these two separate communities, the Buddhist and the Hindu, redefining themselves again, not as two but as one, and this in response to both the introduction of a (largely foreign) "brotherhood of religions" motif into the Bodhgayā discourse, and also to the growing political discourse of "Indianness" that gains momentum at around the time of Independence.

The ceremony at Bodhgayā that was held in May of 1953 was actually a conclusion—a very tentative, temporary sort of conclusion, as it turns out, as we shall see in the next chapter—of a half-century of dispute about Bodghayā. Nearly sixty years earlier, on the morning of February 25, 1895, there was an equally remarkable occurrence at Bodhgayā, an event that would radically shape the future of Buddhism in India and in the world at large and would, in some sense, lead to that apparent moment of harmony in 1953. On that morning in 1895, a Sri Lankan Buddhist, Anagarika Dharmapala, accompanied by several assistants, entered the Mahābodhi Temple, the main structure at Bodhgayā. The men were carrying a stone sculpture of the Buddha. They ascended the steps leading to the second story of the temple, and then entered its inner chamber. There they set the image up on an altar. As they were doing this, a small group of curious onlookers had also entered the now-crowded chamber to observe the goings-on. Once the image had been set up, Dharmapala and his group began to arrange flowers, incense, and candles in front of it; as they were doing so, two more men, Hossain Baksh and Jagganath Singh, entered the chamber, surveyed the scene, and then left.

In the meantime, Dharmapala had sent one of his assistants off to summon Sumangala Bhikkhu, a Sri Lankan Buddhist monk who at the time resided with Dharmapala in the Sri Lankan guest house at Bodhgayā. Sumangala eventually joined the group in the temple, and then began to light a candle as part of the formal ritual that accompanies the installation of a Buddha image in a temple. Before he could finish, however, a group of men, led by Hossain Baksh and numbering between ten and forty (the accounts vary widely), entered the chamber. One of them grabbed the candle from Sumangala while several others climbed onto the altar. An argument ensued, but after several moments of tense negotiation, most of this group left. Dharmapala then sat down in the relative calm to meditate before the image. A few minutes later, however, the group reentered, snatched the image from the altar, and carried it away, eventually to deposit it unceremoniously on the temple lawn.

In an interesting sort of way, this group bears a surface resemblance to the ecumenical gathering at the site fifty-some years later: Here was a Christian-educated Sri Lankan Buddhist, embraced and "adopted" by an American Theosophist (Henry Steele Olcott) and his Russian counterpart ("Madame" Blavatsky), and introduced to the plight of Bodhgayā by a highly romanticized poem (*The Light of Asia*) about the Buddha's life written by an English educator (Edwin Arnold); he goes into an Indian Buddhist temple—one that had in fact been controlled by Śaiva Hindus for over three hundred years and had been operated as a Vaiṣṇava Hindu temple which had seen only a trickle of Buddhist pilgrims since the fifteenth century—in order to set up a Japanese image of the *jina* Buddha Āmitabha. And once that image was installed, it was then promptly removed by the followers of a Śaiva priest, the Mahant in control of the temple, a group led by the Muslim spokesman for the Mahant, Hossain Baksh. This is a complicated scene, and I want to begin by considering the main actor, the polysemous and paradoxical figure of Anagarika Dharmapala. Dharmapala was himself caught up in the drama at Bodhgayā in ways more complex than he could possibly have been aware, and although on the surface it may seem that he was simply trying to restore the image of the Buddha to its rightful place in the Mahābodhi temple, he was himself responding to, and at the same time perpetuating, a long-standing Orientalist conception of Hindu-Buddhist relations in which Hindus, through their idolatrous and fetishistic ritualizing, were viewed as having perverted the pure image of the Buddha.

4.2 Act One: Buddhism Rediscovers Its Center and Reconstructs Its Other

Oh, how unlike in each degree
The Hindoo's foul idolatry,
Whose pond'rous pyramidal pile,
What strange disgusting rites defile!
Where crafty Brahmins guard those shrines,
On which no lively sunbeam shines,
Where never strangers' searching eyes
Can pierce their horrid mysteries,
And where in many a dark recess
Forms that no language can express,
Vile beastly idols grin around,
And grisly monstrous gods abound!
May never such a horrid creed,
To Buddha's simple faith succeed.
—*Captain Anderson of the 19th Infantry*[9]

In the early years of the nineteenth century, the British East India Company began to show a new interest in the people and culture of the regions of northeastern India, and in 1807 the Court of Directors of the Company commissioned a Scottish physician with a particular interest in botany, Francis Buchanan, to "inquire" into the habits and conditions of the people (and, while he was at it, to survey the resources of the country as well).[10] Part of this massive project, which took seven years to complete,[11] was a survey of what is now the modern Indian state of Bihar, which Buchanan visited in 1811–1812. Although this was the birthplace of Buddhism, Buchanan records that in the entire region he had encountered only one indigenous Buddhist,[12] and this a former Śaiva *sannyāsin* who had been converted by two Burmese Buddhists on pilgrimage to Bodhgayā.[13] On its face, there is nothing particularly surprising about this absence of Buddhists; Bodhgayā had been essentially abandoned by Buddhists since the twelfth century, except for sporadic visits by foreign monks on pilgrimage,[14] and those of various groups of Sri Lankan and Burmese monks working to restore and maintain the temple.[15] What is surprising, however, is that only seventy-five years later, Edwin Arnold would, in a series of articles about his 1886 pilgrimage to India published in the *London Daily Telegraph*, describe what seemed to be hordes of Buddhist pilgrims, "wending their way to the immeasurably holy place towards which we also are bound."[16] If both accounts are correct, then the number of Buddhists *in situ* had increased from one to a multitude in only seventy years, which seems nothing short of miraculous.

It was these newspaper articles, and not Arnold's more famous *Light of Asia*, that were the impetus of what became a kind of Buddhist revival centered at Bodhgayā, for as Anagarika Dharmapala, the most prominent of the Buddhists acting at Bodhgayā, would later write: "The idea of restoring the Buddhist Jerusalem into Buddhist hands originated with Sir Edwin Arnold after having visited the shrine, and since 1891 I have done all I could to make the Buddhists of all lands interested in the scheme of restoration."[17] The attempts to restore Buddhism to Bodhgayā, and the conflict that ensued between 1886 and the eventual handover of control of the temple in 1953, have been well documented,[18] but two intertwined aspects of Dharmapala's statement warrant further thought here: the idea that Bodhgayā needed to be returned *from* the Hindus, and that it then would become the domain of "Buddhists of all lands." I will discuss the first of these in this section, and the second in the fourth part of this chapter.

At the time of Arnold's visit, Bodhgayā had been occupied by a lineage of Śaiva ascetics, the Giris, who traced their inhabitancy of the temple to the late sixteenth century, when Gosain Ghamandi Giri, according to Śaiva histories,[19] arrived at the abandoned temple complex. He was then succeeded by Caitanya Giri (1615–1642), who was succeeded by Mahādeva Giri, who is said to have set up the *math* that is still in existence after having received a grant from Shah Alum.[20] According to Mitra, there were between fifty and one hundred *sannyāsins* at the *math* at the end of the nineteenth century,[21] although Buchanan records that there were thousands,[22] an almost certain inflation and a significant negative mirror image to his report that there was only one Buddhist to be found.[23] At any rate, it is certain that there were virtually no Buddhists in residence, and this greatly upset Arnold: "I was grieved to see Mahratta peasants performing 'Shraddh' in such a place and thousands of precious ancient relics of carved stone inscribed with Sanskrit lying in piles around.... Buddha-Gaya is the most dear and sacred to Asiatic Buddhists. Why, then, is it to-day in the hands of Brahman priests, who do not care about the temple, except for the credit of owning it, and for the fees which they draw?"[24] Arnold proposed that Bodhgayā be returned to the Buddhists, so that it could once again become "what it should be, the living and learned centre of purified Buddhism."[25]

If then Arnold's *Daily Telegraph* piece is taken to be the beginning of an attempt to restore not only Bodhgayā, but Buddhism itself, it becomes apparent that at the center of this discourse is not, in fact, the *axis mundi* of Bodhgayā, but rather a vilified Hindu other. This anti-Hindu/pro-Buddhist dichotomy was not new to either colonial or Orientalists discourse, and to a degree Arnold was merely replicating a general characterization of Hinduism, in contrast to Buddhism, that had been in the air for at least a century.[26] Buchanan, for instance, although he could not exactly be characterized as a champion of Buddhism,[27] portrayed Buddhism as possessing an ethical system that was "perhaps as good as that put forth by any of the religious doctrines prevailing among mankind"; Hinduism, by contrast, he describes as "the most abominable, and degrading system of oppression, ever invented by the craft of designing men."[28] Similarly, other influential Westerners who wrote about Bodhgayā in the early nineteenth century had little positive to say about Hinduism. Alexander Cunningham wrote of "the menaces of the most powerful and arrogant priesthood in the world."[29] In the same vein, Mitra described the Śaivas this way: "The monks lead an easy, comfortable life; feasting on rich cakes (*malpulya*) and puddings (*mohanbhog*), and freely indulging in the exhilarating beverage of *bhanga*. Few attempt to learn the sacred books of their religion, and most of them are grossly ignorant."[30]

In comparison to these administrators and scholars, Arnold himself was relatively moderate in his views of Hinduism, and seemed to be at least tentatively respectful of the Mahant and his Śaiva followers, writing, "I think the Mahunt a good man. I had never wished any but friendly and satisfactory arrangements with him."[31] However, Arnold also felt that the only reason that the Hindus were at Bodhgayā at all was to collect fees from Vaiṣṇavas who came as part of their *śraddhā* rituals centered at nearby Gayā—a fairly typical view of the "wily Brahmin." Thus in his view, they were outsiders who did not belong, and in a letter to Sir Arthur Gordon, Governor of Ceylon, appealing for assistance in the restoration of Bodhgayā, Arnold complains that "Buddha-Gaya is occupied by a college of Saivite priests, who worship Mahadeva there, and deface the shrine with emblems and rituals foreign to its nature."[32] This last phrase is extremely important, for it raises what would become perhaps the most central question in the growing storm over control of Bodhgayā, the question of origins, a discourse that resonated with what had become an incredibly powerful and persuasive argument in the late-nineteenth- and early-twentieth-century British intellectual milieu, the basic belief that if one could uncover the origins of a given phenomenon, then one would also uncover the essence of the thing itself (witness Max Müller's influence on the study of religion).[33]

This is also, of course, an issue that is intimately related to the nineteenth-century construction of an original, purified Buddhism. The Buddha was viewed, as Gregory Schopen has put it, as a "kind of sweetly reasonable Victorian Gentleman,"[34] and Buddhism was seen as rational, ethical, devoid of superstition and ritual—the exact opposite of the simultaneous Western construction of Hindusim.[35] Furthermore, because Bodhgayā represented the fount of Buddhism, what the second-century author Aśvaghoṣa referred to as "the navel of the world,"[36] and what Arnold celebrated as the Buddhist Mecca and Jerusalem,[37] the presence of the Hindu Other was all the more offensive. In sum, then, what we see in discussions about Bodhgayā in the latter part of the nineteenth century is a not only a discursive polarization of Hinduism and Buddhism that had been developing since Orientalists in the early eighteenth century had first realized that they were different traditions, but the construction of a Hindu Other who had usurped the Buddhists' rightful place of origins. Thus the Śaivas who effectively owned the temple, and the Vaiṣṇavas who came there to worship, were portrayed by the non-Indian scholars who opined on the matter as outsiders—*mlecchas*—in their own country, polluting the birthplace of Buddhism.

What is more, we see evidence of this not only in the derisive comments of the Orientalists experts whose worked informed Dharmapala and the others who championed the Buddhist position, but also in Western visual representations of the site. Thus the Indians who would have been present at Bodhgayā (in other words, the Hindus) were all but absent from the drawings and paintings of the temple and its environs that were created by Western artists for a Western audience eager for images of the mystical Orient; as Janice Leoshko has noted, "For the Indians included in such views, their presence is at best cursory, decorating the magnificent monuments which were so admired by those of the picturesque persuasion."[38] This can be seen in virtually all of the popular drawings produced by Charles D'Oyly in the 1820s and 1830s, and in another set of illustrations, *Oriental Annual, or Scenes from India*, by William Danell, the accompanying text describes the temple as "entirely deserted so that a scene of gloomy desolation is at the foresaken sanctuary."[39] But as much as the Western champions of Bodhgayā tried to exclude them from the site, the Hindu Other proved rather more difficult to avoid on the ground, and when attempts were made to remove them, they proved to be far more active and far more vocal than the indolent natives in Mitra's writings and D'Oyly's drawings.

4.3 *Act Two: Dharmapala and the Anti-Hindu Polemic*

A powerful Buddhist's eloquent voice is needed to show the knavery of the selfish bigoted Brahman priests.

—ANAGARIKA DHARMAPALA[40]

No matter how one views him—as a rabble rousing extremist or as righteous defender of the true tradition—Anagarika Dharmapala is a decidedly complex and often ambiguous figure. Although I do not wish to consider his entire life—which has been much analyzed[41]—in any real depth, but rather only those aspects of his life that are immediately germane to his involvement at Bodhgayā, at least a little background is helpful in understanding the particular events of that morning in February 1895. Dharmapala was born Don David Hewavitarane, in Colombo, Sri Lanka, in 1864. Although his family was Buddhist, he himself was educated at Christian mission schools, a situation that seems to have deeply disturbed Dharmapala from a very early age.[42] At the age of sixteen, Dharmapala first met the Theosophists Henry Steele Olcott and Helena Petrova Blavatsky, who had come to Sri Lanka in 1880 from their headquarters in southern India at the behest of the island's Buddhist leaders to aid in the Buddhist struggle against the rising influence of Christian missionaries there. The young Dharmapala was immediately struck by their presence: "I remember going up to greet them. The moment I touched their hands I felt overjoyed. The *desire for universal brotherhood*, for all the things they wanted for humanity struck a responsive chord in me."[43] When Olcott and Blavatsky returned to Sri Lanka in 1884, Dharmapala was formally initiated into the Theosophical Society, and later that same year he accompanied Olcott and Blavatsky to the Theosophical Society headquarters in Adyar, outside of Madras.

In the late 1880s and early 1890s, Dharmapala and Olcott traveled extensively in India and elsewhere in Asia, attempting to spread the Theosophical Society's message. It was during his travels with Olcott that Dharmapala first became aware of the state of Bodhgayā. The two were in Kyoto, Japan, in 1891, and Dharmapala was sick in the hospital with rheumatic fever; he had been given a copy of Edwin Arnold's immensely popular poem *The Light of Asia*, and as he read it in his sick bed he there came across Arnold's highly romantic account of the temple. At about the same time, Dharmapala also first read Arnold's account of his pilgrimage to India, and his visit to Bodhgayā, published serially in the *London Telegraph*. These were profoundly transformative moments for him, and in his diary, Dharmapala writes: "The idea of *restoring the Buddhist Jerusalem* into Buddhist hands originated with Sir Edwin Arnold after having visited the sacred spot in 1886. It was he who gave me the impulse to visit the shrine, and since 1891 I have done all I could to make the Buddhists of all lands interested in the scheme of restoration."[44] Later that same year Dharmapala founded the Maha Bodhi Society, ostensibly to restore Bodhgayā to its former state and to establish the site as the sacred center of pilgrimage for the world's Buddhists. But the goal of Dharmapala's "scheme of restoration" was not simply to restore the crumbling glory of Buddhism; on the contrary, his Bodhgayā "mission" was caught up in a web of sentiments that would eventually evolve into a sustained and sometimes vicious anti-Hindu polemic. When, reflecting on the sorry state of Bodhgayā in his journal, he writes that a "a powerful Buddhist's eloquent voice" is needed to combat the Brahmins in control of the Mahābodhi temple, he means, of course, his own voice, which would certainly grow more powerful, although it hardly became more eloquent, but instead grew increasingly ugly and anti-Hindu. Indeed, his relationship with his mentor Olcott had begun to sour during their travels together, largely because he was becoming disenchanted with Olcott and his sympathetic attitude toward Hinduism.[45] For while his early mentor pursued his peculiar theosophical agenda, which Olcott once described as a desire to uncover the "omnipotence of truth" at the root of all religions and to pursue an "unqualified devotion to its discovery and propagation,"[46] Dharmapala's attention increasingly lay elsewhere.

He gradually began to turn away from the Theosophical Society's "desire for universal brotherhood"—that commitment to the good of all humanity that had initially "struck a responsive chord" in him—and he began to turn more and more toward the specific plight of Theravāda Buddhism. While Olcott and Dharmapala were in Calcutta in 1892, for instance, Olcott delivered a lecture, titled "The Kinship Between Hinduism and Buddhism," in which he decried "the baseless antagonism and inexcusable prejudice" felt by many elite Hindus toward Buddhism.[47] He appealed to the common roots of the two "sister cults," and argued that it was not only possible for the two religions to coexist in peace and harmony at Bodhgayā, but it was natural for them to do so, because for Olcott, Hinduism and Buddhism were in essence the same. Although at first sympathetic to Olcott's plea for tolerance and harmony—Dharmapala himself wrote the introduction when the lecture was eventually published—he also began actively to pursue a considerably more divisive agenda. In particular, he took issue with Olcott's conflation of the two traditions. Indeed, years later he would reflect back on his relationship with his old mentor and write that in "the time of Mdme. Blavatsky, most of the theosophists embraced Buddhism and took *pansil*,"—the observance of the five basic ethical principals for Theravādins—but ever since Blavatsky's death in 1891, which was the point at which Olcott became the sole leader of the movement, "the Theosophical Society upholds Hinduism as the supreme cult."[48] In the end, Olcott and his followers, according to Dharmapala, were "only consolidating Krishna worship."[49]

Even a brief sampling of Dharmapala's opinions about Hinduism makes it clear that his attempt to install the Buddha image at Bodhgayā cannot be seen as a purely Buddhist attempt at restoration, but also must be seen as an open act of aggression aimed at Hinduism in general and at the Bodhgayā Mahant and his followers in particular: "India by right belongs to Buddha," Dharmapala said.[50] "Brahmans through sheer selfishness ejected the Noble Aryan Dharma from its native soil and India fell";[51] "[W]hen the Kshatriya Dharma was supplanted by Brahminical priestcraft and ritualism, when rulers became victims of sensuality, and illegitimate luxury, when duty was perverted for satisfaction of one's own self, the teachings of the Lord Buddha were abandoned for idiotic superstitions and insane sensualism"[52] At the center of this extended invective was the Hindu treatment of the Buddha images at Bodhgayā. "It was most painful for me to witness the vandalism that was taking place there constantly," he wrote in *The Buddhist* in 1891 after visiting Bodhgayā for the first time. "The most beautiful statues of the teacher of the Nirvana and the Law... are still uncared for and quietly allowed to perish by exposure."[53] Bodhgayā was run—and, in Dharmapala's opinion, run-down—by Śaiva priests who, he argued, "have no religious interests at the shrine," but were only interested in Bodhgayā as a source of income.[54] He further lamented that the main temple was in ruins, the Buddha images broken and decaying and "allowed to rot and be trampled by cattle... having rubbish thrown upon them."[55] "Is the temple held sacred by the Hindus?" Dharmapala asked rhetorically. "Old Hindu residents at Gaya will tell you that the temple was looked upon with desecration by the orthodox Hindus as a place associated with heterodoxy, who use [*sic*] to scowl and spit upon the image of the BUDDHA and throw stones at the temple."[56]

It is, however, by no means clear—even in Dharmapala's own account—that the Hindus at Bodhgayā were, in fact, scowling and spitting on the Buddha images, nor is it at all clear that the Śaiva priests had "no religious interest" in the place. On the contrary, it would seem that they were indeed venerating the Buddhist images at the site, and had been doing so for centuries. In fact, early on, shortly after he had become aware of the plight of Bodhgayā, Dharmapala had used this very veneration as part of his appeal to the Hindus, urging them to give Bodhgayā back to the Buddhists; in his first public lecture in English, "Buddhism in Its Relationship with Hinduism," delivered in 1891, he pointed out, "As Buddha is held at least by the Hindus as an Avatar there should be no hostility shown to the Buddhists in their attempt to re-occupy the place."[57] Indeed, Dharmapala observed—rather bizarrely—that many of the Hindu images in the Calcutta Museum actually had small images of the Buddha inscribed in their foreheads, and he went so far as to suggest that the "image of Vishnu and Brahma and other gods are of Buddhist origin."[58] Initially, at least, both Dharmapala and Olcott attempted to gain Buddhist control of Bodhgayā by appealing to the common roots and intertwined histories of Buddhism and Hinduism. They talked of the "blending of Buddhist and Hindu symbols" in Buddhist art and practice, and also of the shared veneration of the image of the Buddha, as proof that there was no basis "to this senseless clamour of a necessary enmity between Hinduism and Buddhism," and they each argued that there was an amicable route of reconciliation open to the two groups.[59] This route, however, did not lead to sharing, but to Hindus "returning" to the Buddhists what was really Buddhist.

Thus although he admitted that Hindus and Buddhists both venerated the Buddha at Bodhgayā, he nonetheless argued that Bodhgayā should be an exclusively Buddhist place. Indeed, although Hindus might indeed have been worshiping the Buddha images at Bodhgayā for centuries, they had been worshiping them in the wrong way. "Priest-craft has been busy in converting purely Buddhist statues into the Puranic Hindu pantheon," wrote Dharmapala, and "the images of BUDDHA and the Bodhisatvas [*sic*] found in the Mahant's *baradari* have undergone transformation in having clothes put on them."[60] He goes on: "How shocking it is to see the noble and majestic statue of our Lord *desecrated and lowered* in the eyes of the lingam worshiping Hindu!"[61]

Dharmapala argued that Buddhists did not actually worship the Buddha image at all, but instead only paid it tribute, honoring the memory of the now-absent teacher;[62] the Hindus, however, turned the image into what they saw as a god, and thus into an idol and a fetish. Part of what is at play here is the perpetuation of a nineteenth-century construction of Buddhism as a non-theistic, non-ritual religion, a rational tradition that stands in stark contrast to fetishistic and idolatrous Hinduism.[63] The Hindus were simply subsuming and in the process perverting the Buddha and his image, "converting" him to Viṣṇu with their "priestcraft and ritualism" and their "idiotic superstitions and insane sensualism."

Nowhere in Dharmapala's polemic is there any mention of the actual Hindus on the ground and their own religious motivations. Rather, mirroring the most egregious sort of Orientalist essentialism, to him all Hindus could be reduced to an unambiguous image of the Other: namely, the avaricious, duplicitous, and mercenary Mahant. Thus, just as Dharmapala was arguing for the return of what he saw as rightfully Buddhist, he was also denying what for a great many Hindus was rightfully Hindu, and he did so using the very rhetoric and opinions of the Orientalist experts who had come to know what was Hindu and what was Buddhist, and who had also established that it was in fact best that, to borrow Kipling's line, never the twain shall meet. Furthermore, not only did Dharmapala deny any legitimate Hindu voice with regard to their veneration of the Buddha images at Bodhgayā, he also seemed at the same time to fabricate the Buddhists' position. For instance, during the course of the trial that followed Dharmapala's attempt to install the image in the Mahābodhi temple, a commission was set up by the Lieutenant Governor of Bengal, James Bourdillon, at the request of the Viceroy Lord Curzon, to prove that the Buddhists did indeed have a rightful claim to Bodhgayā. In the course of their investigation, however, they found it difficult to locate actual Buddhists who were actually offended by Hindu veneration at the site. According to Bourdillon's report, the various Mahāyāna Buddhists who visited the site, it seemed, were in fact "pro Hindu," while the Burmese Theravādins had a long-standing and amicable relationship with the Mahant; it was only the Sinhalese, led by Dharmapala, who were "quite intolerant and they form the chief source" of opposition to the Hindus.[64] And perhaps even more ironically, when the Government of India pushed to at least ban the painting and clothing of the Buddha images at Bodhgayā—recall that Dharmapala had expressed outrage that the images "have undergone transformation in having clothes put on them"—and to ban the affixing of sandalwood-paste *tilaks* on the foreheads of the Buddha images, it was found by Bourdillon's commission to be the case that "some sects of Buddhists do make offerings of that material nature."[65]

Who, then, besides Dharmapala was so upset about the Hindu presence at Bodhgayā, and by the Hindus' veneration of the Buddha image? Apparently not very many Buddhists. There were, however, a great many Europeans who found the Hindu presence, and in particular the Hindu treatment of the image of the Buddha, offensive. Indeed, the general nineteenth-century attitude towards Hinduism, as has been well documented, was that it was, in the lamentably memorable words of Buchanan, "the most abominable, and degrading system of oppression, ever invented by the craft of designing men."[66] Buddhism, by contrast, was championed as a highly rational religion rivaling Protestant Christianity, and the Buddha was frequently held up as something like an ideal Victorian gentleman, or in the words of one writer, a "verry parfit gentle knight."[67] As Almond has noted, the "status of the Buddha was enhanced enormously by the perception that he had been an opponent of Hinduism, for in this he was aligning himself with the vast majority of Victorians."[68] The Buddha was thus compared to Martin Luther, and described as being, according to Alexander Cunningham, "a great social reformer who dared to preach the perfect equality of all mankind and the consequent abolition of caste, in spite of the menaces of the most powerful and arrogant priesthood in the world."[69] We see, then, recalling Judith Butler's analysis of the formation of the self, that the construction of Buddhist identity in this context very much entailed the positing of an inimical Hindu other.

Dharmapala was thus hardly alone in his attacks on Hinduism, nor alone in his denunciation of the Hindus at Bodhgayā and their abuses of the Buddha image, and when he pronounced that after the restoration—or, perhaps, more properly the reformation—of the site, Bodhgayā was destined to become "what the holy sepulchre is to the Christians, Zion to the Jews and Mecca to the Mohammedans,"[70] he was in fact replicating, nearly word for word, one of the most popular pro-Buddhist Orientalist spokesmen of his day, Sir Edwin Arnold.

4.4 *Act Three: The Romantic Fantasy of the Buddha and Bodhgayā*

Gautama did for India what Luther and the Reformers did for Chistendom; like Luther, he found religion in the hands of a class of men who claimed a monopoly of it, and doled it out in what manner and in what measure they chose; like Luther, he protested that religion is not the affair of the priest alone, but is the care and concern of every man who has a reasonable soul: both labored to communicate to all the knowledge which had been exclusively reserved for the privileged class.

—Journal of Sacred Literature, 1865[71]

But he arose—made strong with that pure meat—
And bent his footsteps where a great Tree grew,
The Bôdhi-tree (thenceforward in all years
Never to fade, and ever to be kept
In homage of the world), beneath whose leaves
It was ordained that Truth should come to Buddha:
Which now the Master knew; wherefore he went
With measured pace, steadfast, majestical,
Unto the Tree of Wisdom. Oh, ye Worlds!
Rejoice! our Lord wended unto the Tree!

—EDWIN ARNOLD[72]

Arnold's rapturous account of the life of the Buddha, *The Light of Asia*, was one of the most popular long poems in Victorian England. First published in 1871, it went through over one hundred printings—Brooks Wright, in his biography of Arnold, has noted that in its time, the book sold about as many copies as *Huckleberry Finn*—and it was translated into numerous languages, including Bengali and Sanskrit.[73] Although it was hardly greeted with unanimously positive reviews—it was denounced, for instance, as "mischievous" and "shallow," and attacked as an affront to Christianity—with the growing interest in things Asia in both England and America, Arnold found a ready market for the book. In particular, the Theosophists celebrated it as a truly momentous work. Dharmapala had thus probably already been acquainted with *The Light of Asia* when he experienced his epiphanic moment in Kyoto. Indeed, it was probably not this work that most piqued his interest and his ire, and which introduced the "Bodhgayā as *axis mundi*" idea to him; for although Arnold's account of Bodhgayā in *The Light of Asia* is unabashedly romantic, it does not particularly celebrate the place and adds little except literary flourish to his sources.[74] Rather, it seems that it was Dharmapala's reading of Arnold's account of his 1886 pilgrimage to Bodhgayā, serialized in *The London Daily Telegraph*, that inspired and incited him, for it is in this essay that Arnold introduces the idea that, in his words, Bodhgayā would become "the Mecca, the Jerusalem, of a million Oriental congregations."[75]

Arnold begins his account with a description of his approach to Bodhgayā, noting that he was not alone on his pilgrimage: "[T]hose whom we shall overtake will be mainly pilgrims of the day, wending their way to the immeasurably holy place towards which we also are bound ... for that most sacred spot of all hallowed places in Asia."[76] He writes here as if there were thousands of pilgrims on the road to Bodhgayā, perhaps already envisioning the "million Oriental congregations" flocking to the site. But few, if any, of these pilgrims would have been Buddhists—they would have more likely been Hindus on the way to Gayā—a detail that seems entirely to escape the enraptured Arnold. When he arrived at Bodhgayā, he was predictably in awe that he was standing at the very place of the Buddha's enlightenment—"this *is* the spot, most dear and divine, and precious beyond every other place on earth"—but he also expresses distress at seeing that the place was occupied by Hindus, and that the temple and grounds were in a shocking state of decay. Thus he writes, "I was grieved to see Mahratta peasants performing 'Shraddh' in such a place and thousands of precious ancient relics of carved stone inscribed with Sanskrit lying in piles around."[77] In other words, for Arnold it was not only that the Hindus were doing inappropriate things in a place where they did not belong in the first place, but that they did not even have the pride and dignity to take care of their own ancient and sacred heritage.

Arnold's account of his visit to Bodhgayā and his subsequent attempts to "return" the site to the Buddhists are particularly significant in the way that he consistently links these two ideas. From his point of view, the Brahmins had no conception of Bodhgayā's true, sacred character; indeed, according to Arnold, they were not doing anything that could have been deemed religiously legitimate, nor, for that matter, anything that could legitimately be called "religious." Thus Arnold reproduces in the *Daily Telegraph* essay part of a letter that he had written to the Governor of Ceylon, Sir Arthur Gordon, in which he disgustedly observes that the "Buddha's images are to be found used as weights to the levers for drawing water.... I have seen three feet high statues in an excellent state of preservation, buried under rubbish to the east of the Mahunt's baradari.... [A]nd the Asoka pillars, the most ancient relics of the site—indeed, 'the most antique memorials of all India'.... are now used as posts of the Mahunt's kitchen."[78]

It is perhaps understandable that Arnold would have been shocked at the apparent state of decay at Bodhgayā—particularly after his own romantic conception and description of the place in *The Light of Asia*, written before he had been there, of course, and thus based entirely on textual sources—and understandable as well that he would express anguish at seeing statues of the Buddha covered in refuse. But this state of disrepair and decay is only part of the issue for Arnold. Indeed, the real outrage for him was that the Hindus were perverting the pure image of the Buddha. Thus in language and logic that seems to have directly informed Dharmapala, he observes that the Hindus "deface the shrine with emblems and rituals foreign to its nature."[79] As we have already seen, though, when this issue was further investigated, it turned out that the Buddhists themselves were engaged in just these sorts of offensive practices. We see here not only an expression of outrage about the perceived desecration of these images, but also an early iteration of the boundaries between religious traditions, a construction that is an essential component of the genealogy of religious studies. Hinduism and Buddhism are separate religions, with distinct practices and beliefs, and if they appear to be intertwined on the ground, it is the Western scholars' duty to rectify this, to keep them separated—as I remarked in the Preface about world religions textbooks: chapter four, then chapter five.

Arnold's solution to the Hindu presence was remarkably straightforward: the Mahant and his followers ought, quite simply, to be bought out. This was an idea that Dharmapala would later attempt to implement, with absolutely no success. As Arnold puts it, "Buddha-Gaya is the most dear and sacred to Asiatic Buddhists. Why, then, is it to-day in the hands of Brahman priests, who do not care about the temple, except for the credit of owning it, and for the fees which they draw?"[80] Since it was only money that kept them at the site, though, Arnold argued that it would be only money that would make them leave; again, we see the image of the avaricious Brahmin, interested only in money. By removing these mercenary Hindu idolaters, Bodhgayā would be returned to its natural state, and it would thus be made into, in Arnold's words, "what it should be, the living and learned centre of purified Buddhism."[81] He closes his *Daily Telegraph* essay with a final assault on the Hindu presence at Bodhgayā, expressing a sentiment that, as we have already seen, Dharmapala later reiterated nearly word for word: "No orthodox Hindoos will be wounded in sentiment" if Bodhgayā were to be sold to the Buddhists, "because, by strict truth, the Mahunt, as a Brahman and follower of Sankaracharya, goes against his shastras by keeping control of a Buddhist's temple."[82] Arnold here is not only saying that it is wrong for the Hindus to control a Buddhist monument, but that it is wrong for a Śaiva Hindu, such as the Mahant, to engage in what were obviously—to Arnold, at least—Vaiṣṇava forms of worship.

Here we see the nineteenth-century Orientalists taxonomic drive in full force, an ideological stance in which it is the West that decides what sorts of religious practices are and are not appropriate based not on actual practices, but on textual descriptions of the order of things. Dharmapala would, as we have seen, later employ precisely the same logic. There is more, however, to Arnold's (and later Dharmapala's) polemic, more than even the perpetuation of the image of the wily Brahmins: namely, the opinion that the countless Hindus who actually came to Bodhgayā to perform *pūjā* to the Buddhist images—those very pilgrims he had encountered "wending their way to the immeasurably holy place"—were either too confused to know the difference between a Buddhist image and a Hindu one, or worse, too ignorant to care.

Arnold was hardly the first to give voice to this attitude. Alexander Cunningham, the first director of the Archeological Survey of India, freely expressed his derisive and derogatory opinions of Hindus, especially of Brahmins, and his learned and authoritative views seemed to have directly informed Arnold. We have already encountered Cunningham's attitude—recall his remark concerning "the menaces of the most powerful and arrogant priesthood in the world." Indeed, in discussing a stone slab that had been used in construction of the Giri's *math* at Bodhgayā and that bore a presumably Buddhist inscription, Cunningham remarked that "Brahmin malignancy has sadly mutilated" the inscription, making it impossible to decipher. For Cunningham, it was not only this inscription that the Hindus had mutilated, though; they had perverted the very purity of Indian sculpture, which in its early, Buddhist state rivaled the Greeks "until its degradation culminated in the wooden inanities and bestial obscenities of the Brahmanical temples."[83]

Cunningham's disdain was not reserved only for the Brahmins, for where the priests were cunning and greedy, the lay Hindus were simply religiously daft. When the Archaeological Survey of India had first begun excavation of Bodhgayā, they had dug several exploratory trenches, and in the process had "disinterred" hundreds of small *stūpas*, which they left *in situ*. When they later returned to the site, the *stūpas* were gone. Cunningham's description of the scene is particularly telling: "Not a single specimen of these hundreds is now to be seen. I suppose they have been carried off to Gaya, and are now doing duty as lingams, or symbols of Mahadeva. No conversion is required, as the people accept one of these votive stupas of the Buddhists as a ready-made lingam."[84] In other words, the average Hindus were willing to worship *anything* as sacred, just as long as it vaguely resembled the real thing. By the same token, then, these same ignorant pilgrims flocked to Bodhgayā to make *pūjā*s to the Buddha image because, quite simply, he looked a lot like Viṣṇu.

This basic attitude was also expressed by one of Cunningham's prominent contemporaries, another authority on Bodhgayā, Mitra. Remarking on what he saw as the Śaiva's indiscriminate worship of anything remotely resembling a Śiva *liṅgam*, he writes that it "would seem that even for neophytes a lingam was held essential, but in the majority of cases its place was supplied by a miniature votive stupa picked up from the Buddhist ruins in the neighborhood. Half-buried on top on the mound, it passes very well for a lingam."[85] In his 1878 monograph on the site, *Buddha Gaya: The Great Buddhist Temple, Hermitage of Sakya Muni*—a book that, incidentally, Dharmapala read and praised as a "splendid work"—Mitra describes the Brahmin priests in residence at Bodhgayā in terms that make even Cunningham's invectives seem mild by comparison: "The monks lead an easy, comfortable life; feasting on rich cakes (*malpulya*) and puddings (*mohanbhog*), and freely indulging in the exhilarating beverage of *bhanga*. Few attempt to learn the sacred books of their religion, and most of them are grossly ignorant."[86] He praises the extensiveness of the Mahant's "fine collection of Sanskrit manuscripts" but then immediately points out that it appeared that he did not—and, he implies, perhaps also could not—read them. But it was not, in Mitra's opinion, just that the Brahmins were grossly ignorant; they were grossly lazy too: "The temple stood there deserted, forsaken, and dilapidated, and they appropriated it to their own use by giving it and its presiding image new names. In doing so they did not even take the trouble to change the image, or to bring to light the inhumed portion of the temple by removing the rubbish around its base."[87] And why did they not go to the trouble to "change" the image from the Buddha to Viṣṇu? Because the iconographically befuddled lay Hindus would not have noticed the difference even if they had.

This view of Hinduism, and particularly of the Brahmins, is not in itself particularly unusual in nineteenth-century Orientalist writings, and one could find countless examples of similar opinions in any number of sources. One further feature of this discourse that bears particular mention in the present context, though, is the degree to which the actual Hindus who came to worship at Bodhgayā are denied any voice and any agency. Thus Mitra points out that certain Buddhist images at Bodhgayā, such as images of the Bodhisattva Padmapāṇi, were "mistaken by the Hindus for those of Vishnu, and worshipped accordingly."[88] Mitra's language is particularly important here, for where the Brahmin priests, as we have already seen, are portrayed by Mitra and Cunningham as cynical and greedy and willing to sacrifice the integrity of their religious practice for a few extra rupees, the lay people are portrayed as being too ignorant to know even the difference between a Hindu and Buddhist figure.

This is significant, because Mitra is not suggesting that the Hindus knowingly worshipped a Buddhist image as a Hindu one; in other words, he does not suggest, as is so frequently the case in the Orientalist discourse on Hindu/Buddhist relations, that the devotees are informed—or misinformed, as the case may be—by the *purāṇic* understanding that the Buddha is simply one of Viṣṇu's many manifestations. This is a charge that we have already seen leveled by Cunningham, Arnold, and Dharmapala, and one that, no matter how problematic it is, at least gave the Hindu worshipers some degree of agency. According to Mitra, though, the Hindus who perform *pūjā* to Buddhist images are so ignorant that they cannot even correctly discern the gender of the image. So, for instance, Mitra describes an image of Padmapani—a popular form of the Bodhisattva Avalokiteśvara who is male—that is "kept leaning against the wall of the terrace to the left of the entrance of the Great Temple, and, in this position, is worshipped by the Hindus under the impression of its being a representation of the goddess Savitri."[89]

The Orientalist discourse on the relationship between Buddhism and Hinduism could be traced considerably further back than to Mitra and Cunningham—back at least to the end of the eighteenth century, when it had yet to be established that Hindus and Buddhists were in fact different. The notion that they were not distinct traditions persisted well into the nineteenth century, with one writer adamantly pronouncing in 1831 that "it has been at once concluded that the ninth incarnation of Vishnu, and the alleged founder of Buddhism, were one and the same person."[90] Part of the confusion lay in the fact that there were few Buddhists in India to question on the matter, and so the early Orientalists relied almost exclusively on the opinions of Brahmin pundits, and these Brahmins consistently informed the Europeans, perhaps not surprisingly, that the Buddha was indeed the ninth *avatāra* of Viṣṇu.

By mid-century, however, the Orientalists had made sufficient textual headway in their study of Buddhism that it became clear that Buddhism and Hinduism were in fact distinct traditions.[91] Once this was established, though, the two traditions were seen as not only distinct, but also as irreconcilably opposed, as mutually hostile toward one another as Protestantism and Catholicism. We clearly see this codification, or perhaps more properly this reification, of the opposition of the two groups borne out in the discussions about Bodhgayā and the Buddha image, as I have demonstrated in tracing the Orientalist genealogy that extends backward from Dharmapala to Arnold to Cunningham and Mitra. For all of these men, the Brahmins wanted money and power; it was simply unthinkable that the Hindus could have any legitimate claim to the Buddha image.

There is, to be sure, a complex syncretic ambivalence that marks the status of the Buddha *avatāra* within the Hindu context itself, for the Buddha *avatāra* is hardly an unambiguously positive figure in the Vaiṣṇava tradition. Indeed, the whole issue of the status of the Buddha *avatāra* involves more than the simple sort of Brahmanical transformation imputed by Dharmapala. First, the Buddha is not even included in all lists of Viṣṇu's *avatāras*. Jan Gonda has suggested that the early Vaiṣṇava concept of the *avatāra* is intimately linked with the need to preserve the *dharma*: "The god is born each time for a specific purpose. When the dharma is not followed Viṣṇu appears on earth in one of his avatāras for the rescue of the good, for the preservation of the world and its culture, for the destruction of the evil-doers and the establishment of dharma."[92] In the *Viṣṇupurāṇa*, for instance, which contains one of the oldest and most elaborate accounts of the Buddha *avatāra*, the Buddha is introduced as one of the many forms of Viṣṇu's *māyāmohā*, his delusive power, and the Buddha uses this power to engage in battle against the evil *daityas*—who are intent on destroying the proper order of things—on behalf of the *devas*, and he accomplishes this goal by spreading what can only, from a Vaiṣṇava point of view, be called "heretical" teachings.[93] The *daityas* adopt these teachings, and in the process abandon the Vedas and *smṛtis*, which inevitably leads to their downfall.

However, the Buddha is not only portrayed in the *Viṣṇupurāṇa* as the purveyor of false views (albeit ultimately for a good cause); the text also describes in some detail the faults of the followers of the Buddha, portraying them as neglecting the most basic rituals prescribed for householders. As Klaus Klostermaier has noted, the *Viṣṇupurāṇa* is "an early and unmistakably hostile Hindu text dealing with Buddhism.... The Hindu who dines with a Buddhist goes to hell. Buddhists are to be considered as unclean, whatever their caste-affiliation may have been. Not only is the Hindu told to have nothing to do with the Buddhist, he must discourage the Buddhist from associating with him."[94]

The idea, then, that the Buddha is simply transformed into Viṣṇu, using the ruse of the *avatāra*, in order to lure the Buddhists to Hinduism, is simply not supported by the texts. But there is a further problem, for in focusing on texts such as the *Viṣṇupurāṇa*, Dharmapala and his orientalist predecessors tended to ignore the long history of Buddhist/Hindu interaction on the ground in northeast India, and in particular, the degree to which the iconography of the two traditions frequently overlapped and intermeshed, a dynamic I explored in the prior chapter. The Pāla rulers of the eighth through twelfth centuries, for instance—who are consistently portrayed throughout the nineteenth century as the last great Buddhist kings in India—clearly patronized both Buddhists and Hindus for some four hundred years, and it is not at all clear that they ever had a single religious allegiance or identity. And perhaps even more germane to the present context, during the same period the Buddha and Viṣṇu were frequently sculpturally depicted in an almost identical manner, differing only in their iconographic details, details that would, no doubt, have been unimportant to the worshiper *in situ*. Certainly, we could follow Mitra and Cunningham and Arnold and Dharmapala, and argue that in blurring the distinctions between a Buddha image and a Viṣṇu image, the artisans who made such images and the patrons who supported them, as well as the monks and lay people who actually encountered such images, were attempting to earn, as it were, two rupees with one stone image. Or alternately, we could take the other route that we have seen these learned men follow, and simply argue that such images were the result of either laziness on the part of the Brahmins, or ignorance on the part of the lay people, or a combination of the two.

Such interpretations are hardly satisfying, though. For one thing that is missing here is a recognition of one essential aspect of the phenomenology of such images, something we have already seen played out in the context of the footprints I discussed in the last chapter: namely, that they are inherently multivalent, sometimes in spite of the very ideological positions that might originally have motivated their construction. This sort of multivalency is also evident at another famous Buddhist pilgrimage site, Rajgir, which lies only a few hours away from Bodhgayā; there, as I noted in the Preface, during certain times of the year one encounters thousands of Hindu pilgrims making the steep trek up the famous "Vulture's Peak," well-known from accounts of the Buddha's lifetime, in order to venerate a massive stone image of the Buddha. Thus, as Frederick Asher has nicely put it, "we must ask whether there is only one interpretation *of any sculpture.* Is the image any more correctly and precisely Avalokitesvara than Rama, or is its identity fluid, dependent on the viewer.... It is not just the relativism that is so inherently Indian and permits varying interpretations but the obvious fact that different beholders may read an image differently."[95]

This is a point that begs further reflection. Richard Davis has written about Hindu images in a similar vein, using the sort of reader-response orientation developed by Stanley Fish and others, arguing that "different ways of seeing animate the object seen in new ways... [and] viewers also bring their own frames of assumptions, understandings, needs, expectations, and hopes to what they see,"[96] and also noting the ways in which different viewers—and different ritual participants—construed and constructed different meaning and significance out of the same image. I think, certainly, that a degree of caution, or skepticism, is warranted here. I am not suggesting that the meaning and significance of a Buddha image is merely dependent on its particular context, since to do so would be to ignore the complex motivations behind the construction of such images, and also to discount the very specific guidelines for the proper ritual orientation toward such images.[97] Nonetheless, the phrase—and the rather complex critical assumptions behind it—"dependent on the viewer" is extremely important in understanding the venerational dynamics at a site such as Bodhgayā. Davis argues that a kind of monopticism has infected a great many contemporary art historians and religious historians who write about icons and temples in India: they focus almost exclusively on the moment that an object is created. Such a focus, however has the effect, in Davis's words, of "restricting our sense of the meaningful possibilities of an object and it draws our attention away from the object's participation in the ongoing social life of its communities."[98]

Dharmapala and company could be seen as having suffered from a similarly restricted vision; for them, the Buddha image could only ever properly, or legitimately, represent what it was originally intended to represent, the Buddha, although the cause of their restricted vision was not so much the lack of imagination sometimes displayed by historians, but an obviously pro-Buddhist ideology that froze the status of Bodhgayā as the site of Śākyamuni's enlightenment. But despite Dharmapala's or

Mitra's or Arnold's wishes to the contrary, the Buddha images at Bodhgayā were and still are situated in the ongoing social life of Bodhgayā, a social life that now once again includes Buddhist pilgrims, but which also has for several centuries also included a great many Hindus as well. In this regard, Davis's remarks about another Buddhist image that finds its way into a Hindu devotional context, the Didargañj Yakṣā now housed in the Patna Museum, are quite relevant. For although this image, too, was originally intended to be situated in a Buddhist setting, the Hindu villagers who worshiped it "would not have worried unduly about the original historical identity of the awesome new icon. They would have been much more concerned to integrate the image into their current world of belief, and they would have assigned identity and worshiped it accordingly."[99]

The whole question of the identity of any single image in India is, as I have suggested, in serious need of revision. There can be no question that Indian images, be they Buddhist or Hindu or Jain, have always been made for specific purposes, made by and for specific people, and made to function in specific contexts. There is ideology at play here, polemics, and iconographic precision. But we would do well to heed Davis's words about obsessing about original intentions. Indeed, recall that Dharmapala himself, when he placed the image in the Mahābodhi temple, placed not an Indian image of Śākyamuni Buddha, as would have been appropriate at the site of the Buddha's enlightenment, but a Japanese image of Āmitabha. Although the image of Āmitabha was certainly Buddhist, it would originally have been situated in a quite different devotional and ideological context, and quite at odds with Dharmapala's own vision of simplified and purified Buddhism. The irony—and perhaps also the hypocrisy—may have been lost on Dharmapala, but it need not be lost on us, for even Dharmapala, by necessity, was participating in the multivalent fluidity of Bodhgayā and its Buddha image.

4.5 *Act Four: Taking It to the Courts*

The question of who is the proprietor of the Temple...is quite irrelevant to this case.

—NANDA KRISHORE LAL[100]

I wish now to return to Dharmapala's attempt to install the image in the Mahābodhi Temple in 1895. He was so outraged at the way he and the Buddha image had been treated that he pressed criminal charges against the Mahant and his followers, charges that included defiling the Buddhist religion, disturbing a religious gathering, and using criminal force. All of these charges rested on the assumption that the Buddhists held some basic, and exclusive, rights of worship at Bodhgayā.[101] Although Dharmapala's legal representative, Nanda Kishore Lal, opened the case for the prosecution by stating that the ownership of the temple was irrelevant to the case, it was precisely this issue that was, in fact, at stake. What we see in this legal case is a fight central to the concerns of this book, a fight over a religiously significant place, a fight that is about the contested definition and identity of that place, a fight about who can use and occupy that place, and ultimately a fight about the boundaries between religious communities and individuals.

The legal wrangling over the proprietorship of Bodhgayā largely revolved around two issues: first, whether it was the Buddhists or the Śaiva Mahant who could rightfully claim control, and legal ownership, of the temple complex; and second, what sorts of worship were appropriately directed toward the Buddha image. The latter issue, one might think, would also intimately involve the Vaiṣṇava community, since it was they who had for centuries been making the short trip from nearby Gayā as part of their extended *śrāddha* rites, and it was they who venerated Bodhgayā's Buddha images as part of the long-standing tradition in Vaiṣṇava circles of responding to Buddha images as Viṣṇu's ninth avatāra. In fact, however, the issue of the Vaiṣṇavas' right to venerate the Buddha image was rather quickly dealt with in the initial court proceedings, and, as we shall see below, it would not be until the 1930s that the Vaiṣṇavas would begin to have a substantive voice in Bodhgayā's ritual life.

The Buddhist side offered what was essentially a two-fold argument. First, since the government of India had neutral guardianship over the temple as an ancient monument,[102] the Buddhists, as a legitimate religious group under government protection, had the right to worship at the temple, a right clearly denied by the Mahant's aggressive removal of Dharmapala's Buddha image. As Lal put it, it was "the long-standing right of every Buddhist to worship and perform any ceremony in accordance with the tenets of his religion in the Temple, and neither Government nor the Mahanth is entitled to prevent the full exercise of that right."[103] Second, Lal argued that the Giris could not contend—as they continuously had in the period leading up to the trial, and as they would repeatedly during the trial itself—that they had removed the Buddha image in order to protect their own religious worship because, according to Lal, no Hindus had ever worshiped there.[104] Indeed, argued Lal, it was agreed upon by any number of the authorities that Bodhgayā was a Buddhist site in both origin and in contemporary practice, and he brought forth several Hindu witnesses to testify that they did not worship there because it was not a Hindu temple and to do so would be to defile themselves. Furthermore, he called the custodian of the temple, Bepin Behari, to testify, and he said that not only did Hindus not worship there, but he had actually heard Brahmin priests on several occasions forbid Hindus from entering the temple. So the issue of who could worship, or who should worship, at the temple became moot in these proceedings. The real issue was who owned and controlled the temple.

The Śaiva side put forth a number of arguments, some of which attempted to establish the Giri's long-standing legal ownership at the temple; they offered as evidence the fact that government officials had felt it necessary to consult with the Mahant before allowing the Burmese to begin renovations of the temple in 1877. Furthermore, they asserted that Dharmapala himself had recognized this ownership when he and the Mahabodhi Society attempted to purchase the Mahābodhi temple from the Mahant, because if he had not thought that the Mahant owned the temple, then why had Dharmapala made such an offer? As additional proof, the Mahant's lawyers put forth a significant amount of textual evidence to prove that the Buddha was in fact an *avatāra* of Viṣṇu, in an attempt to establish that the Buddha image did not really belong to the Buddhists at all.[105]

This last argument may seem self-defeating, given that the trial centered on the Hindus' *removal* of the Buddha image (which was, according to such logic, not a Buddha image at all, but a Viṣṇu *mūrti*). However, the Mahant and his legal team were attempting to legitimize their own religious—as opposed to proprietary—rights in order to establish that Dharmapala, as a Buddhist, himself had no rights to worship in a Hindu temple. Most of the defense's evidence was, as one would expect, based on the Vaiṣṇava textual tradition—notably, the *Bhagavata, Agni,* and *Vāyu purāṇas*—as well as scholarly studies by orientalists such as Alexander Cunningham, J. D. Beglar, and Rajendrala Mitra, which attested to the very old Hindu presence at the temple.[106] The defense also cross-examined the prosecution's witness, the temple manager Behari, and got him to admit that Hindus did, in fact, bow down before the Bodhi tree and the Buddha image in the main part of the temple (although he did stipulate that the latter practice had begun only recently).

As might be expected, the argument over the essential nature of the figure of the Buddha proved to be a slippery legal slope, for although it is true that from a Hindu point of view the Buddha *avatāra* had defeated the enemies of Hinduism and restored *dharma*, for the Buddhists the *avatāra* discourse was nothing but a bold-faced polemical attack on Buddhism;[107] in other words, from the perspective of the Buddhists and their orientalist sympathizers, this was incontrovertible evidence of Brahmanical hegemony at its worst. Thus in raising the Buddha as *avatāra* issue, the Mahant's legal representatives opened themselves up to a blistering rebuttal from not only Dharmapala's lawyers, but also from the judge himself, who was already predisposed against the Hindus, and viewed this claim as nothing more than an obfuscating ploy, a smokescreen intended to hide their duplicity and greed. Indeed, in a stunningly partisan and dismissive remark, George Macpherson, the local magistrate who heard the case, pronounced that the purported Hindu bowing down before the Buddha image was, "I dare say, of no more significance than my taking off my hat, as I do, when I enter the sanctum."[108]

But the slippery legal slope proved to be even more treacherous than merely raising doubts as to the credibility and objectivity of the evidence. When the Hindus argued that the existing Buddha image on the first floor of the Mahābodhi temple was indeed venerated as Viṣṇu (Dharmapala, it is worth noting, had attempted to install the Japanese image in the empty sanctuary on the second floor of the temple), the Buddhists' lawyers countered by denouncing this as nothing more than an attempt to influence the court's decision based on a recent innovation instituted by the scheming Mahant—and here Behari's testimony under cross-examination proved to be a nasty double-edged sword—in order to create the appearance of Hindu worship in the Mahābodhi, and therefore the precedent of normal and customary worship, which gave them certain legal rights, when in fact no such worship had ever been performed until the Buddhists began to claim a right to the temple. Furthermore, the Buddhist side argued that even if the Buddha image in the Mahābodhi were venerated as a Viṣṇu *mūrti*, as a Śaiva the Mahant had no business regulating such a temple, since it was only Vaiṣṇava theology that recognized the Buddha.

Magistrate Macpherson for his part accepted none of the Hindu side's argument, and he echoed Arnold's logic almost exactly when he pronounced: "If in any case, it was felt expedient to endeavor to establish Vaisnavite worship of Buddha Bhagavan at Mahabodhi, it was an anomaly for the Mahant, a Śaivite, to set himself up as its founder."[109]

This pronouncement became a crucial moment in the establishment of Bodhgayā's religious community, because, in effect, the judge was asserting that if Hindus had any legitimate religious interest in the temple, only a particular kind of Hindu could claim such interest: namely, the Vaiṣṇavas. And since the Vaiṣṇavas themselves were not, in fact, staking any claim to the temple, Buddhist rights to the temple were, by default, *prima facie* valid. It is important here to stress that Macpherson was explicitly avoiding the issue of legal ownership of the temple; his opinions were, ironically enough, limited to the religious status of Bodhgayā, and to him it was clear that nothing put forth by the Hindu side's lawyers altered the essentially Buddhistic nature of the temple. However, in his final remarks on the case, Macpherson went so far as to denounce the "semblance of Hindu worship" performed by a priest who "passes a light in front of the image, sounds bells and leaves the image and altar,"[110] and he castigated the Mahant for the ploy, which he saw as a mere "strategem for giving him a pretext for interfering with the dealings of the Buddhists in the temple and strengthening whatever prescriptive rights he may possess to the usufruct of the offering made at the temple."[111] Not surprisingly, Macpherson found the Mahant's followers guilty of interfering with Dharmapala's lawfully assembled religious congregation; he sentenced each of them to one month in jail and fined each one hundred rupees.

In this trial, there can be no doubt that Macpherson was highly biased; indeed, on the day that Dharmapala placed the Amitābha image in the Mahābodhi temple, Macpherson himself had been summoned (by the Mahant, ironically enough), and upon arriving on the scene was said to have remarked that "a great desecration has been committed." He was not referring to Dharmapala's installation of the Buddhist image, but to the Mahant's followers' removal of the image.[112] By contrast, when the Viceroy of India, Lord Elgin, came to Bodhgayā shortly after Dharmapala's image had been removed—a testimony to the potential volatility that the colonial Government of India saw in the situation—he had expressed the hope that an amicable solution could be found, although he himself felt that the Buddhists' rights to worship in the temple must be protected. He stressed, however, the need for a solution that would also protect the Mahant's rights and noted that a certain amount of tact would be required, since, as he put it, "on some of the minor points of religious controversy a wrong word might be very unfortunate."[113]

When the new Mahant, Hem Narayan Giri, appealed the case in June 1895, it was not heard at the local level, but in the Sessions Court at Gayā, and the judge in that venue, Herbert Holmwood, was quick to castigate his fellow judge Macpherson for his meddling, which he perhaps too charitably described as "a good deal of unnecessary animadversion on Mr. Macpherson's assumed unconscious bias in the matter."[114] Holmwood, however, was not impressed with the Mahant's defense, and in particular took issue with the defense's insistence that their legitimate and long-standing religious rights had been threatened by Dharmapala's action. On appeal, the Hindu side explained that in removing the Buddha image, the Śaivas were only protecting their own right of worship. Holmwood, however, agreed with the Buddhists' position that Dharmapala's right to worship had been blocked by the removal of the Amitābha image, and he thus disregarded the Śaiva's claims.

In particular, Holmwood singled out the current Mahant's offer to place Dharmapala's image back in the Mahabodhi, but only if it first underwent the *Hindu installaton* ritual, an offer that was rejected by the Buddhists outright.[115] This offer was a remarkable gesture on the Mahant's part, and it is difficult to discern Hem Narayan Giri's precise motives in making it. Was he suggesting that the image could at once represent the Buddha and at the same time embody Viṣṇu? If so, this would have been a striking recognition on his part of the inherently polyvalent identity of sculptural images in India, and, in particular, at Bodhgayā. This was not, at any rate, how Holmwood interpreted the offer; he said that when the Mahant expressed his willingness to enshrine the image, "whatever his theories may be as to Buddha being an avatar of Vishnu, he must thereby have intended to prevent Buddhists from ever offering impure articles of food, candles, scent, etc.," because the Hindus found the kinds of things offered by the Buddhists to the Buddha image—Huntley and Palmer's biscuits, candles of lard, cheap English eau-de-cologne—to be utterly impure, and therefore unacceptable in a Hindu temple.[116] In other words, the Mahant was, according to the judge, trying to prevent Buddhist worship of the Buddha image on the grounds that any such worship would be offensive and polluting to the Hindu community. Notice, however, that in contrast to Macpherson and his "assumed unconscious bias," Holmwood went to considerable lengths to avoid any judgment of the validity or appropriateness of a particular form of worship.

In the end, the conviction was upheld, although Holmwood suspended the jail terms (but let the fines stand). The defendants again appealed, this time in the Calcutta High Court, and the case was heard before Goroo Das Banerjee and Justice William Macpherson (no relation to the magistrate George). The latter specifically addressed the question of whether the Mahant, as a Hindu, had any right to interfere with Buddhist worship at Bodhgayā; but like Holmwood, this Justice Macpherson made a point to avoid any pronouncements on the religious aspects of the matter and held that because the case at hand was a criminal one, "No such broad questions arise."[117] Instead, he focused on the issue of proprietorship, and found that it was clear that the Mahant "held 'possession' of the Temple and had control and superintendence over it, subject to the right of Buddhists to worship there."[118] He raised the real possibility that Dharmapala's veneration of the image, just after he had installed it, might not, in fact, have been genuine—and might have simply been intended, as the defense alleged, to incite the Mahant's followers—but he refused further speculation on the matter. However, according to the High Court, Dharmapala's actions had to be seen in the larger context of his motives and attitudes toward the Mahant and his community, which were clearly the eventual removal of the Śaivas (and here Dharmapala's own writings, including his diaries, were brought into the discussion).[119] In this context, his veneration of the recently installed (and soon to be removed) Amitābha image did not, contra his lawyers' claims, constitute normal or customary worship at Bodhgayā. Instead, Macpherson focused on the fact that the legal proprietor of the temple, the Mahant, had explicitly refused Dharmapala permission to install the image (although he had never refused him admission to the temple, nor the right to worship there). Thus Macpherson concluded: "They went to enshrine an image in a place where they had no right to enshrine it."[120] As such, the removal of the image on the part of the Hindus was justified. He then set aside the original conviction, although this would prove to be merely a brief intermission.

4.6 Act Five: Hinduism, Buddhism, and Sanātana Dharma

> *I am sure it will be admitted by all Hindus who are true to their own ideals that it is an intolerable wrong to allow the temple raised on the site where Lord Buddha attained His enlightenment to remain under the control of a rival sect.... I consider it to be a sacred duty for all individuals believing in freedom and justice to help to restore this historical site to the community of people who will reverently*

carry on that particular current of history in their own living faith.

—RABINDANATH TAGORE[121]

It had taken three years to resolve the case between Dharmapala and the Mahant, far longer than anyone had foreseen. However, given the years that the issue would continue to simmer and occasionally boil over, with what seemed to be an unending succession of suits and countersuits being filed every few years, this was in hindsight a speedily resolved dispute. Indeed, it would take another fifty years to settle the issue, to get to the apparently ecumenical moment with which I began this chapter, and even then, as I have earlier suggested, it would be hard to see the handover of control of the temple to the Bodhgayā Temple Management Committee as anything like closure.[122] Nonetheless, it is perhaps surprising, given the discomposed and acrimonious state of things in 1896, that such a sharing of the stage could ever be affected at all: the Buddhist and Śaiva communities were openly hostile toward each other, the Vaiṣṇavas were without a voice, and the government had managed to alienate and offend virtually everyone involved with its open disdain for the Mahant and its ruling against the Buddhists.[123]

After the ruling against him, Dharmapala's authority at Bodhgayā was greatly diminished, and although he continued to be involved in the disputes about the place until his death in 1933, with his removal to the wings the tenor of the discourse over the constitution of Bodhgayā's identity and its religious community changed dramatically. Alan Trevithick has suggested that a pivotal figure in this change was Kakuzo Okakura, a Japanese intellectual who brought his hybridized Buddhist vision—as much influenced by Swami Vivekananda's neo-Vedanta and Rabindranath Tagore's humanism as by anything contained in the Pāli canon—to Bodhgayā in 1903.[124] Although I am somewhat skeptical as to the particular influence that Okakura had on the debate, simply because it is impossible to tell exactly what he said and to whom,[125] he does stand, at the very least, as an important figure symbolically, because his rhetoric seems to bring together the hitherto hostile factions at Bodhgayā into a single Asian brotherhood with a mutual understanding and commitment to the true *dharma*, a discourse that was, as Trevithick rightly notes, strikingly similar to the theosophical vision put forth by Dharmapala himself, prior to his break with Olcott.[126] The different Asian religions, sects, and subsects were, in Okakura's opinion, just so many offspring of a single mother: "The great Vedantic revival of Sankaracharyya is the assimilation of Buddhism, and its emergence in a new dynamic form. And now, in spite of the separation of ages, Japan is drawn closer than ever to the motherland of thought."[127]

Okakura had come to Bodhgayā specifically to ask the Mahant for a small plot of land and permission to build a rest house for Japanese pilgrims; although the Mahant was at the time engaged in another legal fight with the Mahabodhi Society (he wanted to evict the Sri Lankans from the Burmese rest house), he was happy to grant Okakura's request.[128] The government of Bengal, however, was not so willing, and refused to grant the Japanese a building permit, professing that there was no need for another rest house at Bodhgayā, and that the further "multiplication of interest there is undesirable."[129] Although on its face this was a relatively small matter, it represents an important development in the formation of Bodhgayā's religious community. On the one hand, it marks a growing reluctance on the part of the government to meddle in matters of religion at Bodhgayā, perhaps because the colonial administrators had learned from the earlier trial what a tangled mess the issue of proper religious practice could become. From this point on, in fact, the government would officially—although it did not always play out this way in practice—maintain this policy of neutrality in religious questions. On the other hand, however, the refusal of the permit to the Japanese is indicative of the government's desire to avoid sectarian disputes and to promote a certain ecumenical spirit amongst the religious communities of India. However, rather than Okakura's very broad pan-Asianism, it was vested in a non-sectarian pan-Indianism, and thus the community that was envisioned at Bodhgayā quite explicitly excluded the Chinese, Japanese, and Tibetan Buddhists, since they did not fall within the political control of the British Empire.[130] The Burmese, who had been an active presence at Bodhgayā, would also eventually be excluded from this community when Burma ceased to fall under the administration of British India in 1935.

Thus what we see developing at Bodhgayā in the early part of the twentieth century is a new sort of community, a single community that is now defined not primarily by its individual components of Hinduism and Buddhism, but by Indianness, and we see members of both the Hindu and Buddhist communities expressing the same commitment to this new Indian brotherhood.[131] As early as 1911, Nanda Kishore Lal—who, recall, had in his representation of Dharmapala in the suit against the Mahant shown little restraint in his anti-Hindu rhetoric—describes the mutual admiration for Bodhgayā: "Nor does the Hindu of the day look upon it with any less reverence than the Buddhists."[132] And one of the most prominent Indian intellectuals of the period, Rabindranath Tagore, expressed great sympathy with the Buddhist cause. Even Dharmapala himself got in on the Indian brotherhood act, however grudgingly: "To the Buddhists the Lord Buddha is the Supreme One. The Hindus have many devatas to receive their worship. The Buddhists do not worship Vishnu; neither do they worship Siva. But Ceylon Buddhists hold Vishnu as the patron God of Ceylon."[133] Thus the Buddhist representatives at the Indian National Congress, although still requesting Buddhist priority at the temple, appealed to their Hindu kin: "will not our Hindu Brothers join hands with us and give us our shrine, at which all are free to worship."[134] And finally, in a 1935 article in the *Mahabodhi Journal*, the Hindu-Buddhist cooperation in the matter of control of Bodhgayā was praised, and an appeal to their shared conception of true *dharma* was made: "The session also demonstrated that Buddhists and Hindus are culturally one and that there should be complete harmony between them, if the true spirit of the Arya Dharma is understood."[135]

This certainly seems to be moving toward something very close to Turner's *communitas*, affected in large part by the cultivation of a kind of cultural liminality in which the substantial differences between and amongst the actors are now being downplayed. As such, it can be seen in the larger context of both the development of a monolithic conception of Hinduism (which, in very many cases, encompassed Buddhism as well) and the emergence of a single Indian identity and a united India that grew particularly powerful in the 1930s and 1940s leading up to Independence in 1947. At the center of this discourse was a shared religious heritage, essentialized as *sanātana* dharma. Dalmia and von Stietencron note that "there was no place in this scheme of things for overlapping identities which had once been possible when the concept of a monolithic 'Hinduism' had not yet come into existence. Its emergence...led to a disregard for, if not suppression of, all the differentiations within 'Hinduism'. The smaller local community which had been accustomed in everyday situations to tolerate and live with difference, was now inflated to much larger, 'national' proportions. These demanded a display of unity and uniformity."[136] In this sense, the individuals gathered at Bodhgayā for the handover ceremony in 1953 can be seen as representing this new community of Indians, a seemingly liminal state in which divisive differences of culture, belief, and practice were negated to give way to the bond of dharmic brotherhood.

If this all sounds a bit to good to be true, it should, because it is essential to recognize that this spirit of inclusion is predicated on exclusion: the necessary condition for membership in the community was not just Indian roots or a common understanding of *dharma* (as the Buddhists of China, Tibet, Japan, and Burma all could legitimately claim), and not just Indian residence (as the Muslims could certainly claim, if they had so chosen), but the combination of the two. Furthermore, these necessary conditions for membership were not unambiguous. For instance, in 1925 the Burmese delegates to the Indian National Congress put forth a proposal for the formation of a committee that would look into the Bodhgayā situation and attempt to find an equable solution to it. The future president of India, Rajendra Prasad, a lawyer from Bihar and a close associate of Gandhi, was chosen to head this committee. In 1926, Prasad presented a proposal for the joint management—by a committee of Hindus and Buddhists—of the Mahābodhi temple, but stipulated that "we should not have Buddhists from outside the British Empire, e.g. from Japan or China or Tibet."[137] Ironically, as I have noted, this would eventually exclude the Burmese themselves. Questions were also raised as to whether the Sinhala Buddhists should be included. Indeed, Sanjit Roy, a Bengali Buddhist and one of the cofounders of the "Buddha Gaya Defense League," a group which pressed both the Indian National Congress and the Hindu Mahasabha to resolve the Bodhgayā matter, eventually became so disenchanted with the Sri Lankans and Burmese because of their treatment of the Indian Buddhists that he wrote to Prasad, complaining that "Indian Buddhists who come here on pilgrimage are not given even as much attention [as] what common courtesy demands.... We the Indian Buddhists want some concessions to do our 'pujas' in our own way."[138]

So, in the end, we see that the formation of Bodhgayā's religious community, like the constitution of the very place itself, has been a tension-filled process, one that has involved both the formation of some unlikely alliances as well as the exclusion of a number of would-be members. As I have noted, this is a process that is still very much in process, as many of India's Dalit Buddhists lobby (and protest) for a greater representation in the running of the Mahābodhi temple. There is also evidence that various members of the extent community wish to exclude other members, and I want to end with a particularly clear, if not also a quite familiar—and, in the end, outrageous—example, one that ironically harkens back to the old Orientalist distinction between proper and improper religious behavior. Here, a Western scholar remarks on the various visitors to Bodhgayā and implies that it is not the Westerners who are flocking to Bodhgayā for the wrong reason, but the Indians: "the Hindus, curiously enough, behave more or less as tourists. They are the ones who look bright and worldly, carrying cameras, and exhibiting only a minimum of ritual behaviour."[139]

5

Bodhgayā, UNESCO, and the Ambiguities of Preservation

5.1 *The Making of a World Heritage Site*

The Mahabodhi Temple Complex has outstanding universal importance as it is one of the most revered and sanctified places in the world.

—Information Dossier for nomination of Mahabodhi Temple Complex as a World Heritage Site[1]

On June 30, 2002 dozens of Buddhist monks processed through and around the Mahābodhi Vihāra at Bodhgayā. They were celebrating the announcement, three days earlier, of the designation of Bodhgayā as a World Heritage Site (WHS) by the United Nations Educational, Scientific, and Cultural Organization (UNESCO). The WHS designation was hailed as a great triumph for Buddhists throughout the world; it was a recognition, by the world's most prestigious arbiter of history and culture, of the significance of Bodhgayā, placing the Mahābodhi Vihāra among the ranks of over eight hundred other World Heritage Sites, including the Taj Mahal, Angkor Wat, Macchu Picchu, and the Great Wall of China. The monks paraded around the temple and town with huge banners, attracting a small crowd of followers. Although it was a rather sober sort of celebration, to anyone who had been in and around Bodhgayā consistently over the prior decade, this celebration would have stood in sharp contrast to many of the processions at the temple in the 1990s: a series of protests and conflicts over control and management of the temple complex which, although never escalating to actual physical violence, always carried with them the threat of conflagration. In the weeks and months after UNESCO's designation, as the implications of this honor began to emerge, questions and anxieties began to surface. What did all this mean, really? Who and what would be affected by the designation? What would complying with the various WHS rules entail? Rumors spread that the shops and tea stalls and dwellings surrounding the temple complex would need to be removed; some worried that the many monasteries that had sprung up over the last century would be demolished. Was this really, in the end, a positive development?

In this chapter I want to reconstruct—and, to a degree, deconstruct—the process by which the WHS designation was made, and to examine some of the implications of such a designation, since much of the debate about Bodhgayā since the WHS designation has been about what sort of place it should be and for whom, a debate that extends some of the issues I have discussed in the last chapter, and that introduces new complexities. Some of the issues in this chapter also mirror those I discussed in Chapter 2, although the specific dynamics of Bodhgayā are very different from those at Park51. On its face, the designation of Bodhgayā as a WHS represents a significant commitment by UNESCO—with its nearly half-billion-dollar annual budget—and the government of India to help preserve this most important of Buddhist sites. But we must ask: why was this designation sought in the first place? what does it mean to preserve such a temple? who decides the mechanisms of such preservation? Unlike the majority of WHS sites in India (there are, at this writing, twenty-nine such sites, out of a world-wide nine hundred), Bodhgayā is not simply an ancient architectural structure; it is a living temple. It is not a museum, but an active and fluid place, one that, as I discussed in the prior chapter, has over the past fifteen hundred years been constantly changing—often as a result of contestation over what sort of place it is. It has been repaired and, essentially, rebuilt numerous times; it has been abandoned at various points in its history; old structures have decayed and been demolished; new structures have been added. It has been both a Buddhist and a Hindu place of worship.

Thus as much as the WHS designation can be celebrated because it seems to ensure that the temple will be preserved, it is not clear at all that this preservation will be for the Buddhists and Hindus who actually participate in the life of the temple. The WHS designation was designed to preserve what are understood, explicitly, to be places of "outstanding universal value" that are "part of the world heritage of mankind as a whole."[2]

These are places that "belong to all the peoples of the world, irrespective of the territory on which they are located." But what does this mean, to say that places such as the Mahābodhi Vihāra "belong" to all the people of the world? Why should UNESCO dictate how an Indian Buddhist temple is managed? Is this yet another example of Western hegemonic discourse and practice, simply colonialism dressed up in the new clothes of cultural globalization? I certainly do not wish to suggest that monuments such as Bodhgayā should not be preserved; rather, I wish to interrogate the processes and politics of such preservation. What I will argue here is that the plan outlined for the Mahābodhi represents, really, the "museumizing" of the temple complex which, far from presenting a neutral program of restoration and preservation, instead poses a real threat to the life of the temple, and is itself as much about transformation as about preservation.

The government of India first submitted a formal application to UNESCO to gain the WHS designation for Bodhgayā in 2001. This nomination was rejected. According to a follow-up report prepared by the International Council on Monuments and Sites (ICOMOS), there was no question that Bodhgayā was worthy of the WHS designation: the site clearly met four of the criteria for WHS designation.[3] Specifically, it met WHS criteria ii, iii, iv, and vi, which essentially cover the architectural significance of the Mahābodhi Temple and its association with crucial events in the life of the Buddha. The problem with the original application was, first, that it did not present a sufficient plan for the ongoing preservation and management of the temple complex, and, second, that it did not consider the complex religious life of the site. ICOMOS officials had visited the site several times between July 2000 and March 2002, and they faulted the initial Indian plan for Bodhgayā because it lacked "a clear indication of the proposed perimeters of the core area" and did not adequately lay out the "expected impact on the spiritual and historical values of the site."[4] The advisory report on the initial application explicitly drew "the attention of the responsible authorities on the need to continuously monitor the impact that such challenges may have on the religious and spiritual significance of the place."[5] The Indian officials responded to the ICOMOS report immediately. Two meetings were held in Delhi in 2002, and a new application was drafted and submitted. This application was accepted.

The "Convention Concerning the Protection of the World Cultural and Natural Heritage" that was adopted by the United Nations in 1972 is UNESCO's root preservationist text, presenting the organization's guiding vision for why preservation of the world's cultural monuments is necessary. It is a fascinating document, a kind of head-on collision between post-colonial inclusivism and proto-globalization arrogance. The *leit motif* of the document is the phrase "outstanding universal value," a phrase that occurs throughout the sixteen-page text. The central concern of the 1972 convention is the creation of an "Intergovernmental Committee for the Protection of the Cultural and Natural Heritage of Outstanding Universal Value, called 'the World Heritage Committee,'" a body of, initially, fifteen states—subsequently expanded to forty—that is charged with collectively identifying and protecting those places in the world that, according to UNESCO, are of "outstanding interest and therefore need to be preserved as part of the world heritage of mankind as a whole."[6] In other words, these are sites that may be owned, literally, by a particular group or a particular state, but which are really the property of the whole world.

WHS sites are also places that are, implicitly, in danger. Indeed, in Article 11 of the convention, it is stated that the WHS Committee shall maintain a "list of World Heritage in Danger." In danger of what, one might well ask?

> The list may include only such property forming part of the cultural and natural heritage as is threatened by serious and specific dangers, such as the threat of disappearance caused by accelerated deterioration, large-scale public or private projects of rapid urban or tourist development projects; destruction caused by changes in the use of ownership of the land; major alterations due to unknown causes; abandonment for any reason whatsoever; the outbreak of the threat of an armed conflict; calamities and cataclysms; serious fires, earthquakes, landslides; volcanic eruptions; changes in water level, floods and tidal waves.[7]

What sort of danger was Bodhgāya in, though, and from what did it need to be protected? Although the answer to this question is in the end quite complex, perhaps the most immediate answer is "change."

The Convention is intended, fundamentally, to protect and preserve those sites of "universal value," but it is not, despite the list, clear what UNESCO is protecting the sites from. There are the obvious natural dangers—serious fires, earthquakes, landslides, volcanic eruptions. There are also less obvious dangers, though, less obvious in the sense that some of these dangers are, in fact, inherent in the very nature of places such as Bodhgayā. The Convention mentions "large-scale public or private projects of rapid urban or tourist development projects; destruction caused by changes in the use of ownership of the land; major alterations due to unknown causes; abandonment for any reason whatsoever." Are all of these in fact dangers?

Let me begin with the first here, "large-scale public or private projects of rapid urban or tourist development projects." When the Government of India drew up its revised application for WHS status for Bodhgayā, it turned to Ashwini Lohani, the Chairman of the Indian Tourism Development Corporation. In 1999 he had been the driving force in gaining WHS designation for the Darjeeling Himalayan Railway, the seventeenth cultural site in India to be declared a WHS by UNESCO. Although there is no question that both of these sites are of cultural and historic significance, the applications for both put a marked emphasis on their potential as tourist attractions; as such, the tourism potential of Bodhgayā and the infrastructure to support it would clearly need to be substantially developed.

The "Justification for Inscription" section of the application begins by stating that Bodhgayā is a "sanctified" place of universal importance.[8] The emphasis in this part of the document is clearly on the historic and cultural significance of Bodhgayā. The "Justification" then goes on to describe the cultural and historic significance of the Mahābodhi Temple; it quotes both Faxian and Xuanzang, the fourth- and seventh-century Chinese pilgrims who described their visits to Bodhgayā; it quotes the *Mahāparinibbāna Sutta* of the Pāli Canon; it quotes Alexander Cunningham, who as we have seen was the director of the Archaeological Survey of India who oversaw the restoration of the site in the 1880s; and it quotes several contemporary Indian archaeologists. The dossier recounts the history of the temple in considerable detail. For the most part, there is nothing surprising or controversial about this historical narrative, although it is almost exclusively presented from a Buddhist perspective, and as we have seen, Buddhists are not the only group with a history at (and of) the temple, or who have made claims on the temple.

One of the key parts of the revised WHS dossier is a twenty-page "Management Plan" which, in response to the rejection of the original application, outlines in great detail the specific management, conservation, and development of the site. One of the unusual things about the Mahābodhi temple is that it is a site that already had a management structure in place, the Bodhgayā Temple Management Committee (BTMC), which was formed in 1949 in response to the decades of wrangling over who should have control of the temple.[9] The WHS application simply states that the BTMC will continue to make all management decisions regarding the temple complex. A major section of the WHS is the "Conservation Plan and Development Plan," which addresses suggestions that were initially made prior to the submission of the first WHS application, in 1999, by the Patna Circle of the Archaelogical Survey of India, at the request of the BTMC.

The Conservation Plan seems, on its face, to be a straightforward document, offering up a list of needed repairs: "Votive stupas in the parapet wall need to be reset and re-plastered so that they do not fall off. Vegetation growth on the Temple structure needs to be removed effectively."[10] Drainage needs to be improved, plaster needs to be restored, the grounds tidied, and so on. None of this is particularly controversial at first glance. Underlying these seemingly innocuous repairs, however, is a notion of what the Mahābodhi Temple "originally" was and therefore the state to which it should be restored. For instance, some plastering that was done in a 1953–1954 restoration, the Conservation Plan states, needs to be replaced with "original materials." "Acrylic emulsion paint has also been used in some places on the sculptural figures. This changes the original character and beauty of the figures and needs to be removed," according to the plan.[11]

These seemingly neutral observations echo, albeit with a more neutral tone, those of Sir Edwin Arnold from a century earlier; the author of *The Light of Asia* had found Bodhgayā to be in a deplorable state, and he complained, as we have seen, that the Hindus who had been using the temple since it was abandoned by the Buddhists in the thirteenth century had defaced "the shrine with emblems and rituals foreign to its nature."[12] Clearly, though, to the Hindus who venerated Buddha images as Viṣṇu, or who worshipped *stūpas* as Śiva *liṅgams*, such rituals were hardly "foreign" to the objects to which they were directed. The underlying assumption here is that physical objects such as temples and sculptural images (as well as the people who venerate them) are static entities with fixed identities. Bodhgayā, like most temples in India—and in the world—has been in an almost perpetual state of restoration; it is nearly impossible to determine what the "original" temple might have been or what it should be. Furthermore, this quest for the "original" is a distinctly Western endeavor, one that cannot easily, or at least not unproblematically, be imposed on the Indian context, and it is an endeavor that is not simply about aesthetics, but about, as we shall see, a particular ideological discourse of control.[13]

As Tzvetan Todorov has quipped, "only dead cultures remain intact."[14] Nonetheless, the Conservation Plan articulated in the WHS application explicitly sought to "fix" the temple, in at least two senses of the word: to repair it, but also to make it permanent. However, to do so was also to make significant changes to both the physical and ritual life of the temple, a paradox that goes unmarked in the WHS application, the consequences of which continue to surface at Bodghayā years after the WHS designation.

The use of acrylic paint and other "non original" repairs did not evoke the same antipathy as Hindus transforming what was once a Buddhist *stūpa* and venerating it as a Śaiva *liṅgam*, but not all of the Conservation Plan is concerned with such seemingly inconsequential matters. The Plan suggests that some of the stones and epigraphs located in the floor of the temple need to be removed to a separate gallery; no reason is given, but presumably they risk damage from pilgrims and other visitors walking on them. There is no mention of how long these objects have been *in situ*, or what their function is. The Plan goes on:

> Devotees have been following the practice of lighting oil lamps or candles along all the walls and railings and on sculpted figures in the Temple complex. This is adversely affecting the ancient monument and spoiling the pathways. The burning of a large number of oil lamps on festive occasions is a threat to the structure of the Temple as well as to the Bodhi Tree. A thorough cleaning of the oily residue on all parts of the Temple needs to be carried out and an alternative found to this practice of burning oil lamps.[15]

It is the last part of this statement that is particularly striking, since it involves not simply restoring the physical structure of the temple, but altering the ritual practices that are an integral part of its life as an active religious place. This issue comes up in the main body of the application as well, where it is stated that this ritual practice "needs very much to be controlled." The document suggests that the "alternative" would be to create a special place for the ritual, out of the way, an alternative that would protect the temple "without offending the sentiments of the devotees." There are, the document goes on to say, "many places where the Buddhist *Rinpoches* have been persuaded to take an enlightened view to discontinue the burning of oil lamps near the place of worship. Instead, they have located a place well removed from the shrine where a single oil lamp is kept burning with the offerings made by devotees."[16] The Conservation

Plan elaborates what the alternative would be: the BTMC "has earmarked a different site south of the Temple where it intends to build a glass house with a modern exhaust system."[17]

There is a significant tension at play here. On the one hand, the WHS application, in keeping with the 1972 UNESCO Convention, outlines a plan of conservation and protection. Bodhgayā, as a site of "outstanding universal value," must be protected and preserved from the various dangers that threaten it. On the other hand, it must also be returned to its "original" state, which means that many of the ritual practices that are integral to its life as a Buddhist *vihāra*—and, to some, a Hindu *mandir*—must be either significantly altered or eliminated. Conservation and protection, in other words, are not value-neutral activities; they are predicated on a particular understanding of what the temple once was and what it, therefore, now should be, a view that is, in the words of the WHS application, "modern," and "enlightened," and "controlled." And although the 1972 Convention notes that it is important to "adopt a general policy which aims to give the cultural and natural heritage a function in the life of the community," it is not at all clear what defines such "function" or "life," or for that matter "the community."[18] Likewise, the Government of India's WHS application for Bodhgayā in several places mentions that the temple is an active, living place: "The Mahabodhi Temple is a living monument where people from all over the world even today throng to offer their reverential prayers to the Buddha."[19] It would seem, though, that such prayers and the rituals that accompany them are only appropriate if they are cleaned up, modernized, and enlightened.

One of the most interesting, and also most ambiguous, sections of the Information Dossier was prepared by the Government of Bihar Directorate of Archaeology. At first glance, this "Annexure," as it is titled, seems to be included in the Dossier to address some of the more technical issues of the archaeological excavations planned for the Mahābodhi complex. However, this document also includes a description of the temple complex that seems to vacillate between two understandings of the site. On one hand, there is the ancient site, and the task of archaeology is said "to restore the formal aspects of the Bodh Gaya Mahabodhi Mahavihara in as much detail as possible."[20] On the other, however, is an understanding of the temple complex as a living place, and the archaeological work must "preserve its urban structure and also ensure the continuation of social life within its precincts and environs."[21]

It would seem, at first glance, at least, that the authors of this section of the WHS application were intent on balancing these two competing understandings of Bodhgayā. Later in the document, however, things are more ambiguous: "One ultimate objective is the preservation of historic sitescape. Our archaeological discipline is intended to ensure that development and planning operations are conducted in accordance with the archaeological findings and technological research as to create optimal living conditions." It would seem, then, that there is a real awareness of the complexity of Bodhgayā's physical and social make-up. Slightly further on, however, the hegemony of the "original" is reasserted. "Unwanted" dwellings—unwanted by whom is not articulated, but implied—will have to be demolished, and new "amenities" will have to be provided: "We aim at restoring the original dignity and honour of this place, the temple and its Mahavihar. In the sphere of site planning, conservation means the preservation of antique architecture and in case the restoration of important and original and creative conception of space and of unique character of every important and inimitable Vihar cluster."[22]

There is, certainly, a clear here recognition that the Mahābodhi temple complex is a dynamic, living space, and that any archaeological work on the site must attend to the competing understandings and uses of the space. That said, however, the historic consistently trumps the contemporary. Restoration and preservation of the "original" temple is the primary goal of the archaeological work to be done. The contemporary is recognized as important to the life of the temple complex, but in a quite limited way: "But the growing dimensions of building construction whose visual density goes to mar the beauty of historic colour, looks wild.... Modern construction...should be in accordance with the principle of harmonic integration in which modern building will be designed in the same spirit as the contemporary traditional buildings."[23] This points to what is perhaps the key tension in restoring a place like Bodhgayā, a tension that is certainly not unique to this context.[24] If one were to read just this section of the Information Dossier, one might come away sanguine that the competing understandings of the temple complex—historic/original vs. contemporary/living—could be balanced. The emphasis on the "original," however, trumps the more dynamic understanding of the Mahābodhi as a dynamic, fluid, living place.

There are at least three visions of Bodhgayā that emerge from the WHS application, three overlapping, inter-related visions, to be certain, but also three visions that stand in tension with one another. The first is the "outstanding universal value" vision that, essentially, would freeze Bodhgayā, or, more accurately, would restore Bodhgayā to what it was originally and then freeze it. I think of this as the "fixing" vision: the temple would be "fixed up," and then it would be "fixed" in time. It would, essentially, be museumized. The second vision is the "living temple" vision. This is, really, a kind of background vision, a rather reluctant recognition that Bodhgayā is not simply a culturally and historically significant place to visit, but a place where devout Buddhists and Hindus go to perform what they understand to be essential religious rituals.[25] It may seem puzzling that so little attention is paid to this aspect of Bodhgayā in the WHS application—I will have significantly more to say on this below, when I discuss the post-WHS developments at Bodhgayā, which very much revolve around this vision—but it is perhaps not so surprising when put into the larger context of India's other World Heritage Sites. At the time the first application was submitted, there were over twenty such sites in India, but only one of these other sites—the historically significant Catholic churches of Goa—could be even remotely considered an active religious complex. Indeed, although several sites on the culture list (there were also five "Natural" sites at the time) were temples—among them the Sun Temple at Konārk, the great temples at Mahābalipūram, and the Chola-period temples in Tamil Nadu—they were primarily understood, at least by UNESCO and the government of India, to be tourist sites, because they were seen not as active temples but as archaeological sites. This thus brings us to the third "vision": Bodhgayā as tourist site.

The lines between tourism and religious pilgrimage have, no doubt, always been blurred; indeed, the very attempt to make a sharp distinction, an either/or distinction, seems misguided—although scholars often attempt to do precisely that.[26] This is not to say, however, that the two modes are without tensions; in the WHS application, there is a marked tension between the desire to preserve/restore the "original" Mahābodhi Vihāra and the desire to promote it as a tourist destination, a tension that the document's authors are at least aware of: "The approach adopted is to prepare a holistic development plan with clearly identified projects including clear implementation strategies. The focus of the development plan will be tourism promotion, while conserving the local environment and the local resources."[27] The BTMC and the Housing and Urban Development Corporation of India (HUDCO) proposed to build a meditation park, a museum of Buddhism, and reception and information centers. Furthermore, the WHS application notes that Bodhgayā is very hot in the summer, which "makes it very difficult for tourists to enjoy the experience of walking around the temple and benefitting from the peaceful atmosphere of the site." It would, then, be "desirable to plant an adequate number of trees" around the temple "which would surely affect the environment positively."[28]

Such developments seem harmless enough. Others, like the proposal to move the ritual lamps to a separate area, are more ambiguous and seem to ignore or at least to discount the ritual and religious aspects of the *vihāra*. For instance, in the Development Plan appended to the application, a great deal of attention is paid to cleaning up and beautifying the temple grounds. "Innumerable monuments, stupas and memorials built by visitors and dignitaries to the temple during past centuries are located haphazardly and need re-orientation... it will be better if the smaller 'stupas' could be re-arranged along the pathways or in the form of [a] Stupa Garden, with proper grills and placards giving its history, if possible."[29] Although the many *stūpas* surrounding the main temple may "clutter" the area, to many Buddhists they are integral to the ritual life of the temple; others serve as reliquaries for significant monks. Their "haphazard" arrangement reflects centuries of use, layers and layers of ritual practice.

Later in the Development Plan, it is proposed that the various small *stūpas* be rearranged and

> ...organized in a systematic manner, around the monument area. This of course can be done if it is approved by the religious leaders.... It is further recommended that all the remains be identified, through the experts, so that their historical importance could be established. Once this is done, the brief may be placed in form of a placard next to each object so that the worshipers and the visitors could realize the importance of each of the remains. In due course an album for reference could also be prepared.[30]

Knowingly or not, the authors of the WHS application, following the lead of the BTMC and HUDCO, are here replicating the language and *modus operandi* of their former colonizers. Among the various ways the British sought to control India was, as we have seen, by collecting and organizing physical objects, particularly art and artifacts. As Bernard Cohn has pointed out, the eighteenth- and nineteenth-century colonial administrators in British-occupied India sought to control—and just as often to fabricate—the history of India in part by controlling the physical objects that were the products of that history.[31]

It may be that what we see in the WHS application is a kind of post-colonial taxonomic hangover that necessitates clear categorical divisions of function and space—Hindus here, Buddhists there; religious activities here, tourist activities there. It may also be that the authors of the application simply recognized—and capitulated to—the orderly, "modern," "scientific," Western, European orientation of an organization such as UNESCO.[32] It is, at any rate, worth recalling that one of the fundamental purposes of the 1972 "Convention Concerning the Protection of the World Cultural and Natural Heritage" was, as the title so clearly denotes, to protect endangered cultural sites, and one of the explicit threats to such sites, as I have noted, is tourist development.

One of the difficulties for the authors of the Bodhgayā WHS application was to come up with a plan for both development and conservation that would also recognize the fluid, polyvalent nature of Bodhgayā, or at least the polyvalent nature as it was conceived by those seeking the WHS designation. This is an attitude that is, certainly, in sharp contrast with the colonial taxonomic ideology that saw temples and objects as necessarily only belonging to a single group. To many Buddhists, however, the Mahābodhi *vihāra* could be nothing but a Buddhist temple. Indeed, as we shall see shortly, in the years after the WHS designation, this would become a decidedly heated issue. At any rate, although I have named three different conceptions of the Mahābodhi complex that can be teased out of the Information Dossier, the authors of the WHS dossier overtly adopted an essentially binary approach:

> In view of the outcome of the analysis and physiographic character of the site, the entire Bodh Gaya Temple Complex Development has been broadly conceived as a two way functional approach as follows:
> 1. Meditation-Religious
> 2. Tourist Attraction
>
> The two aspects of the design are entirely diverse and do not go hand in hand. A religious person wants peace to worship for prayers and to listen to the religious discourses whereas a tourist visits the Temple to have glimpses, pay his regards as well as enjoy the time that he is in the complex.[33]

The problem, according to the authors of the Development Plan, is that, at the time of the application, the two aspects, and their respective visitors, were not distinct in the temple complex, and "the result is chaos."[34]

They offered up a plan that would substantially transform the space and therefore the way in which that space could be used by those who claim it, a transformation that, as we shall see below, would come to have serious unintended consequences. It separates the two groups, moving the various religious "functions"—meditation platforms, sculptures, *stūpas*—out of the way of the tourists. What the plan fails to recognize or acknowledge is that there are, as I have already noted, no clear distinctions between religious visitors and pilgrims; it is a false distinction, one that is more informed by the post-Enlightenment West's distinction between the secular and sacred than it is by the reality played out on the ground at a place such as Bodhgayā. Furthermore, what does it mean to say that the temple complex is chaotic? What is the implied (normative) model of order?

5.2 *Conflicting Stakeholders: Whose Temple Is It?*

> *Notwithstanding anything contained in this Act or in the rules framed thereunder, Hindus and Buddhists of every sect shall have access to the temple and the temple land for the purpose of worship or pindadan.*
>
> —The Bodhgaya Temple Act

Bodhgayā has long been a shared and, at times, contested site, a multivalent place that is claimed by more than one group: this much is clear. It is a striking example of what Michel Foucault has famously called a heterotopia, an "ill constructed jumbled space" constituted by "complex references to other spaces."[35] There are shrines specifically identified and treated as Buddhist; there are shrines specifically identified and treated as Hindu; there are Buddhist temples and monasteries belonging to a variety of sects; there is a Śaiva monastery. Despite these seemingly clear identities, however, Hindus venerate "Buddhist" objects and Buddhists venerate "Hindu" objects. One of the most striking aspects of the WHS application, however, is that it makes virtually no mention of this fact. Indeed, to read the dossier is to come away with a distinctly monothetic history of the place—an exclusively Buddhist history, really. The WHS application contains a lengthy account of the Mahābodhi's historical significance, one that draws on a standard set of Orientalist sources—Alexander Cunningham, Rajendralala

Mitra, Benimadhab Barua, etc.[36] According to this history, the temple was built first by the great Buddhist king Aśoka, after his pilgrimage there in the third century B.C.E.; as recorded by Aśvaghosa (first century C.E.), by the Chinese pilgrims Faxian (fifth century) and Xuanzang (seventh century), Bodhgayā was the Buddhists' most important place of pilgrimage in the world. After Buddhism's gradual disappearance from India, however, which seems to have taken place between the twelfth and thirteenth centuries, the temple was essentially abandoned, although Buddhist pilgrims continued to visit and, on occasion, do restoration work on the Mahābodhi.[37]

In the late eighteenth century, British explorers and amateur archeologists began to make sporadic mention of the Mahābodhi temple; the romantic painters William and Thomas Daniell, for instance, visited Bodhgayā in the 1780s and made several sketches and painted a number of watercolors of the temple and its environs.[38] It was not, however, until Francis Buchanan, during his government-sponsored survey of Bihar and Patna, visited the temple that any sustained interest was taken in Bodhgayā. Buchanan reported that the Mahābodhi was in a state of decay and was being dismantled by people in the area in need of brick and stone for building. He mentions, also, that the shrines around the temple had been demolished to provide bricks for construction work at the Hindu Mahant's monastery.[39] Despite this early interest in the temple, the first formal archaeological work was not done by the British until 1847, when Captain Markham Kittoe dug several trenches at the temple; he unearthed parts of the railing and several statues, some of which were left lying there, while others were carried off to museums. He also made an album of drawings of some of the sculptures. Alexandar Cunningham began the most extensive archaeological work at the temple in 1861, with the assistance of Major Mead and J. D. Beglar. At around the same time, the Burmese, who had continued to make pilgrimages to Bodhgayā after it had been abandoned by Indian Buddhists, had begun several restoration projects. These raised concerns in the British administration.

Sir Charles Stuart Bayley, the Secretary to the Government of India, wrote to Mitra, who was one of the most respected contemporary archaeologists in India, and asked him to visit Bodhgayā and report on what the Burmese were doing. He was particularly concerned that the Burmese were not taking proper care of Bodhgayā's antiquities:

> It is not desired to interfere with the Burmese gentlemen beyond giving them such guidance as may prevent any serious damage

> being done to the temple, of which there seemed at one time some danger from their laying bare a portion of the foundation; and to arrange for such of the antiquities as are worth preserving being properly taken care of. They are at present building them into walls, and sticking foolish heads on to ancient torsos, etc. Mr Eden wishes to know if you can make it convenient to pay a visit to Buddha Gaya to inspect the work and the remains collected, and to give advice as to their value and to their disposition, and whether there are any that should go to the Asiatic Society; and generally to advise the Government in regard to the manner in which the operations of the Burmese excavations should be controlled.[40]

When Mitra did visit Bodhgayā he was appalled by what he saw. The Burmese, he wrote, were, "perfectly innocent of archaeology and history, and the mischief they have done by their misdirected zeal has been serious. The demolitions and excavations already completed by them have swept away most of the old landmarks, and nothing of ancient times can now be traced on the area they worked upon."[41] In Mitra's opinion, however, the Hindus were ultimately to blame: "The temple stood there deserted, forsaken, and dilapidated, and they appropriated it to their own use by giving it and its presiding image new names. In doing so they did not even take the trouble to change the image, or to bring to light the inhumed portion of the temple by removing the rubbish around its base."[42] Mitra's attacks on the Hindus at Bodhgayā, particularly on the Mahant, would, as we have seen with Dharmapala, be repeated over and over again by various Buddhists and their supporters as they tried to gain control of the temple in the latter part of the nineteenth century. Mitra's report seemed to have convinced the British administration to begin restoration of the temple; under the direction of Cunningham, a major restoration was begun in 1880.[43]

The WHS application, as I have noted, goes to great lengths to praise, in particular, Cunningham's restoration of the temple: "The care and concern of the devout Buddhist lay people and governments of these countries has been expressed meaningfully both in terms of financial contributions and also efforts for preserving the integrity of the monument.... Care was taken by the restorers to use the stone model found of the temple as a reference and to restore it in accordance with the model."[44] Cunningham had intended, explicitly, to restore the temple to its "original" condition—which, to him, meant recreating the temple as it was depicted in a small model he had uncovered in his excavations. In doing so, however, he used an idealized model of the temple, a static, frozen model that would have borne little resemblance to the dynamic, living temple that Bodhgayā had been (let alone the Hindu temple that it had long ago become); he was, essentially, replicating the Picturesque aesthetic, imposing an idealized view of what the British thought India should be onto the reality of what India was.[45] As Matthew Edney puts it, "the British did not find a naturally Picturesque landscape in India: they created it in line with the highly selective and appropriate nature of the Picturesque aesthetic."[46] However, in the case of Bodhgayā it was not merely a visual representation that was created: it was the temple complex itself. Significantly, one of the first things Cunningham suggested was to change the name of the temple site, wishing, in the process, to sever any links to the Hindu pilgrimage center at nearby Gayā: "I have thought it right to drop the erroneous title of Buddha Gaya.... In giving the name of *Mahabodhi* to the most famous place in Buddhist history, I am only restoring the true name which has been in use for many centuries." He goes on to say, careful to distinguish the Buddhist temple from nearby Gayā—one of the most important pilgrimage places for Hindus—that the "Great Temple of Mahābodhi...has no connexion whatever with the name of Gayā."[47] Cunningham's position here is consistent with the taxonomic hegemony of the British in India, with what, in a different context, Foucault calls the "ceremony of objectification."[48] People and places are labeled, ordered, and thereby separated; using a kind of Linnaean logic, a temple, like an animal or a plant, can only belong to one group. Just as Gayā could be only Hindu, Bodhgayā could be only Buddhist.

Although the WHS report praises the British restorations, it fails to mention that at the time of Buchanan's visit, as well as during Cunningham's restorations, the temple was not, as in the Daniells' paintings and writings, empty. William Daniell, for instance, describes the temple as "entirely deserted so that a scene of gloomy desolation is at the foresaken sanctuary."[49] As I have already noted, it was, however, inhabited. Bodhgayā had been reöccupied after the Buddhists abandoned it, by a lineage of Śaiva ascetics, the Giris, who traced their inhabitancy of the temple to the late sixteenth century. However, virtually all the British archaeologists who conducted archaeological work at Bodhgayā—and I think it important to note here that not all of this work could be even generously considered "restoration," since the British also hauled away innumerable images to be placed in museums and their own private collections, and many of the restorations were in the end every bit as slipshod as those they decried—saw the Hindu presence at Bodhgayā, if they even acknowledged it at all, as aberrant.

There was, then, a clear conception in the nineteenth century of what Bodhgayā "originally" was, and, thus, what it should be: an exclusively Buddhist temple, the birthplace of Buddhism, the most sacred of all Buddhist places. The Hindu presence at the temple, in this view, was an affront, even a pollution, and must be removed.[50] No matter that there had been no Buddhists in residence at the site for half a millennium; no matter that the Hindus had been living in and worshipping at the site for hundreds of years. We have seen this dynamic before, with both Ayodhya and the Park51 project; what is important to point out, again, is that there is nothing "natural" about this linking of origins and propriety. Places do not, ever, exist in some sort of cultural and historical vacuum, and the claim to the "original" is just that, a claim. It is an argument to be made.

When Cunningham and Beglar began the restoration of the Mahāvihāra, they did so not, certainly, to restore and return it to the Buddhists. They did so because, in keeping with the basic aim of the ASI,[51] the colonial administration felt that it was necessary to preserve and restore the great monuments of India. As George Nathaniel Curzon, who was the British Viceroy in India from 1899 to 1905 and a great champion of the ASI, put it: "It is . . . equally our duty to dig and discover, to classify, reproduce and describe, to copy and decipher, and to cherish and conserve."[52]

Embedded in the ASI's extensive nineteenth-century restoration/preservation project is a basic Orientalist discourse, really a hegemonic colonial discourse: "The key to British self-representation, and therefore their representation of Indians, lay in their claim to possess an innate rationality and scientific nature," a rationality that the Indians, in their view, lacked.[53] "The British," as Edney puts it, "made themselves the intellectual masters of the Indian landscape. And they did so with all the certainty and correctness granted by the Enlightenment's epistemology."[54] And like the British project of mapping the subcontintent, the ASI's restoration projects were very much intended to impose a particular vision of India on the land; such activities were part of a much larger systemic "disciplinary mechanism, a technology of vision and control, which was integral to British authority in South Asia."[55] Denis Byrne has referred to this as the "totalizing ambition of the conservation ethic."[56] He points out that there is an unmarked assumption in Western archaeological discourse, the roots of which go back at least as far as the early nineteenth century and which is more recently articulated in such documents as the Vienna Charter of 1966 and the International Committee on Archaeological Heritage Management Charter of 1996: "If the West has been mistaken in thinking that the conservation charters have global applicability . . . this is largely a result of an archaeological discourse acting hegemonically to exclude other discourses, other 'voices,' whose salient characteristic in this context is that they do not conceive or construct the objects in question as archaeological."[57]

Indeed, the ASI was hardly engaged in innocent archaeology in the nineteenth century, but rather undertook a systematic effort to demonstrate British colonial superiority, to demonstrate—to both the Indians they ruled and the home government by which they were employed—that they were a superior, enlightened civilization that would never let its great monuments and artifacts be turned into rubbish heaps. There is a consistent tone in all of these writings—Buchanan's, Cunningham's, Mitra's—a mixture of outrage and derision; the Hindus are idolaters and spoilers, too lazy to bother with cleaning these great monuments, and too greedy or ignorant to know not to plunder them for building materials. We have already encountered Cunningham's remark that "Brahmin malignancy has sadly mutilated" many of the inscriptions and images at Bodhgayā; this was, in Cunningham's view, in keeping with the basic character of Hindu art, which was little more than "wooden inanities and bestial obscenities."[58] The Buddhists, by contrast, were consistently portrayed by the British as rational and noble.[59]

When Beglar and Cunningham set out to restore the Mahābodhi, they used earlier models of the temple to carry out their work, models that may have been intended to be pilgrims' mementos.[60] In so doing, they ignored the organic nature of the temple, the way it had changed as a result of use, by changing populations of Buddhists who, since its initial construction by Aśoka—if that is indeed its origin—had altered the *vihāra* to conform to their particular forms of Buddhism. This is, I would suggest, part of the basic life of temples in India: they are never static physical structures, but living, changing places.[61] They are in motion. Indeed, a temple in many ways contains and is constituted by its history; it is, palimpsest like, made up of layers and layers of use. Bruce Owens has put this particularly well:

> The constant transformation of sacred places through devotional practice is very much a part of South Asian religious traditions. . . .

> All over South Asia images identified as gods are painted, repainted, plastered over with devotional offerings, clothed, bejeweled, and even worn down by worshipful caresses. In fact, without the benefit of these kinds of transformations, these gods "die" in so far as their devotees are concerned, the maintenance of their life and power being dependent upon human intervention and its transformational consequences.... Inspired by devotion or desire to acquire merit (among many other motivations), South Asians have also long restored, improved, decorated, remodeled, and rebuilt temples, including ancient ones.[62]

Thus like a canonical Sanskrit or Pāli manuscript which is always embedded in and surrounded by its commentaries—making it folly, albeit a commonly practiced sort of folly, to attempt to uncover its "original" meaning—the layers of the temple are both a record of prior use and part of current practice.

To strip away what was "added," as the British routinely did, was to radically alter—really, it was to do violence to—the character of the temple. As Byrne, writing about the Thai context, has noted, the archaeologist's zeal for the "original" is, ultimately, misguided in the Buddhist context: "The ethic of merit making in Thai Buddhism, moreover, puts a premium on the proliferation, reconstruction and rebuilding of *stupas*—practices which routinely imperil or consume the original fabric and structure of old and often ancient *stupas*."[63] Interestingly, although his analysis is very much critical of the sorts of "fixing" that leads to Foucault's "ceremony of objectification," Byrne slips into the very language of those whom he is critiquing here—"routinely imperil" the "original." Indeed, we are so used to thinking in these terms that the very language we use is bound by the ideology of preservation.

What Byrne describes is true not only in the Thai context: the history of Indian temples is fundamentally a fluid history, a history of images—as I discussed in the two previous chapters—being altered or "converted" from one tradition to another, of the fluidity of objects and materials. Western methods of preservation and conservation have tended to ignore such material fluidity, however; the effects of such methods are on display in virtually any art museum that contains Hindu or Buddhist sculptures.[64] Such images are transformed into art, and as such bear almost no resemblance to what they would have been in their temple settings. Indeed, as we have just seen, one of the things that Anagarika Dharmapala was most incensed about was the Hindu "decoration" of the Buddha images and *stūpas* at Bodhgayā when, in fact, the few Buddhists (mostly Tibetan) who continued to worship at Bodhgayā were just as likely to have been responsible for such adulteration.

The "monumental heterogeneity"—to use Owen's term—of a place like Bodhgayā is ignored in the WHS application,[65] as is the larger complex, messy history and context of the temple and its environs; there is no mention, for instance, of the lengthy dispute over control of the temple following Cunningham's restoration, after it was celebrated by Edwin Arnold in his *Light of Asia*, and the zealous attempt by Dharmapala and his Western Buddhist champions to "regain" Buddhist control of the temple. This omission is significant and can hardly be accidental. It must, though, be placed in the context of the more immediate history of the Mahābodhi complex. The decade prior to the WHS designation was one of renewed conflict at the Mahābodhi, with the emergence of an increasingly outspoken Buddhist movement—the "All-Indian Mahabodhi Temple Liberation Action Committee"—a group largely made up of so-called "Ambedkar Buddhists,"[66] who called for the "return" of the temple to Buddhists hands.

This dispute has its roots in 1949 when the BTMC was formed to resolve the protracted dispute about control of the temple that began with Dharmapāla's agitations in the 1890s. The BTMC Act recognized that the Mahāvihāra was claimed by two groups, and thus attempted to articulate a vision of shared management of the temple and its environs. Significantly, there is, in the Act, no mention of what the temple might have originally been, or to whom it might have originally belonged. Rather, the BTMC Act is very obviously concerned with the actual Hindus and Buddhists who use the temple:

> 10. Subject to the provisions of this Act or of any rules made thereunder, it shall be the duty of the Committee –
>
> (1) to arrange for –
>
> (a) the upkeep and repair of the temple;
> (b) the improvement of the temple land;
> (c) the welfare and safety of the pilgrims; and
> (d) the proper performance of worship at the temple and pindadan (offering of pindas) on the temple land;
>
> (2) to prevent the desecration of the temple or any part thereof or of any image therein;

(3) to make arrangements for the receipt and disposal of the offerings made in the Temple, and for the safe custody of the statements of accounts and other documents relating to the temple or the temple land and for the preservation of the property appertaining to the temple;
(4) to make arrangement for the custody, deposit and investment of funds in its hand; and
(5) to make provision for the payment of suitable emoluments to its salaried staff.

11. (1) Notwithstanding anything contained in this Act or in the rules framed thereunder, Hindus and Buddhists of every sect shall have access to the temple and the temple land for the purpose of worship or pindadan.[67]

This is in sharp contrast to the monothetic colonial understanding of the temple, certainly, as well as the WHS application's later conception of the temple. That said, however, the Act would be seriously challenged in the 1990s by the so-called Dalit, or Ambedkar, Buddhists.

In 1991, Laloo Yadav became the Chief Minister of the state of Bihar, where Bodhgayā is located. Yadav is a Dalit, or member of the so-called scheduled castes (formerly known as untouchables); he is not, however, a Buddhist. However, he quickly took up the Ambedkarite calls for complete Buddhist control of the Mahābodhi. In 1992, he circulated a draft of a substantial revision of the BTMC Act that would give the Buddhists full control of the Mahāvihāra. Yadav's amendment went further: it proposed to ban Hindu weddings in the temple complex, and also to ban Hindu images from being ritually bathed in the temple's sacred tanks. The Hindu Mahant and his followers were outraged. Later that year, on the significant Buddhist holy day, Vaisakh, a large group of Ambedkar Buddhists arrived at the temple; according to reports, this group was approached by the chief priest in the *Pancapandav Mandir*—a Hindu temple within the Mahāvihāra complex—and asked for donations. The Buddhists refused, and an exchange of insults (if not an actual physical altercation) ensued. Significantly mirroring Dharmapala's storming of the temple a century earlier, the angry Buddhists entered the *Pancapandav Mandir* and removed the Hindu garments that were draped on the Buddhist statues, and then attempted to break off the temple's Śiva *liṅgam*. Fearing violence and particularly mindful of the recent violence surrounding Ayodhya, the government called in troops to be stationed outside of the temple.

At the heart of the issue was the BTMC Act. There is a certain irony here, to be sure, since the Act was created to resolve the dispute over control of the temple that had begun in the 1890s. By the time the BTMC Act was put into place, Dharmapala had been dead for over a decade, and a spirit of ecumenicism seems to have replaced Dharmapala's pro-Buddhist, anti-Hindu polemics. This ecumenical spirit—which certainly was as much wishful thinking as actuality—was replaced in the 1990s by a renewed pro-Buddhist, anti-Hindu rhetoric at Bodhgayā. Although on its surface this new movement, lead by the monk Bhadant Nagarjun Surai Sasai, replicated Dharmapala's efforts, this new Buddhist call for Buddhist control of the Mahābodhi was rather more complex, enmeshed in the politics of the Ambedkarite Buddhist movement and the larger context of Dalit assertions of their own identity in India, as well as the communal politics of north India.[68] One consistent element here, however, is the monothetic conception of Bodhgayā as exclusively Buddhist. For Sasai and his followers, this was not simply a matter of the exclusively Buddhist identity of Bodhgayā; it was also complexly tied to the identity politics of the Ambedkar Buddhists. As Tara Doyle notes, "Like Ambedkar before him, Sasai utilizes anti-Hindu rhetoric and emphasizes that to be a Buddhist in this community is very much wrapped up with *not* being a Hindu."[69] Like Ambedkar, and also very much like Dharmapala.

While the original WHS application might have been timed to resolve the ongoing tensions over control of the Mahābodhi, it failed to do so. For as I have noted, one thing that is all but absent from the WHS dossier is the recognition that Bodhgayā is a living temple, not a static archaeological site. As Michael Herzfeld has pointed out in an entirely different context, the restoration of a monument—"fixing," as I have called it—is "never immune to contestation."[70] As we have seen at Park51 and Ayodhya, and as we will see particularly at what is known as Devils Tower, there will always be a polyphony of voices, a cacophony, even, making different, competing claims on the place and space. This is perhaps an obvious point, but one that seems totally lost on UNESCO and the WHS project. It is thus not surprising that Sasai and some of his followers have continued, although in a rather more muted manner, to push against UNESCO's involvement at Bodhgayā. Part of the issue is that the BTMC remained in place after the WHS designation; indeed, the BTMC would continue to be the governing body for Bodhgayā, charged, under UNESCO's WHS guidelines, with assuring that the Temple Management Plan be implemented.[71] For Sasai and his followers, this is unambiguously offensive, since the BTMC is made up of Hindus and Buddhists, but must be headed by a Hindu. But this is not the only irritant. The WHS designation, as I have noted, puts strict controls on any developments within the temple complex and mandates that buildings not originally part of that complex must be removed, which many Ambedkar Buddhists feel will leave them out of the temple's future.

5.3 *An Illusionary Account of the Real Landscape*

If the management of temples, churches, mosques and gurdwaras are not under control of other sects, then why not so in the case of the Mahabodhi temple?

—BHADANT ANAND[72]

When the WHS designation was announced, Sasai almost immediately challenged UNESCO to return Bodhgayā fully to the Buddhists. Significantly, it was not the restrictions required by the WHS designation that provoked his ire, but, rather, the continued control of the temple complex by the BTMC. He wrote a letter to Mary Robinson, the UN Commissioner for Human Rights, complaining of "the continued illegal occupation of the most sacred and holiest place of the Buddhists and the Entire world . . . by high caste Hindu Brahmins," Brahmins who, according to Sasai, were responsible for Buddhism's disappearance in India. He goes on, charging that the Hindus "have been playing tricks to show to the world that Lord Buddha was a Hindu God and nothing else," and that "criminal elements" encouraged by the Brahmin priests had misused donations, that "Hindu Gods have been smuggled inside the Mahavihar . . . to dilute and defame Buddhism," and that "all sorts of Hindu Rituals and Rites are being followed inside the Mahabodhi Mahavihar to defame and bring impurity in Buddhism." For Sasai, the remedy was quite straightforward: "Hand over entire management of Mahabodhi Mahavihar" and "prevent confrontation between the Buddhists and Hindu Brahmins."[73]

The UN, as was perhaps to be expected, did not grant Sasai's request, and the issue continues to fester, with sporadic calls by Buddhists to abolish the BTMC and give them full and exclusive control of the temple complex. In March of 2008, for instance, the head of the Akhil Bharatiya Bhikkhu Mahasang, an influential body of Buddhist monks, charged that the government, in continuing to uphold the Hindu/Buddhist makeup of the BTMC, was merely cowing to "the forces of Hindutva."[74] Here, again, a basic tension is evident: although the WHS dossier recognizes that the Mahābodhi is a living temple, and although UNESCO—in their various reviews of the application and subsequent assessments of the implication of the Development Plan—seems to recognize the various religious groups who have a stake in the temple, the very structure of the WHS designation precludes any real engagement with the complex issues on the ground. Owens has examined a similar situation at Swayambhu, in Nepal:

> The struggles now being waged over cement, stone, and turf at places like Swayambhu are often struggles over whether cultural practices or their material consequences should be privileged as worthy of preservation, and determining whose culture, as of when, is at stake for whom. Thus distinguishing between new and old kinds of transformations at these places is more than an exercise in distinguishing post-modernity from modernity, or modernity from whatever came before. These distinctions lie at the heart of debates taking place between those determining what these places will look like in the future, or even whether or not they will continue to exist.[75]

These, however, are precisely the complex issues that the authors of the WHS dossier for Bodhgayā do not consider, and, really, precisely the tensions that UNESCO strategically does not engage.

The makeup of the BTMC and management of the Mahābodhi by it are not the only issues that continue to simmer at Bodhgayā, however. As I have already noted, the WHS designation reflects an essentially monothetic, static conception of Bodhgayā; the Mahāvihāra is, according to this conception, an archaeological site, an ancient monument that must be restored to its original state and preserved for the whole world. In this sense, then, UNESCO becomes the ultimate arbiter of what is and what is not legitimate at Bodhgayā; in so doing, however, it stands outside of the fray, apparently uninvolved in the mess on the ground, objective, rational, and scientific, in much the same way that the British Orientalists did in the eighteenth and nineteenth centuries: "Eighteenth and early nineteenth-century epistemology was thus rooted," writes Edney, "in a vision which, with its surrogates, established an almost physical distance between the viewer and the viewed, between the subject and the object of vision."[76] In a study of the eighteenth- and nineteenth-century genre of landscape painting in Britain, Ann Bermingham has argued that the landscape painter presents "an illusionary account of the real landscape while alluding to the actual conditions existing in it."[77] This is relevant to the colonial context, of course, because the observers of India were informed by this same basic ideology. Much the same sort of "illusory account" can be seen in Bodhgayā's WHS dossier as well, an account endorsed, after all, by UNESCO. But it is important to recognize that, much like the "objective" view presented in British landscape painting, "the claim to possess a realist and naturalistic view is itself an ideological statement of power."[78] Again, we see the West, as embodied by UNESCO, holding the Indian other at a distance just as it controls it with its discourse of order, rationality, and science. As the Subaltern Project has demonstrated, the irony is that this discourse has been internalized;[79] in order to receive the approval of UNESCO, the Indian applicants for the WHS designation necessarily had to adopt the assumptions of UNESCO, and, as we have seen, they did so using the vision of India—religion, culture, art—constructed by the Orientalists, an illusionary, idealized, static vision.

One important element of this WHS program of preservation is the creation and maintenance of the "buffer zone," the area where only those structures designated as "original" can be located. Accordingly, the revised Master Plan submitted to UNESCO by HUDCO dictates that all shops and commercial complexes within the one-kilometer buffer be relocated. In early 2008, a group made up of members of a diverse collection of business organizations, independent traders, hotel associations, and travel agencies marched in protest in Bodhgayā because the "clean up" of the buffer zone would imperil their livelihoods. Here, again, we see a clash of visions about what the temple complex should be and, what is more, the ironic inconsistency of any single vision of the temple. The WHS designation, following closely in the footsteps of orientalists such as Cunningham and Mitra, envisions the temple complex as a historical monument, reconstructed and preserved according to an objective, scientific, and, perhaps most importantly, universal standard; as with the landscapes produced by the Daniells and others, this is a vision largely devoid of people. The Ambedkar Buddhists, in contrast, see the Mahāvihāra as a living, exclusively Buddhist, temple, a temple that they should control, in the same way that other religious groups control their places of worship.

It is difficult to see how these two groups can reconcile their very different visions of the temple complex, or how the other significant religious group that makes claims on the temple, the Hindus, figure into the equation. But what of the merchants and traders? Although they are not part of UNESCO's vision of the temple—which of course simply assumes the Enlightenment separation of the sacred and the secular—such people and the various activities in which they are engaged have always been an integral part of the life of Indian temples. As Vincent Berdoulay has pointed out, "a place comes explicitly into being in the discourse of its inhabitants."[80] Ironically enough, the Master Plan itself also depends on them; a substantial component of this vision of Bodhgayā—not unlike what we have seen in Chapter 2 in the complex negotiations over the redevelopment of the World Trade Center site—is commercial. As with the candles and "new" images and all of the other "additions" to the Mahābodhi complex, however, it seems that they must be put in their proper place—they must be ordered and controlled—outside of the temple complex itself.

It is hard to imagine that the hegemonic vision of UNESCO will not, in the end, prevail, and that Bodhgayā will, finally, be transformed into a kind of religious Disneyland, transformed into what Fredric Jameson has called the dead style of "the imaginary museum of a now global culture."[81] It would not be alone. The medieval Portuguese city of Porto, for instance, became a WHS in 1996. There is no question that Porto is a gem of a city, with its narrow winding streets, its cafes and restaurants, its port warehouses along the river Duoro, its majestic bridges. But whole blocks of Porto have stood uninhabited, slowly crumbling; many of the long-term residents who remain in the medieval part of the city are too poor to restore their homes in accordance with UNESCO guidelines. Many of them live with only spotty electricity, no telephone access, no Internet; many of them have simply moved away from the old part of the city. There is a vibrant tourist industry, certainly, that keeps the city "alive," but large parts of medieval Porto are only a kind of virtual city, devoid of people. These are the ambiguities of preservation. Such sites may, as UNESCO says, be "part of the world heritage of mankind as a whole," may "belong to all the peoples of the world," but this global ownership may very well be at the expense of the very people who live and worship in such sites.

One of the consequences of UNESCO's ideology may be, then, that places such as Bodhgayā will, for all intents and purposes, be killed in order to be preserved. In an interesting article on the great temple at Borobodur, Shelly Errington has adopted the framing language of Irving Goffman to analyze the different ways in which the government of Indonesia, UNESCO, and others have created a particular vision of Borobodur that, in significant ways, has become its own on-the-ground reality. These various agents, and the government of Indonesia and UNESCO in particular, have created a kind of "totalizing" frame for Borobudur—which was declared a WHS in 1991—thereby "eliminating other 'frames,' other 'lives,'" other stories about it."[82] Errington picks up Appadurai's notion of the "social life of things"[83] and suggests that understanding physical objects, including monuments and temples, in this way "has the virtue of encouraging us to notice that an object's meaning is not located in a single moment of its history" and that what "an object is may change in the course of time, as it is moved from one place to another and changes hands and contexts."[84] Significantly, Errington was told by one person whom he interviewed that after Borobodur had become a WHS, it had "lost its soul" and was, essentially, dead.[85]

It is perhaps surprising that the globalizing ideology behind UNESCO's World Heritage Sites is so seldom critiqued or even questioned. This may be a consequence of the fact that its ideology so effectively obscures the fact that there is an ideology at work at all. One might well ask: Where is Foucault—or Marx, for that matter—when we need him? A dramatic exception to this kind of passive acquiescence was the Taliban's destruction of the great Buddhas at Bamiyan in 2000. A collective gasp of horror went up at the sight of these magnificent images crumbling, an initial visceral reaction that was quickly followed by universal condemnation by the world's intellectual and religious and artistic communities. The outrage was, to be sure, warranted. Few, however, have pushed the "why" here; few have asked what was behind the Taliban's dramatic act of iconoclasm, settling, typically, for the simple "religious fanaticism" explanation.[86] One important element at play, though, was the WHS designation of these Buddhas, and plans to spend millions of foreign dollars on their restoration. These were, after all, objects of "outstanding universal value" which were "part of the world heritage of mankind as a whole." From the Taliban's perspective, however, they were idolatrous objects, vestiges of a foreign religion, fetishes, and their destruction was religiously mandated, as evinced by the *fatwa* issued by Mullah Mohammad Omar in the spring of 2001. But they were fetishes in a different sense as well; the international community, as symbolically and materially embodied by UNESCO, had, in the eyes of the Taliban, deemed these inanimate objects more important than the people of Afghanistan; the WHS designation of Bamiyan was not, therefore, in the eyes of the Taliban an archaeological designation, but an undeniably political strategy. To put it inelegantly and far too simplistically, UNESCO and its international backers had committed millions to restoring these physical objects, these vestiges of a long-dead religion in the region, while thousands of Afghan children starved in refugee camps.[87]

Bodhgayā will not likely become a Bamiyan, and the point of my comparison is not, certainly, to suggest that these are analogous issues. Rather, it is to make the simple point that there is a kind of neo-colonial politics at work here, an ideology that has so effectively masked its own mechanisms of power that it is able to create the very world it envisions—the world of an apparently shared but radically sanitized universal culture, Jameson's "imaginary museum of a now global culture," that both constitutes and is constituted by the mechanisms of globalization—with hardly a protest from those most affected by it.

At Bodhgayā, the Buddhists see the Hindus, and the Indian government that is constituted by them, as the enemy, as the other; the Hindus, in turn, see the Buddhists, with their exclusive and exclusionary demands on the Mahābodhi, as the enemy. UNESCO, however, remains remote and neutral and, therefore, blameless. Certainly the Taliban's violent iconoclasm at Bamiyan is outrageous. That granted, however, it must be recognized that it was an act of violence intended to powerfully communicate a blunt message: UNESCO and the West cannot tell us what to do with our own material culture. The Taliban's shocking, desperate act of protest is the exception; capitulation to the ideology behind the WHS is the rule.[88] Indeed, if there is any real doubt about the power of UNESCO's neo-colonial project of preservation, this doubt should be dispelled by a simple and consistent response to this project: silence. The issue, in the end, is not whether a place like Bodhgayā will be transformed; certainly it will, as it has continuously been transformed since its beginnings. Rather, the question is who will dictate the terms of this ongoing transformation.

6

The Power and the Politics of Emplacement

6.1 *Itinerant Heads*

The inmates of two rival French monasteries used to exhibit, the one the skull of John the Baptist "when he was a boy," the other his cranium after he had become a man. The effrontery of the modern relic-maker is scarcely less heroic, and it has had one good result. It has acted as an antidote to silly relic-worship.

—*The New York Times*, January 16, 1881

In the *Los Angeles Times* of May 21, 2008, the following headline was buried deep in the blog section of the online edition of the paper: "Sacred surprise behind Israeli hospital." The short article reports that a rocket fired from Gaza hit a shopping mall in the coastal city of Ashkelon, injuring several people, and that the victims were treated at Barzilai Medical Center, in Ashkelon. The focus of the article is not the rocket attack, however, but rather the hill just behind the hospital; the mound marks the spot where the head of Husayn ibn 'Ali, the prophet Mohammed's grandson and the central figure in all of Shi'a Islam, is said to have been interred in the tenth century. The head is long gone, having been relocated to Damascus, and there is now little more than a mound of dirt behind the hospital to mark the spot where it once rested, although several years ago a Shi'a pilgrim received permission to build a small marble prayer area behind the hospital. A trickle of pilgrims visits the site. "They are quite peaceful people. They come in silence, sometimes barely uttering a sound," remarked the deputy director of the hospital, Ron Lobel. It is, he observed, an "island of Shiite Muslim prayer in an Israeli hospital in a Jewish state. It really is unique."[1]

As fascinating as this confluence is on its face, there is much more to the story, a complex series of movements and transformations of places and objects. On October 10, in the year 680 of the common era, Husayn and a group of his followers were on their way to Kufa, in Iraq, to contest the rule of Yazid I, the second ruler of the Umayyad dynasty and the fourth leader of the Muslim community after the death of the Prophet Mohammed. Yazid had been appointed Caliph in May of 680 (he would rule for only three years, until his death in 683) amidst a flurry of debate and disagreement about rightful leadership of the Islamic community. Many opposed his rule, including Husayn and his followers; they believed that leadership of the community should stay within the prophet's family. Furthermore, they saw Yazid as an oppressive, morally corrupt leader, and thus they refused to pledge their support and allegiance to him. Husayn was beseeched by the Caliph's oppressed subjects to come to Iraq and incite and lead a rebellion. He and a group of his relatives and soldiers set out to oppose Yazid's rule. On their way, in the desert in what is now southern Iraq, they were ambushed by an army sent by Yazid. Although they were vastly outnumbered, Husayn and his followers refused to surrender, and after a tense standoff that lasted ten days, all of the adult men in the group were slaughtered.

The accounts of this event are the stuff of legend, with long, elaborate versions of the story accruing over the centuries, some in written form, some dramatically reenacted; it is a story well known by all Shi'as, and it is really the orienting story of Shi'a Islam, a story of resistance to tyranny and injustice, a story of heroic suffering and martyrdom. Husayn and his slain troops' bodies were left where they lay, but Husayn's head was severed and skewered on a pole and triumphantly paraded to the governor of Kufa, Ubayd Allah ibn Ziyad, along with the women and children who survived the attack. Husayn's head was then sent to Yazid himself in Damascus. He displayed the head to his court, a most potent symbol of victory over his political and religious opposition, and then had it buried in a courtyard outside of what is now the Umayyad Mosque.

I begin this chapter by focusing on this head, for what interests me about this highly charged object is its fluid and ambiguous status within several different contexts, and in particular its relationship to several different religiously significant places. For Yazid and his followers it was a kind of war trophy, a physical symbol of the Sunni triumph over the heretical followers of Husayn (who eventually become the Shi'a community). Its presence in the Great Mosque in Damascus certainly added to that place's significance in the Islamic world. The head itself is a highly charged religious object—in the context of Islam, it would not be quite right to call it a relic—since Husayn was a direct descendent of the prophet Mohammad. For the Sunni community, however, there is an inherent ambivalence, which at times becomes a fierce rejection, regarding such objects: worship of anything that is not Allah is *shirk*, idolatry, a violation of the fundamental principle of *tawhid*, the absolute oneness of Allah. Indeed, initially it seems that Yazid hid the head precisely because he did not want it to become an object of worship. There is thus both a theological principle behind this act as well as a political one I will have more to say on this below.

For what eventually becomes the Shi'a community, the head of their martyred leader is an embodiment of their community's persecution at the hands of the Sunni, and as such is intimately linked to the Shi'a ethos of suffering for their faith, and also to the momentous significance of the events at Karbala. As Kamran Scot Aghaie puts it, Karbala "has become the root metaphor upon which many of their religious beliefs and practice are based. It has served as a vindication of the Shi'i cause in the face of Sunni criticism, as well as constituting the central event in their understanding of human history."[2] Karbala becomes much more than a place in this regard, in much the same way, say, that Ayodhya becomes symbolically overdetermined in contemporary Hindu and Muslim relations in India, becoming much more than just a place but also a symbol of identity. In both Shi'a and Sunni Islam, although in very different ways, Karbala and "the rituals associated with the battle have historically served as a vehicle for expressing and strengthening a variety of political and social relationships, associations, and identities."[3] I will have much more to say about Karbala later in this chapter.

The Great Mosque in Damascus in fact contains two significant heads: Husayn's, and that of the apocalyptic proto-Christian evangelizer John the Baptist. Interestingly, this is not the only head that is identified as having belonged to John: his head has also been said to be located in the Amiens Cathedral in France, in Antioch, Turkey, and in Tenterden, England; there are currently heads in the Residenz Museum in Munich and the San Silvestro in Capite in Rome; and a recent report from Bulgaria indicates that part of his head was uncovered in a monastery on an island in the Black Sea.[4] Regardless of the purported existence of these other heads, Muslims and Christians both believe that the head in the Great Mosque belonged to John the Baptist, although its significance is different for these two communities. For Christians, of course, John the Baptist is a central figure in the development of the tradition, the baptizer of Jesus and one of his most important early associates. For Muslims, John—or, as he is known in Arabic, Yaḥyā ibn Zakariyyā—is a significant figure in the long line of prophets leading up to the final prophet.[5]

A shrine containing the body of Husayn—along with the remains of the seventy-two other martyrs who died with him—seems to have been erected almost immediately after the massacre. Leaders of the majority Sunni community had this and subsequent shrines destroyed. Again, part of the impetus was theological, but part was also political (as if the two are ever completely separate). They sought to deny the Shi'a a place to worship this most important of martyrs; it was not just worship that was being denied, but a spatial association with Husayn and the events of Karbala. Nonetheless, a permanent shrine and an associated mosque were built at Karbala in the late tenth century, and it has since then been one of the central places of pilgrimage for Shi'a Muslims, rivaled only by, for some, Najaf. Karbala is visited by millions of predominantly Shi'a pilgrims each year. It is the place where Shi'a Islam resisted what is understood by Shi'as to be persecution and injustice by the Caliphate, and as such it is for many the center of the Shi'a world. Pilgrims end the annual forty-day period of mourning Husayn's death, *Muharram*, at Karbala, where dramatic reenactments of the event are played out, with some pilgrims symbolically reenacting his martyrdom. The pilgrimage to Karbala has in recent years become a familiar anti-Islamic trope in the West, with images of men whipping themselves bloody broadcast by the mainstream media to demonstrate, among other things, the fanatical nature of Islam.

The fate of Husayn's head is less well-known than that of his body, and its history rather more difficult to trace. It seems to have remained in its obscure burial place in Damascus until the tenth century, when the Abbasid emperor Al-Muqtadir attempted to put an end to Shi'a pilgrimage to the site by having the head moved to Ashkelon, where it was buried in a secret place. It was eventually re-discovered—there are many versions of the story, some of which recount the efforts of various Shi'a leaders to find the head—and a shrine was erected over it, with an associated mosque eventually erected as well. At some point it was moved to Egypt—perhaps to protect it from those who rejected Shi'a pilgrimage practices as un-Islamic—until it eventually made its way back to Damascus, where it is now located in a shrine within the Great Mosque.[6] The fact that the head ends up in the Great Mosque is, if nothing else, symbolically charged; the building of the Great Mosque itself was a political act, an assertion of Islam's presence in what had been a predominantly Christian place, and the installation of Husayn's head in the mosque can be seen as an extension of this political assertion, since John the Baptist's head was already located there.

The installation of Husayn's head in the Great Mosque in Damascus raises all sorts of issues relevant to the major concerns that have run through this book: Why would the Sunni Caliph wish to have the head of the key figure of Shi'a Islam, who was killed by Sunnis, installed in the central place of worship in their political capital? Was this an act of appropriation, or aggression (or both)? Given the frequent Sunni critiques of pilgrimage practices directed at anything but Mecca, why would they enshrine this relic knowing that it would become the object of pilgrimage? Why was it placed in the Great Mosque, which itself was built on the very site of the destroyed Basilica of Saint John, and where the head of John the Baptist was already located?[7] What became of the mosque in Ashkelon where Husayn's head had been located? And what about the relation between the head in the Great Mosque and the body in Karbala?

Again, so many questions. My interest in this chapter is the ways in which these physical objects, the actual events to which they are related, and the various narratives that convey these events intersect and interact with particular places, and the ways in which all of these elements are intimately entangled in the assertions of particular identities. The places that I discuss in this chapter—the Umayyad Mosque in Damascus, Syria, and the shrine of Husayn in Karbala, Iraq—are certainly physical places, locatable on the map, but they become more than just physical places. The Umayyad Mosque, for instance, was itself a physical symbol of a new kind of Sunni political and social power in the still emerging Muslim communities; the city of Karbala, and the shrine and mosque associated with the body of Husayn, are likewise vitally important in the constitution of Shi'a identity, and "Karbala" comes to be far more than a physical place—it comes to be an essential part of Shi'a identity throughout the Muslim world; and although the site where Husayn's head had been interred in Ashkelon is a minor sort of place, it too is significantly enmeshed in the assertion of a particular Israeli identity.

6.2 The Umayyad Mosque and the Power of Palimpsests

The strong marks of present space merge in the imaginary traces of the past, erasures, losses, heterotopias.

—ANDREAS HUYSSEN[8]

The appropriation of the site upon which the focal shrine of Damascus had stood, and the subsequent construction of a monumental place of worship for Muslims, marks a watershed in the development of the city. The construction of the Damascus mosque not only irrevocably altered the urban landscape of that city, inscribing upon it a permanent affirmation of Muslim hegemony, but giving the Syrian congregational mosque its definitive form it also transformed the subsequent history of the mosque in general.

—FINBARR BARRY FLOOD[9]

The Umayyad Mosque, more commonly known in the West as the Great Mosque of Damascus, was commissioned by the Caliph al-Walid in 706. He is said to have told the Damascus people, as building began (some sources say the Caliph himself began the work): "Inhabitants of Damascus, four things give you a marked superiority over the rest of the world: your climate, your water, your fruits, and your baths. To these I want to add a fifth: this mosque."[10] The site chosen for the mosque was highly symbolic: the Cathedral of St. John, the basilica that housed the head of John the Baptist and which was located in the center of the city, and that itself had been built on the site of the Temple of Jupiter. Damascus had long been one of the central cities in the Middle East, and it was a city with a decidedly polyglot population. Since its establishment, control of the city had passed from Assyrian, Greek, Roman, and then Byzantine rule. In 636 the city was captured by the Muslim general Khalid ibn al-Walid.

Here, as we have seen with Babar's construction of the Babri Masjid on the legendary site of Rāma's birth in Ayodhya, is at once a kind of tapping into the long-established religious and social power of the place and a symbolic—and also real—gesture of domination. The basilica was razed, but significant parts of the old structure were incorporated into the mosque. Flood, in his study of the architecture of the Great Mosque, suggests that the reuse of materials from the basilica was an intentional and symbolically charged act, an act of visual translation, and that as

> with any translation, the very act itself constitutes an appropriation conveying multiple messages about patronage and power. In the case of Damascus the literal force of this subtext was conveyed not only by the location of the mosque, but by the fact that it was constructed using columns, doors, and other materials drawn from the buildings which had formerly stood in and around the site.[11]

The pre-Islamic temenos, according to Flood, was shared by both Christians and Muslims, "with the latter worshipping in a simple *muṣallā* constructed in the south-eastern part of the sanctuary. The demolition of the church and the construction of the vast congregational mosque upon its site radically altered this arrangement." Indeed, the building of the mosque on that very site constituted a highly charged political act in Damascus, one that had the effect of "inscribing upon it a permanent affirmation of Muslim hegemony."[12]

In the case of the Umayyad mosque, the Caliphate needed to legitimize its new religious and political center; first, it was not, obviously, Mecca. It was not just the religious significance of the mosque that was at issue, though; the mosque itself was a powerful symbol of the Umayyad Caliph's political power, a power that was significantly contested within the Muslim world. In 656, Ali, the cousin of the Prophet, was elected to the Caliph, succeeding the third Caliph, Uthman. Some in the community disputed this election, however, and their opposition resulted in a long period of strife. Fearing for his safety, Ali moved his political base from Medina to Kufa, in modern Iraq. One of those most opposed to Ali's leadership was Muawiyah, a follower of Uthman and the governor of Damascus. Muawiyah asserted that he was in fact the rightful leader of the Muslim community, and he and his followers fought several battles with Ali and his supporters.

Ali was assassinated in 661, allegedly by a group of his former supporters, the Kharjites, and after his death Muawiyah and his forces marched to Kufa to persuade Ali's followers to declare him, rather than Ali's son Hasan, as the rightful Caliph. Muawiyah emerged as Caliph; Hasan signed a treaty with him and did not contest his rule. The newly appointed Caliph then went back to Damascus and established that city as the new political center of the Muslim world. Damascus had long been a Christian city, though; the newly-arrived Muslim leaders thus needed to legitimize their new center, and they did so in part by building the Great Mosque, and building it in a way that at once erased the old Christian presence and also tapped into the power of this presence. Indeed, part of the sacrality and political power of the Umayyad Mosque is that it stands over the Christian—and, before that, the Pagan—site. It replaces it, certainly, but it also gets part of its sacredness and power from the relation. As Flood puts it:

> The later transposition of Jerusalemite and Mekkan *topoi* is indicative of an attempt to increase the religious significance of the Syrian capital, reflecting an attempt to overcome the difficulties arising from a divergence of centres of political authority and religious sanctity. Like the transposition of material objects, the phenomenon represents an attempt to capitalize on the sanctified or mythologised relics of an historical past in order to bolster the status and significance of the Umayyad capital, to garner for its cathedral mosque the visible trappings of religious authority and political power.[13]

Again, we see a kind of physical example of Derrida's *sous rature*, writing under erasure: the Christian structure is at once demolished, erased, and at the same time very much present. Indeed, part of the symbolic power of the mosque is connected with the structures with and upon which it was built. The reuse of some of the physical materials from the Christian and Pagan structures, then, is a kind of "selective quotation which appropriates some of the kudos of the source structure while simultaneously signaling the supercession of the religio-political order responsible for its creation."[14]

The presence of the head of John the Baptist in the Umayyad Mosque is, certainly, symbolically significant. Flood points out that one of the tasks faced by al-Walīd in constructing the mosque was creating a "visual text" that "had to address both an internal audience (the Muslim *umma*) and an external one (those outside the *umma* and, ultimately perhaps, those outside the *dār al-Islām*)."[15] Flood refers to this as the "somewhat schizophrenic requirement" to at once assert a Muslim hegemony, one that physically replaces the Christian and Pagan significance of the place, and at the same time to render the "new" place "legible" to these pre-existing groups. In other words, the presence of the head of John the Baptist in the new mosque at once incorporates this object within a Muslim context, and at the same time makes that context "open" to non-Muslims.

It is unclear when the head of John the Baptist was moved to the new mosque. Indeed, the relic's history is difficult to trace: after Herod ordered John killed, his head was presented to Salome on a platter; she then gave it to her brother, Herodias. According to the Gospels of both Mark and Matthew, John's followers retrieved his body and placed it in a tomb, although neither source mentions whether his followers also retrieved his head. It is not until the fourth century that John's relics reappear in the sources, when John's tomb is recorded to have been located in Palestine, where it was said to be in the possession of a group of monks and nuns.[16] According to Georges Kazan, the tomb was attacked by pagans in 361, and John's bones were scattered; they were then collected by a group of monks who were on pilgrimage to the site and who then brought them to Philip, the founder of their monastery.[17] The relics were then sent to Alexandria for safe keeping, where they were interred in a wall, not to be discovered for another century. Patriarch Theophilus then constructed a martyrium for them in Alexandria; apparently John's head was included. The relics were moved again, however, this time to Cosilaos.

In 391, the emperor Theodosius moved the relic—this time apparently it was only the head—to Constantinople, where he eventually built a church to enshrine it. Prior to the Battle of Frigidus, when Theodosius reunified the Empire, the emperor is said to have prayed over the head relic, and he attributed his victory in part to its power. John's relics did not stay stationary, a common enough occurrence in the early Christian milieu,[18] and they seem to have multiplied as well: "There are probably a dozen or so other reliquaries from our period from Western Europe, almost all of them clustered in North Italy and the upper Adriatic. In the Balkans, on the route to Constantinople, numerous others have been discovered."[19] John's relics appear in Palestine, in Syria, in Jerusalem; a "second head" appears in Emesa. According to Kazan, the twelfth-century Benedictine abbot Guibert of Nogent remarked that if there were in fact two heads, this would suggest "that there were either two John the Baptists or one John who had two heads—both equally impossible assertions!"[20]

The head was "discovered" during the demolition of the basilica in Damascus—Arabic sources report that it was found in chest with a marble slab on which was written "this is the head of John, son of Zacharias"[21]—and then subsequently placed inside of the Umayyad Mosque. It is, I think, noteworthy that this was done substantially before the arrival of

Husayn's head. My point here, certainly, is not to present an exhaustive history of the relics of John the Baptist. Rather, I want to emphasize that John's head was a most powerful relic, one that would have been not just an object of worship, but also a potent political object, a kind of palladium for whoever possessed it.[22] Thus the placement of John's head in the mosque was, if nothing else, a charged act, an act of appropriation and, inherently, symbolic domination. Flood points out that the "use of a religious sanctuary as a repository for semiotically charged antiquities follows a well-established Umayyad precedent, but the gathering of such relics in the Great Mosque of Damascus should probably be seen as part of a more widespread endeavor to incorporate into the mosque insignia of a religio-political nature."[23] Indeed, John's head was not the only significant relic that was interred in the mosque, nor the only relic that the Umayyad dynasty had moved to Damascus.

There was, for instance, an attempt to transport the Prophet's staff from Medina to Damascus: "Just as the earlier accumulation and agglomeration of relics in the churches of Jerusalem coincides with a bid by the Jerusalem episcopate to increase its power, one might see the unearthing of John the Baptist's head during the construction of the Damascus mosque as standing in a long line of politically expedient discoveries of saintly relics (including alternative heads of the same saint)."[24] Flood here echoes one of the central points of Jonathan Z. Smith's discussion in *To Take Place*, a point that has been at the heart of my analysis in this book: namely, that places become significant, sacred even, in part because of the objects that are put there, and that the placing of such objects is very much a politically charged act. "Sacrality is," Smith says, "above all, a category of emplacement."[25]

Interestingly, a kind of reversal of this sort of emplacement could be seen in post-independence Israel, when, under the direction of general Moshe Dayan, a great many mosques were destroyed in an attempt to at once erase the Muslim presence in newly founded Jewish Israel, and at the same time to assert a kind of dominance over those Muslims that remained. It was during this campaign that Mash'had Nabi Hussein, the eleventh-century shrine that was said to have housed the remains of Husayn in Ashkelon, was reportedly demolished—although not without protest. One of the chief archeologists in the Israeli Department of Antiquities, Shmuel Yeivin, complained about the destruction of what he saw as places that were part of the heritage of Israel, whether they were Muslim structures or not.[26] This is an interesting point, because there was a recognition, at least by some, that these "foreign" religious places were nonetheless significant and important, that they were part of what constituted nascent Israeli identity.

The ruins of the Mash'had Nabi Hussein in Ashkelon are still there, a reminder of the place that was, and thus there is still power there, what might be called a two-dimensional power: for the Israeli forces, the ruined mosque is a reminder of their military might; for the Muslims, though, it is a reminder of what was there and is still, somehow, there. Thus as much as it might be someone else's sacred place, it is, even in ruin, still powerful.

When the Taliban destroyed the two Buddhas at Bamiyan, they were engaged in a similar act, but, again invoking Derrida, this is a complex act of erasure, because the Buddhas are still there in a significant sense.[27] After their destruction, however, some Hazara residents of the region—the Hazaras are a persecuted ethnic Shi'a minority in Afghanistan, and in the Bamiyan region they have mostly lived in crushing poverty—who had been living in the many monastic caves built into the same hills as the Buddhas expressed a deep sense of loss over the destruction of the Buddhas. Yes, these were foreign objects, idols, but they were also something like living relatives, and their loss was very personal. Indeed, they were not alone in decrying the destruction of the Buddhas at Bamiyan and other Buddhist antiquities throughout the country. "These were part of our culture, part of our identity," was a commonly expressed sentiment. I raise this point here because, again, we see the blurring of the lines between religious and cultural identities. Certainly, in the context of Afghanistan, the Buddhas were vestiges of a foreign religion; but they were so much more than this, part of the heritage of the country and thus interwoven with Afghan identity.

6.3 Karbala and the Politics of Pilgrimage

Whoever undertakes ziyarat of his own free will, thereby confirming the wish of the imams, for him the imams will intercede with God on the day of resurrection.

—'ALI AL-RIDA[28]

[T]he contours of Karbala have been mapped and remapped in innumerable colors by succeeding generations

of chroniclers, poets, mystics, reformers, and devotees. From the Tartars of modern-day Azerbaijan to Tunisian playwrights like Muhammad Aziza, from Musa al-Sadr in Lebanon to the Ayatollah Khomeini in Iran, from the first English poetry anthology of Pakistani writers in the diaspora to the festive Muharram processions of Trinidad, Karbala and its heroes have been envisaged and invoked, commemorated and celebrated, enacted and emulated time and again, although not always with apparent consensus. The longevity of this event's legacy is tied to its malleability, which itself inheres in its symbolic resilience.

—SYED AKBAR HYDER[29]

It is the stabilizing persistence of place as a container of experiences that contributes so powerfully to its intrinsic memorability. An alert and alive memory connects spontaneously with place, finding in it features that favor and parallel its own activities. We might even say that memory is naturally place-supported.

—EDWARD CASEY[30]

Jonathan Z. Smith has frequently reminded us that sacrality is relational, not just oppositional. Thus Smith points out that even Constantine, in constructing his empire, did not simply lay waste to what had been and then rebuild a Christian land—a kind of ancient version of the contemporary urban phenomenon of the "scrape"—but rather "created, for the first time, a Christian 'Holy Land,' laid palimpsest-like over the old, and interacting with it in complex ways, having for its central foci a series of imperial-dynastic churches. It was a venture made possible at least as much by Hadrianic 'erasure' "—the quotation marks are noteworthy here—"of elements of the past as it was by the discovery of new modes of Christian topographical significance."[31] But how does a place become significant? How is this sort of topographical significance created? This, of course, has been the central question of this book.

Also writing about the early Christian context—in an article appropriately titled "How on Earth Could Places Become Holy?"—Robert Markham has observed that there is something fundamentally counterintuitive about the development of Christian pilgrimage places in the ancient world. He cites the fourth-century Roman historian and Christian apologist Eusebius, for instance, and his view that unlike Jews and Pagans, for whom place was very important, "Christianity had no room for physical holy places. If there is a holy city now, it can only be the heavenly Jerusalem."[32] Up until the fourth century, Christians seem not to have had holy places; part of this, certainly, was a theological position, rooted in the Pauline idea that the community—and not some physical place—was the temple on earth, as expressed in Acts 17.24: "The God who made the world and everything in it, being the lord of heaven and earth, does not dwell in shrines made by man." Markham suggests that it was the Christian concept of sacred time that led, in the fourth century, to the emergence of sacred places: "The great contribution of the fourth century was to intensify a long established system of Christian sacred time; and one of the consequences—very indirectly—was the emergence of holy places and of a sacred Christian topography."[33] Echoing Smith's basic thesis that religiously significant sites are placed, Markham notes that the presence of a relic in a church transformed that church into a sacred place, "housing the saint, in a sense they could not while they housed only the worshipping congregation. A network of 'holy places' thus came into being, in which suburban burials, urban churches, and the more remote destinations of pilgrimage came to define a whole sacred topography of the Roman, and now also Christian, world."[34]

Although there was real tension centered on such practices in the early Christian context, with significant authorities rejecting the veneration of the saints and their relics, the spread of relic veneration was an essential component in the spread of Christianity. Thus as Peter Brown has documented in *The Cult of the Saints,* by "the end of the sixth century, the graves of the saints, which lay in the cemetery areas outside the walls of most of the cities of the former Western Empire, had become centers of the ecclesiastical life of the region."[35] The places where the saints' corporeal remains were located became the central pilgrimage places in European Christendom.

In the Islamic context, the matter of pilgrimage (*ziyarat*) is rather more complicated and contested, and there are significant tensions that cut across Islamic communities, tensions between Shi'a and Sunnis and tensions within the Shi'a and the Sunni communities as well. Sunnis have typically held that pilgrimage should only be directed to Mecca, and some clerics and jurists have been quite critical of any Shi'a pilgrimage practices that are not centered on Mecca. There is a complex and extensive sacred geography in Shi'a Islam, and, as S. H. Nasr has pointed out, the "tombs of all the imams are considered extensions of the supreme centers of Mecca and Medina, and, thus, pilgrimage to these sites ... [is] strongly encouraged by the jurists and the official religious hierarchy and play a very important role in the Shia religious life."[36] Indeed, according to Surinder Bhardwaj, citing R. B. Serjant, some Shi'a communities permit the substitution of pilgrimage to Mecca by pilgrimage to one of the tombs of the Shi'a saints.[37]

Non-Hajj pilgrimage is, certainly, a contested aspect of Muslim practice, with a long and complicated history: some early scholars recommended that pilgrimage to the Ka'ba should include the mosque of the Prophet in Medina,[38] whereas some Sunni scholars have been very critical of any pilgrimage directed to any place other than Mecca, including even Medina; some, such as the thirteenth-century scholar Ibn Taymiyyah, rejected any veneration at any shrine or mosque that even approached the honor directed to Mecca and Medina; other jurists and clerics have argued that there are three legitimate places to which pilgrimage is permitted—Mecca, Medina, and Kufa (in some instances the latter is replaced by Jerusalem, and in others Jerusalem becomes a fourth); and the Sufis hold such a huge list of places worthy of pilgrimage that they seem to put essentially no restrictions on the practice.

Although there were frequent attempts to limit the number of religiously significant places in Islam, new pilgrimage places continued to emerge. M. J. Kister remarks that "Damascus gained a prominent position among the cities frequented by the believers very early on in Islamic times, becoming in effect the fourth holy sanctuary."[39] As in Christianity, part of what imbued power and sacredness to a place was the presence of relics of significant figures; as Kister—citing the ninth-century Muslim historian Al-Fākihī—puts it, the "number of graves of prophets and saints in a given city serves as a measure of its status and position on the map of holy places as drawn by the Muslim community."[40] Thus although there have been frequent criticisms of the practice of venerating at the tombs of various figures—as was the case in the early Christian context as well—there has also been a consistent recognition, even if in the cause of opposition, of the social and political power of such places.

Part of what makes Karbala a religiously significant place, then, is what happened there—the murder of Husayn—and what is located there, his body. According to Ingvild Flaskerud, Muslims began to visit to the place where Husayn's body was buried as early as 684, and by the ninth century Karbala had become a major pilgrimage destination, such that the imams attempted to institutionalize the pilgrimage cult for *ashura*."[41] *Ashura*, broadly translated as "mourning," is, as we shall see in a moment, a major part of the commemoration and remembrance of the martyrdom of Husayn. The visitation of the shrines of the imams, however, is a major component of Shi'a devotional life, not limited to Karbala. Every year some twelve million pilgrims visit the shrine of Imam Reza at Mashad.[42] "The most prominent of these shrine cities was Najaf, which by the early twentieth century exercised an enormous religious and political influence far beyond the limits of Iraq."[43] Najaf is where the tomb of Ali, the cousin and son-in-law of the Prophet and the fourth leader of the Muslim community,[44] is located; Najaf became especially important in the shifting political landscape of nineteenth century Iran and Iraq, and by the early twentieth century there were at least nineteen schools in Najaf. "It was often the seat of the leading Shi'i mujtahid of the day," notes Yitzhak Nakash, "who would receive large contributions from Shi'i followers around the Muslim world."[45]

For the vast majority of those Shi'a and Sunnis who visit Najaf, it is the shrine of Ali that is the attraction; not only is it a place to be visited by pilgrims, but it is also where many Shi'a long to be buried. As Vali Nasr puts it, "It is a blessing to be buried near the imams' great shrines. Shias believe that one who is buried in the shadow a shrine will have a quicker passage to the after life."[46] These are, to use Peter Brown's term, "the special dead," and like the Christian martyrs Brown discusses—who are the "invisible companions" of the living, and who help bridge the gap between earth and heaven—the imams are understood not simply as historical religious leaders, but as powerful figures capable of interceding with god on behalf of the pilgrim. As Nakash puts it, "It was believed that through the visitation, prayers said by the tomb, and votive offering, the supplicants could obtain the help and intercession (*shafa'a*) of the saints with God on their behalf."[47]

In the early Christian context, the tombs of the saints were powerful places where the nascent Christian community came to understand itself as a community. As Brown describes it, these sites drew people from a wide social swath, and the rituals associated with the saints affected a kind of *communitas*, a link not only between the dead saint and the worshipper, but also between the worshippers themselves: "The Christian definition of the urban community was notably different from that of the classical city. It included two unaccustomed and potentially disruptive categories, the women and the poor. The cult of the saints offered a way of bringing precisely these two categories together, under the patronage of the bishop, in such a way as to offer a new basis of the solidity of the late-antique town"[48] Something analogous is at play in the Shi'a context. "The essential function of the visitation is to acknowledge their authority as the leaders of the Muslim community following the death of Muhammad and to reinforce the bond between the believers and their imams."[49] In the case of Karbala, in particular, the shrine containing the body of the imam was also a highly charged symbol of the suffering and persecution of the Shi'as: "Besides serving as an act of covenant renewal between the believer and the imam, the visitation is also aimed at preserving the collective Shi'i memory and group identity as distinguished from that of the Sunnis."[50] Place clearly matters in the Islamic context, and such places—like the other places I have discussed in this book—were and continue to be freighted with a great deal of theological and ritual and political power. As I have noted, though, places and the practices centered on such places is contested; not all within the Muslim world have condoned such place-centered practices. In the eighteenth century, for instance, the Wahhabis, as part of their broad reform—some would say fundamentalist—agenda destroyed all the Shi'a shrines in Arabia, and in 1801 sacked Karbala, stripping the shrine of Husayn of all ornamentation and gold. Significantly, such attacks have become part of the ethos and pathos of Shi'a Islam, and have amplified the powerful symbolic resonance of Karbala. As Flaskerud, in her study of the visual dimensions of Shi'a practices, has put it, the tent and shrine at Karbala "are polysemic signs that absorb and amalgamate historiography, mythology, theological conceptions, ritual practice and personal experience."[51] Like the site where the World Trade Center towers stood, and like Ayodhya as well, "Karbala" becomes a synecdoche for a whole range of associations, emotions, and attitudes, the amalgamation of which Hamid Dabashi has called the "Karbala Complex." I will have more to say on this below.

Shortly after the fall of Saddam Hussein, in the spring of 2003, thousands of Iranian Shi'as crossed into Iraq on their way to Karbala, Najaf, and other pilgrimage cities. The distance to Karbala from the Iranian border is nearly two hundred miles. Most of these pilgrims walked. Many of them were abjectly poor, carrying with them only small bundles of food, not even bringing with them a change of clothes; the journey was dangerous and difficult, across fields of landmines and through the desolate and forbidding landscape of southern Iraq. Why make such a journey? Why take such risks? This was the first chance in decades that these pilgrims could visit these sites, since Saddam Hussein had banned Iranian pilgrimage to the Iraqi holy cities, where the tombs of the great figures of the Shi'a tradition are located: the tomb of Husayn in Karbala, the shrine of Imam Reza at Mashad, in addition to the shrines of Musa al-Kazem (the seventh Imam) and Muhammad al-Taqi (the ninth Imam) near Baghdad, the tomb of Ali al-Reza (the eighth Imam) in Mashad, the tomb of Ali, in Najaf, and others. Although it is the tomb of Ali that is regarded by many Shi'a as the most religiously powerful of all of these shrines—in part because of the healing powers of the place and the blessings bestowed to the pilgrim who visits Ali's tomb, and the belief that burial near Ali is especially auspicious—it is Karbala that is freighted with the most symbolic power and which for many Shi'a is the center of their religious world.

Indeed, the physical power of Karbala was such that Shi'a traditions "attach blessing to its water and soil, and promise rewards to the believers to be gained from their pilgrimage to the city."[52] In India and what is now Pakistan, rulers have had soil and water brought from Iraq to be incorporated into mosques, and have, in turn, sent substantial sums of money back to Iraq for the construction and maintenance of religious shrines and for the performance of rituals. Syed Akbar Hyder, in his *Reliving Karbala: Martyrdom in South Asian Memory*, points out that for centuries, "Shias, during the performances of their devotions, prostrate time and again on the clay tablets fashioned from this holy earth."[53] Thus even outside of Iraq, Karbala is present, is put in place: "Karbala is embraced and nurtured, not to mention redesigned and mobilized, around the world. Its geographical and religious displacements do not necessitate its dissolution."[54]

Certainly, for many Shi'a pilgrims it is the tomb that contains Husayn's body in Karbala that is the focus of their devotion, but the power of that specific place is not simply contained in the physical, but permeates out, extending far beyond the boundaries of Karbala, and is also entwined in Husayn's murder and the murder of his followers and also the long history of Shi'a persecution—both experienced and imagined. It is perhaps tempting to call this a spiritual place, even a sacred place, but, again, we have to ask: spiritual how? in what way sacred? In a significant way, Karbala could be called an *axis mundi*, but not in the sense that Eliade means—the meeting place of the earth and the heavens. Rather, Karbala is the orienting center for many Shi'a Muslims, the embodiment of their religious world and worldview, a highly charged metaphor, a physical place that transcends the bounds of both location and temporality. "Every Place is Karbala" was a familiar Shi'a slogan during the Iran-Iraq war in the 1980s, and also during the United States' invasion of Iraq in the early 2000s. Karbala is thus at once a place, an event that happened long ago and also that continues to be played out, and also a way of being in and understanding the world. Karbala has both ontological and epistemological valence.

This is perhaps a too woolly construction, and thus calls for some unpacking. As I have earlier noted, there is a substantial body of theoretical scholarship on the topic of space and place. A sub-genre of this work, or really an ancillary field, is what, for lack of a better term, is place theory, sometimes called Human Geography. A starting point for much of this scholarship is Martin Heidegger's basic observation, in *Being and Time*, that to be human is to dwell in a place.[55] Early theoretical work on place drew on the insights of both phenomenology and existentialism. Thus the influential theorist of place Yi-Fu Tuan articulates an approach to place that focuses on the concept of "topophilia," a term he uses to describe what he calls the "affective bond between people and place."[56] Tuan is a complex and sometimes frustrating thinker, but his work is relevant here because he shifts the focus away from space, per se, to what makes it become place. Drawing particularly on the phenomenological tradition, Tuan shifts some of the discussion about space to the human use of space, and the way this use—our attachments and associations and memories—transforms the physical realities of space into place. As Edward Relph puts it, where space is amorphous and intangible, place is something different, because "however we feel or explain space, there is nearly always some associated sense or concept of place."[57] Relph points out that places do not derive their meanings merely from locations; rather, the "essence of place lies in the largely unselfconscious intentionality that defines places as profound centers of human experience."[58] We have seen this sort of transformation throughout this book: the empty space of Ground Zero is transformed into a particular sort of place; it is freighted with all sorts of meanings and associations; people are emotionally invested in the place; and, of course, different—and contested—understandings of the place emerge.

It is certainly tempting to invoke the Turners here, and their notion of normative *communitas* that I discussed in Chapter 1. Recall that in their discussion of Lough Derg in *Image and Pilgrimage*, they talk of the way in which "Irishness is raised to a more abstract plane of generalization and normativeness,"[59] and that this "Irishness" is intimately linked to and enmeshed in a kind of pathos of persecution and martyrdom, in much the same way that we have seen with Shi'a identity, particularly as it is caught up in conceptions of Karbala. In this sense, Karbala conforms in ways that few other places do to what Heidegger seems to mean when he talks of *Dasein*, a word that conveys far more, for Heidegger, than simply dwelling, as the term is typically translated; indeed, *Dasein* connotes for him something like the ontological ground of our being. Hamid Dabashi, in his engaging *Shi'ism: A Religion of Protest*, uses the phrase—as I have noted—"Karbala Complex" to get at something of the deep, polysemous resonance of Karbala:

> The Karbala complex is thus the gradual mutation of the central trauma of Shi'ism (the battle of Karbala) into a nexus of emotive responses and political instincts that are then doctrinally codified and cast into a full panoramic history. This trauma is ultimately not just emotively untenable, but more important it is narratively untellable. It cannot be fully told to any Shi'i's full satisfaction, and thus there is a central mimetic crisis at the heart of Shi'ism.[60]

Dabashi's analysis is too complex and detailed to really do it justice here, but the central thrust of his argument is that Karbala is something like the ground of a kind of existential pathos for Shi'as, a real and metaphoric trauma that is at the very core of their understanding of self and community. In this sense, then, Karbala is almost the mirror image of what Heidegger means—or, more accurately, the way many have used Heidegger in the context of place and space: it is not the comforting, grounding cabin in the woods that Heidegger talks of,[61] but more like the open wound at the heart of every Shi'a's self, a wound in which the very source of Shi'a identity dwells. John Haugeland has described *Dasein* as "neither people nor their being, but rather *a way of life* shared by the members of some community. It is ways of life, in this sense, that have the basic structure of being-in-the-world."[62]

I am perhaps forcing the metaphor here—and certainly it is not my aim to add anything new to the analysis of the work of Heidegger—but I am doing so intentionally, because although Karbala is indeed a physical place, as I have said it is far more than that. Again, I think Dabashi is useful; he discusses the way in which Karbala is "parabolically metaphoric. It can easily metamorphose into multiple parables." In this sense, there is a fluid quality to Karbala, such that the narrative, mythic, ritual, and theological dimensions of Karbala flow into any number of "containers." As Dabashi puts it, by "varied acts of metaphoric and doctrinal osmosis it has in fact spread into any number of adjacent narratives and emotive territories—both Islamic and non-Islamic, theistic or agnostic, worldly or other-worldly."[63] Writing from the theoretical perspective, Rob Shields introduces the term "spatialisation"—which is closely related, as Shields notes, to Bourdieu's *habitus*, and which also owes no small debt to Heidegger's association of place and being—to talk about the ways that space, and place, are part of our existential (and ontic) makeup.[64] The spatial, he writes, "has an epistemic and ontological importance—it is part and parcel of our notions of reality, truth, and causality. As an initial hypothesis, we could suggest that a 'discourse of space' composed of perceptions of places and regions, of the world as a 'space' and of our relationships with these perceptions are central to our everyday conceptions of ourselves and of reality."[65]

Thus when Habashi says that Karbala "can easily metamorphose into multiple parables," in part what he means is that all sorts of conceptions of Shi'a identity are harnessed to Karbala, both the place and the full panoply that extends out from that particular place. Ali Shariati, a Marxist Shi'a intellectual who died before the Iranian revolution, saw in Karbala a revolutionary drama, such that "Karbala was no longer an eternal manifestation of the truth but a revolutionary act by a revolutionary hero, which could be duplicated in the late twentieth century."[66] Dabashi points out that one critical component of the broad discourse of Karbala is the concept of insurrection (*qiyam*): "Tyranny is not to be tolerated. Tyranny is to be resisted. Hossein's *qiyam* against Yazid is the archetypal model of a small band of revolutionaries rising against tyranny."[67]

This was played out in the early 1960s in Iran, when clerics critical of the Shah's regime "referred to Husayn as the example for rising against tyranny and oppression. Again, during the Iranian revolution in 1978–1979, the battle at Karbala was used to mobilize the masses in overthrowing the Shah."[68] Indeed, the Shah was explicitly associated with Yazid, as, a decade later, was the Iraqi president, Saddam Hussein, and, more recently, United States President George W. Bush. "Not only did the symbols of Karbala frame the discourse of anti-imperialism and anti-colonialism"—and here it is important to remember that the Iraqis received a great deal of support from the United States during their war with Iran—"but the lack of access to this sacred Iraqi city prompted many Shias to speak of the

Iraqi president as a modern incarnation of Yazid."[69] As I have mentioned, Iranians had long been prohibited from visiting Karbala, and although there were many complicated political reasons for the Iran-Iraq war, Karbala was a potent symbol for the Iranians, and the aim of "retaking" Karbala was a consistent theme throughout the war.

From December of 1986 until April of 1987, the Iranians launched the Karbala campaign, one of the major thrusts of the entire war, thereby harnessing the pathos of Karbala that Dabashi describes as part of the "Karbala Complex." This campaign consisted of six major battles, the explicit aim of which was to first capture Basrah, and then move to take Karbala. The first few battles consisted of tens of thousands of Iranian soldiers streaming into Iraq, soldiers who were symbolically cast as "pilgrims" on the road to Karbala. They sang songs with lyrics such as "Karbala, Karbala we are coming," and "We'll give our lives to conquer Karbala / Rise up brave warriors! Seize back your homeland from the enemy / The road to victory passes through the land of Karbala," and "I am joining you, O caravan of Karbala, I am joining you!"[70] There was also the ubiquitous chant, a sentiment echoed throughout Shi'a history: "Every day is Ashura, Everywhere is Karbala." Stephen Pelletier describes these waves of pilgrim-soldiers, and remarks that the "essential nature of which was their torrential quality. The attackers flowed inexorably forward."[71] Some 70,000 of these pilgrim-soldiers were killed, thus adding to the tragic suffering associated with Karbala, suffering which begins with Husayn's murder at Karbala the physical place, and then radiates out.[72] Indeed, the observance of *Ashura*, the day on which Husayn was murdered, was "used to bolster support for the cause of the Iran-Iraq War."[73]

Ashura is an essential aspect of Karbala. On one level, it is the ritual observance of the events at Karbala that took place in 686, but as Aghaie points out, it "is not a word limited only to a certain location or time. Rather, it is often considered to be timeless and universal in scope."[74] *Ashura* is, essentially, the ritual performance of Karbala, both the events and the place at which these events took place. Again, in this sense, for many Shi'a every place becomes, through these rituals, Karbala.

Although *Ashura* is observed in virtually all places where there are Shi'a Muslims, it is Karbala itself that is the locative center and orienting place of these ritual practices. Pilgrims visit the tomb of Husayn, actors perform his murder, there are processions of mourners, and, most dramatically, ritual acts of self-flagellation. The latter is perhaps the most symbolically potent of these ritual observances—it is certainly the ritual that is most condemned outside of the Shi'a community—having developed in the mid-nineteenth century and become an important way in which some Shi'a articulate their distinct identity and their deep connection to Karbala. Flagellation has been a particularly contested form of commemorating and reliving the events of Karbala, consistently criticized, not surprisingly, by Sunni clerics, but also by some Shi'a religious leaders. As Nakash points out, "Leading Shi'i *mujtahids* [religious scholars] and religious families were divided, however, over the legality and usefulness of the rituals of '*Ashura*' as practiced by the laity."[75] Various Iraqi governments, as well as the British before them, have sought to control and limit these rituals, particularly the practice of flagellation.

In contrast, in Iran the ritual observances of *Ashura* have been exceedingly important. For instance, throughout the 1950s the Shah regularly gave donations to a group of breast beaters, and in the 1970s the Pahlavi court attempted to patronize the dramatic representation of the battle of Karbala "and transform it into a type of Iranian folklore."[76] These rituals became an important way to mark various forms of Shi'a identity, with different ethnic and national Shi'as developing distinct forms and ways of ritually commemorating and enacting Karbala; Nakash notes that during the Ottoman period, Arab pilgrims directed their *Ashura* rituals to the shrine of Husayn, whereas "the Persian participants used to perform before the Iranian consult-general" in Karbala, "thereby stressing their Persian identity and strong communal sense."[77] Brian Spooner, an anthropologist who did field work in Iran in that late 1950s and early 1960s, observed that "Iranians became preoccupied with various observances and ceremonies of Husayn's death, dedicating half of their life to that end."[78]

Iranians may historically have been unable to visit the actual place of Karbala, as were many Shi'a—and Sunnis as well—in South Asia, but this did not lessen the importance of Karbala as a place. Indeed, in a significant way, for those Shi'a communities the rituals became a way of transforming the locative fixity of Karbala the place into the portable sense of Karbala, and thereby into a place that was ritually available in time. As Jonathan Z. Smith argues in *To Take Place*, writing specifically about Christians and Jerusalem but making a point that is equally applicable to Shi'a Muslims and Karbala, "If Jerusalem were to be accessible, it was to be gained through participation in a temporal arrangement of events, not a spatial one."[79] An important distinction here is that unlike the early Christian sense of Jerusalem, which Smith suggests became a kind of fantasy, accessible only through narrative, Karbala—like Jerusalem for many contemporary Jews and some Christians—continues to be fundamentally linked to Shi'a identity and to be accessible through ritual action. These rituals became and continue to be essential ways in which Shi'as make the events at Karbala perpetually present.

Smith remarks that ritual "is a relationship of difference between 'nows'—the now of everyday life and the now of ritual place; the simultaneity, but not the coexistence, of the 'here' and 'there.'"[80] Karbala, however, seems to push against this assertion, such that the differences between these different "nows" is collapsed, as, likewise, are the differences between the "here" and the "there." There is thus an inherent fluidity to Karbala, such that the place flows out and is capable of filling any other place, in part through ritual. Again, such rituals transform otherwise neutral spaces into religiously charged places.

In his recent study of religiously significant places that have involved violence, *War on Sacred Grounds*, Ron Hassner suggests that one of the distinct features of what he calls sacred places is their indivisibility: "Sacred spaces are unique in this regard because all sacred spaces fulfill the three conditions for indivisibility. Sacred places are integrated monolithic spaces that cannot be subdivided; they have clearly defined and inflexible boundaries; they are unique sites for which no material or spiritual substitute is available."[81] Hassner is self-consciously deeply indebted to Eliade here; sacred places become sacred because they are hierophanies, places where the sacred irrupts. They are in the well-known Eliadian term, *axis mundi*, the places where heaven and earth are conjoined. I have quite obviously argued in precisely the opposite direction, in the present chapter, and throughout this book. To reiterate a point I have made throughout, no place is inherently sacred, but is made sacred—and, again, it is not at all clear that this is typically, or only, how such places are regard by those who value them—through events, through associations, through discourse, through political machinations. "Sacrality is, above all, a category of emplacement."[82]

I would not, however, say that a place such as Karbala is divisible; I think that is the wrong metaphor. As I have said, places such as Karbala are fluid, a liquid metaphor, after all, and liquids cannot be divided in quite the same way as solids. In another, less abstract way, the power of a place such as Karbala is not contained in the physical confines of Karbala the city, but flows outward, such that this power is fully available in potentially any place. Karbala is fluid and, to perhaps force my own metaphor, can be tapped into. Thus water or soil from

Karbala can make a mosque in Hyderbad a religiously charged place, a place that evokes and contains the symbolic and, for many Shi'a, makes available the real power of Karbala itself. Likewise, the rituals of *Ashura* performed during Muharram not only invoke Karbala the place, but also affect that place, bringing it into being, even make it sacred, if "sacred" is how those who worship in it choose to perceive it. "Every day is Ashura, Everywhere is Karbala."

7

Public Space or Sacred Place?

7.1 Nature Set Apart: On the Sacrality of the National Parks

How do you design plans to protect sacred places when you are dealing with people who have never held anything sacred? People who probe the earth, probe the sky and oceans, tread upon all the earth, touch everything all without feeling the mother earth under them.

—Tribal Elders at the Medicine Wheel Alliance[1]

The burden that the Acropolis bares is that it simultaneously "belongs" to radically divergent imagined communities. And the question as to whom it "truly" belongs has no direct theoretical answer: it is determined through political contestation and struggle and, hence is a relatively unstable determination.

—DAVID HARVEY[2]

I turn in this chapter back to the United States, and the contested rock formation located in the Black Hills of Wyoming known popularly as Devils Tower National Monument. For a great many citizens of the United States, National Parks are sacred places. The actual term "sacred" is not always used, but this was how they were conceived from the outset. Thus when Yellowstone, the first National Park, was so designated in 1872, the language used to describe the place very much echoed Durkheim's description of the sacred as that which is set apart, prohibited, inviolable: "Be it enacted…That the tract of land in the Territories of Montana and Wyoming, lying near the head-waters of the Yellowstone river... is hereby reserved and withdrawn from settlement, occupancy, or sale... and dedicated and set apart as a public park or pleasuring-ground for the benefit and enjoyment of the people."[3] Although the overt language here—"pleasuring-ground," "enjoyment"—does not immediately evoke the sacred or sacrality, the parks were very definitely conceived from the outset as sacred places; as Lynn Ross-Bryant points out, "Nature 'set apart' in the parks becomes the embodiment of an archetypal America, which is the ever-pristine source of the greatness of the nation and the people and, as such, serves as a sacred site and a unifying symbol in U.S. American culture."[4]

Overtly religious language was also frequently used to describe the parks. As Stephen Mather, then Director of the National Parks, put it in 1921, "They are the first in the worthwhile things in our national life that make for better citizens. And there is no finer opportunity in the Americanization movement than to spread the gospel of the parks far and wide."[5] Ross-Bryant points out that in the early literature on the parks, "Yosemite was described as America's national cathedral, and Greek temples and Gothic cathedrals paled in comparison. Not only were the U.S. sacred shrines far vaster in scale, they were also far older in time—and made by God, not humans."[6] The parks were integrally connected to a particular sort of American identity—the chosen people given this chosen land, an expression of divine favor. Simon Schama describes Yosemite as coming to stand for Americans, after Carleton Watkins' iconic stereographs were displayed in New York in 1861, as "a symbol of a landscape that was beyond the reach of sectional conflict, a primordial place of such transcendent beauty that it proclaimed the gift of the Creator to his new Chosen People."[7]

There are some deep ironies at play here, for as I have argued throughout this book, marking a place as sacred in this way is seldom a unilateral move—and also seldom a neutral one. The sacredness of the national parks, as conceived by those who initially proposed them—and by those who have championed and protected them since the late nineteenth century—is a sacredness based on opposition and exclusion. On its face, marking such places as sacred is, certainly, a form of prohibition: prohibited are activities that would alter and therefore pollute these places, such as logging and building. As Frederick Law Olmstead put it in 1865, speaking here specifically about Yosemite but, implicitly, about all of the National Parks: "The first point to be kept in mind is the preservation and maintenance as exactly as it is possible of the natural scenery; the restriction, that is to say, within the narrowest limits consistent with the necessary accommodation of visitors, of all artificial constructions and the prevention of all constructions markedly inharmonious with the scenery or which would unnecessarily obscure, distort or detract from the dignity of the scenery."[8] This is more than a statement of practice, but a reflection of an ideology, the basic tenor of which would later be articulated, as we have already seen, by UNESCO in the description of World Heritage Sites.

Of course, there are all sorts of artificial and inharmonious constructions in American National Parks: roads, luxury hotels, playgrounds, restaurants, visitors' centers, and so on. It was not, however, only "artificial" building that was prohibited, but also "inharmonious" people. The rhetoric of the various acts designating the National Parks is certainly one of inclusiveness; they are places to be left "unimpaired for the enjoyment of future generations," as the Organic Act of 1916 puts it; they are to be preserved "for the benefit and enjoyment of the people." These future generations, however, did not include the very people who had for centuries lived in these places. As Ross-Bryant points out, "As each park was 'discovered' by the white man, Native Americans were expelled or hidden away, except when 'authentic Indians' were brought before the white visitors to perform. There was never a thought that Native Americans should continue to live in the parks."[9] Like the picturesque eighteenth-century paintings of the Indian landscape that I discussed in Chapter 4, which were all but devoid of the Indians who actually lived in India, the National Parks were to be an idealized landscape devoid of Native Americans.

Michael Harkin has analyzed the way places in North America have been co-opted by Euro-Americans, not only in the physical sense of taking the land, but also in how they have been discursively depicted and viewed, and he notes that something as seemingly innocuous as the picture window, a staple of middle-class life, creates landscapes with the quality of the picturesque, and that this affects what "is inherently a stance of appropriation. It assumes possession of prominent spaces and at least partial control of the space between the viewer and the horizon."[10] This panoramic view is inherently linked to control and power, and brings to mind, at least metaphorically, Foucault's discussion of the Panopticon in *Discipline and Punish*, in which the very panoramic view afforded by the tower is a means of control: "It is a type of location of bodies in space, of distribution of individuals in relation to one another, of hierarchical organization, of disposition of centres and channels of power."[11] As Harkin puts it, "The panoramic point of view reflects an elevated social position; those with the ability to see the big picture are those who are given the power to control and alter social as well as physical landscapes, in this case to rationalize them according to principles of colonial administration."[12] In a significant way, it is precisely this "big picture" that we see articulated in the early conception of the National Parks.

The indigenous, original occupiers of the land—and even this idea, of the land as something to be occupied, is highly problematic—are thus removed from view. Not entirely, though, because white America linked the presence of "Indians" to the sacredness of these places, but only in a symbolic sense. Thus not unlike the way in which the Umayyad Caliphate linked the Great Mosque to the prior Christian presence there, and so consciously and visually reüsed some aspects of Saint John's Basilica in the building of the mosque, so too was the native presence in the National Parks preserved, but it was also significantly erased in Derrida's sense of erasure: their continued presence, even in their absence, was necessary, as both a marker of the dominance of white America and also as a reminder of the "original," or aboriginal, state of the places. Thus "Native Americans, as a symbol of pristine American land, have been preserved and play an important role in the space of national parks—whether in person or through their (supposed) artifacts, which often become the 'relics' the pilgrims take home with them. They, like the land, must be unchanging, outside the dynamics of the living world."[13] As Harkin puts it, "the presence of aboriginals signifies a link with romantic ideas of the past, of authentic traditional cultures existing in harmony with the landscape. This gaze is sympathetic, as long as the aboriginals conform to expectations."[14] I will return to this last point in a moment, because this is one of the things at the root of the Euro-American side of the conflict over Mato Tipila: the Native Americans are not conforming. Conforming to what, though?

The dispute over the National Monument called Devils Tower emerged in the early 1990s, when Native American groups and rock climbers came into conflict over their mutual claims on the place. In an article focusing on the main legal case in the conflict, the 1998 *Bear Lodge Multiple Use Ass'n v. Babbitt*, Allison M. Dussias has nicely summarized the issues involved in this conflict:

> The *Bear Lodge* case involves conflicting views of several groups as to the proper use and treatment of the Tower. The plaintiffs,

> reflecting the attitudes of mainstream American culture, focus on recreational and commercial uses of the Tower, which they regard as an attractive site for rock climbing. Certain Native American tribes see the Tower as having a deeper, sacred significance, and travel to the Tower to engage in traditional practices. The Tower is also important to birds of prey that nest on the Tower's crags and ledges. Many of these birds' nesting activities have been disrupted by climbers. In addition, the public at large has an interest in the preservation of the Tower because of its status as a national monument and its eligibility, as a traditional cultural property, for inclusion on the National Register of Historic Places.[15]

This is indeed a messy place, a place with multiple—and often conflicting—associations and meanings for different people.

Devils Tower—known as Mato Tipila to the Lakota, which translates as "Bear Lodge"—was the first national monument so designated under the 1906 Antiquities Act; then-President Theodore Roosevelt said of it that "the lofty and isolated rock tower known as 'Devils Tower' . . . is such an extraordinary example of the effect of erosion in the higher mountains as to be a natural wonder and an object of historic and great scientific interest."[16] Here, Roosevelt's conception of this place is that it is really not a place at all, but a space. Yes, he notes that there is some "historic" importance to the rock formation, and therefore some cultural significance—a phrase that Roosevelt, of course, would never have used—but this is really an afterthought. Devils Tower is an object, a physical space to be preserved for scientific study. He makes no mention of its importance to Native Americans, and it is impossible to tell if this is because he is unaware of this significance—which is hard to imagine—or if it is simply of no matter to him; like Alexander Cunningham and his Archaeological Survey of India colleagues, for Roosevelt how the place might be used by actual people for whom it is important seems of no consequence.

Several Native American groups perform important rituals at Bear Lodge, rituals that date back thousands of years. The Lakota, for instance, perform the Sun Dance there in June to mark the summer solstice. Many groups leave prayer bundles at the tower's base, colorfully wrapped offerings of sage or tobacco left for the various spirits who dwell around the tower. Devils Tower has also been a climbing destination—something of a climbing Mecca, even—since the late nineteenth century; there are over two hundred established climbing routes on the tower, many of which are fixed routes. By the early 1990s, there were hundreds of bolts and pitons permanently embedded in the tower, and thousands of climbers visited the site each year. Other visitors frequently remark that the bolts and pitons left by climbers, as well as the chalk that remains on the rock, disturb the visual aesthetic of the monument. Some climbers eschew such methods, and instead rely on the natural cracks in the rock to support themselves, using various camming devices which are temporarily inserted into cracks and crevices to protect themselves from falls. Although these devices do not remain in the rock, they can and do damage the tower; climbers also disturb the vegetation on and around the tower, which can lead to erosion.

As we have seen throughout this book, places—pilgrimage places, so-called sacred places, really any place—are never static, but are always, as Appadurai says, "in motion." Tim Cresswell, synthesizing the work of, among others, David Seamon, Allen Pred, Nigel Thrift, and Michel de Certeau, has put it this way: "Place provides the conditions of possibility for creative social practice. Place in this sense becomes an event rather than a secure ontological thing rooted in notions of the authentic. Place as an event is marked by openness and change rather than boundedness and permanence."[17] This points to one of the main problems with UNESCO's activities at Bodhgayā and elsewhere: what it wants to do is stop the movement. But it is not just a matter of making static that which is inherently dynamic; it is also a matter of who gets to decide what sort of place a place is. This is why all of the places I have been discussing in this book are contested: because their importance is open to interpretation and to competing claims.

Many of the same sorts of tensions that we have seen played out at the various religiously significant places I have discussed in this book have also been played out at Devils Tower. The competing and conflicting conceptions of the place have not led to violence, but they have led to protracted legal debates about just what sort of place it is, and who gets to use it and how it gets to be used. John Eade and Michael Sallnow, in their volume on pilgrimage, point out that "pilgrimage is above all an arena for competing religious and secular discourses, for both the official co-optation and the non-official recovery of religious meanings, for conflict between orthodoxies, sects, and confessional groups, for drives towards consensus and communitas *and* for counter-movements towards separateness and division."[18] They could be describing the conflict over Devils Tower.

In this chapter, I return to where I began at the start of this book, with the question of the sacred. At the heart of the debate about Devils Tower are a series of questions about the sacred: Is Devils Tower a sacred place? Sacred for whom? Sacred how? What does this sacredness mean? As I noted in my discussion of UNESCO's involvement at Bodhgayā, one of the issues that emerges is the question of who gets to determine and control what sort of site it is. This issue is also very much in play at Devils Tower. Indeed, the very name that is affixed to the place, "Devils Tower," is itself a means of control. This is a Euro-American label, after all, and as such a kind of discursive claim of ownership. For the Native Americans it is Mato Tipila, "Bear Lodge," a place where important spiritual beings—not devils—reside, and a place where, through various rituals, individuals and communities can interact with these beings. It is a dwelling place, and, as such, carries some of the existential and ontological resonances of Heidegger's *Dasein*. As a national park, it is also, for some Euro-Americans, caught up in certain essential conceptions of the self—freedom, expansion, domination, and control.

7.2 *The Dignity of Scenery and Conflicting Sacreds*

> *It's not that Indians should have exclusive rights there, it's that that location is sacred enough so it should have time of its own, and once it has time of its own then the people who know how to do ceremonies should come and minister it. That's so hard to get across to people.*
>
> —VINE DELORIA JR., in the Film *In the Light of Reverence*

> *In the face of perceived threats to the identity of place and landscapes ideas about the uniqueness and singularity of both have become in many cases re-entrenched with people wishing to find a refuge, to defend a notion of bounded place with which they can identify.*
>
> —CHRISTOPHER TILLEY[19]

The conflict over Devils Tower began when groups of Native Americans protested the disruption of their rituals by rock climbers. The presence of the climbers on the tower and in its environs upset tribe members who charged that the climbers were inhibiting their ability to perform their rituals, and that the bolts and anchors damage what to them is a living place, thereby polluting, essentially, what one tribal member called "the spiritual quality of the site."[20] Climbers (and other visitors) were also accused of removing the prayer bundles that are part of some Native rituals.[21]

The National Park Service (NPS) is the agency charged with managing the tower and its environs, with balancing the competing uses of the site, and the NPS has quite clearly recognized that the place is religiously significant for many Native Americans; on the NPS website, for instance, there is a short essay titled "How Is Devils Tower a Sacred Site to American Indians?" that lists over twenty tribes who have a "potential cultural affiliation with Devils Tower National Monument.[22] Native Americans have important cultural links to the place, the NPS points out, that need to be respected and protected. Some in the climbing community—and all indications are that it is a decided minority of climbers—have bristled at any restrictions on public use of Devils Towers (as long as that use was in keeping with the NPS guidelines for acceptable use of the parks), seeing the attempts of the NPS and others to limit climbing on the site as a restriction on their basic freedom as United States citizens and as a violation of the Establishment Clause of the U.S. Constitution (arguing that any restrictions intended to protect Native American religious practices are a governmental establishment of religion).[23] As tensions between some climbers and the Native American community and their supporters grew, the NPS assembled a working group made up of different stakeholders that met over the course of several years in an attempt to reach a compromise solution that would allow for the various groups to cooperate and respect each other's claims.

The NPS had, initially, been in favor of an outright ban on climbing during the month of June, but tribal leaders urged that they work to institute a voluntary ban—an idea that seems actually to have originated with the climbers themselves—that was rooted in the climbers' understanding and appreciation of the cultural and religious importance of the tower for Native Americans.[24] The NPS created a 100-page document, the "Final Climbing Management Plan" (FCMP), which was put into place in March of 1995. The FCMP outlines the cultural significance of the tower for Native American groups, outlines the terms of the voluntary ban, and calls for the suspension of commercial climbing licenses during June.

Although the climbing community was generally cooperative and had in fact been an active participant in the negotiations leading up to the

FCMP being put into place, and most climbers observed the voluntary June ban, not everyone in the community was in favor of the voluntary ban. In the spring of 1996 a lawsuit was filed in U.S. district court in Casper, Wyoming, by the umbrella group Mountain States Legal Foundation which represented a non-profit organization called the Bear Lodge Multiple Use Association, as well as a commercial guide, Andy Petefish, and several recreational climbers. The suit alleged that the voluntary ban violated the U.S. Constitution's separation of church and state, and argued that it represented the promotion of religion, charges that had been at the root of the climbers' agitation since the beginning of the conflict.

There are many issues swirling around Devils Tower, but the central question really is what sort of place it is. Is it a sacred place for Native Americans that must be protected, and at times closed off, in order for it to be sacred? Or is it a different sort of protected place, a public place for all people to use, as long as they use it in a particular way, a way that would be in keeping with Olmstead's nineteenth-century vision of the parks, so that use is "within the narrowest limits consistent with the necessary accommodation of visitors, of all artificial constructions and the prevention of all constructions markedly inharmonious with the scenery or which would unnecessarily obscure, distort or detract from the dignity of the scenery"? Olmstead used the phrase "the dignity of the scenery," but what does this mean? Why is it the scenery that must be protected? Olmstead's pronouncement here seems precisely what Harkin means when he talks about the way the panoramic view, with its fetishizing of the scenic, "reflects an elevated social position," and is both an expression of power—over place, and over those who contest this particular view of place—and a mechanism for exercising power. This is discourse, certainly, but it is discourse that informs and reflects the implementation of a broad ideology of control.

About Mato Tipila, this much is uncontested: for several different groups of Native Americans, the rock structure is a special place, what the West would call a sacred religious place. For the Lakota, the tower figures prominently in their mythology: in one Lakota story, seven young girls—and sometimes a boy—are playing when a bear (or in some versions several bears) begins to chase them. They jump onto a small rock, and beseech it for help; the rock grows up into the sky and the children are saved from the bear (who tries to reach them and in the process scrapes the sides of the structure with its claws, creating the distinct striations that mark the tower). The girls eventually become the stars in the Big

Dipper constellation. There is much that could be said about this myth, but my point here is that the tower is part of an indigenous cosmography, and thus essentially linked to Native American identity.[25] As Harkin has put this, drawing on both Heidegger's analysis of dwelling and Keith Basso's important work on space and place in the Apache context, "a particular place entails the ongoing lived relations among people and places, and those places contain the concatenation of past events and ways of being."[26]

In much of the discussion about the conflict over Mato Tipila the word "sacred" is used. This is problematic for several reasons. First, there is the fact that "sacred" is a European category, not an indigenous designation. Second, there is the sheer murkiness of the term itself, particularly as it is applied in the Native American context. Third, there is a legal problem that emerges when judges are asked to make rulings based on claims of sacredness.

The sacred is a decidedly slippery and decidedly Western context, a construct that carries with it all sorts of assumptions. As I have noted, I have tried to avoid the term in this book precisely because it is so murky and freighted with unmarked significance and assumptions. That said, in much of the discussion of the sacred, there is an assumed distinction between the sacred and the non-sacred. As Durkheim famously posited early in the twentieth century:

> All known religious beliefs, whether simple or complex, present a common quality: they presuppose a classifications of things—the real or ideal things that men represent for themselves—into two classes, two opposite kinds, generally designated by two distinct terms effectively translated by the word *profane* and *sacred*. The division of the world into two comprehensive domains, one sacred, the other profane, is the hallmark of religious thought."[27]

The sacred for Durkheim is that which is set apart, that object or place that cannot be touched or tread upon (except by ritual specialists). As Durkheim puts it, "The religious prohibition necessarily implies the notion of the sacred; it comes from the respect the sacred object inspires, and its aim is to prevent any lack of that respect."[28] This understanding of the sacred is taken for granted in the Euro-American discussions of religion, in religious and academic and civil discourse; there is, to be sure, a complicated genealogy of the sacred, one that warrants further attention—a future book—but the Durkheimian definition has come to be a given, assumed to be both normative and universal.

In this regard, it then makes good strategic sense to say that Devils Tower is a sacred place. This claim is a means to argue against development; as Alf Hornborg puts it, such a claim is "a successful revolt against the language of modernity."[29] We see this in the earliest discussions of the place as a National Park: it is a place that must be preserved as it is, in its pristine natural state, and this preservation necessitates the prohibition of certain kinds of activities—those activities that would, essentially, disrupt or pollute the sacredness of the place. This conception of the sacred is a particularly secular American one, in line with Roosevelt's pronouncement that the tower and its environs are "a natural wonder." This is not, however, the sense of the sacred employed by those who wish to defend the Native Americans' claims on Mato Tipila. Theirs tends to be a more overtly religious sense of the sacred. The NPS website, for instance, states that "American Indians have regarded the Tower as a sacred site long before climbers found their way to the area.... Some perceive climbing on the Tower as a desecration to their sacred site.... The National Park Service has decided to advocate this closure in order to promote understanding and encourage respect for the culture of American Indian tribes who are closely affiliated with the Tower as a sacred site."[30]

Many scholars, Native and non-Native, have pointed out that even applying the term "sacred" to indigenous peoples is anachronistic.[31] Where the category sacred implies prohibition and separation, a zone of purity set aside, the indigenous concepts of land and place and personhood tend to be far more integrated. "The Euro-American concept of what is sacred is vastly divergent from the Native American concept," points out Rayanne Griffin, because in Native American contexts time and space and personhood are intimately intermeshed.[32] Notice, though, that even as she critiques the use of "sacred" in Native American contexts, she still uses the term, a subtle sort of anachronism of which I am also guilty. Donald Fixico writes that the earth is understood to be "the principal focus of life, and sacred sites like the Black Hills, Blue Hills of the Taos, Mackinac Island, Mount Rainer, Mount Taylor, Bear Butte, and Devils Tower were blessed with special powers."[33] In this sense, what is described as sacred is not something set apart, but rather a force or power that is integrally involved in all of life. Living beings are imbued with this force, but so are places and objects. In effect, everything would be sacred here.

7.3 *The Legal Ambiguity of the Sacred*

When a sacred site is owned by believers, or by tribal societies associated with them, protection is either straightforward or an internal question for the tribal society. Conversely, when a site is privately owned by others, legal protection of believers' interest in the site is limited or absent.

—RICHARD B. COLLINS[34]

Bruce G. Miller, in his analysis of the potential to use the category of the sacred as a means to defend Native land rights, has suggested that although such a claim is valid, such a general conception hinders efforts to protect particular places. He proposes a typology of places, which would allow those working to protect such places to "present a conceptually more differentiated landscape in legal settings, and to regard the landscape as constituted by various sorts of cultural resources, thereby employing a vocabulary already in use. This strategy," Miller suggests, "may skirt questions such as this: if all the landscape is sacred, how can one differentiate and why should measures be made to protect particular locations?"[35]

Daniel Dubuisson, in his insightful critique of the implications of the way the West has constructed "religion," makes a similar point. Dubuisson argues that applying the term "religion" to the South Asian Indian context, for example, implies that there is a distinctly religious realm, a realm of experience that is somehow separate from the social or the cultural or the political or the economic. In so doing, Dubuisson argues, we forget "to stipulate that this complex is, in India, artificial, that it corresponds to nothing, since, from the Indian point of view, it refers to no distinct domain or notion."[36] The same basic critique applies to the way scholars have discussed Native American conceptions of what are called sacred places; a place such as Mato Tipila is not significant because it is set apart, but because there is a power at and of the place, a power that is an ontological—and not just a physical—presence.

To label certain places as sacred in the Native American context is a potent rhetorical strategy, in that the language of the sacred does have a certain purchase in popular discourse. Even if Euro-Americans do not agree with the designation, they certainly understand that something called "sacred" is special. "Special," however, is hardly an unambiguous category, and the problem with calling "sacred" certain places that are religiously and culturally significant for Native Americans, as I noted above, is that this term carries with it a set of meanings for Euro-Americans that do not really fit the Native American context. Vine Deloria Jr., one of the most widely-read Native American scholars of religion, has explicitly used the language of the sacred—as well as the larger category "religion"—in discussing Native understandings of particularly significant places, but he has insisted that Native American understandings of the sacred—like Native understandings of religion—are not the same as those of Euro-Americans.

In his widely anthologized article, "Sacred Lands and Religious Freedom," Deloria lays out four ways in which Native Americans conceive of the sacred, and he does so using explicitly Western terms. There is almost an exasperation to Deloria's discussion, though, a tone of frustration because he seems very aware that in his attempt to compare Native categories to Western ones, he is translating, and this act of translation is an interpretation and, in the end, a distortion. It is a paradox, since Native American groups must adopt the language of the West in order to defend themselves against Western understandings of land and property and ownership. Deloria says that some sites possess an "inherent sacredness, sites that are holy in and of themselves.... These holy places are locations where human beings have always gone to communicate and be with higher spiritual powers."[37]

The American Indian Religious Freedom Act (AIRFA), put into place in 1978, attempts to address the legal issue of the sacredness of certain places for Native Americans. The act is explicitly intended "to protect and preserve for American Indians their inherent right of freedom to believe, express, and exercise the traditional religions of the American Indian, Eskimo, Aleut, and Native Hawaiians, including but not limited to access to sites, use and possession of sacred objects, and the freedom to worship through ceremonials and traditional rites."[38] The problem, though, is that this Act has done little to aid Native groups in protecting places they regard as sacred. "Lacking a workable metric to determine the importance and authenticity of religious claims," points out Collins, "judges rest their decisions almost entirely on the adequacy of secular justifications for denying religious claims, and most contested claims lose."[39]

Deloria is blunt on this point, calling AIRFA "simply a policy statement with 'no teeth.'"[40] Discussing a dispute involving the U.S. Forest Service's attempt to build a highway on the Chimney Rock area of the Six Rivers National Forest in northern California, Deloria points out that the court's understanding of religion and the sacred is not the same as that held by Native Americans. There is, Deloria argues, a "great gulf that exists between what traditional Westerners think about religion and the Indian perspective."[41] Deloria wants, then, to retain the language of the sacred in discussing the importance of particular places for Native Americans, but not necessarily the meaning that is typically affixed to the sacred. It is a dilemma, and it gives rise to a rather vicious paradox, since perhaps the greatest irony in the claim for the sacredness of Mato Tipila is that as much as such language has power in influencing public sentiment about the conflict, "sacred" generally has no legal purchase in the United States. As Miller puts it, specifically discussing a legal case in Washington State involving a proposed quarry site on private land claimed as sacred by indigenous groups, efforts "to construct a notion of sacredness in court as a means of creating legal space appears akin to a cultural defense in criminal litigation in that the court must accept premises which are neither shared by the judges' own cultures or the legal sub-culture and thereby stand outside of their values and experiences."[42]

There are, of course, all sorts of culturally significant objects and places that are protected by the United States' legal system. For instance, the Antiquities Act, which the United States Congress put into place in 1906, allows the president to designate a wide range of publicly owned places as national monuments: "historic landmarks, historic and prehistoric structures, and other objects of historic or scientific interest."[43] Under the provisions of this act, not only the place, but also the significant objects located there are protected: any "person who shall appropriate, excavate, injure, or destroy any historic or prehistoric ruin or monument, or object of antiquity" without permission is subject to punishment.[44] There is also the National Register of Historic Places, which was established by the National Historic Preservation Act of 1966, which protects, among other places, "traditional cultural property," which refers to "those beliefs, customs, and practices of a living community of people that have been passed down through the generations, usually orally or through practice." This designation encompasses buildings, neighborhoods, communities, and locations that possess "traditional cultural significance," and this significance is "derived from the role the property plays in a community's historically rooted beliefs, customs, and practices."[45] Devils Tower is listed on the National Register of Historic Places.

However, such designations are very frequently contested, and are themselves no guarantee that a place will be protected. In the case discussed by Miller, Native American groups protested the quarry site because they considered it a spiritually charged place, a "Hot Place" in the

Lushootseed language of the Upper Skagit Tribe.[46] This in itself was not enough to prevent a quarry on the site. As Miller notes, although physical objects such as petroglyphs and historic buildings are protected, excluded from protection "are perhaps the majority of cultural resources defined by the tribes themselves. Vision quest sites, for example, are said to have left no 'footprints;' spiritual beings and Aboriginal supplicants are not well preserved in the archaeological record, often leaving nothing or only small anthropogenic stone structures."[47] Thus it is not enough for a place to be considered religiously significant: there must be a physical object to mark this significance. In the case Miller discusses, the area in which the proposed quarry was to be located was also mythologically significant to the Upper Skagit Tribe: "In short, this small area was among the most spiritually freighted locations in the Skagit Valley."[48] When Deloria writes, "Tradition tells us that there are, on this earth, some places of inherent sacredness, sites that are Holy in and of themselves,"[49] he knows that the best he can hope for is that such language will sway public opinion. It is a moral sentiment, certainly, and also perhaps a theological claim, but it is not enough to legally protect such places.

During surveys of the area in Washington discussed by Harkin, archaeologists discovered what they believed to be a petroglyph of a double-headed snake in the immediate vicinity. As Miller notes, "The site therefore appeared to qualify for protection under Washington state law, Chapter 27.44, Indian Graves and Records, which protects 'glyphic or painted record of any tribe.' "[50] As attorneys for both sides argued the case before the courts, the petroglyph became the focus of the case, with attorneys for the plaintiffs arguing that it was not, in fact, a cultural artifact. The family who owned the contested land brought in a variety of experts, one of whom used radiocarbon dating on the rock, concluding that the object in question was not a petroglyph at all, but marks on a rock made by a bulldozer. One person's sacred, it appears, is another person's construction damage. In the end, the Native American claims were rejected, and the quarry project moved forward. Miller points out that in this case, "a positivistic, scientific narrative was preferred to oral traditions of the tribe," and the courts failed "to distinguish between what was culturally significant, namely a site where the spirit powers reside, and the secondary representation of the site, namely the petroglyph."[51]

The idea, then, that a place might be regarded as spiritually or religiously significant because it is the place where powerful beings reside is not recognized by the courts. Thus an object regarded as culturally or historically significant is enough to legally protect a place, but mythic or spiritual associations are not. Miller cites another case, a 1990 British Columbia land claim in which a judge rejected native claims on a territory that was mythologically significant to them: a supernatural bear caused an avalanche at the site. As Miller puts it, "the court recognizes no concept of land tenure in which land belongs to the supernatural, rather than to the Aboriginal people who express their relation to the immortal beings as one of subordination or supplication."[52] There is, in short, no legal test for sacredness, and this is not unrelated to the fact that there is no agreed-upon definition of what the sacred is, or on what makes a place sacred. It is a category that proves every bit as slippery in the legal as in the cultural context. Again, Miller puts it well: "The very idea of sacred sites requires judges to endow the landscape with cultural properties beyond the reach and outside the conventional rules of local civil authorities because of the problems of establishing sacredness as a legal fact, and because of the court's requirement of differentiating between sacred, partially sacred, and non sacred landscapes."[53]

In an interesting and ironic sort of way, those who have sued for the right to climb on Devils Tower have also tapped into the discourse of the sacred, and, in so doing, have also attempted to make a kind of ontological connection to place. The main thrust of the climbers' claim is that the tower is a publicly owned place, a national park, and as such a place intended for all Americans, and at times they use religiously charged language in articulating this. "Climbing on Devils Tower is a spiritual experience for me," pronounced Andy Petefish, the commercial guide who was one of the plaintiffs in the 1996 lawsuit.[54] The climbers argue that they should be free to use the park in a manner appropriate to the vision of the National Parks, a vision, as we have seen, that is intimately enmeshed in a particular vision of America. The original vision of the parks—a vision that is really an ideology, one that is very much alive today—as the Organic Act of 1916 puts it, was that they were to be pristine places to be preserved "for the benefit and enjoyment of the people." The parks embody all sorts of American values, but the notion of freedom is particularly prominent. Much can be said about the place of the idea of freedom in the United States' ethos, but it is not, I think, a stretch to say that freedom is at the ontological core of the United States of America's, and Americans', sense of self. Thus for those climbers who have objected to the climbing ban, and who filed the first lawsuit in 1996, the ban was seen as a restriction on their freedom, and in a sense a restriction on their very being.

The district court agreed with the climbers in June of 1996, citing the First Amendment and arguing that the ban amounted to "government entanglement with religion."[55] The court pronounced: "While the government has the right and even the obligation to accommodate American Indian religious practices at Devils Tower, it cannot do so by forcing guides to refrain from leading ascents of the tower in June solely because some Indians find the activity offensive."[56] Then-Secretary of the Interior Bruce Babbitt promptly revoked the ban. In April of 1998, however, the case was dismissed: the ban, the court ruled two years after the initial decisions, was "in the nature of accommodation, not promotion, and consequently is a legitimate secular purpose."[57] This was in keeping with legislation, beginning in the 1970s, which was intended to promote greater understanding of and tolerance for Native American practices. Indeed, in 1996 President Bill Clinton issued an Executive Order that required federal agencies to accommodate Native American ritual practices at their sacred sites and to "avoid adversely affecting the physical integrity of such sacred sites."[58]

The ruling to dismiss the case was appealed, and the United States Court of Appeals for the Tenth Circuit affirmed the lower court's decision, holding that the plaintiffs lacked standing to challenge the ban because they were not, by their own admission, prohibited from climbing because of the ban, and also because the guide, Petefish, had not demonstrated that he had suffered any economic injury because of the ban. Furthermore, the court did not, because the plaintiffs lacked standing, consider the constitutional issue. The plaintiffs then sought to have the case reviewed by the United States Supreme Court. They argued that the ban was not really voluntary, and that they were adversely affected as a result of the government privileging of religious activities on federal land: "When the federal government demands adherence to religious orthodoxy by threatening to close public lands in the absence of such adherence, that action constitutes coercion in violation of the Establishment Clause."[59] In their written refusal to consider the case, the Supreme Court, significantly, quoted parts of the amici brief that was filed in response to the original case—parts of which did indeed appeal to the Native Americans' conception of the sacredness of Mato Tipila—noting the cultural significance of the place for Native Americans.

In the struggles over Mato Tipila, some have adopted the language of sacred in regard to the place, whereas others have rejected such a label. Although such language has obvious theological—and particularly Biblical—associations, and although "sacred" is a Euro-American category, it is a word that has also been used as a powerful rhetorical tool. As I have said, "sacred" is an argument to be made, but it can also be used to more powerfully make an argument. In the Native American context, Mato Tipila is certainly a special place, a powerful place where powerful beings are thought to reside, and where important rituals related to those powerful beings are performed. For some Native Americans it is called a sacred place. As such, it is a place that is intimately linked to ontology, with the very core of being; as Heidegger might put it—as paraphrased by David Harvey—place is the "locale of the truth of being."[60]

Of course, as much as Heidegger may speak to the focus of this book—the centrality of place in the lives of religious communities and individuals—the sentiment does little to resolve the very real, on-the-ground struggles over place. These struggles are, as I have maintained throughout, as much about identity as they are about property and ownership. It has certainly not been my intent to provide a solution to such disputes; when it comes to place, it is indeed doubtful that we can all just get along. Viewed from one angle, the dispute over Mato Tipila/Devils Tower offers up a model for how such disputes might be resolved, in that the various groups with claims on the tower did indeed talk to one another, and for the most part they did so in an intentional spirit of cooperation and accommodation. That said, though, I am quite certain that such conflicts over religiously significant places will continue as long as external groups—such as the Archaeological Survey of India, or UNESCO, or real estate developers, or the United States government—wield disproportionate power in deciding what sort of places these are and what sorts of people are permitted to use them and what sorts of uses are permitted.

8

Fences and Walls: A Not-So-Final Reflection on Preservations, Prohibitions, and Places in Motion

He only says, "Good fences make good neighbors."
Spring is the mischief in me, and I wonder
If I could put a notion in his head:
"Why do they make good neighbors? Isn't it
Where there are cows?
But here there are no cows.
Before I built a wall I'd ask to know
What I was walling in or walling out,
And to whom I was like to give offence.
Something there is that doesn't love a wall,
That wants it down."

—ROBERT FROST, *"Mending Wall"*

The question of boundaries is the first be encountered; from it all others flow. To draw a boundary around anything is to define, analyze and reconstruct it.

—FERNAND BRAUDEL[1]

A FENCE IS, among other things, a means of definition, specifically a means to define a place, or, more properly, two places. A fence marks a here and a there, a "this side" and a "that side"—or, as is perhaps more usually the case, a "my side" and a "your side." Fences are, typically, arbitrary things;

place a fence in the middle of an open field, anywhere in that field, and there are then two fields where there had been one. But of course fences are much more than that, as Frost, I think, is intimating,

A fence, a wall in this case, is also a walling out, a means of separating and defining—this is, after all, what definition is all about—and this separating is more often than not likely to give offense, likely to be perceived, by someone who finds themselves on the wrong side of the wall, or on any side at all, as aggressive. The massive wall that separates the Palestinians from the Israelis—the so-called Israeli West Bank Barrier—is an offense to those Palestinians; it is a prohibition, a restriction, a means of walling them in and walling them out. The notion of the sacred, as it is applied to a place such as Devils Tower, is also a kind of wall, albeit a metaphorical wall. It is a means of defining, and, as such, of limiting and prohibiting.

David Chidester, in his important book *Savage Systems*, uses the term "apartheid comparative religion" to describe the ways in which academics have constructed these sorts of fences, or borders:

> [A]partheid comparative religion sought local control in global terms...this approach to comparative religion has been committed to identifying and reifying the many languages, cultures, peoples, and religions of the world as if they were separate and distinct regions. Each religion has to be understood as a separate, hermetically sealed compartment into which human beings can be classified and divided.[2]

There are, as Chidester demonstrates, real effects of this sort of discourse; again, it is a discourse that came to be, in the Southern African case as well as throughout the colonized world, a means of control and exploitation. Such "hermetically sealed" compartments are a means of othering, a means of producing an "us" and a "them"—and a "them" that, frequently, needs to be dominated. As Daniel Boyarin starkly puts it, "Borders themselves are not given but constructed by power to mask hybridity, to occlude and disown it."[3]

As we have seen throughout these chapters, to define a place—or an object or a person—is also, always, to define what it or he or she is not. Bodhgayā is a Buddhist place, not a Hindu place; America is for Americans, not Muslims; Bear Lodge is a sacred place, not a playground, and so on. But as Boyarin insists, religious people, and I would extend this to religious places, are hybrid: "The religious dialect map is a hybridized one, and the point is that that hybridity extends even to those religious groups that would consider themselves 'purely' Jewish or 'purely' Christian in their self-understanding."[4] For many scholars and students of religion, though, this is a very difficult idea to accept, and even when a nod is given to Bhabha's notion of hybridity, it is typically business as usual when we go about teaching our courses and writing our books and articles, with neat divisions between what is Jewish and what is Christian, or what is Buddhist and what is Hindu.[5]

Borders, like definitions, are tentative things. I write this from my office in Denver; if I had been sitting here two centuries ago I would be in Mexico, and two centuries before that I would be in land not defined at all, or at least not in terms of borders and states and nations. One of the most dramatic recent examples of this was the partitioning of India and Pakistan in 1947; suddenly, there was a border where there had been none, an arbitrary line that defined not just territory, but, in very significant ways, identity. Suddenly one belonged to either Pakistan or India, with all of the attendant religious complexities of those belongings—and these quickly became political and social and economic and military complexities as well. The problem, however, the devil in these particular details, is the way such borders become fixed, become reified. Borders, labels, definitions—these are peculiar things, because they pose as natural and permanent entities, when, as we know, as we have seen throughout this book, they are very much not permanent and not static, but in constant flux.

In my discussion of UNESCO's involvement at Bodhgayā in Chapter 5, I was quite critical of the sorts of "fixing" that an organization such as UNESCO engages in, because, among other things, it involves an imposition by an outside group—a very powerful Western organization, after all—of a particular view of the world, a particular *epistemé*, to use Foucault's term. And as I argued in that chapter, and as I also argued in my discussion in Chapter 3 of the ways the Archaeological Survey of India "fixed" temples and images, there is a not-so-subtle hegemony at work here. These organizations impose a particular order of things.

When the National Park Service was created in 1916, its mandate was to preserve the natural beauty of the parks, to freeze them, as it were, and preserve them in their pristine, original state. As Ross-Bryant nicely puts this:

> Central to the symbolic power of the national park has been the connection between the actual site and the idea of a *changeless*

> pristine America and an understanding of the sacred that is coincident with this unchanging reality. The discourse surrounding this symbol, however, is constantly changing, as are the parks. The creative tension between this attachment to a timeless ideal and the actualities of change is at the heart of the national park as a sacred site, a place that is seen as set apart, immune to the passage of time and the imperfections of life in the world. Sacred places are often said to have these characteristics. In a sacred place, things do not change.[6]

But things do change—that is Ross-Bryant's point. "Of course, this doesn't actually happen in any sacred space— humans and their cultural creations are always in the process of change." Firstspace is rarely just that, and becomes Thirdspace through use and through the sorts of Secondspace imaginings that all of these places participate in. The sort of "creative tension" Ross-Bryant is interested in can mean that one worshiper sees Viṣṇu's footprint, another the Buddha's; this can mean that one person sees a gnarly place to climb, while another sees a place for the performance of solemn rituals. And as much as these sorts of tensions can be creative, they can also be strikingly destructive.

Where does religion end and the secular begin in all of this? It is a rhetorical question, but one worth posing nonetheless. When the climbing guide Andy Petefish says, "Climbing on Devils Tower is a spiritual experience for me," is he really making a religious claim? For the Hindus who claim Ayodhya as the birthplace of Rāma, it is certainly a claim about religion, but it is also about many other things: about power, crudely put, but also about identity and social location and about straight-up alienation and aggression. For the young men who stormed the mosque, they were surely acting as much as disenfranchised underemployed youth as militant Hindu fundamentalists.

It is in part we who decide to foreground a particular identity, labeling certain sorts of actors religious, others secular. For the Dalits who have agitated at Bodhgayā in recent years, their aims are as much about religious access to the temple as about a rejection of an imputed social identity and location. Likewise, Pamela Geller's attacks on Islam, as distasteful as they are, are not simply attacks on religion, but also assertions of what she, and her followers, perceive as normative American identity, which for many of Geller's followers precludes Islam. What I think is interesting about the resolution of the Devils Tower dispute—if it is indeed a resolution—is that the place continues to be understood by those who claim it as both a sacred and a secular place, and a sacred place with multiple resonances. In other words, it continues to be in motion.

I have perhaps too quickly moved on from my point about walls and definitions and labels; surely it is not as simple as the labels that we scholars—or any other observer, for that matter—put on particular places and the disputes that swirl around them. Part of what determines what sort of conflict is involved is the orientation of the actors on the ground. The Native Americans protesting what they see as the desecration of a sacred place are acting first as Native Americans, and their objection is in large part a matter of what we—and not necessarily they, since "religion" is not necessarily something Native Americans think they are engaged in—call religion. The issue, for them, is the pollution of their sacred place. The rock climbers, typically although not exclusively, are not making a religious claim, although religion is obviously at the heart of the matter, since their lawsuit was based on an interpretation of the Establishment Clause of the United States Constitution. When Imam Feisel Abdul Rauf rejected the designation "sacred space" for the area around Ground Zero, he was in part attempting to remove religion from the discussion, which for some Americans is nonsensical, since the center planned for Park51 is a Muslim community center, not simply a community center. And here is the complexity of the wall: even if only one person or group erects a wall, it is a wall, nonetheless, for both groups.

Walls, like borders, are temporary things. Walls go up, certainly, as is painfully evident to the Palestinians living in the shadows—and quite obviously on the wrong side—of the so-called Israeli West Bank Barrier. Walls come down as well; there is no longer an East and a West Berlin, just Berlin. Likewise, the wall separating the religious and the non-religious, the sacred and the secular, is never absolute. The sacred is contagious in a way somewhat different from that meant by Durkheim. It seeps in and out. As Frost puts it, "Something there is that doesn't love a wall / That wants it down." I began this book with Robert Orsi's provocative injunction: "This is a call, then, for attention to religious messiness, to multiplicities, to seeing religious spaces as always, inevitably, and profoundly intersected by things brought into them from outside, things that bear their own histories, complexities, meanings different from those offered within the religious space." In motion, messy, hybrid—such is the nature of the places I have been discussing in this book.

I hope, in the end, to have provoked an attention not just to messiness—although I think that is crucial—but also to the particularity of religiously charged places and the actors who engage and constitute them. What is at stake? In part, it is a matter of understanding the complexity of place and responding to this complexity appropriately. Take as an example the Taliban's destruction of the Buddhas at Bamiyan in 2001, which I have discussed at several junctures of this book. This was an act that was certainly about place, about a place designated by UNESCO as culturally significant, a place that was marked by some in the West as belonging to the entire world. The Taliban did not see it this way. This was their place, and UNESCO had no right to designate or dictate anything to do with it. If they wanted to destroy it and all of the other vestiges of foreign religion in their country, then that was their right. To stop there, however, is to miss what was going on, to miss the political and the human dimensions of their act of iconoclasm. Jonathan Z. Smith has remarked more than once that the role of the scholar is to seek more and more complexity. As I said in the Preface of this book, my own question is always some variation of "What's going on here?" There can be no static answer to this question. The places I have discussed here are in motion, as Appadurai would have it, and the conflicted and tense negotiations over their significance, on the ground, is ongoing, as should be our analysis of them. I have noted at several junctures that I am suspicious of the very term "sacred space"—or "sacred place," as the case may be—and although I have used "sacred" a great deal throughout this book, I remain uneasy with the term. But it is my dis-ease with the easy label, with the unexamined generalization, that has held my interest.

Place matters, we might say. The questions remain, though: how? why? when? for whom? In these chapters, I have provided, I think, some specific, contextual answers to these questions. I have tried to demonstrate what is at stake in a particular context. It is an ongoing discussion, in part, as I have argued, because these places do not sit still—they are in motion.

Notes

PREFACE

1. Robert A. Orsi, *Between Heaven and Earth: The Religious Worlds People Make and the Scholars Who Study Them* (Princeton, NJ: Princeton University Press, 2005), 167.
2. Barbara Bender, "Place and Landscape," in *Handbook of Material Culture*, ed. C. Tilley, W. Keene, S. Kuechler, R. Rowlands, and P. Spyer, 303–314 (London: Sage, 2006), 303.
3. James Legge, *A Record of Buddhistic Kingdoms, Being an Account by the Chinese Monk Fa-Hien of his Travels in India and Ceylon (A.D. 399–414) in Search of the Buddhist Books of Discipline* (Oxford: Clarendon Press, 1886), 124.
4. See my "Reevaluating the Eighth-Ninth Century Pala Milieu: Icono-Conservatism and the Persistence of Śākyamuni," *Journal of the International Association of Buddhist Studies* 20, no. 1 (1997): 281–300; see also John Huntington's series of articles, "Sowing the Seeds of the Lotus: A Journey to the Great Pilgrimage Sites of Buddhism, part I," *Orientations* 16, no. 11 (1985): 46–61; "Sowing the Seeds of the Lotus: A Journey to the Great Pilgrimage Sites of Buddhism, part II," *Orientations* 17, no. 2 (1986): 28–43; "Sowing the Seeds of the Lotus: A Journey to the Great Pilgrimage Sites of Buddhism, part I," *Orientations* 17, no. 3 (1986): 32–46; "Sowing the Seeds of the Lotus: A Journey to the Great Pilgrimage Sites of Buddhism, part IV," *Orientations* 17, no. 6 (1986): 28–40; and his "Pilgrimage as Image: the Cult of the Aṣṭamahāpratiharya, Part I, *Orientations*18, no. 4 (1987): 55–63, and "Pilgrimage as Image: the Cult of the Aṣṭamahāpratiharya, Part II, *Orientations* 18, no. 8 (1987): 56–68.
5. Edward Soja, *Thirdspace: Journeys to Los Angeles and Other Real-and-Imagined Places* (Oxford: Blackwell, 1996), 56.
6. John Berquist, "Theories of Space and Construction of the Ancient World," paper presented in the Constructs of the Social and Cultural Worlds of Antiquity Group, 1999, 6.
7. Soja, 56–57.
8. Ibid., 10.

9. Ibid., 5.
10. For a fuller articulation of her methodology, see Wendy Doniger, *The Implied Spider: Politics and Theology in Myth* (New York: Columbia University Press, 1998).
11. Jonathan Z. Smith, "Differential Equations: On Constructing the Other," in *Relating Religion: Essays in the Study of Religion* (Chicago: University of Chicago Press, 2004), 230–251.
12. Shields, *Places on the Margin: Alternative Geographies of Modernity* (London: Routledge, 1991), 6.
13. For a difficult but fecund overview—which is really much more than just an overview—see Soja's *Postmodern Geographies: The Reassertion of Space in Critical Social Theory* (London: Verso, 1989), or, for a different sort of overview, Edward S. Casey, *The Fate of Place: A Philosophical History* (California: University of California Press, 1997). For a more accessible survey of some of the major thinkers here, see Tim Cresswell, *Place: A Short Introduction* (London: Blackwell, 2004), as well as Shields, *Places on the Margin*, particularly chapter one, and also Margaret Rodman's very useful article, "Empowering Place: Multilocality and Multivocality," *American Anthropologist* 94, no. 3 (1992): 640–656.
14. Soja, *Thirdspace*, 2.
15. Shields, *Places on the Margin*, 10.

CHAPTER 1

1. Victor Turner and Edith Turner, *Image and Pilgrimage in Christian Culture* (New York: Columbia University Press, 1978), 9.
2. Charles Tilly, "Contentious Conversation," *Social Research* 65, no. 3 (1998): 491–510, 493.
3. Pierre Bourdieu, *In Other Words: Essays Toward a Reflexive Sociology* (Stanford, CA: Stanford University Press, 1990), 134.
4. Jonathan Z. Smith, *To Take Place: Toward Theory in Ritual* (Chicago: University of Chicago Press, 1987), 28.
5. For instance, James J. Preston, in a very useful piece that articulates an interdisciplinary methodology and typology for the study of pilgrimage, nonetheless writes of what at times is a peculiarly agentless, and I think theologically suspect, "spiritual magnetism" created by and present at pilgrimage places; see James J. Preston, "Spiritual Magnetism: An Organizing Principle for the Study of Pilgrimage," in *Sacred Journeys: The Anthropology of Pilgrimage*, ed. Alan Morinis, 31–46 (Westport, CT: Greenwood Press, 1992); see also Belden C. Lane, who writes that "sacred place is not chosen, it chooses.... Sacred place, therefore, is a construction of the imagination that affirms the independence of the holy. God chooses to reveal himself only where he wills." *Landscapes of*

the Sacred: Geography and Narrative in American Spirituality (Baltimore: Johns Hopkins University Press, 2001), 19.

6. David Chidester and Edward T. Linenthal, "Introduction," *American Sacred Space*, ed. David Chidester and Edward T. Linenthal, 1–42 (Bloomington: Indiana University Press, 1995), 17.
7. George Marcus, "Imagining the Whole: Ethnography's Contemporary Efforts to Situate Itself," *Critique of Anthropology* 9, no. 3 (1989): 7–30, 25.
8. See Claude Lévi-Strauss, *Introduction to the Work of Marcel Mauss*, trans. Felicity Baker (London: Routledge, 1987); cited in J. Z. Smith, *To Take Place*, 107. Smith cites the French original, *Sociologie et anthropologie: pécédé d'une introduction à l'oeuvre de marcel Mauss* (Paris: Presses universitires de France, 1950), xlix.
9. Roger Friedland and Richard D. Hecht, "The Politics of Sacred Place: Jerusalem's Temp Mount/*al-haram al-sharif*," in *Sacred Places and Profane Spaces: Essays in the Geographies of Judaism, Christianity, and Islam*, ed. Jamie Scott and Paul Simpson-Housley, 21–61 (Westport, CT: Greenwood Press, 1991), 55; see also their "The Bodies of Nations: A Comparative Study of Religious Violence in Jerusalem and Ayodhya," *History of Religions* 38, no. 2 (1998): 101–149, and "Changing Places: Jerusalem's Holy Places in Comparative Perspective," *Israel Affairs* 5, nos. 2–3 (1999): 200–225. For more on the social construction of place and space, see Henri Lefebvre's now classic *The Production of Space*, trans. D. Nicholson-Smith (Oxford: Basil Blackwell, 1991).
10. See, for instance, Richard Davis, *Lives of Indian Images* (Princeton, NJ: Princeton University Press, 1997), for an account of the various identities a single image can take on.
11. For a clear treatment of this in the American context, see the Pew Forum on Religion and Public Life's 2008 "U.S. Religious Landscape Survey," accessed November 11, 2011, http://religions.pewforum.org/.
12. There is a great deal of literature on the topic: see for instance Sebastian Kim, *In Search of Identity: Debates on Religious Conversion in India* (Oxford: Oxford University Press, 2005), and Rowena Robinson and Sathianathan Clark, *Religious Conversion in India: Modes, Motivations, and Meanings* (Oxford: Oxford University Press, 2007), and also Sumit Sarkar "Hindutva and the Question of Conversions," in *The Concerned Indian's Guide to Communalism*, ed. K. N. Panikkar, 73–106 (New Delhi: Viking, New Delhi 1990).
13. Daniel Boyarin, *Border Lines: The Partition of Judaeo-Christinity* (Philadelphia: University of Pennsylvania Press, 2004), xi.
14. Ibid., 19.
15. See Homi K. Bhabha, *The Location of Culture* (London: Routledge, 1994).
16. Victor Turner, *The Ritual Process* (Ithaca, NY: Cornell University Press, 1969), 139.
17. For a discussion of the broad impact of the Turnerian approach to the study of pilgrimage, see Simon Coleman, "Do You Believe in Pilgrimage?"

Anthropological Theory 2, no. 3 (2002): 355–68, 356; the articles in John Eade and Michael Sallnow, eds., *Contesting the Sacred: The Anthropology of Christian Pilgrimage* (Urbana: University of Illinois Press, 2000); and Ann Gold, "Still Liminal after All These Years," in *Teaching Ritual*, ed. Catherine Bell, 29–45 (Oxford: Oxford University Press, 2007).

18. For one of the most concise treatments of the sort of contestation I mean, see Friedland and Hecht, "The Politics of Sacred Place."
19. More violence would break out in Gujarat and elsewhere in March of 2002, after a fire "broke out" on a train filled with pilgrims—or activists, depending on whose account is believed—on their way to Ayodhya; see Agsar Ali Engineer, *The Gujarat Carnage* (Hyderbad: Orient Longman, 2003); M. L. Sondhi, and Apratim Mukarji, eds., *The Black Book of Gujarat* (Delhi: Manak Publications, 2002); and Siddharth Varadarajan, *Gujarat, the Making of a Tragedy* (London and Delhi: Penguin Books, 2002).
20. This attempt to create a pan-Indian Hindu national identity dates to the late nineteenth century, and the emergence of Hindu political groups such as the Brahmo Samaj, Arya Samaj, Rashtriya Swayamsevak Sangh, and others.
21. One could also argue that the very construct "communitas" is only a romanticized—and perhaps also theologically utopian—ideal that does not, and I would say cannot, actually exist on the ground; I will address this issue below.
22. Victor Turner, *Dramas, Fields, and Metaphors: Symbolic Action in Human Society* (Ithaca, NY: Cornell University Press, 1974), 202.
23. Victor Turner, "Variations on a Theme of Liminality," in *Secular Ritual*, ed. Sally Moore, 27–41 (Leiden: van Gorcum, 1978).
24. Turner, *Dramas, Fields, and Metaphors*, 274.
25. Turner quotes Hume here, referring to his sense of an "egalitarian 'sentiment for humanity'," ibid., 274.
26. Turner, *The Ritual Process*, 132.
27. Ibid., 136.
28. Ibid., 137.
29. Ibid., 132.
30. Turner and Turner, *Image and Pilgrimage*, 135.
31. It is important to point out, I think, that this is a late work, written with his wife, Edith Turner, and as such is very much a meditative and retrospective look back at his own substantial body of work.
32. Turner and Turner, *Image and Pilgrimage*, 135–137.
33. Ibid., 136–137.
34. Turner, *The Ritual Process*, 132.
35. Turner and Turner, *Image and Pilgrimage*, 137.
36. Caroline Walker Bynum, "Women's Stories, Women's Symbols: A Critique of Victor Turner's Theory of Liminality," in *Anthropology and the Study of Religion*, ed. Frank Reynolds and Robert Moore, 105–25 (Chicago: Center for the Scientific Study of Religion, 1984), 106.

37. See Jonathan Z. Smith, "The Bare Facts of Ritual," *History of Religions* 20 (1980): 112–127, and also his *To Take Place*, especially chapter five.
38. This may seem counterintuitive, given that ritual is almost universally agreed to be marked by invariance, but one needs only think of the many instances in which ritual agents improvise and respond, ad hoc, to unforeseen developments. Furthermore, there are countless examples of the ritual "creation" of chaos—and here we can thank Turner for consistently emphasizing anti-structure—such as the Indian practice of Holi; see Lawrence Babb, *The Divine Hierarchy: Popular Hinduism in Central India* (New York: Columbia University Press, 1975), 168–175.
39. Sudhir Kakar, *The Colors of Violence: Cultural Identities, Religion, and Conflict* (Chicago: University of Chicago Press,1996), 41.
40. Among the many treatments on the subject, see in particular Peter van der Veer, *Religious Nationalism: Hindus and Muslims in India* (Berkeley: University of California Press, 1994); Amrita Basu, "Mass Movement or Elite Conspiracy? The Puzzle of Hindu Nationalism," in *Contesting the Nation: Religion, Community, and the Politics of Democracy in India*, ed. David Ludden, 55–80 (Philadelphia: University of Pennsylvania Press, 1996); Tapan Basu et al., *Khaki Shorts and Saffron Flags: A Critique of the Hindu Right* (Hyderbad: Orient Longman, 1993); and Ashis Nandy et al., *Creating a Nationality: The Ramjanmabhumi Movement and Fear of the Self* (Delhi: Oxford University Press, 1995). More generally, on the topic of how to understand and analyze religious violence in South Asia, see Gyanedra Pandey's, "In Defense of the Fragment: Writing about Hindu-Muslim Riots in India Today," *Representations* 37 (1992): 27–55; E. Valentine Daniel, *Charred Lullabies: Chapters in an Anthropography of Violence* (Princeton, NJ: Princeton University Press, 1996); and Stanley J. Tambiah, *Leveling Crowds: Ethnonationalist Conflicts and Collective Violence in South Asia* (Berkeley: University of California Press, 1996).
41. Ludden, *Contesting the Nation*, 10.
42. Tapan Basu et al., *Khaki Shorts*, 1; see also 4–6.
43. See William R. Pinch, "Soldier Monks and Militant Sadhus," in Ludden, *Contesting the Nation*, 140–161.
44. Richard H. Davis, "The Iconography of Rama's Chariot," in Ludden, *Contesting the Nation*, 27–54, 38; Davis suggests that the very idea of the Babri Masjid as marking the place of Rāma's birth probably originated in this act. The British, at any rate, seemed to take this as a fact from this point on. For more on the political and religious uses of the figure of Rāma in the context of communal violence in India, see Anuradha Kapur, "Deity to Crusader: The Changing Iconography of Ram," in *Hindus and Others: The Question of Identity in India Today*, ed. Gyanendra Pandey, 74–109 (New Delhi: Viking Penguin, 1993).
45. Davis, "The Iconography of Rama's Chariot," 40; see also H. V. Seshyadri, ed., *RSS: A Vision in Action* (Bangalore: Sahitya Sindhu Prakashana, 1988).
46. Davis, "The Iconography of Rama's Chariot," 40.

47. The symbolic language of the "liberation" of the temples was, quite explicitly, charged with the image of Rāma himself freeing the captive Sita from the evil Ravana, a story that is at the very center of the *Ramayana* narrative.
48. Davis, "The Iconography of Rama's Chariot," 40.
49. Ibid., 41.
50. Ibid.; see also Tapan Basu et al., *Khaki Shorts*, 60.
51. Amrita Basu, "Mass Movement or Elite Conspiracy?" 64.
52. Tapan Basu et al., *Khaki Shorts*, 59.
53. The choice of Gujarat was intended, surely, to provoke violence, given the particular political and religious unrest there at the time. This sort of violence would erupt again in early 2002, when a group of Muslims clashed with Hindus on board a train on "pilgrimage" way to Ayodhya. The specific details of this event remain contested, but it is unquestionable that the Muslims were not unprovoked, nor that the route taken by the pilgrims, and the behavior of some of them, was not at least in part intended to increase tensions.
54. This media coverage was extremely important to the BJP, for although the crowds were enormous along the Yatra's path, the majority of those gathered were poor. The press coverage, as Thomas Blo Hansen has noted, was clearly targeted at the middle class; see Hansen, *Saffron Wave: Democracy and Hindu Nationalism in Modern India* (Princeton, NJ: Princeton University Press, 199), 169.
55. Davis, "The Iconography of Rama's Chariot," 44.
56. Nandy et al., *Creating a Nationality*, 95.
57. This is a highly charged issue, dating back at least a century—the cow is a potent signifier, the image of a pure, Hindu India, and the Muslims, as both butchers and consumers of beef, stand as the threat to this powerful image; see, for instance, Beth Roy, *Some Trouble with Cows: Making Sense of Social Conflict* (Berkeley: University of California Press, 1994).
58. Nandy et al., *Creating a Nationality*, 96–98.
59. See K. Roy, "Coming Storm," *Frontline* (October 13–26, 1990): 26–29.
60. Tapan Basu et al., *Khaki Shorts*, 62.
61. Nandy et al., *Creating a Nationality*, 123.
62. Ibid., 135.
63. Ibid., 28.
64. Ibid., 29.
65. Ibid., 31.
66. Hansen, *Saffron Wave*, 165.
67. Ibid., 168–170.
68. Hansen has referred to a certain "Ayodhya fatigue" that had by then set in, marked by a decidedly lukewarm public reaction; see *Saffron Wave*, 182–183, and 262–263n54.
69. There can be little doubt that the Bajrang Dal and karsevaks were carefully trained. Advani, at a meeting in Azangarh in Uttar Pradesh on December 2

went so far as to say that the young men would be "physical with bricks and shovels," an utterance that he would later deny. Furthermore, eyewitnesses reported that an RSS member was stationed atop a tower, shouting directions to the karsevaks and blowing a whistle, like the coach of an athletic team. See in particular Nandy et al., *Creating a Nationality*.

70. In an official "White Paper" published by the BJP in 1993, the destruction of the Babri Masjid is called "unexpected" and "spontaneous" (131–132).
71. Émile Durkheim, *The Elementary Forms of Religious Life*, trans. Carol Cosman (New York: Oxford University Press, 2001), 230.
72. Tapan Basu et al., *Khaki Shorts*, 58.
73. Van Gennep, *The Rites of Passage*, trans. Monika B. Vizedom and Gabrielle L. Caffee (Chicago: University of Chicago Press, 1960).
74. Victor Turner, *Process, Performance, and Pilgrimage: A Study in Comparative Symbology* (New Delhi: Concept, 1979), 19.
75. Ibid., 41.
76. Hansen, *Saffron Wave*, 184.
77. Ibid., 185.
78. Kakar, *Colors of Violence*, 43. One might also invoke René Girard's conception of the ritual scapegoat here; see his chapter "Generative Scapegoating," in *Violent Origins: Walter Burkert, René Girard, and Jonathan Z. Smith on Ritual Killing and Cultural Formation*, ed. Robert G. Hamerton-Kelly, 73–148 (Stanford, CA: Stanford University Press, 1987). Certainly the nearly ubiquitous practice of possession and exorcism at the culmination of pilgrimage can be seen as a means through which an other is ritually constructed and then banished or defeated, a process that fundamentally leads to group identity if not actual communitas. In this sense, the anonymous Muslim is substituted for the demon or scapegoat.
79. Kakar, *Colors of Violence*, 43.
80. Ibid., 45.
81. David Kertzer, *Ritual, Politics, and Power* (New Haven, CT: Yale University Press, 1988), 40. For a useful discussion of the limitations of Durkheim for understanding ritual and politics, 67–68; see also, for a rather different view, Charles Tilly, "Contentious Conversations and his interesting discussion of what he calls the "conversational dynamics of such disputes," which contrasts somewhat with Kakar's more individual-centered analysis, and in which he articulates an useful critique of the tendency toward instrumentalist reductionism in the analysis of the socio-religio-political conflict. As he nicely puts it, "the Hindu/Muslim conversation engages multiple interlocutors in varied settings. It therefore takes place in many modes.... Which idioms they actually deploy and which histories they invoke, furthermore, varies with who else is participating. Because of learning and of constraint by relations to third parties, to be sure, conversations within similar and connected pairs share many properties. Yet we must understand that contentious conversation proceeds through

incessant improvisation within limits set by the previous histories and relations of particular interlocutors" (494).

82. Turner and Turner, *Image and Pilgrimage*, 38.
83. Tapan Basu et al., *Khaki Shorts*, 56.
84. Turner, *Dramas, Fields, and Metaphors*, 37–41; Turner breaks these dramas into four phases: breach, crisis, redressive action, and reintegration.
85. Turner, *Process, Performance, and Pilgrimage*, 65.
86. Ibid., 66–67.
87. Pierre Bourdieu, *Outline of a Theory of Practice*, trans. Richard Nice (Cambridge: Cambridge University Press, 1977), 72.
88. Tilly, "Contentious Conversation," 495.
89. Nandy, *Contesting the Nation*, 148.

CHAPTER 2

1. Shields, *Places on the Margin*, 6.
2. See Alan E. Morinis, *Pilgrimage in the Hindu Tradition: A Case Study of West Bengal* (Delhi: Oxford University Press, 1984), especially 165–201.
3. See David Kinsley, *Tantric Visions of the Divine Feminine: The Ten Mahāvidyās* (California: University of California Press, 1997), 92–111.
4. See Morinis, *Pilgrimage in the Hindu Tradition*.
5. See Diana Eck, *Darśan: Seeing the Divine in India* (Chambersburg, PA: Anima Books, 1981); Joanne Punzo Waghorne and Norman Cutler, eds., *Gods of Flesh/Gods of Stone: The Embodiment of Divinity in India* (Chambersburg, PA: Anima Books, 1985); and also Kathleen M. Erndl, *Victory to the Mother: The Hindu Goddess of Northwest India in Myth, Ritual, and Symbol* (New York: Oxford University Press, 1993).
6. See Diana Eck, *Banaras: City of Light* (London: Routledge and Kegan Paul, 1983); and Jonathan Parry, *Death in Banaras* (Cambridge: Cambridge University Press, 1995).
7. Kinsley, *Tantric Visions of the Divine Feminine*, 96.
8. Ibid., 97.
9. Morinis, *Pilgrimage in the Hindu Tradition*, 167.
10. Andreas Huyssen, *Present Pasts: Urban Palimpsests and the Politics of Memory* (Palo Alto, CA: Stanford University Press, 2003).
11. I do not wish to delve much further into the complex debate about memory and history, which has been raging on and off since the end of the nineteenth century, but it is worth remembering that Nietzsche, in the second of his *Untimely Meditations* (Cambridge: Cambridge University Press, 1997), talks of the hypertrophy of memory that characterizes the modern, industrial world of the nineteenth century; true enough, perhaps, although his is perhaps a rather too monoptic, Euro-centric view of the way societies remember;

among the many sources on the topic, see Paul Connerton, *How Societies Remember* (Cambridge: Cambridge University Press, 1989); and Eric Hobswan and Terrence Ranger, eds., *The Invention of Tradition* (Cambridge: Cambridge University Press, 1992).

12. I want what you have not because I want it, Girard suggests, but because you have it; René Girard, *Violence and the Sacred*, trans. Patrick Gregory (Baltimore: Johns Hopkins University Press, 1977); also see Girard, "Generative Scapegoating."
13. For more on this larger debate, see Rogers Brubaker, *Ethnicity without Groups* (Cambridge: Harvard University Press, 2004).
14. Tilly, Charles, "Contentious Conversation, 493.
15. Ibid., 498.
16. Quoted in Setha Low, "The Memorialization of September 11: Dominant and Local Discourses on the Rebuilding of the World Trade Center Site," *American Ethnologist* 31, no. 3 (2004): 326–39, 335.
17. Marita Sturken, *Tourists of History: Memory, Kitsch, and Consumerism from Oklahoma City to Ground Zero* (Durham, NC: Duke University Press, 2007), 205.
18. Sam Lubell, "Reflecting Absence Chosen as World Trade Center Memorial," *Architectural Record* 192, no. 2 (2004): 21–21, 21.
19. Sturken, *Tourists of History*, 227.
20. Jay Winter, *Sites of Memory, Sites of Mourning: The Great War in European Cultural History* (Cambridge: Cambridge University Press, 1995), 105.
21. Sturken, *Tourists of History*, 239.
22. Ibid., 227.
23. *New York Times Magazine*, November 23, 2001.
24. See David Simpson, *9/11: The Culture of Commemoration* (Chicago: University of Chicago Press, 2006), 79.
25. *New York Times*, July 2, 2002.
26. *9/11*, Jules Naudet, Gedeon Naudet, and James Hanlon, directors (Paramount Pictures, 2002).
27. Patricia Yaeger, "Rubble as Archive, or 9/11 as *Dust, Debris, and Bodily Vanishing*," in *Trauma at Home: After 9/11*, ed. Judith Greenberg, 187–194 (Lincoln: University of Nebraska Press, 2003); and Sturken, *Tourists of History*.
28. Jonathan Z. Smith, *Map Is Not Territory: Studies in the History of Religions* (Chicago: University of Chicago Press, 1978), 291.
29. *New York Daily News*, March 24, 2007.
30. Philip Nobel, *Sixteen Acres: Architecture and the Outrageous Struggle for the Future of Ground Zero* (New York: Metropolitan Books, 2004), 22.
31. Quoted in Paul Goldberger, *Up from Zero: Politics, Architecture, and the Rebuilding of New York* (New York: Random House, 2005), 37.
32. *New York Times*, June 10, 2005.
33. According to Michael Tomasky, "ground zero" was first used in relation to the attacks on the World Trade Center just hours after the event, by Larry McShane,

an Associated Press reporter; Tomasky, "Battleground Zero," *New York Review of Books*, May 1, 2003, 18; http://www.nybooks.com/articles/archives/2003/may/01/battleground-zero/, accessed October 19, 2011.

34. See Marita Sturken, *Tourists of History*, 167; see also Amy Kaplan, "Homeland Insecurities: Transformations of Language and Space," in *September 11 in History: A Watershed Moment*, ed. Mary L. Dudziak, 55–69 (Durham, NC: Duke University Press, 2002).
35. *New York Times*, September 17, 2001.
36. *New York Times*, September 23, 2001.
37. Sturken, *Tourists of History*, especially chapter 5, "Architectures of Grief and the Aesthetics of Absence"; see also Nathan Carlin and Heba Khan, "Mourning, Memorials, and Religion: A Psychoanalytic Perspective on the Park51 Controversy," *Religions* 2 (2011): 114–131.
38. *New York Times*, October 22, 2010.
39. *New York Times*, July 20, 2010.
40. Quoted in Setha Low, "The Memorialization of September 11," 333.
41. *New York Times*, December 9, 2009.
42. http:/www.cordobainitiative.org/about/, accessed October 15, 2011.
43. Newt Gingrich, for one, has called it a "deliberately insulting term" that points to Muslim conquest; statement issued on July 21, 2010, www.newtdirect.org; the statement, and indeed the website itself, has since been removed.
44. Nancy Fuch Kreimer, *Huffington Post*, May 21, 2010.
45. *Financial Times*, August 13, 2010.
46. Ibid.
47. *New York Times*, May 26, 2010.
48. *New York Daily News*, May 19, 2010. Ironically enough, this association of Islam and monkey worship has been in the air for a very long time; see Sophia Shafi, "Muslim Monsters from Prophet Muhammad to Bin Laden: Stereotypical Images of the Muslim Male," Ph.D. dissertation, Iliff School of Theology and the University of Denver, 2010.
49. http://religiousliberty.tv/transcript-of-mayor-bloombergs-speech-on-ground-zero-mosque.html, accessed October 17, 2011.
50. The Koran burning was eventually carried out in March of 2011 after Jones and his congregation, Dove World Outreach, put the sacred text "on trial" and pronounced it guilty, an event that provoked violent outrage in several countries.
51. M. Kedar and D. Yerushalmi, "Sharia and Violence in American Mosques," *The Middle East Quarterly* 18, no. 3 (2011): 59–72.
52. Slovoj Zizek, *Welcome to the Desert of the Real* (New York: Verso, 2002), 11.
53. When Anders Behring Breivik detonated a bomb in Oslo on July 22, 2011 and then proceeded to shoot to death some ninety campers on the nearby island of Utoya, news reports immediately pointed to Islamic terrorists as being responsible for the attacks (and, indeed, several groups claimed responsibility). It was

simply assumed. For several hours, the suspected Islamic links to these attacks were reported in the media, including interviews with Muslims in Norway who denounced the attacks. Breivik, it turned out, was a white Norwegian right-wing anti-Islam crusader. Equally rampant speculation followed the bombings at the Boston Marathon in April 2013, and the assumed Islamic motivations of the accused bombers, Dzhokhar and Tamerlan Tsarnaev.

54. On the idea of religious violence as motivated by or oriented toward the notion of cosmic war, see Mark Juergensmeyer, *Terror in the Mind of God: The Global Rise of Religious Violence* (Berkeley: University of California Press, 2003); see also Bruce Lincoln, *Holy Terrors: Thinking about Religion after September 11* (Chicago: University of Chicago Press, 2003), and, for a rather different approach to the question of motivation, Talal Asad, *On Suicide Bombing* (New York: Columbia University Press, 2007).
55. For an insightful and devastating account of this process, see Michael Sells, *The Bridge Betrayed: Religion and Genocide in Bosnia* (Berkeley: University of California Press, 1998), and also Kakar, *The Colors of Violence.*
56. Judith Butler, *Giving an Account of Oneself* (New York: Fordham University Press, 2005), 10.
57. Ibid.
58. A simple but graphic illustration of Butler's point could be seen in the ubiquitous "United We Stand" bumper stickers in America after September 11—this is both an assertion of identity ("United" . . . "We") and opposition ("Stand").
59. See Samuel Huntington, "The Clash of Civilizations?" *Foreign Affairs* 72, no. 3 (1993): 22–50, and the expanded version of this article, *The Clash of Civilizations and the Remaking of World Order* (New York: Simon & Schuster, 1996).
60. See Peter Gottschalk and Gabriel Greenberg, eds., *Islamophobia: Making Muslims the Enemy* (Plymouth, UK: Rowman and Littlefield, 2008); Andrew Shyrock, ed., *Islamophobia/Islamofilia: Beyond the Politics of Enemy and Friend* (Bloomington: Indiana University Press, 2010); Christopher Allen, *Islamophobia* (Surrey, UK: Ashgate, 2010); Gabriele Marranci, "Multiculturalism, Islam and the Clash of Civilisations Theory: Rethinking Islamophobia," *Culture and Religion* 5, no. 1 (2004): 105–117; Michael Welch, *Scapegoats of September 11th: Hate Crimes and State Crimes in the War on Terror* (Trenton, NJ: Rutgers University Press, 2006); Salman Sayyid and Abdulkaroom Vakil, eds., *Rethinking Islamophobia* (New York: Columbia University Press, 2010); and John Esposito and Ibrahim Kalin, eds., *Islamophobia: The Challenge of Pluralism in the 21st Century* (New York: Oxford University Press, 2010).
61. http://thinkprogress.org/politics/2010/11/24/131936/pam-geller-park51/?mobile=nc, accessed October 19, 2011.
62. An equally inflammatory movie, *Obsession*, that, among other things, equated political Islam with the Nazis, was produced in 2007 and sent to some 30 million households leading up to the 2008 elections.

63. http://www.reuters.com/article/2011/01/20/idUS61419+20-Jan-2011+PRN20110120, accessed October 19, 2011.
64. http://action.afa.net/Blogs/BlogPost.aspx?id=2147497353, accessed October 16, 2011.
65. *New York Times*, June 25, 2005.
66. Anne Barnard, "'Everything Is on the Table,' Imam Says of Plans," *New York Times*, September 13, 2010.
67. Eboo Patel, in a speech at the Aspen Institute, actually stated as much, although his point was about inclusiveness, not exclusivity: "I believe Ground Zero is sacred. I believe every inch of America is sacred." "America's Sacred Ground," Aspen Institute, March 30, 2011, http://www.aspeninstitute.org/policy-work/justice-society/americas-sacred-ground, accessed October 24, 2011.
68. Durkheim, *The Elementary Forms*, 38.
69. Pierre Bourdieu, *The Logic of Practice* (Stanford, CA: Stanford University Press, 1990), 62.
70. "Atheists Sue to Block Display of Cross-Shaped Beam in 9/11 Museum," Elissa Gootman, *New York Times*, July 28, 2011.
71. See for instance Robert Bellah, *The Broken Covenant: American Civil Religion in Time of Trial* (Chicago: University of Chicago Press, 1992), and José Casanova, *Public Religions in the Modern World* (Chicago: University of Chicago Press, 1994); this issue will reappear in Chapter 6, with my discussion of the dispute over Devils Tower.
72. Paul Vitello, "Amid Furor on Islamic Center, Pleas for Orthodox Church Nearby," *New York Times*, August 3, 2011.
73. Richard Comstock, "A Behavioral Approach to the Sacred: Category Formation in Religious Studies," *The Journal of the American Academy of Religion* 49, no. 4 (1981): 625–43, 632.
74. Quoted in Lincoln, *Holy Terrors*, 101. In his insightful analysis of the parallel rhetoric of this speech and Osama Bin Laden's speech following Bush's, Lincoln notes Bin Laden's creation of the United States as The Other as well—"they measured the relative power of two antithetical cultural formations" (17)—and they both did so using religious language and imagery.
75. Javier C. Hernandez, "Planned Sign of Tolerance Bringing Division Instead," *New York Times*, July 13, 2010, http://www.nytimes.com/2010/07/14/nyregion/14center.html, accessed October 18, 2011.
76. Lauren Green, "Plan to Build Mosque Near Ground Zero Riles Families of 9/11 Victims," *Foxnews.com*, May 14, 2010, http://www.foxnews.com/us/2010/05/14/plan-build-mosque-near-ground-zero-riles-families-victims/, accessed October 19, 2011.
77. William Saletan, "Muslims Keep Out," *Slate*, August 2, 2010, http://www.slate.com/articles/news_and_politics/frame_game/2010/08/muslims_keep_out.html, accessed October 23, 2011.

78. The project was denied funding by the LMDC in September 2011, however, not because it was promoted by Muslims, but because Park51 had not, at the time of the distribution of funding, been granted non-profit status; see http://www.dnainfo.com/new-york/20110907/downtown/downtown-nonprofits-get-17m-grants, accessed October 18, 2011.

CHAPTER 3

* An early iteration of this chapter appeared as "The Polyvalent *Padas* of Visnu and the Buddha," *History of Religions* 40, no. 1 (2000): 32–57.

1. L. P Vidyarthi, *The Sacred Complex in Hindu Gaya* (Bombay: Asia Publishing House, 1961), 24.
2. Ibid.
3. Certainly, the *pādas* do frequently bear various marks, but as I shall discuss below, the markings on the footprints at both Bodhgayā and Gayā seem to be intentionally intermingled and blurred, drawn from a shared Hindu and Buddhist iconographic vocabulary.
4. See the essays collected in Waghorne and Cutler, *Gods of Flesh/Gods of Stone*, as well as Waghorne's article, "Dressing the Body of God: South Indian Bronze Sculpture in its Temple Setting," *Asian Art* 3 (1992): 9–34; for an interesting case study of the Buddhist context, see Donald K. Swearer, "Hypostatizing the Buddha: Buddhist Image Consecration in Northern Thailand," *History of Religions* 34 (1995): 263–280. Museum curators have begun to recognize the degree to which the image is out of place in the museum, and there has been some attempt in recent years to recreate something like a temple setting in shows such as the "Manifestations of Shiva" curated by Stella Kramrisch at the Philadelphia Museum of Art in the early 1980s, or the "Gods, Guardians and Lovers" show at the Asia Society in New York in the early 1990s.
5. Bernard S. Cohn, "The Transformation of Objects into Artifacts, Antiquities and Art in Nineteenth Century India," in *The Powers of Art: Patronage in Indian Culture*, ed. Barbara Stoler Miller, 301–329 (Delhi: Oxford University Press, 1992), 302, 304.
6. For a discussion of the practices of arrangement and display of non-Western art in general, see Sally Price, *Primitive Art in Civilized Places* (Chicago: University of Chicago Press, 1989).
7. Richard Davis, *Lives of Indian Images*, 262.
8. Ibid., 261. Davis discusses the interesting case of the Dadarganj yakśī, an early Buddhist image that was found near Patna in 1917, which serves to illustrate this point nicely. After the sculpture was disinterred, it was secretly moved to a makeshift shrine, where it was worshiped by local Hindus as a Hindu goddess. When the curator of the Patna museum learned of this, he and several

officials (and a number of policemen) went to the shrine and put a stop to this impromptu devotion. The image was then moved to the Patna museum, where its brief life as a Hindu deity ended, and it resumed its former life as a Buddhist yakṣī (see ibid., 3–6). A similar scenario, but with a rather different outcome, is mentioned by Alexander Cunningham in his discussion of the excavations at Bodhgayā: when the Archaeological Survey of India team disinterred hundreds of small Buddhist *stūpas*, they found that before the images could be properly labeled and stored, they were carted off by local Hindus who, much to Cunningham's dismay, then apparently set them up as Śiva *liṅgams* at nearby Gayā; see Alexander Cunningham, *Archaeological Survey of India Report*, vol. VIII (Calcutta: Office of the Superintendent of Government Printing, 1878), 100.

9. Mikhail M. Bhaktin, *The Dialogic Imagination*, ed. Michael Holquist, trans. by C. Emerson and M. Holquiest (Austin: University of Texas Press, 1981), 276.
10. Frederick M. Asher, "Gaya: Monuments of the Pilgrimage Town," in *Bodhgaya: Site of Enlightenment*, ed. J. Leoshko, 74–88 (Bombay: Marg Publications, 1988), 86; Asher here is specifically discussing an image of the Bodhisattva Avalokiteśvara located at Gayā that is venerated as Rāma by Hindu pilgrims who visit the site.
11. See David Kinsley, *Tantric Visions of the Divine Feminine*, 92–111.
12. I will have more to say on this in the next chapter.
13. See Philip Almond, *The British Discovery of Buddhism* (Cambridge: Cambridge University Press, 1988), especially chapter one.
14. For the effects of this on the academic study of Buddhism, see Gregory Schopen, "Archaeology and the Protestant Presuppositions in the Study of Indian Buddhism," *History of Religions* 31 (1991): 1–23.
15. I will return to this issue in the next chapter; see Almond, *The British Discovery of Buddhism*, especially 70–77. As he puts it, the "status of the Buddha was enhanced enormously by the perception that he had been an opponent of Hinduism, for in this he was aligning himself with the vast majority of Victorians" (70). For a more detailed account of the British view of Hinduism, see Peter Marshall, ed., *The British Discovery of Hinduism in the Eighteenth Century* (Cambridge: Cambridge University Press, 1970).
16. Witness Max Müller's influence on the study of religion. For a very insightful discussion of this topic, see Tomoko Masuzawa, *In Search of Dreamtime: The Quest of the Origin of Religion* (Chicago: University of Chicago Press, 1993).
17. Samuel Beal, *Si-Yu-Ki: Buddhist Records of the Western World Translated from the Chinese of Hiuen Tsiang* (AD 629) (London: Trübner, 1884), 90.
18. Benimadhab Barua, *Gayā and Buddha-Gayā (Early History of the Holy Land)*, 2 vols. (Calcutta: Indian Research Institute, 1934), II: 63; contrast Barua's view of *pāda* veneration with that of Rajendralala Mitra below.
19. It is also a favorite trope in secondary accounts of the tradition; witness the film, *The Footprint of the Buddha*, used in countless introductory courses, or

the existence of any number of books with "footprint" in their titles, such as R. Raven-Hart's *Where the Buddha Trod: A Buddhist Pilgrimage* (Colombo: Lake House, 1966), or S. Muthiah's *Where the Buddha Walked* (Madras: T. T. Maps and Publications, 1990), or Thich Nhat Hanh's *Old Path White Clouds: Walking in the Footprints of the Buddha* (Berkeley: Parallax Press, 1991), and Kate Blackstone's *Women in the Footsteps of the Buddha: Struggle for Liberation in the Therīgāthā* (London: Curzon Press, 1998).

20. For the origins of this thesis, see Alfred Foucher, "L'Origine grecque de l'image du Bouddha," *Annales du Musee Guimet* (Chalon-sur-Saone: Bibliotheque de vulgarisation, 1913), 231–272, and also Foucher's "The Beginnings of Buddhist Art," in his *The Beginnings of Buddhist Art and Other Essays in Indian and Central Asian Archaeology*, 1–29 (Paris: Paul Geuthner, 1917); for an opposing view, see Ananda Coomaraswamy, "The Origin of the Buddha Image," *The Art Bulletin* 9 (1927): 1–43, and also see his "The Indian Origin of the Buddha Image," *Journal of the American Oriental Society* 46 (1926): 165–170. Also see Paul Mus's article, "The Iconography of an Aniconic Art," *RES* 14 (1987): 5–28. For a more recent foray into the subject, see Susan Huntington, "Early Buddhist Art and the Theory of Aniconism," *Art Journal* 49 (1990): 401–407, and also Vidya Dehejia, "Aniconism and the Multivalence of Emblems," *Ars Orientalis* 21 (1992): 45–66; and S. Huntington's response, "Aniconism and the Multivalence of Emblems: Another Look," *Ars Orientalis* 22 (1993): 111–156 [and Dehejia's brief response, on 157], as well as my own articles, "The Field of the Buddha's Presence," in *Embodying the Dharma: Buddhist Relic Veneration in Asia*, ed. Kevin Trainor and David Germano, 117–143 (Albany: State University of New York Press, 2004), and "Amaravati as Lens: Envisioning Buddhism in the Ruins of the Great Stupa," in *Buddhism in the Krishna River Valley of Andhra*, ed. Sree Padma and Tony Barber, 81–103 (Albany: State University of New York Press, 2008).

21. David Snellgrove et al., *The Image of the Buddha* (Paris: UNESCO, 1978), 28, 33.

22. Schopen makes these remarks in his essay, "Relic," in *Critical Terms for Religious Studies*, ed. Mark C. Taylor (Chicago: University of Chicago Press, 1998), 259. On its most basic level, this ambiguity is rooted in the tension between the basic Buddhist ideals of impermanence and non-attachment, and the desire, if not the need, for the Buddha's continued presence. For a discussion of this tension, see Kevin Trainor, *Relics, Ritual, And Representation in Buddhism: Rematerializing the Sri Lankan Theravāda Tradition* (Cambridge: Cambridge University Press, 1997), especially chapter 2, as well as my "The Field of the Buddha's Presence." It is worth noting, however, that the problematic nature of relics has been greatly inflated by Western scholars of Buddhism (as Schopen himself has demonstrated throughout his *oeuvre*; the French Buddhologist André Bareau, for instance, suggested that, unable to comprehend the finality of the Buddha's

parinibbana, early Buddhists clung on to his physical remains "comme un jeune enfant aux vêtements de sa mere." A. Bareau, "La *Parinirvāṇa* du Bouddha et la naissance de la religion bouddhique," *Bulletin de l'Ecole Française d'Extrême-Orient* 61 (1964): 285.

23. For a good idea of just what can be considered a relic, see Yael Bentor, *Images and Stūpas in Indo-Tibetan Tantric Buddhism* (Leiden: E. J. Brill, 1996), as well as her article, "The Content of *Stūpa*s and Images and the Indo-Tibetan Concept of Relics," Tibet Journal 28, nos. 1–2 (2003): 21–48.
24. I am, necessarily, oversimplifying here, since the very notion of "traditional" is itself neither unambiguous nor uncontested in Buddhist discourse. Furthermore, the concept of a relic became considerably expanded as Buddhism developed historically. The three-fold categorization is perhaps most succinctly expressed in the *Khuddakanikāya*, which states that the Bodhi tree is a relic of use, an image of the Buddha is a relic of commemoration, and a *stūpa* that contains a relic is a corpeal relic. There is a more complete discussion of these categories in the *Kalinga-bodhi-Jātaka*, in *The Jātaka, or Stories of the Former Lives of the Buddha*, vol. 4, E. B. Cowell, ed., W. H. D. Rouse, trans. (Cambridge: Cambridge University Press, 1901), 142–47.
25. The *uddeśika* category is itself a rather ambiguous and problematic category, having developed quite late in the tradition; see Walpola Rahula, *History of Buddhism in Ceylon: The Anurādhapura Period, 3rd Century BC–10th Century AC*, 2d ed. (Colombo: Gunasena, 1966), 121–128.
26. The fact that the majority of the extant footprints throughout the Buddhist world are much larger than any human footprint is not, on its face, a problem, but rather is seen as a product of the Buddha's supernatural stature.
27. See Snellgrove et al., 44.
28. John Irwin, "Viṣṇu in the Archaic Cosmology," in *Indian Art and Connoisseurship: Essays in Honour of Dougless Barnett*, ed. John Guy, 75–85 (Middletown, NJ: Grantha, 1995), 82. Calling a relic a "symbol," however, rather misses the significance of what a relic does, since a relic does not simply point to something else (as a symbol, by definition, does), but rather is, or at least partakes of, that thing (or person) itself; see Schopen's discussion in "Burial 'Ad Sanctos' and the Physical Presence of the Buddha in Early Indian Buddhism," *Religion* 17 (1987): 193–225, 203, as well as in his "On the Buddha and his Bones," *Journal of Indian Philosophy* 108, no. 4 (1990): 181–217. Peter Brown, on whom Schopen draws, presents a particularly detailed account of this same idea in his *The Cult of the Saints: Its Rise and Function in Latin Christianity* (Chicago: University of Chicago Press, 1981), especially in chapters three ("The Invisible Dead") and five ("Praesentia").
29. The Pāli is "*tatha ye māla vā gandha vā vaakam vā āropessanti abhivādessanti vā, citta vā pasādessanti, tesa ta bhavissati dīgharatta hitāya sukhāya*," *The Dīgha Nikāya*, vol. 2, ed. T. W. Rhys Davids and J. Eslin Carpenter (London: Oxford University Press, 1947), 142.

30. I say "general preference" because, clearly, *sariraka* relics were not the only acceptable form of relics. In the *Kāliṅga-bodhi-jātaka*, for instance, the Buddha rejects commemoration shrines (*uddeśika cetiya*) because he says that such a shrine "[i]s improper because the connection depends on the imagination only." Relics of contact or use, such as the *Bodhi* tree, are, however, appropriate.
31. A ninth clan, which had arrived after the eight portions are distributed, is given a ninth portion, the embers from the funeral pyre, which would also appear to be relics of use, and not corporeal remains.
32. See Trainor, *Relics, Ritual, and Representations*, 122–123.
33. *The Dispeller of Delusion (Sammohavinodanī)*, part I, trans. Bhikkhu Ñāṇamoli (London: Pali Text Society, 1987), 175.
34. The *Buddhavaṃsa* is one of the last texts to be added to the Pāli canon; see K. R. Norman, *Pāli-Literature, Including the Canonical Literature in Prakrit and Sanskrit of All the Hinayāna Schools of Buddhism* (Wiesbaden: Otto Harrassowitz, 1983), 94.
35. Trainor, *Relics, Rituals, and Representations*, 122.
36. *Papañcasūdanī Majjhimanikāya aṭṭhakathā of Buddhagosācariya*, ed. I. B. Horner (London: Pali Text Society, 1938), V: 91–92; the relevant Pāli reads: *So: mayha bhante paricaritabba dethā ti yāci. Bhagavā Nammadānadītire padacetya dassesi. Ta vīcīsu āgatāsu pithīyati gatāsu vivarīyati mahāsakkarappata ahosi.*
37. For a discussion of how such objects function in *buddha anussati*, see my "The Field of the Buddha's Presence," as well as Paul Harrison's "Buddhānusmṛti in the Pratyutpanna-Buddha-Samukhāvasthita-Samādhi-Sūtra," *Journal of Indian Philosophy* 6 (1978): 35–57, and also his *The Samādhi of Direct Encounter with the Buddhas of the Present* (Tokyo: The International Institute for Buddhist Studies, 1990).
38. See the discussion of this in chapter three of my *Imaging Wisdom: Seeing and Knowing in the Art of Indian Buddhism* (London: Curzon Press, 1999).
39. *Papañcasūdanī Majjhimanikāya aṭṭhkathā*, V: 92.
40. See my *Imaging Wisdom*, especially 72–78.
41. For a useful overview of the terms *caitya* and *cetiya*, see V. R. R. Dishitar, "Origin and Early History of Caityas," *Indian Historical Quarterly* 14 (1938): 440–451, and also Jotiya Dhirasekara, "Cetiya," *Encyclopaedia of Buddhism*, vol. 4 (Colombo: Government of Sri Lanka, 1979), and B. C. Law, "'Cetiya' in the Buddhist Literature," in *Studia Indo-Iranica: Ehrengabe für Wilhelm* Geiger, ed. Walther Wüst, 42–48 (Leipzig: Harrasowitz, 1931). Bareau, "La construction et le culte des stūpa d'aprés les *Vinayapiṭaka*," *Bulletin l'Ecole Française d'Extrême-Oriente* 50 (1962): 229–74, 240.
42. A. Bareau, "La construction et le culte des stūpa d'aprés les *Vinayapiṭaka*," 240.
43. See Bareau's "La *Parinirvāṇa* du Bouddha. Also see Schopen's discussion in "The Phrase *sa pṛthivīpradeśaś caityabhūto bhavet* in the Vajracchedikā: Notes on the Cult of the Book in Mahāyāna," *Indo-Iranian Journal* 17 (1975): 147–81, as well as his revision of his original argument in "An Old Inscription from Amarāvatī

and the Cult of the Local Monastic Dead in Indian Buddhist Monasteries," *Journal of the International Association of Buddhist Studies* 14.2 (1991): 281–329, particularly 322n38, and "The Stūpa Cult," 91.

44. This is a topic about which Schopen has extensively written in his "Burial 'Ad Sanctos'" and "On the Buddha and his Bones" articles.

45. *Monarathapūranī: Buddhaghosa's Commentary on the Anguttara Nikāya*, ed. M. Walleser and H. Kopf (London: The Pali Text Society, 1924), I: 382–284. An interesting parallel to this sort of "self made" relic is found in the many versions of the Prasenajit story. The story, as recorded by Faxian, goes as follows: "When the Buddha went up to heaven for ninety days to preach the Faith to his mother, king Prasenajit, longing to see him, caused to be carved in sandal-wood from the Bull's head mountain an image of Buddha and placed it where Buddha usually sat. Later on, when Buddha returned to the shrine, the image straightaway quitted the seat and came forth to receive him. Buddha cried out, 'Return to your seat: after my disappearance you shall be the model for the four classes in search of spiritual truth.' At this, the image went back to the seat. It was the very first of all such images, and is that which later ages have copied," *The Travels of Fa-hsien*, trans. H. A. Giles (Cambridge: Cambridge University Press, 1966) 30–31. A story similar to the Prasenajit story occurs at the beginning of the *Pratimālakṣaṇam*, a text that describes in great detail the proper proportions of a Buddha image. In this version it is Śāriputra who asks the Buddha how he is to be honored when he is away (in the Tuṣita heaven), to which the Buddha responds: "*Śāriputra mayi gate parinirvte vā nyagrodhaparimaala kāya kartavya*" (Oh Śāripuptra! When I am gone or when I attain *parinirvāṇa*, [my] body is to be made [as a] well-proportioned body [or image]). *Pratimālakṣaṇam* (Calcutta: Calcutta University Press, 1933).

46. Schopen, "On the Buddha and his Bones," 535.

47. Benimadhab Barua, *Gayā and Buddha-Gayā*, 63.

48. Rajendralala Mitra, *Buddha Gaya: The Great Buddhist Temple, Hermitage of Sakya Muni* (Calcutta: Bengal Secretariat Press, 1878), 125. Mitra offers an elaborate reading of the Gāyasura story in the *Vāyu Purāṇa* as an allegory for the Hindu displacement of Buddhism at Gayā.

49. Debjani Paul, "Antiquity of the Visnupada at Gaya: Tradition and Archaeology," *East and West* 35, nos. 1–3 (1985): 103–141, 140.

50. See Tomoko Masuzawa, *In Search of Dreamtime*; for a very useful survey of some of the key figures in the origin of religions discourse, see also Garry Trompf, *In Search of Origins* (New Delhi: Sterling, 1990).

51. Vijay Kumar Thakur, "Evolution of Gayā as a Religious Complex: An Historical Note," in *Pilgrimage Studies: Text and Context*, ed. D. P. Dubey 172–191 (Allahabad: Society of Pilgrimage Studies, 1990), 178.

52. M. Bhaktin, *The Dialogic Imagination*, 276.

53. Barua, *Gayā and Buddha-Gayā*, 87 and 95; see also Pandranga Vamana Kane, *History of Dharmaśāstra: Ancient and Medieval Religious and Civil Law in India*

(Pene: Bhandarkar Oriental Research Institute, 1975), 660. The *Likhita-Smṛti* puts particular emphasis on this aspect of Gayā: "In whosesoever name a *piṇḍa* is offered at Gayāśiras, whether for oneself or for another, that person, if in hell, goes to heaven and if in heaven that man secures release" (quoted in Kane, *History of Dharmaśāstra*, 654); in the *Vāyupurāṇa*, ch. 105, ll. 14–15, *śrāddha* offered at Gayā is said to lead one directly to Brahmā.

54. *Udāna: Verses of Uplift and Itivuttaka: As it Was Said*, trans. F. L. Woodward (London: Pali Text Society, 1935), 9. For further elaboration, see also the commentary, the *Udāna Aṭṭhakathā*.

55. *The Majjhima Nikāya*, vol. I, ed. V. Trenckner (London: Pali Text Society, 1888), 39; see also the verse from the *Vatthūpama Sutta* (quoted in Barua, 94); in the *Theragāthā*, there is mention of an annual spring festival at Gayā in which titthābiseka in the Phalgu is described and critiqued as so much worthless bobbing and dunking; see the Senaka chapter, as well as the chapter on Kassapa of Gayā (who may be the same Kassapa in the Jaila episode).

56. *The Majjhima Nikāya*, vol. I, 47.

57. Debjani Paul writes: "Admittedly, to our great consternation, the Buddhist texts do not explicitly mention the foot-print of Savit-Āditya-Viṣṇu at the site." But she sees in this silence not evidence of absence, but, on the contrary, a strong indication of the presence of the *viṣṇupāda*: "[I]t follows that those practices in Brahmanism which seemed in no way so superfluous [as the ablutions], were not subjected to criticism and, as such, called for little or no particular attention in the Buddhist writings. One such item of universal appeal in the preexisting system might have been the convention of foot-print worship which, as we know, played an ever greater role in religious concept and artistic expression of the Buddhists themselves." "Antiquity of the Visnupada at Gaya," 111–112. Following this line of reasoning, one can only wonder here about all of the other things that the Buddhists did not see fit to mention, but which must have existed nonetheless.

58. *Gacchet tata udyanta parvata gītanāditam / sāvitra tu padam tatra daśyate bharatābha*, 3.82.81. *Mahābharata: Text as Constituted in Its Critical Edition* (Poona: Bhandarkar Oriental Research Institute, 1971), I: 505.

59. Paul, "Antiquity of the Visnupada at Gaya," 108. Hans Bakker has drawn attention to the fact that Paul seems to base her argument almost entirely on Kane's discussion of Gayā, and he notes that she has entirely ignored the evidence presented by Claude Jacques in his *Gayā Māhātmya: Edition critiue, traduction française et introduction* (Pondichéry: Publications de l'Institut Française d'Indologie, 1962); see Hans Bakker, "The Footprints of the Lord," in *Devotion Divine: Bhakti Traditions from the Regions of India: Studies in Honour of Charlotte Vaudeville*, ed. Diana L. Eck and Françoise Mallison, 19–37, Groningen Oriental Studies, vol. 8 (Groningen: Egbert Forsten, 1991). Jacques consistently argues that there is in fact no evidence—save "*l'argumentum a silentio*" championed by Kane—that the image of the *viṣṇupāda* predates the *Mahābharata*: "Nous

pouvons donc quasi affirmer que le Viṣṇupada n'existait pas à Gayā à l'epoque où fut composé ce passage du Mbh" (xxxvi). Furthermore, Jacques rather convincingly maintains that the origin of the footprints is in fact Buddhist: "ce qui confirme notre hypothése qu'à l'origine, ces empreintes de pied étaient dispersées sur tout le territoire de Gayā; elles devaint provenir très vraisemblement de Bodh-Gayā." Jacques, lxiii.

60. Paul, "Antiquity of Viṣṇupāda at Gayā," 108.
61. For useful discussions on the general dangers of such methodological moves, albeit in a very different context, see the essays in *Iconography at the Crossroads: Papers from the Colloquim Sponsored by the Index of Christian Art, Princeton University, 23–24 March 1990*, ed. Brendan Cassidy, (Princeton, NJ: Department of Art and Archaeology, Princeton University, 1993), especially Cassidy's introduction.
62. Paul, "Antiquity of Viṣṇupāda at Gayā," 119f.
63. Hendrik Kern writes: "The origin and history of the *Śrīpādas* are as yet wrapt in darkness, but we have sufficient data to warrant the inference that their worship is connected with the strides, *vikrama*, of Puruottama, Viṣṇu." *Manual of Indian Buddhism* (Strassburg: Verlag Von Karl J. Trubner, 1896), 98.
64. See Diana Eck's article, "India's *Tīrthas*: Crossings in Sacred Geography," *History of Religions* 20 (1981): 323–344, especially 336, for a discussion of the relationship of the *tīrtha* as the place where the god is located, and the *avatāra* as its manifestation.
65. This is Wendy O'Flaherty's translation, from *The Rig Veda* (New York: Penguin, 1981), 226. It is worth noting that the three main commentators on the *Ṛg Veda*, Aurṇavābha, Yāska, and Śākapūni, are themselves not in agreement as to the exact meaning of the image of the three strides. See Kane, *History of Dharmaśāstra*, 645, as well as Jacques' discussion of the matter in his introduction to the *Gayā Mahātmya*.
66. The *Gayāmāhātmya* constitutes chapters 105–112 of the *Vāyupurāṇa*; see Kane, *History of Dharmaśāstra*, for a discussion of that dating of the text. For his part, Kane calls the *Gayāmāhātmya* a "*post facto* attempt to account for the sanctity of the place" (ibid., 660).
67. This is Kane's translation, 657; see the *Gayāmahātmya*, 109.20, 43–45 for the Sanskrit. Viṣṇu is said to be *vyaktāvyakta*, manifest and unmanifest, in the *pāda*. Viṣṇu, interestingly, is not the only god represented by a footprint in the Gayā region—there are also references to the footprints of Rudra, Brahmā, Śakra, and Sūrya.
68. Although I know of no discussions about what sort of *mūrti* the *viṣṇupāda* might be, it would seem to fall into a special class of *mūrti*, *svayambhū*, or "self-created." For a general discussion of the various classifications of images within the Brahmanical tradition, as well as speculation about their origins, see Jitendra Nath Banerjea, *Development of Hindu Iconography* (Calcutta: University

of Calcutta, 1956), and the general introduction to T. A. Gopinatha Rao's *Elements of Hindu Iconography*, 2 vols. (Madras: Law Printing House, 1914–1916).

69. See Bakker, "The Footprints of the Lord."
70. See Jacques's discussion of dating in his edition of the *Gayā Māhātmya*.
71. See Paul, "Antiquity of the Visnupada at Gaya," 116n37, for a list of references to these early *buddhapādas*.
72. Mitra, *Buddha Gaya*, 127.
73. Paul, "Antiquity of the Visnupada at Gaya," 114.
74. Nalinaksha Dutt, ed., *Bodhisattvabhūmih* (Patalīputtram: Kadiprasada-Jayas avala-Anusilanasamsthanam, 1978), 10. The Sanskrit is: *adhasthāt pādatalayoś cakre jāle sahasrare sanābhike sanemike sarvākāraparipūre.*
75. See N. A. Jayawickrama, ed. *Buddhavamsa and Cariyapitaka* (London: Pali Text Society, 1974); E. H. Johnston, *The Buddhacarita; or, Acts of the Buddha* (Delhi: Motilal Banarsidass, 1984), 6; and P. L. Vaidya, ed., *Lalitavistara*, Buddhist Sanskrit Texts, no. 1 (Dharbhanga: Mithila Insititute, 1958), 75.
76. Mitra, *Buddha Gaya*, 125.
77. Barua, *Gaya and Buddha Gaya*, 63.
78. Probably the most complete description of the marks on Viṣṇu's feet is found in the *Skanda Purāṇa*; see Mitra, *Buddha Gaya*, 126.
79. Mitra, *Buddha Gaya*, 127; see plate XLIII for the images themselves.
80. Barua, *Gaya and Buddha Gaya*, 18n2.
81. Ibid., 63.
82. B. C. Law did not know what to make of the physical referent of the term "*pādacetiya*"; this image discussed by Paul certainly provides an intriguing possibility, although without a better sense of its original context, it would be difficult to draw any conclusions simply on the basis of this one unusual image.
83. See Mitra, *Buddha Gaya*, 100, as well as Cunningham, *Archeological Reports*, vol. I., pl. VII. According to both Cunningham and Mitra, it contains the word "*madana*," which Paul suggests appears to be a reference to Viṣṇu; this, in my opinion, is simply puzzling, since "*madana*" typically refers to Kāma.
84. Paul, "Antiquity of the Visnupada at Gaya," 123; oddly, Paul bases her understanding of the "actual rendering of *Viṣṇupāda* in art" on a nineteenth-century Pahari painting.
85. I will have more to say on this in the next chapter.
86. J. Ph. Vogel, "The Earliest Sanskrit Inscriptions in Java," in *Publications van den Oudheidkundigen Dienst in Nederlandsch-Indie I: Uitgegeven door het Koninklijk Bataviaasch Genootschap van Kunsten en Vetenschappen* (1925): 17.
87. See S. Paranavitana, *The God of Adam's Peak*, Ascona, Artibus Asiae Supplementum XVIII (Artibus Asiae Publishers, 1958): 11–22, and also Markus Aksland, *The Sacred Footprint* (Oslo: YETI Consult, 1990).
88. For an interesting discussion of the various ways in which Europeans have viewed this footprint, see J. Charpentier, "Heilige Fussabdrücke in Indien, I &

II," *Ostasiatische Zeitschrift. Beiträge zur Kenntnis der Kultur und Kunst des Fernen Ostens* 7 (1918–19): 1–30.

89. In Beal, *Si-Yu-Ki*, 29.

CHAPTER 4

* Parts of this chapter earlier appeared as "When Is the Buddha Not the Buddha? The Hindu/Buddhist Battle over Bodhgaya and the Buddha Image," *Journal of the American Academy of Religion* 66, no. 4 (1999): 817–839, and "When the Buddha Sued Viṣṇu," in *Constituting Communities: Theravāda Traditions in South and Southeast Asia*, ed. John Holt, Jacob N. Kinnard, and Jonathon Walters, 85–106 (Albany: State University of New York Press, 2003). Reprinted with changes with permission from Oxford University Press and the State University of New York Press.

1. W. J. T. Mitchell, *What Do Pictures Want? The Lives and Loves of Images* (Chicago: University of Chicago Press, 2005), 76.
2. Amartya Sen, *Identity and Violence: The Illusion of Destiny* (New York: Norton, 2006), 19.
3. According to the report in the *Times of India*, May 29, 1953, 7, there were some 100,000 people in the crowd; Michael Trevithick, rather more conservatively, has suggested (without corroboration) that there were more like 5,000 people in attendance; see his *The Revival of Buddhist Pilgrimage at Bodh Gaya (1811–1949): Anagarika Dharmapala and the Mahabodhi Temple* (Delhi: Motilala Banarsidass, 2006), 201.
4. Sir Edwin Arnold, *East and West: Being Papers Reprinted from the "Daily Telegraph" and Other Sources* (London: Longman's, Green, and Co., 1896), 311.
5. Victor Turner, *Dramas, Fields, and Metaphors*, 202.
6. Victor Turner, *The Forest of Symbols: Aspects of Ndembu Ritual* (Ithaca, NY: Cornell University Press, 1967), 100.
7. Vasudha Dalmia and Heinrich von Stietencron, eds., *Representing Hinduism: The Construction of Religious Traditions and National Identity* (New Delhi: Sage Publications, 1995), 28.
8. For the fullest treatment of this topic to date, see Philip Almond, *The British Discovery of Buddhism*.
9. Quoted in Almond, *The British Discovery of Buddhism*, 71.
10. For the history of the East Indian Company, see Stanley Wolpert, *A New History of India* (New York: Oxford University Press, 1977); for more on Buchanan and other similar early Orientalists, see also John Keay, *India Discovered* (London: Collins, 1988), as well as Abu Imam, *Sir Alexander Cunningham and the Beginnings of Indian Archaeology* (Dacca: Asiatic Society of Pakistan, 1966).
11. Buchanan's complete manuscript is located in the Indian Office Library and Records; his account of Bihar is published as *An Account of the Districts of Bihar*

and Patna in 1811–1812 (Patna: Bihar and Orissa Research Society, 1986; first published in 1934); a partial account, with illustrations, was published in 1838 as Montgomery Martin, ed., *The History, Antiquities, Topography and Statistics of Eastern India* (Delhi: Cosmo Publications, 1976).

12. Buchanan, *An Account of the Districts of Bihar and Patna*, 100.
13. Ibid., 140.
14. Most notable among these is the Tibetan Dharmasvāmin, who left a detailed account of his travels in Bihar; see *Biography of Dharmasvāmin: A Tibetan Monk Pilgrim*, trans. George Roerich (Patna: K. P. Jayaswal Research Institute, 1959).
15. For details of the Burmese mission in particular, see W. S. Desai, "History of the Burmese Mission to India, October 1830–July 1833," *Journal of the Burma Research Society* 26 (1936): 71–109; for more general treatments of the various missions to Bodhgayā, see Rajendralala Mitra, *Buddha Gaya*, Alexander Cunningham, *Mahabodhi or the Great Buddhist Temple Under the Bodhi Tree at Buddha-Gaya* (London: W. H. Allen, 1892), and Benimadhab Barua, *Gayā and Buddha-Gayā (Early History of the Holy Land)*, 2 vols. (Calcutta: Indian Research Institute, 1934); for more specific discussions of the activities of these missions, particularly as they affected the Mahābodhi temple itself, see Geri H. Malandra, "The Mahabodhi Temple," in *Bodhgayā: The Site of Enlightenment*, ed. Janice Leoshko, 10–28 (Bombay: Marg, 1988), and Jeremiah P. Losty, "The Mahabodhi Temple Before its Restoration," in *Aksayanivi: Essays Presented to Dr. Debala Mitra in Admiration of Her Scholarly Contributions*, ed. G. Bhattacharya, 335–357 (New Delhi: Sri Satguru, 1991).
16. Arnold, *East and West*, 307.
17. In Ananda Guruge, *Return to Righteousness: A Collection of Speeches, Essays, and Letters of Anagarika Dharmapala* (Colombo: Government Printing Press, 1965), 336.
18. See Tara Doyle's Ph.D. dissertation, "Bodh Gayā: Journeys to the Diamond Throne and the Feet of Gayāsur" (Harvard University, 1997); see also Trevithick, *The Revival of Buddhist Pilgrimage*, and the recent collection of essays in David Geary, Matthew Sayers, and Abhishek Singh Amar, eds., *Cross-disciplinary Perspectives on a Contested Buddhist Site* (Oxford: Routledge, 2012).
19. For details on the Giris, and the larger Dasanāmi orders of which they are generally considered to be a part, see Bahadur Sing and Rai Ram Anugrhraha Narain, *A Brief History of Bodh Gayā Math, District Gayā* (Calcutta: Bengal Secretariat Press, 1893), and also Wade Dazey, "Tradition and Modernization in the Organization of the Dasanāmi Samnyāsins," in *Monastic Life in the Christian and Hindu Traditions*, ed. Austin Creel and Vasudha Narayanan, 281–321 (Lewiston: Edwin Mellen Press, 1992).
20. See Mitra, *Buddha Gaya*, 5.
21. Ibid., 6.
22. Buchanan, *An Account of the Districts of Bihar and Patna*, 90.

23. Significant in that in at once so radically over estimating the number of Śaivas and at the same time reporting a single Buddhist, Buchanan was implicitly drawing attention to the fact that the Buddhists had been forced out of their sacred center by the Hindus.
24. Arnold, *East and West*, 310–311.
25. Ibid., 314
26. See Almond, especially 29–32.
27. There were, however, abundant nineteenth-century characterizations of the Buddha as one of the great men of history; see Almond, 69–77.
28. Ibid., 166.
29. Alexander Cunningham, *The Bhilsa Topes, or Buddhist Monuments of Central India: Comprising a Brief Historical Sketch of the Rise, Progress, and Decline of Buddhism* (Varanasi: Indological Book House, 1966), 33.
30. Mitra, *Buddha Gaya*, 6.
31. Arnold, *East and West*, 313.
32. Ibid., 312.
33. For a very insightful discussion of this topic, see Masuzawa, *In Search of Dreamtime*. Ironically, though, it is precisely this claim of origins that appears, inverted, in subsequent polemical efforts to create a space—both a physical and a rhetorical space—for Viṣṇu and the Vaiṣṇava community at Bodhgayā, and the focus of many of these efforts has not been on the Buddha images at all, but rather on the footprints *in situ* at Bodhgayā and their relationship to the famous *viṣṇupāda* at Gayā, both of which Vaiṣṇavas claim significantly predate the arrival of Buddhism; see Chapter 3.
34. Gregory Schopen, "The Buddha as an Owner of Property and Permanent Resident in Medieval Indian Monasteries," *Journal of Indian Philosophy* 18 (1990): 181–217, 181; for more on the character of the Buddha as viewed by nineteenth-century Westerners, see also Almond, *The British Discovery of Buddhism*, and Étienne Lamotte, "La légende du Buddha," *Revue de l'histoire des religions* 134 (1948): 37–71.
35. See Peter Marshall, ed., *The British Discovery of Hinduism*, and Brian Pennington, *Was Hinduism Invented? Britons, Indians, and Colonial Construction of Religion* (Oxford: Oxford University Press, 2005); see also Partha Mitter, *Much Maligned Monsters: A History of European Reactions to Indian Art* (Chicago: University of Chicago Press, 1992).
36. In E. B. Cowell, *The Buddhacarita of Asvaghosa*, in *Buddhist Mahayana Texts*, trans. E. B. Cowell, F. Max Muller, and J. Takakusu, *Sacred Books of the East*, vol. XLIX (New Delhi: Cosmo Publications, 1977), 115 of the Sanskrit portion of the text.
37. Arnold, *East and West*, 311.
38. Janice Leoshko, "On the Construction of a Buddhist Pilgrimage Site," *Art History* 19, no. 4 (1996): 573–97, 580. This exclusion was not, however, limited

to the Hindus. Indeed, only a particular sort of Buddhism—the Theravāda—was included in the Western imagination of Bodhgayā, a perception that persist to this day. For as Leoshko notes, "Many scholars have tried to construct a singular truth about a site at the expense of a more complicated picture offered by the evidence of subsequent developments" (573).

39. For more on this topic, see Jeremiah P. Losty, "The Mahābodhi Temple Before its Restoration"; on the broader issue of the ways in which nineteenth-century Orientalists constructed ancient religious sites in India, see my "Amarāvatī as Lens: Envisioning Buddhism in the Ruins of the Great Stūpa."
40. Cited by Trevithick, *The Revival of Buddhist Pilgrimage*, 42.
41. See for instance Gananath Obeyesekere, "Personal Identity and Cultural Crisis: The Case of Anagarika Dharmapala," *The Biographical Process: Studies in the History and Psychology of Religion*, ed, F. Reynolds and D. Capps, 573–97 (The Hague: Mouton and Company, 1976); Kitsiri Malalgoda, *Buddhism in Sinhalese Society: 1750–1900* (Berkeley: University of California Press, 1976); Richard Gombrich and Gananath Obeyesekere, *Buddhism Transformed: Religious Change in Sri Lanka* (Princeton, NJ: Princeton University Press, 1988); George Bond, *The Buddhist Revival in Sri Lanka: Religious Tradition, Reinterpretation and Response* (Columbia: University of South Carolina Press, 1988); L. A. Wickremeratne, "Religion, Nationalism and Social Change in Ceylon, 1865–85," *Journal of the Royal Asiatic Society* 2 (1969): 123–150; Ananda Guruge, *Return to Righteousness;* Ananda Guruge, *From the Living Fountains of Buddhism* (Colombo: Ministry of Cultural Affairs, 1984); *Rick Fields, How the Swans Came to the Lake: A Narrative History of Buddhism in America* (Boston: Shambala, 1992), 83–118; Stephen Prothero, *The White Buddhist: The Asian Odyssey of Henry Steel Olcott* (Bloomington: Indiana University Press, 1996); Trevithick, *The Revival of Buddhist Pilgrimate.*
42. See Mark Juergensmeyer, ed., *The Oxford Handbook of Global Religions* (New York: Oxford University Press, 2006), 76ff.
43. Guruge, *Return to Righteousness*, 685.
44. Ibid., 336.
45. See Steven Kemper, "Dharmapala's Dharmaduta and Buddhist Ethnoscape," in *Buddhist Missionaries in the Era of Globalization*, ed. Linda Learman, (Honolulu: University of Hawai'i Press, 2005), 22–50.
46. Henry Steel Olcott, "The First Leaf of the Theosophical Society," *The Theosophist* 12, no. 2 (1890): 60.
47. Reprinted in Guruge, *Return to Righteousness*, 368–386.
48. Guruge, *Return to Righteousness*, 167.
49. Cited by Prothero, *The White Buddhist*, 167.
50. Guruge, *Return to Righteousness*, 571.
51. Ibid., 580.
52. Ibid., 728.

53. Ibid., 590.
54. Ibid., 625.
55. Ibid., 603.
56. Cited by Trevithick, *The Revival of Buddhist Pilgrimage*, 88.
57. In Guruge, *Return to Righteousness*, 358. In a review of this lecture published in the November 3, 1891 *Indian Mirror*, the reviewer hopefully asked: "Why should not this unlooked for return of Buddhism in the form of a Buddhist colony at Buddha Gaya bring back with it the hope that the Hindus will recover their place among the great nations of the world...? Why should we, then, hesitate to take the hand which the Buddhists now proffer us in right, pure friendship?"
58. Guruge, *Return to Righteousness*, 603.
59. Ibid., 381.
60. Ibid., 603.
61. Cited in Trevithick, *The Revival of Buddhist Pilgrimage*, 77.
62. This itself is a common Orientalist take on Buddhist image veneration, extending a textual argument made in the Pāli canon, and paying no attention to the ways actual Buddhists actually understood their ritual practices; see my "The Field of the Buddha's Presence."
63. See Philip Almond, *The British Discovery of Buddhism*, and also David McMahan, *The Making of Buddhist Modernism* (New York: Oxford University Press, 2008).
64. Cited in Trevithick, *The Revival of Buddhist Pilgrimage*, 157.
65. Ibid., 159.
66. Cited in Almond, *The British Discovery of Buddhism*, 70.
67. Ibid., 74.
68. Ibid., 70.
69. Cunningham, *The Bhilsa Topes*, 33.
70. Guruge, *Return to Righteousness*, 688.
71. *Journal of Sacred Literature*, 1865, 287.
72. Edwin Arnold, *The Light of Asia* (London: Trübner, 1879), 155–156.
73. Brooks Wright, *Interpreter of Buddhism to the West: Sir Edwin Arnold* (New York: Bookman Associates, 1957), 1–3.
74. Wright, however, in his essentially hagiographic account of Arnold's life, says of Arnold's use of his Buddhist sources: "Arnold was able to animate the rather dry Buddhist scriptures with color, warmth, and imaginative vigor." *Interpreter of Buddhism to the West*, 88.
75. Arnold, *East and West*, 311.
76. Ibid., 307.
77. Ibid., 311.
78. Ibid., 313–314.
79. Ibid., 312.
80. Ibid., 310.
81. Ibid., 314.

82. Ibid., 321.
83. Cunningham, *Archaeological Survey of India Report*, 87.
84. Mitra, *Buddha Gaya*, 100.
85. Ibid., 4.
86. Ibid., 6.
87. Ibid., 66.
88. Ibid., 136.
89. Ibid.
90. Cited in Almond, *The British Discovery of Buddhism*, 16.
91. Almond, *The British Discovery of Buddhism*, and Pennington, *Was Hinduism Invented?*
92. Jan Gonda, *Aspects of Early Viṣṇuism* (Utrecht: Nva Oostoek's Uitgevers MIJ, 1965), 125.
93. These include: 1. The killing of animals in sacrifice must be stopped; 2. The world is only a product of the mind, *vijñānamāya* (which goes against the principle that the world is the body of Viṣṇu); 3. The world is without support, *anādhāram* (which goes against the principle that Viṣṇu is the support of the world); and 4. The world is engaged in the pursuit of error which it mistakes for knowledge. For more on the *Viṣṇupurāṇa*'s view of Buddhism, see Klaus Klostermaier, "Hindu Views of Buddhism," in *Canadian Contributions to Buddhist Studies*, ed. R. Amore, 60–82 (Waterloo: Wilfred Laurie University Press, 1979).
94. Ibid., 65–66.
95. Asher, "Gaya: Monuments of the Pilgrimage Town," 86.
96. Davis, *Lives of Indian Images*, 186–221.
97. In the Buddhist context, for instance, texts such as the *Niṣpannayogāvalī* and the *Sādhanamālā*, are very specific in laying out the ritual place of any number of Buddhist images.
98. Davis, *Lives of Indian Images*, 263.
99. Ibid., 5.
100. *Mahabodhi Journal* 4, no. 6 (October 1895).
101. It is worth noting that Dharmapala was acting against the advice of his mentor, Olcott—as I have noted, their relationship was at the very least strained by this point—who urged further negotiations instead of legal actions, and also against the advice the Sri Lankan monk to whom he frequently turned for authority in religious matters, Hikkauve Sumangala.
102. When Lord Elgin visited Gayā and Bodhgayā in the spring of 1895, he explicitly stated the government's policy of neutrality in matters regarding religion, and although the specific context was the contemporary "cow controversy," his words, delivered as they were on the very day that he visited the Mahābodhi temple, were clearly meant to pertain to the conflict there as well: "Government, as you are aware, must preserve a strict, perhaps even stern impartiality of which

you have indicated your appreciation, but it has seemed to me that when we approach spots or deal with institutions which others hold in veneration and affection, our first object should be to do our best to appreciate the feelings inspired by them, and our second to see that we do nothing by word or deed to injure those feelings." *Mahabodhi Journal* 4, no. 1 (1895): 44.

103. *Mahabodhi Journal* 4, no. 6 (1895): 45.
104. Lal did note, however, that it was possible that some Hindus had begun worshipping in the temple in the months leading up to the image incident, but that this was merely a recent innovation intended to establish a precedent for precisely such a legal claim; more on this point below.
105. For a list of texts cited by both the prosecution and the defense, see *Mahabodhi Journal* 4, no. 10 (1896): 80.
106. It is of course ironic that the defense would choose Cunningham and Mitra, since as we have already seen, both professed highly unfavorable views of Hinduism, and Mitra, in particular, was unrelenting in his castigation of the Mahant and the Giri *sannyāsin*: recall his remarks about their laziness and ignorance cited above.
107. Indeed, in the *Viṣṇupurāṇa* itself, there is no question as to the derisive position regarding Buddhism: according to this text, Buddhists are unclean and impure, and the Hindu who so much as dines with a Buddhist goes to hell. See Klostermeir, 65–66.
108. *Mahabodhi Journal* 4, nos. 7–8 (1896): 56.
109. *Mahabodhi Journal* 4, no. 11 (1896): 93.
110. Ibid., 79.
111. Ibid., 80.
112. See Trevithick, *The Revival of Buddhist Pilgrimage*, 106.
113. Ibid., 111.
114. Ibid., 122.
115. This is an offer that had first been made when Dharmapala initially approached the Mahant about installing the Amitābha image; see *Mahabodhi Journal* 4, nos. 7–8 (1896): 56.
116. Quoted in Trevithick, *The Revival of Buddhist Pilgrimage*, 126.
117. *Indian Law Reports* (Calcutta Series) 23 (1896): 62.
118. Ibid.
119. It is interesting that Macpherson would explicitly consider what he saw as Dharmapala's ulterior motives, since in the first trial, Macpherson noted: "I do not think there is any ground for believing that Dharmapala was animated by any other motive than a genuine one to discharge the trust he had undertaken in Japan to enshrine a suitable image of Buddha in the sanctum sanctorum, where one was needed." *Mahabodhi Journal* 4, nos. 7–8 (1896): 56.
120. *Indian Law Reports* (Calcutta Series) 23 (1896): 72.
121. From the *Mahabodhi Journal* (1922), reprinted in *Mahabodhi Journal: Diamond Jubilee Souvenir, 1891–1951* (Calcutta: MBJS, 1952), 95.

122. Most recently, Dalit Buddhists, who were left out of the discourse during the original negotiations, have agitated for greater representation; see Doyle, 387–422.
123. See Trevithick, *The Revival of Buddhist Pilgrimage*, 141–143, and also Doyle, 170–172.
124. Okakura, who served as curator of the Department of Japanese and Chinese Art at the Museum of Fine Arts, Boston, from 1903 to until his death in 1913, was a complex figure, at once a staunch defender of the traditional arts and culture of Japan, and at the same time a key interlocutor in the early East-West dialogue. See in particular his works in English, *The Ideals of the East, with Special Reference to the Art of Japan* (New York: Dutton, 1903), *The Awakening of Japan* (New York: The Century Co., 1904), and *The Book of Tea* (New York: Duffield, 1906). For a useful study of his interactions with various American intellectuals, see Satoko Tachiki, "Okakura Kakuzo (1862–1913) and Boston Brahmins" (Ph.D. dissertation, University of Michigan, 1986).
125. Dharmapala mentions his visit to Bodhgayā in his diaries and states elsewhere that Okakura "with the help of the Bengaless belonging to a neo-Hindu school opened negotiations with the Saivite Mahant stating that Japanese Buddhism is similar to Hinduism, and that they have no relationship with the Buddhist of Ceylon." Anagarika Dharmapala, *Buddhism in Its Relationship to Hinduism* (Calcutta: Mahabodhi Society, 1918), 205.
126. See Trevithick, *The Revival of Buddhist Pilgrimage*, 170
127. Okakura, *The Ideals of the East*, 81.
128. It is not clear what the Mahant's motives were here, but certainly he did not wish to continue to alienate the entire Buddhist world, and this minor gesture afforded him the opportunity to appease those who had been angered by his legal fights with the Mahābodhi temple. Furthermore, he must have known that the Japanese and Sri Lankan Buddhists were hardly allies, and thus siding with the former—and bringing them into the Bodhgayā community—might lessen the latter's influence.
129. Quote in Trevithick, *The Revival of Buddhist Pilgrimage*, 172
130. There was an important political dimension to both the government's refusal of Okakura's request, and also its view of non-Indian Buddhist groups, because the government was increasingly concerned about the issue of foreign influence in India, and it had no desire to allow the Japanese or any other foreigners even this minor outpost.
131. It is important to note, however, that the Mahant and his followers continued to assert their own rights and did not cease their polemical attacks on Buddhism.
132. *Mahabodhi Journal* 19, no. 12 (1911): 6–8.
133. *Mahabodhi Journal* 33, no. 4 (1925) : 203.
134. Ibid.
135. *Mahabodhi Journal* 43, no. 5 (1935): 207–213.
136. Dalmia and von Stietencron, *Representing Hinduism*, 20.

137. Quoted in Trevithick, *The Revival of Buddhist Pilgrimage*, 185.
138. Ibid., 194.
139. Albertina Nugteren, "Ritual Around the Bodhi-Tree in Bodhgaya," in *Pluralism and Identity: Studies in Ritual Behaviour*, ed. J. Platvoet and K. van der Toorn (Leiden: E. J. Brill, 1995), 156.

CHAPTER 5

1. "Information Dossier for nomination of Mahabodhi Temple Complex, Bodhgaya as a World Heritage Site," 4; http://whc.unesco.org/p_dynamic/sites/passfile.cfm?filename=1056rev&filetype=pdf&category=nominations, accessed 8 November 2009; this document has since been removed.
2. "Convention Concerning the Protection of the World Cultural and Natural Heritage," adopted by the General Conference of the United Nations Educational, Scientific and Cultural Organization, at its seventeenth session, Paris, November 16, 1972, 1.
3. ICOMOS No. 1056; Robert Shepherd has pointed out, however, the criteria UNESCO provides "are so broad and general that it seems reasonable to wonder what might not qualify." "UNESCO and the Politics of Cultural Heritage in Tibet," *Journal of Contemporary Asia* 36, no. 2 (2006): 243–257, 248.
4. Ibid., 8.
5. Ibid.
6. "Convention Concerning the Protection of the World Cultural and Natural Heritage," 1; a second document specifically addressing non-material aspects of culture—aspects as diverse as the watertight-bulkhead technology of Chinese junks and Cambodia's Royal Ballet to Indonesian puppet theater and the French gastronomic meal. The "Convention for the Safeguarding of Intangible Cultural Heritage" was created in 2003.
7. Ibid., 6.
8. "Information Dossier," 4.
9. See Trevithick, *The Revival of Buddhist Pilgrimage*, and Tara Doyle, "Bodh Gayā."
10. "Information Dossier," 3.
11. Ibid.
12. Sir Edwin Arnold, *East and West*, 310.
13. That said, however, it has been a typical modus operandi in Buddhist Studies since the discipline began, with numerous claims to uncover the "true," "original," "primitive," etc. teachings of the Buddha. For a specifically archaeological treatment of this issue, see Denis Byrne, "Buddhist Stupa and Thai Social Practice," *Buddhist Archaeology* (1985): 266–281.
14. Tzvetan Todorov, "Tribunals, Apologies, Reparations, and the Search for Justice: In Search of Lost Crime," *The New Republic* (January 2001): 9.
15. "Information Dossier," 3.

16. "Information Dossier;" it is unclear if the use of "enlightened" is meant to be an ironic pun.
17. Ibid., 4.
18. "Convention Concerning the Protection of the World Cultural and Natural Heritage," 3
19. "Information Dossier," 5.
20. "Information Dossier," Annexures, "Archaeological Project," 8.
21. Ibid., 11.
22. Ibid., 11 [*sic*].
23. Ibid., 12.
24. See J. O. Blatti, ed., *Past Meets Present: Essays about Historic Interpretation and Public Audiences* (Washington, DC: Smithsonian Institution Press, 1987); Jean Misitelli, "World Heritage, Between Universalism and Globalization," *International Journal of Cultural Property* 11, no. 2 (2002): 323–336. For UNESCO, see Thomas Erickson, "Between Universalism and Relativism: A Critique of the UNESCO Concept of Culture," in *Culture and Rights: Anthropological Perspectives*, ed. Jane Cowan, 127–148 (Cambridge: Cambridge University Press, 2001).
25. There are, really, two "subvisions" here: one is a Buddhist vision of the temple, one a Hindu vision. But even this is too simple, as we shall see below, because different Buddhist communities have different visions of the temple complex.
26. See, for instance, Erik Cohen, "Pilgrimage and Tourism: Convergence and Divergence," in *Sacred Journeys: The Anthropology of Pilgrimage*, ed. Alan Morinis, 47–61 (Westport, CT: Greenwood Press, 1992). Cohen takes a structuralist approach, and argues—following Turner—that there is a basic difference, in that pilgrims travel to a center of the world whereas tourists travel from a center to a periphery. Cohen critiques those scholars who have seen a modern/pre-modern distinction, or a material/spiritual distinction, but in the end I find his own binary analysis altogether too neat.
27. "Information Dossier," 21.
28. Ibid., 27.
29. Ibid., 7.
30. Ibid., 11.
31. Bernard S. Cohn, "The Transformation of Objects into Artifacts," 302 and 304. See also James Clifford, "On Collecting Art and Culture," in *The Predicament of Culture: Twentieth Century Ethnography, Literature, and Art*, ed. James Clifford, 215–251 (Cambridge: Harvard University Press, 1988). For more on the taxonomic tenor of British Orientalists in India, see Cohn, *Colonialism and Its Forms of Knowledge: The British in India* (Princeton, NJ: Princeton University Press, 1996), and Nicholas B. Dirks, *Castes of Mind: Colonialism and the Making of Modern India* (Princeton, NJ: Princeton University Press, 2001); see also Tim Barringer and Tom Flynn, eds., *Colonialism and the Object: Empire, Material Culture and the Museum* (London: Routledge, 2004), and Tony Bennett, *Pasts Beyond Memory: Evolution, Museums, Colonialism* (London: Routledge, 2004).

32. For a formative view of UNESCO, see Julian Huxley (the first director of UNESCO), *UNESCO: Its Purpose and Philosophy* (Washington, DC: American Council on Public Affairs, 1947); see also Thomas Ericksen, "Between Universalism and Relativism: A Critique of the UNESCO Concept of Culture" in *Culture and Rights: Anthropological Perspectives*, ed. Jane Cowan, 127–148 (Cambridge: Cambridge University, 2001); Jean Musitelli, "World Heritage, Between Universalism and Globalization," *International Journal of Cultural Property* 11, no. 2 (2002): 323–336; Robert Shepherd, "UNESCO and the Politics of Cultural Heritage in Tibet," *Journal of Contemporary Asia* 36, no. 2 (2006): 243–257.
33. "Information Dossier," 9.
34. Ibid.
35. Michel Foucault, "Of Other Spaces," *Diacritics* 16, no. 1 (1986): 22–27.
36. The Mahābodhi's history has been exceedingly well documented; see Rajendralala Mitra, *Buddha Gaya: The Great Buddhist Temple, Hermitage of Sakya Muni*; Alexander Cunningham, *Mahabodhi or the Great Buddhist Temple Under the Bodhi Tree at Buddha-Gaya*; and Benimadhab Barua, *Gayā and Buddha-Gayā*. See also, more recently, Alan Trevithick, *The Revival of Buddhist Pilgrimage at Bodh Gaya (1811–1949)*; Janice Leoshko, *Sacred Traces: British Explorations of Buddhism in South*; and Frederick M. Asher, *Monumental Legacy: Bodh Gaya*.
37. For details of the Burmese missions in particular, see W. S. Desai, "History of the Burmese Mission to India, October 1830–July 1833," *Journal of the Burma Research Society* 26 (1936): 71–109; for more specific discussions of the activities of these missions, particularly as they affected the Mahābodhi temple itself, see Geri H. Malandra, "The Mahabodhi Temple," and Jeremiah P. Losty, "The Mahabodhi Temple Before Its Restoration."
38. See Mildred Archer, *Early Views of India: The Picturesque Journeys of Thomas and William Daniell, 1786–1794* (London: Thames and Hudson, 1980). Significantly, most of these paintings are devoid of people, presenting an idealized, empty landscape. As Matthew Edney has pointed out, the Picturesque mode of these early painters was one in which the world "is viewed, represented, and through that representation is cured and improved." Bodhgayā here is idealized as a static monument, an archaeological object; see Matthew Edney, *Mapping an Empire: The Geographical Construction of British India, 1765–1843* (Chicago: University of Chicago Press, 1997).
39. Buchanan's complete manuscript is located in the Indian Office Library and Records; his account of Bihar is published as *An Account of the Districts of Bihar and Patna in 1811–1812* (Patna: Bihar and Orissa Research Society, 1986; first published in 1934); a partial account, with illustrations, was published in 1838 as *The History, Antiquities, Topography and Statistics of Eastern India*, ed. Montgomery Martin (Delhi: Cosmo Publications, 1976).
40. Mitra, *Buddha Gaya*, ii.

41. Mitra, Government of India, Foreign Department, Political Branch, Part A, February 1878, nos. 129–251.
42. Mitra, *Buddha Gaya*, 66.
43. Leoshko, "On the Construction of a Buddhist Pilgrimage Site," 580.
44. "Information Dossier," 8.
45. See Nicholas Dirks, "Guiltless Spoliations: Picturesque Beauty, Colonial Knowledge, and Colin Mackenzie's Survey of India," in *Perceptions of South Asia's Visual Past*, ed. Catherine B. Asher and Thomas R. Metcalf, 211–232 (New Delhi: Oxford and IBH Publishing for the American Institute of Indian Studies, 1994).
46. Edney, *Mapping an Empire*, 61.
47. Cunningham, *Mahabodhi*, 3; this is a ridiculous claim, since Bodhgayā has always been intimately linked to Gayā and Buddhist and Hindu pilgrims have from the beginning visited both sites.
48. Michel Foucault, *Discipline and Punish: The Birth of the Prison*, trans. Alan Sheridan (New York: Random House, 1977), see in particular 184–192. See also Thomas Metcalf, *Ideologies of the Raj*, vol. 3, no. 4, *The New Cambridge History of India* (Cambridge: Cambridge University Press, 1994), as well as C. A. Bayly, "Knowing the Country: Empire and Information in India," *Modern Asian Studies* 27 (1993): 3–43; and David Ludden, "Orientalist Empiricism: Transformations of Colonial Knowledge," in *Orientalism and the Postcolonial Predicament: Perspectives on South Asia*, ed. Carol A. Breckinridge and Peter van der Veer, 250–278 (Philadelphia: University of Pennsylvania Press, 1993).
49. For more on this topic, see Losty, "The Mahābodhi Temple Before its Restoration."
50. This attitude is embedded in a larger colonial epistemology, which understood Indian culture in binary and oppositional religious terms, so that labels such as "Hindu" and "Muslim" and "Buddhist" were not simply descriptive, but prescriptive, and these antagonistic divisions became what Ludden has called "an iconic principle of governance." Ludden, "Orientalist Empiricism," 266. What is significant in this context is that these sharp divisions were not restricted to people, but applied to places as well. As Ludden further elaborates, the "the colonial invention of tradition became irrelevant to experience of the village and communalism.... The empire made orientalism as a body of knowledge appear as a verified representation of reality by building it into both the construction of empirical evidence and the social experience of people in governance and education" (268).
51. For an exhaustive history, see Dilip K. Chakrabarti, *A History of Indian Archaeology from the Beginning to 1947* (New Delhi: Munshiram Monoharlal, 1988).
52. Quoted in Benedict Anderson, *Imagined Communities: Reflections on the Origin and Spread of Nationalism* (London: Verso, 1983), 179n30.
53. Edney, *Mapping an Empire*, 34.
54. Ibid., 16; see Arjun Appadurai, "Number in the Colonial Imagination," in *Orientalism and the Postcolonial Predicament: Perspectives on South Asia*, ed. Carol A. Breckinridge and Peter van der Veer, 314–339 (Philadelphia: University of Pennsylvania Press, 1993).

55. Edney, *Mapping an Empire*, 25.
56. Byrne, "Buddhist Stupa and Thai Social Practice," 267. See also Denis Byrne, "Western Hegemony in Archaeological Heritage Management," *History and Anthropology* 5 (1991): 269–276.
57. Byrne, "Buddhist Stupa and Thai Social Practice," 267.
58. Cunningham, *Archaeological Survey of India Report*, 87.
59. Almond, *The British Discovery of Buddhism*.
60. A. B. Griswold, "The Holy Land Transported: Replicas of the Mahābodhi Shrine in Siam and Elsewhere," in *Paranavitana Felicitation Volume on Art and Architecture and Oriental Studies*, ed. N. A. Jayawickrama, 173–221 (Colombo, Sri Lanka: M. D. Gunasena and Co., 1965).
61. See Richard Davis, *Lives of Indian Images*.
62. Bruce McCoy Owens, "Monumentality, Identity, and the State: Local Practice, World Heritage, and Heterotopia at Swayambhu, Nepal," *Anthropological Quarterly* 75, no. 2 (2002): 269–316, 277; see also Joanne P. Waghorne and Norman Cutler, eds., *Gods of Flesh, Gods of Stone: The Embodiment of Divinity in India* (New York: Columbia University Press, 1996).
63. Byrne, "Buddhist Stupa and Thai Social Practice," 267.
64. There is, perhaps, reason to hope that there has been something of a shift in the practices of museum collection and display; see Moira Simpson, *Making Representations: Museums in the Post-Colonial Era* (London: Routledge, 1996).
65. Owens, "Monumentality, Identity, and the State," 275.
66. See Tara N. Doyle, "'Liberate the Mahabodhi Temple!' Socially Engaged Buddhism, Dalit-Style," in *Buddhism in the Modern World: Adaptations of an Ancient Tradition*, ed. Steven Heine and Charles S. Prebish, 249–280 (Oxford: Oxford University Press, 2003).
67. The Bodhgaya Temple Act, 1949, (Bihar Act 17 of 1949); available at http://www.mahabodhi.com/en/b-gaya_tempact.htm.
68. See Doyle, "'Liberate the Mahabodhi Temple!'" for the specifics concerning the Ambedkar Buddhists at Bodhgayā; for the larger Dalit context, see Eleanor Zelliot, *From Untouchable to Dalit: Essays on the Ambedkar Movement* (New Delhi: Manohar, 2001).
69. Doyle, "'Liberate the Mahabodhi Temple!'", 261. For an interesting and, I think, extremely useful discussion of the issue of communalism and identity, see Rogers Brubaker, *Ethnicity without Groups*.
70. Michael Herzfeld, *A Place in History: Social and Monumental Time in a Cretan Town*, (Princeton, NJ: Princeton University Press, 1991), 14; quoted in Owens, "Monumentality, Identity, and the State."
71. This has been a decidedly thorny issue, and UNESCO has at several junctures not only criticized the implementation of the TMP, but has gone so far as to threaten to remove the WHS designation.

72. As reported by IANS, http://www.buddhistchannel.tv/index.php?id=42,6138,0,0,1,0, accessed March 12, 2011.
73. See http://www.ambedkar.org/News/letter.htm, accessed March 12, 2011.
74. As reported by IANS, http://www.buddhistchannel.tv/index.php?id=42,6138,0,0,1,0, accessed March 12, 2011.
75. Owens, "Monumentality, Identity, and the State," 271.
76. Edney, *Mapping an Empire*, 48.
77. Ann Bermingham, *Landscape and Ideology: The English Rustic Tradition, 1740–1860* (Berkeley: University of California Press, 1996), 3.
78. Edney, *Mapping an Empire*, 57.
79. The literature on this topic is extensive; see, for instance, the varied essays in Gautam Badhra, Gyan Prakash, and Susie Tharu, eds., *Subaltern Studies X*, (New Delhi: Oxford University Press, 1999); Dipesh Chakrabarty, *Habitations of Modernity: Essays in the Wake of Subaltern Studies* (Chicago: University of Chicago Press, 2002); Vinayak Chaturvedi, ed., *Mapping Subaltern Studies and the Postcolonial* (Verso: London and New York, 2000); and David Ludden, ed., *Reading Subaltern Studies: Critical History, Contested Meaning and the Globalization of South Asia* (London: Anthem South Asian Studies, 2002).
80. Vincent Berdoulay, "Place, Meaning, and Discourse in French Language Geography," in *The Power of Place*, ed. John A. Agnew and James S. Duncan, 124–39 (London: Unwin Hyman, 1989), 135.
81. Fredric Jameson, "The Cultural Logic of Capital," *New Left Review* 46 (1984): 66.
82. Shelly Errington, "Making Progress on Borobudur: An Old Monument in New Order," *Visual Anthropology Review* 9, no. 2 (1993): 32–59.
83. Arjun Appadurai, *The Social Life of Things: Commodities in Cultural Perspective* (New York: Cambridge University Press, 1986).
84. Errington, "Making Progress on Borobudur," 32; see also Davis, *The Lives of Indian Images*.
85. Errington, "Making Progress on Borobudur," 56.
86. A notable exception is Finbarr Barry Flood's "Between Cult and Culture: Bamiyan, Islamic Iconoclasm, and the Museum," *The Art Bulletin* 84, no. 4 (2002): 641–659.
87. UNESCO's official response to this, published in the *American Journal of Archaeology*, ignored the complexity of the Taliban's iconoclasm: "UNESCO is not only concerned by the threats to the cultural heritage in Afghanistan but with the totality of the human condition there. Alongside its efforts to protect the material expressions of culture and religion, UNESCO also strives to address the problems of the lack of respect for human rights in the country, the poor status of women there, the present famine conditions, and the catastrophic living conditions in the Afghan refugee camps." Christian Manhart, "The Afghan

Cultural Heritage Crisis: UNESCO's Response to the Destruction of Statues in Afghanistan," *American Journal of Archaeology* 105, no. 3 (2001): 387–88, 388.

88. Significantly, one of Owens's informants at Swayambhu complains: "It used to be that you could put a god wherever you wanted. Nowadays they even tell you what kind of brick to use." Owens, "Monumentality, Identity, and the State," 281.

CHAPTER 6

1. http://articles.latimes.com/2008/may/21/world/fg-mosque21, accessed May 21, 2012.
2. Kamran Scot Aghaie, *The Martyrs of Karbala: Shi'i Symbols and Rituals of Modern Iran* (Seattle: University of Washington Press, 2004), 9.
3. Ibid.
4. Not a great deal is known about this recent discovery; see Rossina Kostova, Kazimir Popkonstantinov, and Tom Higham, "Relics of the Baptist: Scientific research planned for finds excavated in Sozopol, Bulgaria in 2010 (Radiocarbon Dating, DNA testing)," paper presented at "Saint John the Baptist and His Cults," colloquium held at St. John's College, Oxford, June 24, 2001.
5. For a discussion of John in Islamic sources, see Geert Jan van Gelder, "A Flood of Bubbling Blood and a Talking Head: John the Baptist in the Islamic Sources," paper presented at the "Saint John the Baptist and His Cults," colloquium held at St. John's College, Oxford, June 24, 2001.
6. It is perhaps more appropriate, given the context, to call this a tomb.
7. See Finbarr Barry Flood, *The Great Mosque of Damascus: Studies on the Makings of an Umayyad Visual Culture* (London: Brill, 2000).
8. Andreas Huyssen, *Present Pasts*, 7.
9. Flood, *The Great Mosque of Damascus*, 5.
10. Ibid., 1
11. Ibid., 11.
12. Ibid., 4.
13. Ibid., 108.
14. Ibid., 202; for more on the politics of this sort of visual "translation," see chapter six of Flood, *The Great Mosque of Damascus*, "Damascus and the Making of an Umayyad Visual Culture."
15. Ibid., 240.
16. Georges Kazan, "The Head of St. John the Baptist—the Early Evidence," paper presented at "Saint John the Baptist and His Cults," colloquium held at St. John's College, Oxford, June 24, 2001.
17. Ibid., 2.
18. See Geary, *Furta Sancta*, and Brown, *Cult of the Saints*.
19. Kazan, "The Head of St. John the Baptist," 3.

20. Ibid., 5.
21. See van Gelder, "A Flood of Bubbling Blood and a Talking Head," 6.
22. For a discussion of the ways in which a relic can become such a politically charged object, the importance of the Buddha's tooth relic for kings in Sri Lanka is illustrative; see A. M. Hocart's classic—and deeply flawed—study, *The Temple of the Tooth in Kandy* (London: Luzac and Co. 1931), and Kevin Trainor, *Relics, Ritual, and Representation.*
23. Flood, *The Great Mosque of Damascus*, 107.
24. Ibid., 108.
25. Smith, *To Take Place*, 104.
26. See Raz Kletter, *Just Past? The Making of Israel Archaeology* (London: Equinox Publishing Ltd, 2006), and Nadia Abu El-Haj, *Facts on the Ground: Archaeological Practice and Territorial Self-Fashioning in Israeli Society* (Chicago: University of Chicago Press, 2001).
27. UNESCO, in what can only be deemed a bizarre response to the Taliban's outrage at the West's idolatrous relationship with the Buddhas, sent a team of scientists to Bamiyan to explore various possibilities of reconstructing the Buddhas, using highly sophisticated means of identifying even the tiniest of particles from the destroyed images. The lead scientist was at the time quite confident that the Buddhas could, in fact, be reconstructed. This has yet to happen.
28. Quoted in Yitzhak Nakash, "The Visitation of the Shrines of the Imams and the Shi'i Mutjahids in the Early Twentieth Century," *Studia Islamica* 81, no. 1 (1995): 153–164, 154.
29. Syed Akbar Hyder, *Reliving Karbala: Martyrdom in South Asian Memory* (Oxford: Oxford University Press, 2006), 7.
30. Edward Casey, *Remembering: A Phenomenological Study* (Bloomington: Indiana University Press, 1987), 186–187.
31. Smith, *To Take Place*, 79.
32. R. A. Markham, "How on Earth Could Places Become Holy? Origins of the Christian Idea of Holy Places," *Journal of Early Christian Studies* 2, no. 3 (1994): 257–71, 259.
33. Ibid., 268.
34. Ibid., 270.
35. Brown, *Cult of the Saints*, 3.
36. S. H. Nasr, "Ithna Ashariyah," ed. Lindsay Jones, *The Encyclopedia of Religion* (Detroit, MI: MacMillan, 2005), 8337.
37. Surinder Bhardwaj, "Non-Hajj Pilgrimage in Islam: A Neglected Dimension of Religious Circulation," Journal of Cultural Geography 17, no. 2 (1988): 69–87, 73.
38. M. J. Kister, "Sanctity Joint and Divided: On Holy Places in the Islamic Tradition," *Jerusalem Studies in Arabic and Islam* 20 (1996): 18–65.
39. Ibid., 21.
40. Ibid., 22.

41. Ingvild Flaskerud, *Visualizing Belief and Piety in Iranian Shiism* (London: Continuum, 2010), 102.
42. Vali Nasr, *The Shia Revival: How Conflicts Within Islam Will Shape the Future* (London: Norton, 2006), 56.
43. Yitzhak Nakash, *The Shi'is of Iraq* (Princeton, NJ: Princeton University Press, 1994), 18.
44. Ali is incredibly significant in the Shi'a tradition, since it is the dispute over succession after the Prophet's death that, ultimately, leads to formation of the Shi'a tradition. Ali is the fourth and last of the "Rightly Guided" caliphs, and although it is Hussein, Ali's son, who is considered by many to be the first of the Shi'a rulers, Ali occupies a place second only to Mohammad for much of the Shi'a community.
45. Nakash, *The Shi'is of Iraq*, 18.
46. Nasr, *The Shia Revival*, 55
47. Nakash, "The Visitation of the Shrines of the Imams," 153.
48. Brown, *Cult of the Saints*, 42.
49. Nakash, *The Visitation of the Shrines of the Imams*, 154.
50. Ibid.
51. Flaskerud, *Visualizing Belief*, 103.
52. Nakash, *The Shi'is of Iraq*, 21.
53. Hyder, *Reliving Karbala*, 16; for more on the place of Karbala in southern Asia, see David Pinault, *Horse of Karbala: Muslim Devotional Life in India* (New York: Palgrave, 2001).
54. Hyder, *Reliving Karbala*, 208.
55. Consider, for instance, J. E. Malpas's assertion that that place is where "subjectivity itself is established—place is not found *on* subjectivity, but is rather that *on which* subjectivity is founded." J. E. Malpas, *Place and Experience: A Philosophical Topography* (Cambridge: Cambridge University Press, 1999), 35.
56. Yi-Fu Tuan, *Topophilia: A Study of Environmental Perception, Attitudes, and Values* (Englewood Cliffs, NJ: Prentice Hall, 1974), 4.
57. Edward Relph, *Place and Placeness* (London: Pion, 1976), 8. For more on this particular emphasis in theoretical discussions of place, see Robert Sack, *Homo Geographicus* (Baltimore: Johns Hopkins University Press, 1997), and Tim Cresswell, *In Place/Out of Place: Geography, Ideology and Transgression* (Minneapolis: University of Minnesota Press, 1996).
58. Relph, *Place and Placeness*, 43.
59. Turner and Turner, *Image and Pilgrimage*, 136.
60. Hamid Dabashi, *Shi'ism: A Religion of Protest* (Cambridge, MA: Belknap, 2011), 6.
61. Martin Heidegger, *Poetry, Language, Thought* (New York: Harper and Row, 1971), 160.
62. John Haugeland, "Reading Brandom Reading Heidegger," *European Journal of Philosophy* 13, no. 3 (2005): 421–28, 423.
63. Dabashi, *Shi'ism*, 87.

64. Shields posits that spatialisation is better than *habitus*, and better than Foucault's related notion of *dispositif*, in that it is more dynamic, more able to "to accommodate the contradictions and schisms." Shields, *Places on the Margin*, 63. As he puts it, "I use the term *social spatialisation* to designate the ongoing social construction of the spatial at the level of the social imaginary (collective mythologies, presuppositions) as well as interventions in the landscape (for example, the built environment). This term allows us to name an object of study which encompasses both the cultural logic of the spatial and its expression and elaboration in language and more concrete actions, constructions and institutional arrangements." Shields, *Places on the Margin*, 31.
65. Ibid., 7.
66. Nasr, *The Shia Revival*, 128.
67. Dabashi, *Shi'ism*, 83.
68. Flaskerud, *Visualizing Belief and Piety*, 81.
69. Hyder, *Reliving Karbala*, 69.
70. The 2007 PBS documentary, *Pilgrimage to Karbala*, contains footage of some of these songs being sung by soldiers on their way to Iraq.
71. Stephen C. Pelletier, *The Iran-Iraq War: Chaos in a Vacuum* (New York: Praeger, 1992), 122.
72. See Mahmoud Ayoub, *Redemptive Suffering in Islam: A Study of the Devotional Aspects of 'Ashura' in Twelver Shi'ism* (The Hague: de Gruyter, 1978).
73. Kamran Scot Aghaie, *The Women of Karbala: Ritual Performance and Symbolic Discourses in Modern Shi'i Islam* (Austin: University of Texas Press, 2005), 94.
74. Aghaie, *The Women of Karbala*,
75. Ibid., 154.
76. Nakash, *The Shi'is of Iraq*, 154.
77. Ibid., 151.
78. Brian Spooner, "The Function of Religion in Persian Society," *Iran* 1 (1963): 91.
79. Smith, *To Take Place*, 117.
80. Ibid., 110.
81. Ron Hassner, *War on Sacred Grounds* (Ithaca, NY: Cornell University Press, 2009), 43; some readers of Hassner may find it puzzling that earlier in the book, he talks of the "contagious" nature of the sacred—a Durkheimian notion—and the way that the sacred power can, in fact, be contained in portable objects such as relics and pilgrims' mementos. For a very different treatment on the topic of the indivisible nature of the sacred, see Richard Sosis, "Why Sacred Lands Are Not Indivisible: The Cognitive Foundations of Sacralising Land," *Journal of Terrorism Research* 2, no. 1 (2011): 17–44.
82. Smith, *To Take Place*, 104.

CHAPTER 7

1. Nicole Price, "Tourism and the Bighorn Medicine Wheel: How Multiple Use Does Not Work for Sacred Land Sites," in *Sacred Sties, Sacred Places*, ed. David L. Carmichael, Jane Hubert, Brian Reeves, and Audhild Schanche, 257–264 (London: Routledge, 1994).
2. David Harvey, *Justice, Nature and the Geography of Difference* (Oxford: Blackwell Publishers, 1996), 310.
3. The Yellowstone Act, 1872.
4. Lynn Ross-Bryant, "Sacred Sites: Nature and Nation in U.S. National Parks," *Religion and American Culture* 15, no. 1 (2005): 31–62, 31.
5. Fifth Annual Report, 1921.
6. Ross-Bryant, "Sacred Sites," 38.
7. Simon Schama, *Landscape and Memory* (New York: Random House, 1995), 191.
8. Frederick Law Olmsted, intro. Laura Wood Roper, "The Yosemite Valley and the Mariposa Big Trees, a Preliminary Report (1865)," *Landscape Architecture* (October 1952): 22.
9. Ross-Bryant, "Sacred Sites," 52.
10. Michael E. Harkin, "Sacred Places, Scarred Spaces," *Wicazo Sa Review* 15, no. 1: 54.
11. Michel Foucault, *Discipline and Punish: The Birth of the Prison*, trans. Alan Sheridan (New York: Pantheon, 1977), 205.
12. Harkin, "Sacred Places, Scarred Spaces," 55.
13. Ross-Bryant, "Sacred Sites," 52.
14. Harkin, "Sacred Places, Scarred Spaces," 56.
15. Allison M. Dussias, "Cultural Conflicts Regarding Land Use: The Conflict Between Recreational Users at Devil's Tower and Native American Ceremonial Users," *Vermont Journal of Environmental Law* 2 (2000–01): 13–40, 1.
16. Quoted in Dussias, "Cultural Conflicts," 2.
17. Cresswell, *Place*, 39.
18. Eade and Sallnow, eds., *Contesting the Sacred*, 2.
19. Christopher Tilley, "Introduction: Identity, Place, Landscape and Heritage," *Journal of Material Culture* 11, nos. 1/2 (2006): 7–32, 13.
20. Bear Lodge Multiple Use Association v. Babbit 175 F.3d 818 (10th Cir. 1999).
21. See Jeffery R. Hanson David Moore, "Applied Anthropology at Devils Tower National Monument," *Plains Anthropologist* 31 (1999).
22. Gear L. San Miguel, "How Is Devils Tower a Sacred Site to American Indian?," 1994, at http://www.nps.gov/deto/historycultur/sacredsite.htm, accessed April 12, 2012.
23. On the issue of religious freedom as it relates specifically to Native Americans, see Russell Lawrence Barsh, "The Illusion of Religious Freedom for Indigenous Americans," *Or. L. Rev.* 65 (1986): 369–372; Celia Byler, "Free Access or Free

Exercise?: A Choice between Mineral Development and American Indian Sacred Site Preservation on Public Lands," *Conn. L. Rev.* 22 (1990): 397–435.; Raymond Cross and Elizabeth Brenneman, "Devils Tower at the Crossroads: The National Park Service and the Preservation of Native American Cultural Resources in the 21st Century," *Pub. Land & Resources L. Rev.* 18 (1997): 5–45; Rebekah J. French, "Free Exercise of Religion on the Public Lands," *Pub. Land L. Rev.* 11 (1990): 197–209; Rayanne J. Griffin, "Sacred Site Protection against a Backdrop of Religious Intolerance," *Tulsa L.J.* 31 (1995): 395–419.; Ann M. Hooker, "American Indian Sacred Sites on Federal Public Lands: Resolving Conflicts between Religious Use and Multiple Use at El Malpais National Monument," *Am. Indian L. Rev.* 19 (1994): 133–158; Dean B. Suagee, "Tribal Voices in Historic Preservation: Sacred Landscapes, Cross-Cultural Bridges, and Common Ground," *Vt. L. Rev.* 21 (1996): 145–224; Fred Unmack, "Equality under the First Amendment: Protecting Native American Religious Practices on Public Lands," *Pub. Land L. Rev.* 8 (1987): 307–339; Anastasia P. Winslow, "Sacred Standards: Honoring the Establishment Clause in Protecting Native American Sacred Sites," *Ariz. L. Rev.* 38 (1996): 1291–1343.

24. Dustin et al, "Cross-Cultural Claims on Devils Tower National Monument," 82.
25. The linkage between place and mythology is ubiquitous in Native American and other aboriginal cultures, and in many court cases involving Native American places, mythological associations are an import part of the legal proceedings; see, for instance, Bruce G. Miller, "Culture as Cultural Defense: An American Indian Sacred Site in Court," *American Indian Quarterly* 22, nos. 1/2 (1998): 83–97, particularly 85.
26. Harkin, "Sacred Places," 50; see also Keith Basso, *Wisdom Sits in Places: Landscape and Language among the Western Apache* (Albuquerque: University of New Mexico Press, 1996).
27. Durkheim, *The Elementary Forms*, 36.
28. Ibid., 223.
29. Alf Hornborg, "Environmentalism, Ethnicity, and Sacred Places: Reflections on Modernity, Discourse, and Power," *Canadian Review of Sociology and Anthropology* 31, no. 3 (1994): 245–267, 245.
30. http://www.nps.gov/deto/faqs.htm.
31. The literature here is vast; for a clear and insightful overview, see Vine Deloria Jr., "Prospects for Restoration of Tribal Lands," *Restoration and Management Notes* 10, no. 1 (1992): 48–58; for more specific discussions of this context, see Eric Freedman, "Protecting Sacred Sites on Public Land: Religion and Alliances in the Mato Tipila-Devils Tower Litigation," *American Indian Quarterly* 31, no. 1 (2007): 1–22; Rena Martin, "Native Connection to Place: Policies and Play," *American Indian Quarterly* 25, no. 1 (2001): 35–41; Joe Watkins, "Place-meant," *American Indian Quarterly* 25, no. 1 (2001): 41–45; Donald L. Fixico, "The Struggle for Our Homes: Indian and White Values and Tribal Lands," in *Defending*

Mother Earth: Native American Perspectives on Environmental Justice, ed. Jace Weaver, 29–46 (Maryknoll, NY: Orbis, 1996); Sandra B. Zellmer, "Sustaining Geographies of Hope: Cultural Resources on Public Lands," *U Col. L. Rev.* 73 (2002): 413–519; Leo McAvoy, "American Indians, Place Meanings and the Old/New West," *Journal of Leisure Research* 34, no. 4 (2002): 383–396; Marietta W. Eaton, "Consultation on Grand Staircase—Escalante National Monument from Planning to Implementation," *American Indian Quarterly* 25, no. 1 (2001): 28–34; and Griffin, "Sacred Site Protection."

32. Griffin, "Sacred Site Protection," 395; and Andrew Gulliford, *Sacred Objects and Sacred Places: Preserving Tribal Traditions* (Boulder: University Press of Colorado, 2000).
33. Fixico, "The Struggle for Our Homes," 9.
34. Richard B. Collins, "Sacred Sites and Religious Freedom on Government Land," *J. Constitutional L.* 5, no. 2 (2003): 241–270, 241.
35. Miller, "Culture as Cultural Defense," 92.
36. Daniel Dubuisson. *The Western Construction of Religion: Myths, Knowledge, and Ideology* (Baltimore, MD: Johns Hopkins, 2007), 64.
37. Vine Deloria Jr., "Sacred Lands and Religious Freedom," in *The Sacred Land Reader*, ed. Marjorie Beggs and Christopher McLeod, 20, www.sacredland.org/reader.html, accessed December 12, 2012. See also Deloria's discussion of the importance of the spatial in Native American traditions in his important *God Is Not Red: A Native View of Religion* (New York: Putnam, 1973).
38. The full text of the Act is available at http://www.cr.nps.gov/local-law/fhpl_IndianRelFreAct.pdf, accessed December 12, 2012.
39. Collins, "Sacred Sites and Religious Freedom," 269.
40. Deloria, "Sacred Lands," 24.
41. Ibid., 17.
42. Miller, "Culture as Cultural Defense," 83.
43. 16 U.S.C. 431; see Dussias, "Cultural Conflicts Regarding Land Use," 2.
44. 16 U.S.C. 433.
45. Patricia L. Parker, "Guidelines for Evaluation and Document Traditional Cultural Properties," U.S. Department of the Interior, National Park Service, 1990, available at http://www.nps.gov/nr/publications/bulletins/nrb38/nrb38%20introduction.htm#tcp, accessed March 16, 2013.
46. Miller, "Culture as Cultural Defense," 84.
47. Ibid., 84; Miller cites John Dormaar and Brian O. K. Reeves, "Vision Quest Sites in Southern Alberta and Northern Montana," in *Kunaitupil: Coming Together on Native Sacred Sites*, ed. Brian O. K. Reeves and Margaret A. Kennedy, 162–178 (Calgary: Archaeological Society of Alberta, 1993).
48. Miller, "Culture as Cultural Defense," 85.
49. Deloria, "Sacred Lands," 18.
50. Ibid.

51. Ibid., 87.
52. Ibid., 88.
53. Bruce G. Miller, "Culture as Cultural Defense," 84.
54. J. T. Thomas, "Climbing Ban Upheld at Devils Tower," *High Country News*, April 27, 1998; see also Charles H. Bonham, "Devils Tower, Rainbow Bridge, and the Uphill Battle Facing Native American Religion on Public Lands," *Law and Inequality* 20 (2002): 157–202, especially n168.
55. Bear Lodge Multiple Use Association v. Babbitt et al., 96-CV-063-D (10th Cir. 1996).
56. Ibid.
57. Bear Lodge Multiple Use Association v. Babbitt et al., 2 F.Supp.2d 1448,1452 (10th Cir. 1998).
58. See Dustin et al., "Cross-Cultural Claims on Devils Tower National Monument," 83.
59. Quoted in Freedman, "Protecting Sacred Sites on Public Land," 14–15.
60. Harvey, *Justice, Nature and the Geography of Difference*, 298.

CHAPTER 8

1. Fernand Braudel, *The Mediterranean and the Mediterranean World in the Age of Philip II*, 2 vols., trans. Sian Reynolds (London: Collins, 1972), 1:18.
2. David Chidester, *Savage Systems:* Colonialism and Comparative Religion in Southern Africa (Charlotesville: University of Virginia Press, 1996), 4.
3. Boyarin, *Border Lines*, 15.
4. Ibid., 18.
5. For a refreshing resistance to such neat divisions, see the chapters in Margaret Cormack's *Muslims and Others in Sacred Space* (Oxford: Oxford University Press, 2013), particularly Peter Gottschalk's introduction and Lance D. Baird's chapter, "Boundaries and Baraka: Christians, Muslims, and a Palestinian Saint."
6. Ross-Bryant, "Sacred Sites," 53–54.

Bibliography

Abu El-Haj, Nadia. *Facts on the Ground: Archaeological Practice and Territorial Self-Fashioning in Israeli Society*. Chicago: University of Chicago Press, 2001.

Aghaie, Kamran Scot. *The Martyrs of Karbala: Shi'i Symbols and Rituals of Modern Iran*. Seattle: University of Washington Press, 2004.

——. *The Women of Karbala: Ritual Performance and Symbolic Discourses in Modern Shi'i Islam*. Austin: University of Texas Press, 2005.

Aksland, Markus. *The Sacred Footprint*. Oslo: YETI Consult, 1990.

Albera, Dionigi. "'Why Are You Mixing What Cannot Be Mixed?' Shared Devotions in the Monotheisms." *History and Anthropology* 19, no. 1 (2008): 37–59.

Albera, Dionigi, and Maria Couroucli, eds. *Sharing Sacred Spaces in the Mediterranean: Christians, Muslims and Jews at Shrines and Sanctuaries*. Bloomington: Indiana University Press, 2012.

Allen, Christopher. *Islamophobia*. Surrey, UK: Ashgate, 2010.

Almond, Philip. *The British Discovery of Buddhism*. Cambridge: Cambridge University Press, 1988.

Anderson, Benedict. *Imagined Communities: Reflections on the Origin and Spread of Nationalism*. London: Verso, 1983.

Appadurai, Arjun. "Number in the Colonial Imagination." In *Orientalism and the Postcolonial Predicament: Perspectives on South Asia*, edited by Carol A. Breckinridge and Peter van der Veer, 314–339. Philadelphia: University of Pennsylvania Press, 1993.

——. *The Social Life of Things: Commodities in Cultural Perspective*. New York: Cambridge University Press, 1986.

Archer, Mildred. *Early Views of India: The Picturesque Journeys of Thomas and William Daniell, 1786–1794*. London: Thames and Hudson, 1980.

Arnold, Sir Edwin. *East and West: Being Papers Reprinted from the "Daily Telegraph" and Other Sources*. London: Longman's, Green, and Co., 1896.

——. *The Light of Asia*. London: Trübner, 1879.

Asad, Talal. *Geneologies of Religion: Disciplines and Reasons of Power in Christianity and Islam*. Baltimore: Johns Hopkins University Press, 1993.

——. *On Suicide Bombing*. New York: Columbia University Press, 2007.
Asher, Frederick M. "Gaya: Monuments of the Pilgrimage Town." In *Bodhgaya: Site of Enlightenment*, edited by J. Leoshko, 74–88. Bombay: Marg Publications, 1988.
——. *Monumental Legacy: Bodh Gaya*. New York: Oxford University Press, 2008.
Ayoub, Mahmoud. *Redemptive Suffering in Islam: A Study of the Devotional Aspects of "Ashura" in Twelver Shi'ism*. The Hague: de Gruyter, 1978.
Babb, Lawrence. *The Divine Hierarchy: Popular Hinduism in Central India*. New York: Columbia University Press, 1975.
Badhra, Gautam, Gyan Prakash, and Susie Tharu, eds. *Subaltern Studies X*. New Delhi: Oxford University Press, 1999.
Bahnassi, Afif. *The Great Omayyad Mosque of Damascus: The First Masterpieces of Islamic Art*. Damascus: TLASS, 1989.
Bakker, Hans. "The Footprints of the Lord." In *Devotion Divine: Bhakti Traditions from the Regions of India: Studies in Honour of Charlotte Vaudeville*, edited by Diana L. Eck and Françoise Mallison, 19–37. Groningen Oriental Studies 8. Groningen: Egbert Forsten, 1991.
Banerjea, Jitendra Nath. *Development of Hindu Iconography*. Calcutta: University of Calcutta, 1956.
Bareau, Andre. "La construction et le culte des stūpa d'aprés les Vinayapiṭaka." *Bulletin l'Ecole Française d'Extrême-Oriente* 50 (1962): 275–299.
——. "La Parinirvāṇa du Bouddha et la naissance de la religion bouddhique." *Bulletin de l'Ecole Française d'Extrême-Orient* 61 (1964): 275–299.
Barsh, Russell Lawrence. "The Illusion of Religious Freedom for Indigenous Americans." *Oregon Law Review* 65 (1986): 369–372.
Barringer, Tim, and Tom Flynn, eds. *Colonialism and the Object: Empire, Material Culture and the Museum*. London: Routledge, 2004.
Barsh, Russell Lawrence. "The Illusion of Religious Freedom for Indigenous Americans." *Oregon Law Review* 65 (1986): 369–372.
Barua, Benimadhab. *Gaya and Buddha-Gaya (Early History of the Holy Land)*. 2 vols. Calcutta: Indian Research Institute, 1934.
Basso, Keith. *Wisdom Sits in Places: Landscape and Language among the Western Apache*. Albuquerque: University of New Mexico Press, 1996.
Basu, Amrita. "Mass Movement or Elite Conspiracy? The Puzzle of Hindu Nationalism." In *Contesting the Nation: Religion, Community, and the Politics of Democracy in India*, edited by David Ludden, 55–80. Philadelphia: University of Pennsylvania Press, 1996.
Basu, Tapan, Sumit Sarkar, Tanika Sarkar, Pradip Datta, and Sambuddha Sen. *Khaki Shorts and Saffron Flags: A Critique of the Hindu Right*. Hyderabad: Orient Longman, 1993.
Baudrillard, Jean. *The Spirit of Terrorism and Requiem for the Twin Towers*. Translated by Chris Turner. London: Verso, 2002.

Bayly, C. A. "Knowing the Country: Empire and Information in India." *Modern Asian Studies* 27 (1993): 3–43.

Beal, Samuel. *Si-Yu-Ki: Buddhist Records of the Western World Translated from the Chinese of Hiuen Tsiang (AD 629)*. London: Trübner, 1884.

Bear Lodge. Multiple Use Association v. Babbitt et al. 2 F.Supp.2d 1448,1452 (10th Cir. 1998).

Bear Lodge Multiple Use Association v. Babbit et al. 175 F.3d 818 (10th Cir. 1999).

Bellah, Robert. *The Broken Covenant: American Civil Religion in Time of Trial*. Chicago: University of Chicago Press, 1992.

Bender, Barbara. "Place and Landscape." In *Handbook of Material Culture*, edited by C. Tilley, W. Keene, S. Kuechler, R. Rowlands, and P. Spyer, 303–314. London: Sage, 2006.

Bennett, Tony. *Pasts Beyond Memory: Evolution, Museums, Colonialism*. London: Routledge, 2004.

Bentor, Yael. "The Content of *Stupas* and Images and the Indo-Tibetan Concept of Relics." *Tibet Journal* 28, nos. 1/2 (2003): 21–48.

——. *Images and Stupas in Indo-Tibetan Tantric Buddhism*. Leiden: E. J. Brill, 1996.

Berdoulay, Vincent. "Place, Meaning, and Discourse in French Language Geography" In *The Power of Place*, edited by John A. Agnew and James S. Duncan, 124–139. London: Unwin Hyman, 1989.

Berminham, Ann. *Landscape and Ideology: The English Rustic Tradition, 1740–1860*. Berkeley: University of California Press, 1996.

Berquist, John. "Theories of Space and Construction of the Ancient World." Paper presented in the Constructs of the Social and Cultural Worlds of Antiquity Group, 1999.

Bhabha, Homi K. *The Location of Culture*. London: Routledge, 1994.

Bhaktin, Mikhail M. *The Dialogic Imagination*. Edited by Michael Holquist. Translated by C. Emerson and M. Holquiest. Austin: The University of Texas Press, 1981.

Bhardwaj, Surinder M. "Non-Hajj Pilgirmage in Islam: A Neglected Dimension of Religious Circulation." *Journal of Cultural Geography* 17, no. 2 (1998): 69–87.

Blackstone, Kate. *Women in the Footsteps of the Buddha: Struggle for Liberation in the Therigatha*. London: Curzon Press, 1998.

Blatti, J. O., ed. *Past Meets Present: Essays about Historic Interpretation and Public Audiences*. Washington, DC: Smithsonian Institution Press, 1987.

Bond, George. *The Buddhist Revival in Sri Lanka: Religious Tradition, Reinterpretation and Response*. Columbia: University of South Carolina Press, 1988.

Bonham, Charlton H. "Devils Tower, Rainbow Bridge, and the Uphill Battle Facing Native American Religion on Public Lands." *Law and Inequality* 157 (2002): 157–202.

Bourdieu, Pierre. *In Other Words: Essays Toward a Reflexive Sociology*. Stanford, CA: Stanford University Press, 1990.

——. *The Logic of Practice*. Stanford, CA: Stanford University Press, 1990.

——. *Outline of a Theory of Practice*. Translated by Richard Nice. Cambridge: Cambridge University Press, 1977.
Boyarin, Daniel. *Border Lines: The Partition of Judaeo-Christianity*. Philadelphia: University of Pennsylvania Press, 2006.
Brady, Joel. "'Land Is Itself a Sacred, Living Being': Native American Sacred Site Protection on Federal Public Lands Amidst the Shadows of *Bear Lodge*." *American Indian Law Review* 24 (1999/2000): 153–186.
Braudel, Fernand. *The Mediterranean and the Mediterranean World in the Age of Philip II*, 2 vols. Translated by Sian Reynolds. London: Collins, 1972.
Brown, Bill. "Thing Theory." *Critical Inquiry* 28 (2001): 1–16.
Brown, Peter. *The Cult of the Saints: Its Rise and Function in Latin Christianity*. Chicago: University of Chicago Press, 1981.
Brubaker, Rogers. *Ethnicity without Groups*. Cambridge: Harvard University Press, 2004.
Buchanan, Francis. *An Account of the Districts of Bihar and Patna in 1811–1812*. Patna: Bihar and Orissa Research Society, 1986.
——. *The History, Antiquities, Topography and Statistics of Eastern India*. Edited by Montgomery Martin. Delhi: Cosmo Publications, 1976.
Butler, Judith. *Giving an Account of Oneself*. New York: Fordham University Press, 2005.
Byler, Celia. "Free Access or Free Exercise?: A Choice between Mineral Development and American Indian Sacred Site Preservation on Public Lands." *Connecticut Law Review* 22 (1990): 397–435.
Bynum, Caroline Walker. "Women's Stories, Women's Symbols: A Critique of Victor Turner's Theory of Liminality." In *Anthropology and the Study of Religion*, edited by Frank Reynolds and Robert Moore, 105–125. Chicago: Center for the Scientific Study of Religion, 1984.
Byrne, Denis. "Buddhist Stupa and Thai Social Practice." *World Archaeology* 27, no. 2 (1985): 266–281.
——. "Western Hegemony in Archaeological Heritage Management." *History and Anthropology* 5 (1991): 269–276.
Calhoun, Craig, Paul Price, and Ashley Timmer, eds. *Understanding September 11*. New York: New Press, 2002.
Carlin, Nathan, and Heba Khan. "Mourning, Memorials, and Religion: A Psychoanalytic Perspective on the Park51 Controversy." *Religions* 2 (2011): 114–131.
Carmichael, David L., Jane Hubert, Brian Reeves, and Audhild Schanche, eds. *Sacred Sties, Sacred Places*. London: Routledge, 1994.
Carpenter, Kristen A. "The Interests of Peoples in the Cooperative Management of Sacred Sites." *Tulsa Law Review* 42, no. 37 (2006): 37–55.
——. "Old Ground and New Directions at Sacred Sites on the Western Landscape." *Denver University Law Review* 83 (2006): 981. University of Denver Legal Studies Research Paper No. 07-03.

Casanova, José. *Public Religions in the Modern World.* Chicago: University of Chicago Press, 1994.

Casey, Edward. *Betting Back into Place.* Bloomington: Indiana University Press, 1993.

——. *The Fate of Place: A Philosophical History.* Berkeley: University of California Press, 1997.

——. *Remembering: A Phenomenological Study.* Bloomington: Indiana University Press, 1987.

——. *Representing Place: Landscape Painting and Maps.* Minneapolis: University of Minnesota Press, 2002.

Cassidy, Brendan, ed. *Iconography at the Crossroads: Papers from the Colloquim Sponsored by the Index of Christian Art, Princeton University, 23–24 March 1990.* Princeton, NJ: Department of Art and Archaeology, Princeton University, 1993.

Chakrabarti, Dilip K. *A History of Indian Archaeology from the Beginning to 1947.* New Delhi: Munshiram Monoharlal, 1988.

Chakrabarty, Dipesh. *Habitations of Modernity: Essays in the Wake of Subaltern Studies.* Chicago: University of Chicago Press, 2002.

Charpentier, J. "Heilige Fussabdrücke in Indien, I & II." *Ostasiatische Zeitschrift. Beiträge zur Kenntnis der Kultur und Kunst des Fernen Ostens* 7 (1918–19): 1–30.

Chaturvedi, Vinayak, ed. *Mapping Subaltern Studies and the Postcolonial.* Verso: London and New York, 2000.

Chidester, David. *Savage Systems: Colonialism and Comparative Religion in Southern Africa.* Charlotesville: University of Virginia Press, 1996.

Chidester, David, and Edward T. Linenthal, editors. *American Sacred Space.* Bloomington: Indiana University Press, 1995.

Choper, Jesse H. *Securing Religious Liberty: Principles for Judicial Interpretation of the Religion Clauses.* Chicago: University of Chicago Press, 1995.

Clark, Jeanne Nienaber, and Kurt Angersbach. "One Hundred Years of National Monuments." *Culture and Society* 43, no. 4 (2006): 76–80.

Clifford, James. "On Collecting Art and Culture." In *The Predicament of Culture: Twentieth Century Ethnography, Literature, and Art,* edited by James Clifford, 215–251. Cambridge: Harvard University Press, 1988.

Cobb, Paul M. "Virtual Sacrality: Making Muslim Syria Sacred before the Crusades." *Medieval Encounters* 8 (2002): 35–55.

Cohen, Erik. "Pilgrimage and Tourism: Convergence and Divergence." In *Sacred Journeys: The Anthropology of Pilgrimage,* edited by Alan Morinis, XX–XX. Westport: Greenwood Press, 1992.

Cohn, Bernard S. *Colonialism and Its Forms of Knowledge: The British in India.* Princeton, NJ: Princeton University Press, 1996.

——. "The Transformation of Objects into Artifacts, Antiquities and Art in Nineteenth Century India." In *The Powers of Art: Patronage in Indian Culture,* edited by Barbara Stoler Miller, 301–329. Delhi: Oxford University Press, 1992.

Coleman, Simon. "Do You Believe in Pilgrimage?" *Anthropological Theory* 2, no. 3 (2002): 355–368.

Collins, Richard B. "Sacred Sites and Religious Freedom on Government Land." *Journal of Constitutional Law* 5, no. 2 (2003): 241–270.

Commins, David. "Religious Reformers and Arabists in Damascus, 1885–1914." *International Journal of Middle East Studies* 18, no. 4 (1986): 405–425.

Comstock, Richard "A Behavioral Approach to the Sacred: Category Formation in Religious Studies." *The Journal of the American Academy of Religion* 49, no. 4 (1981): 632.

Connerton, Paul. *How Societies Remember.* Cambridge: Cambridge University Press, 1989.

Coomaraswamy, Ananda. "The Indian Origin of the Buddha Image." *Journal of the American Oriental Society* 46 (1926): 165–70.

——. "The Origin of the Buddha Image." *The Art Bulletin* 9 (1927): 1–43.

Cormack, Margaret, ed. *Muslims and Others in Sacred Space.* Oxford: Oxford University Press, 2013.

Cowell, E. B. *The Buddhacarita of Asvaghosa*, in *Buddhist Mahayana Texts.* Translated by E. B. Cowell, F. Max Muller, and J. Takakusu. Sacred Books of the East XLIX. New Delhi: Cosmo Publications, 1977.

——, ed., *The Jātaka, or Stories of the Former Lives of the Buddha.* Vol. 4. H. D. Rouse, trans. Cambridge: Cambridge University Press, 1901.

Creswell, K. A. C. *Early Islamic Architecture.* 2d ed., vol. 1. Oxford: Oxford University Press, 1969.

Cresswell, Tim. *In Place/Out of Place: Geography, Ideology and Transgression.* Minneapolis: University of Minnesota Press, 1996.

——. *Place: A Short Introduction.* London: Blackwell, 2004.

Cross, Raymond, and Elizabeth Brenneman. "Devils Tower at the Crossroads: The National Park Service and the Preservation of Native American Cultural Resources in the 21st Century." *Public Land and Resources Law Review* 18 (1997): 5–45.

Cunningham, Alexander. *Archaeological Survey of India Report*, vol. VIII. Calcutta: Office of the Superintendent of Government Printing, 1878.

——. *The Bhilsa Topes, or Buddhist Monuments of Central India: Comprising a Brief Historical Sketch of the Rise, Progress, and Decline of Buddhism.* Varanasi: Indological Book House, 1966.

——. *Mahabodhi or the Great Buddhist Temple Under the Bodhi Tree at Buddha-Gaya.* London: W. H. Allen, 1892.

Curtis, William Eleroy. "Our National Parks and Reservations." *Annals of the American Academy of Political and Social Science* 35, no. 2 (1910): 15–24.

Dabashi, Hamid. *Shi'ism: A Religion of Protest.* Cambridge, MA: Belknap, 2011.

Dalmia, Vasudha, and Heinrich von Stietencron, eds. *Representing Hinduism: The Construction of Religious Traditions and National Identity.* New Delhi: Sage Publications, 1995.

Daniel, E. Valentine. *Charred Lullabies: Chapters in an Anthropography of Violence.* Princeton, NJ: Princeton University Press, 1996.

Davids, T. W. Rhys, and J. Eslin Carpenter, eds., *The Dīgha Nikāya*. Vol. 2. London: Oxford University Press, 1947.

Davis, Richard. "The Iconography of Rama's Chariot." In *Contesting the Nation: Religion, Community, and the Politics of Democracy in India*, edited by David Ludden, 27–54. Philadelphia: University of Pennsylvania Press, 1996.

——. *Lives of Indian Images*. Princeton, NJ: Princeton University Press, 1997.

Dazey, Wade. "Tradition and Modernization in the Organization of the Dasanāmi Samnyāsins." In *Monastic Life in the Christian and Hindu Traditions*, edited by Austin Creel and Vasudha Narayanan, 281–321. Lewiston: Edwin Mellen Press, 1992.

Dehejia, Vidya. "Aniconism and the Multivalence of Emblems." *Ars Orientalis* 21 (1992): 45–66.

Deloria, Vine, Jr. "Prospects for Restoration of Tribal Lands," *Restoration and Management Notes* 10, no. 1 (1992): 48–58.

——. *God Is Not Red: A Native View of Religion*. New York: Putnam, 1973.

——. "Sacred Lands and Religious Freedom," In *The Sacred Land Reader*, ed. Marjorie Beggs and Christopher McLeod, 20, www.sacredland.org/reader.html, accessed December 12, 2012.

Desai, W. S. "History of the Burmese Mission to India, October 1830–July 1833." *Journal of the Burma Research Society* 26 (1936): 71–109.

Dharmapala, Anagarika. *Buddhism in its Relationship to Hinduism*. Calcutta: Mahabodhi Society, 1918.

Dhirasekara, Jotiya. "Cetiya." *Encyclopaedia of Buddhism*. Vol. 4. Colombo: Government of Sri Lanka, 1979.

Dirks, Nicholas B. *Castes of Mind: Colonialism and the Making of Modern India*. Princeton, NJ: Princeton University Press, 2001.

——. "Guiltless Spoliations: Picturesque Beauty, Colonial Knowledge, and Colin Mackenzie's Survey of India." In *Perceptions of South Asia's Visual Past*, edited by Catherine B. Asher and Thomas R. Metcalf, 211–232. New Delhi: Oxford and IBH Publishing for the American Institute of Indian Studies, 1994.

Dishitar, V. R. R. "Origin and Early History of Caityas." *Indian Historical Quarterly* 14 (1938): 440–451.

Doniger, Wendy. *The Implied Spider: Politics and Theology in Myth*. New York: Columbia University Press, 1998.

Dormaar, John, and Brian O. K. Reeves, "Vision Quest Sites in Southern Alberta and Northern Montana," In *Kunaitupil: Coming Together on Native Sacred Sites*, ed. Brian O. K. Reeves and Margaret A. Kennedy, 162–178. Calgary: Archaeological Society of Alberta, 1993.

Dorst, John. "Postcolonial Encounters: Narrative Constructions of Devils Tower National Monument." In *Postcolonial America*, edited by C. Richard King, 303–320. Champaign: University of Illinois, 2000.

Doss, Erika. *Memorial Mania: Public Feeling in America*. Chicago: University of Chicago Press, 2010.

Douglas, Mary. *Purity and Danger: An Analysis of Concepts of Pollution and Taboo.* London: Routledge, 2002.

Doyle, Tara. "Bodh Gayā: Journeys to the Diamond Throne and the Feet of Gayāsur." PhD diss., Harvard University, 1997.

——. "'Liberate the Mahabodhi Temple!' Socially Engaged Buddhism, Dalit-Style." In *Buddhism in the Modern World: Adaptations of an Ancient Tradition*, edited by Steven Heine and Charles S. Prebish, 249–280. Oxford: Oxford University Press, 2003.

Dubuisson, Daniel. *The Western Construction of Religion: Myths, Knowledge, and Ideology.* Baltimore, MD: Johns Hopkins, 2007.

Durkheim, Émile. *The Elementary Forms of Religious Life.* Translated by Carol Cosman. New York: The Free Press, 1995.

——. *Professional Ethics and Civic Morals.* Glencoe, IL: Free Press, 1958.

Dussias, Allison M. "Cultural Conflicts Regarding Land Use: The Conflict between Recreational Users at Devil's Tower and Native American Ceremonial Users." *Vermont Journal of Environmental Law* 2 (2000–2001): 13–40.

Dustin, Daniel L., Ingrid E. Schneider, Leo H. McAvoy, and Arthur N. Frakt. "Cross-Cultural Claims on Devils Tower National Monument: A Case Study." *Leisure Sciences* 24, no. 1 (2002): 79–88.

Dutt, Nalinaksha, ed. *Bodhisattvabhūmih.* Patalīputtram: Kadiprasada-Jaya savala-Anusilanasamsthanam, 1978.

Eade, John, and Michael Sallnow, eds. *Contesting the Sacred: The Anthropology of Christian Pilgrimage.* Urbana: University of Illinois Press, 2000.

Eaton, Marietta W. "Consultation on Grand Staircase—Escalante National Monument from Planning to Implementation." *American Indian Quarterly* 25, no. 1 (2001): 28–34.

Eck, Diana. *Banaras: City of Light.* New York: Columbia University Press, 1999.

——. *Darśan: Seeing the Divine in India.* New York: Columbia University Press, 1998.

——. "India's *Tīrthas*: Crossings in Sacred Geography." *History of Religions* 20 (1981): 323–344.

Eck, Diana, and Françoise Mallison, eds. *Devotion Divine: Bhakti Traditions from the Regions of India: Studies in Honour of Charlotte Vaudeville.* Groningen Oriental Studies 8. Groningen: Egbert Forsten, 1991.

Edney, Matthew. *Mapping an Empire: The Geographical Construction of British India, 1765–1843.* Chicago: University of Chicago Press, 1997.

Emmet, Chad. "The Citing of Churches and Mosques as an Indicator of Christian-Muslim Relations." *Islam and Christian-Muslim Relations* 20, no. 4 (2009): 451–476.

Engineer, Agsar Ali. *The Gujarat Carnage.* Hyderbad: Orient Longman, 2003.

Erickson, Thomas. "Between Universalism and Relativism: A Critique of the UNESCO Concept of Culture." In *Culture and Rights: Anthropological Perspectives*, edited by Jane Cowan, 127–148. Cambridge: Cambridge University Press, 2001.

Erndl, Kathleen M. *Victory to the Mother: The Hindu Goddess of Northwest India in Myth, Ritual, and Symbol.* New York: Oxford University Press, 1993.

Errington, Shelly. "Making Progress on Borobudur: An Old Monument in New Order." *Visual Anthropology Review* 9, no. 2 (1993): 32–59.

Esposito, John L., and Ibrahim Kalin, eds. *Islamophia: The Challenge of Pluralism in the 21st Century*. New York: Oxford University Press, 2011.

Evans, Bette Novit. *Interpreting the Free Exercise of Religion: The Constitution and American Pluralism.* Chapel Hill: The University of North Carolina Press, 1997.

Fields, Rick. *How the Swans Came to the Lake: A Narrative History of Buddhism in America.* (Boston: Shambala, 1992).

Fixico, Donald L. "The Struggle for Our Homes: Indian and White Values and Tribal Lands." In *Defending Mother Earth: Native American Perspectives on Environmental Justice*, edited by Jace Weaver, 29–46. Maryknoll NY: Orbis, 1996.

Flaskervud, Ingvild. *Visualizing Belief and Piety in Iranian Shiism.* London: Continuum, 2010.

Flood, Finbarr Barry. "Between Cult and Culture: Bamiyan, Islamic Iconoclasm, and the Museum." *The Art Bulletin* 84, no. 4 (2002): 641–659.

——. *The Great Mosque of Damascus: Studies on the Makings of an Umayyad Visual Culture*. London: Brill, 2000.

Foote, Kenneth E. *Shadowed Ground: America's Landscape of Violence and Tragedy.* Austin: University of Texas Press, 2003.

Foucault, Michel. *Discipline and Punish: The Birth of the Prison.* Translated by Alan Sheridan. New York: Random House, 1977.

——. "Of Other Spaces." *Diacritics* 16, no. 1 (1986): 22–27.

Foucher, Alfred. "L'Origine grecque de l'image du Bouddha." In *Annales du Musee Guimet.* Chalon-sur-Saone: Bibliotheque de vulgarisation, 1913.

——. "The Beginnings of Buddhist Art." In *The Beginnings of Buddhist Art and Other Essays in Indian and Central Asian Archaeology*, edited by Alfred Foucher, 1–29. Paris: Paul Geuthner, 1917.

Fowden, Elizabeth Key. "Sharing Holy Places." *Common Knowledge* 8, no. 1 (2002): 124–146.

Freedman, Eric. "Protecting Sacred Sites on Public Land: Religion and Alliances in the Mato Tipila-Devils Tower Litigation." *The American Indian Quarterly* 31, no. 1 (2007): 1–22.

French, Rebekah J. "Free Exercise of Religion on the Public Lands." *Public Land Law Review* 11 (1990): 197–209.

Friedland, Roger, and Richard D. Hecht. "The Bodies of Nations: A Comparative Study of Religious Violence in Jerusalem and Ayodhya." *History of Religions* 38, no. 2 (1998): 101–149.

——. "Changing Places: Jerusalem's Holy Places in Comparative Perspective." *Israel Affairs* 5, nos. 2–3(1999): 200–225.

——. "The Politics of Sacred Place: Jerusalem's Temple Mount/*al-haram al-sharif*." In *Sacred Places and Profane Spaces: Essays in the Geographics of Judaism, Christianity, and Islam*, edited by Jamie Scott and Paul Simpson-Housley, 21–61. Westport, CT: Greenwood Press, 1991.

Geary, David, Matthew Sayers, and Abhishek Singh Amar, eds. *Cross-disciplinary Perspectives on a Contested Buddhist Site*. Oxford: Routledge, 2012.

Geffen, Joel, and Bron Taylor. "Battling Religions in Parks and Forest Reserves: Facing Religion in Conflicts over Protected Places." *The George Wright Forum* (2003): 56–68.

Gibb, Hamilton A. R. "Arab-Byzantine Relations under the Umayyad Caliphate." *Dumbarton Oaks Papers* 12 (1958): 219–233.

Giles, H. A., trans. *The Travels of Fa-hsien*. Cambridge: Cambridge University Press, 1966.

Girard, René. *Violence and the Sacred*. Translated by Patrick Gregory. Baltimore: Johns Hopkins University Press, 1977.

——. "Generative Scapegoating." In *Violent Origins: Walter Burkert, René Girard, and Jonathan Z. Smith on Ritual Killing and Cultural Formation*, edited by Robert G. Hamerton-Kelly, 73–148. Stanford, CA: Stanford University Press, 1987.

Gold, Ann. "Still Liminal after all these Years." In *Teaching Ritual*, edited by Catherine Bell, 29–45. Oxford: Oxford University Press, 2007.

Goldberger, Paul. *Up from Zero: Politics, Architecture, and the Rebuilding of New York*. New York: Random House, 2005.

Gombrich, Richard, and Gananath Obeyesekere. *Buddhism Transformed: Religious Change in Sri Lanka*. Princeton, NJ: Princeton University Press, 1988.

Gonda, Jan. *Aspects of Early Viṣṇuism*. Utrecht: Nva Oostoek's Uitgevers MIJ, 1965.

Gottschalk, Peter, and Gabriel Greenberg. *Islamophobia: Making Muslims the Enemy*. Plymouth, UK: Rowman and Littlefield, 2008.

Grafman, Rafi, and Myriam Rosen-Ayalon. "The Two Great Syrian Umayyad Mosques: Jerusalem and Damascus." *Muqarnas* 16 (1999): 1–15.

Granoff, Phyllis, and Koichi Shinohara, eds. *Pilgrims, Patrons, and Places: Localizing Sanctity in Asian Religions*. Toronto: UBC Press, 2003.

Greenberg, Judith, ed. *Trauma at Home: After 9/11*. Lincoln: University of Nebraska Press, 2003.

Griffin, Rayanne J. "Sacred Site Protection Against a Backdrop of Religious Intolerance." *Tulsa Law Journal* 31 (1995): 395–419.

Grimes, Ronald. *Rite Out of Place: Ritual, Media, and the Arts*. Oxford: Oxford University Press, 2006.

Griswold, A. B. "The Holy Land Transported: Replicas of the Mahābodhi Shrine in Siam and Elsewhere." In *Paranavitana Felicitation Volume on Art and Architecture and Oriental Studies*, edited by N. A. Jayawickrama, 173–221. Colombo: M. D. Gunasena and Co., 1965.

Gulliford, Andrew. *Sacred Objects and Sacred Places: Preserving Tribal Traditions*. Boulder: University Press of Colorado, 2000.

Guruge, Ananda. *From the Living Fountains of Buddhism.* Colombo: Ministry of Cultural Affairs, 1984.

——. *Return to Righteousness: A Collection of Speeches, Essays, and Letters of Anagarika Dharmapala.* Colombo: Government Printing Press, 1965.

Hamerton-Kelly, Robert, ed. *Violent Origins: Walter Burkert, Rene Girard, and Jonathan Z. Smith on Ritual Killing and Cultural Formation.* Palo Alto, CA: Stanford University Press, 1988.

Hanh, Thich Nhat. *Old Path White Clouds: Walking in the Footprints of the Buddha.* Berkeley, CA: Parallax Press, 1991.

Hansen, Thomas Blom. *Saffron Wave: Democracy and Nationalism in Modern India.* Princeton, NJ: Princeton University Press, 1999.

Hanson, Jeffery R., and David Moore. "Applied Anthropology at Devils Tower National Monument." *Plains Anthropologist* 44, no. 170 (1999): 53–60.

Harkin, Michael. "Sacred Places, Scarred Spaces." *Wicazo Sa Review* 15, no. 1: 54.

——. "Towering Conflicts: Bear Lodge/Devils Tower and the Climbing Moratorium." *The International Journal of Environmental, Cultural, Economic and Social Sustainability* 2, no. 3 (2002): 181–188.

Harrison, Paul. "Buddhānusmṛti in the Pratyutpanna-Buddha-Samukhāvasthita-Samādhi-Sūtra." *JIP* 6 (1978): 35–57.

——. *The Samādhi of Direct Encounter with the Buddhas of the Present.* Tokyo: The International Institute for Buddhist Studies, 1990.

Harvey, David. *Justice, Nature and the Geography of Difference.* Oxford: Blackwell Publishers, 1996.

Hassner, Ron. *War on Sacred Grounds.* Ithaca, NY: Cornell University Press, 2009.

Hauerwas, Stanley, and Frank Lentricchia, eds. *Dissent from the Homeland: Essays after September 11.* Durham, NC: Duke University Press, 2003.

Haugeland, John. "Reading Brandom Reading Heidegger." *European Journal of Philosophy* 13, no. 3: 421–428.

Heidegger, Martin. *Poetry, Language, Thought.* New York: Harper and Row, 1971.

Heller, Dana, ed. *The Selling of 9/11: How a National Tragedy Became a Commodity.* New York: Palgrave Macmillan, 2005.

Herzfeld, Michael. *A Place in History: Social and Monumental Time in a Cretan Town.* Princeton, NJ: Princeton University Press, 1991.

Hobswan, Eric, and Terrence Ranger, eds., *The Invention of Tradition.* Cambridge: Cambridge University Press, 1992.

Hocart, A. M. *The Temple of the Tooth in Kandy.* London: Luzac and Co., 1931.

Hooker, Ann M. "American Indian Sacred Sites on Federal Public Lands: Resolving Conflicts between Religious Use and Multiple Use at El Malpais National Monument." *American Indian Law Review* 19 (1994): 133–158.

Hornborg, Alf. "Environmentalism, Ethnicity, and Sacred Places: Reflections on Modernity, Discourse, and Power." *Canadian Review of Sociology and Anthropology* 31, no. 3 (1994): 245–267.

Horner, I. B., ed. *Papañcasūdanī Majjhimanikāya atthkathā of Buddhagosācariya*. Vol V. London: Pali Text Society, 1938.

Huntington, John. "Sowing the Seeds of the Lotus: A Journey to the Great Pilgrimage Sites of Buddhism, part I." *Orientations* 16, no. 11 (1985): 46–61.

——. "Sowing the Seeds of the Lotus: A Journey to the Great Pilgrimage Sites of Buddhism, part II." *Orientations* 17, no. 2 (1986): 28–43.

——. "Sowing the Seeds of the Lotus: A Journey to the Great Pilgrimage Sites of Buddhism, part III." *Orientations* 17, no. 3 (1986): 32–46.

——. "Sowing the Seeds of the Lotus: A Journey to the Great Pilgrimage Sites of Buddhism, part IV." *Orientations* 17, no. 6 (1986): 28–40.

——. "Pilgrimage as Image: the Cult of the Aṣṭamahāpratiharya, Part I." *Orientations* 18, no. 4 (1987): 55–63.

——. "Pilgrimage as Image: the Cult of the Aṣṭamahāpratiharya, Part II." *Orientations* 18, no. 8 (1987): 56–68.

Huntington, Samuel. "The Clash of Civilizations?" *Foreign Affairs* 72, no. 3 (1993): 22–50.

——. *The Clash of Civilizations and the Remaking of World Order*. New York, Simon & Schuster, 1996.

Huntington, Susan. "Aniconism and the Multivalence of Emblems: Another Look." *Ars Orientalis* 22 (1993): 111–156.

——. "Early Buddhist Art and the Theory of Aniconism." *Art Journal* 49 (1990): 401–407.

Huxley, Julian. *UNESCO: Its Purpose and Philosophy*. Washington, DC: American Council on Public Affairs, 1947.

Huyssen, Andreas. *Present Pasts: Urban Palimpsests and the Politics of Memory*. Palo Alto, CA: Stanford University Press, 2003.

Hyder, Syed Akbar. *Reliving Karbala: Martyrdom in South Asian Memory*. Oxford: Oxford University Press, 2006.

Imam, Abu. *Sir Alexander Cunningham and the Beginnings of Indian Archaeology*. Dacca: Asiatic Society of Pakistan, 1966.

Irwin, John. "Visnu in the Archaic Cosmology." In *Indian Art and Connoisseurship: Essays in Honour of Dougless Barnett*, edited by John Guy, 75–85. Middletown, NJ : Grantha, 1995.

Jacques, Claude. *Gayā Māhātmya: Edition critiue, traduction française et introduction*. Pondichéry: Publications de l'Institut Française d'Indologie, 1962.

Jameson, Fredric. "The Cultural Logic of Capital." *New Left Review* 46 (1984): 53–92.

Jayawickrama, N. A., ed. *Buddhavamsa and Cariyapitaka*. London: Pali Text Society, 1974.

Johnston, E. H. *The Buddhacarita; or, Acts of the Buddha*. Delhi: Motilal Banarsidass, 1984.

Juergensmeyer, Mark, ed. *The Oxford Handbook of Global Religions*. New York: Oxford University Press, 2006.

——. *Terror in the Mind of God: The Global Rise of Religious Violence.* Berkeley: University of California Press, 2003.

Kakar, Sudhir. *The Colors of Violence: Cultural Identities, Religion, and Conflict.* Chicago: University of Chicago Press, 1996.

Kane, Pandranga Vamana. *History of Dharmaśāstra: Ancient and Medieval Religious and Civil Law in India.* Pune: Bhandarkar Oriental Research Institute, 1975.

Kapferer, Bruce, ed. *The World Trade Center and Global Crisis.* New York: Berghahn Books, 2004.

Kaplan, Amy. "Homeland Insecurities: Transformations of Language and Space." In *September 11 in History: A Watershed Moment?*, edited by Mary L. Dudziak, 55–69. Durham, NC: Duke University Press, 2003.

Kapur, Anuradha. "Deity to Crusader: The Changing Iconography of Ram." In *Hindus and Others: The Question of Identity in India Today*, edited by Gyanendra Pandey, 74–109. New Delhi: Viking Penguin, 1993.

Kazan, Georges. "The Head of St. John the Baptist—the Early Evidence." Paper presented at "Saint John the Baptist and His Cults" colloquium held at St. John's College, Oxford, June 24, 2001.

Keay, John. *India Discovered.* London: Collins, 1988.

Kedar, M., and D. Yerushalmi. "Sharia and Violence in American Mosques." *The Middle East Quarterly* 18, no. 3 (2011): 59–72.

Kemper, Steven. "Dharmapala's Dharmaduta and Buddhist Ethnoscape." In *Buddhist Missionaries in the Era of Globalization*, ed. Linda Learman, 22–50. Honolulu: University of Hawai'i Press, 2005.

Kern, Hendrik. *Manual of Indian Buddhism.* Strassburg: Verlag Von Karl J. Trubner, 1896.

Kertzer, David. *Ritual, Politics, and Power.* New Haven, CT: Yale University Press, 1988.

Kim, Sebastian. *Search of Identity: Debates on Religious Conversion in India.* Oxford: Oxford University Press, 2005.

Kinnard, Jacob. "Amaravati as Lens: Envisioning Buddhism in the Ruins of the Great Stūpa." In *Buddhism in the Krishna River Valley of Andhra*, edited by Sree Padma and A. W. Barber, 81–104. Albany: State University of New York Press, 2008.

——. "The Field of the Buddha's Presence." In *Embodying the Dharma: Buddhist Relic Veneration in Asia*, edited by Kevin Trainor and David Germano, 117–144. Albany: State University of New York Press, 2004.

——. *Imaging Wisdom: Seeing and Knowing in the Art of Indian Buddhism.* London: Curzon Press, 1999.

——. "Indeterminate Sacrality and the Subjectivity of Sacred Space." *Material Religion* 7, no. 2 (2011): 275–277.

——. "The Polyvalent *Pādas* of Viṣṇu and the Buddha," *History of Religions* 40, no. 1 (2000): 32–57.

——. "Reevaluating the Eighth-Ninth Century Pala Milieu: Icono-Conservatism and the Persistence of Śākyamuni." *Journal of the International Association of Buddhist Studies* 20, no. 1 (1997): 281–300.

——. "When Is the Buddha Not the Buddha? The Hindu/Buddhist Battle over Bodhgaya and the Buddha Image." *Journal of the American Academy of Religion* 66, no. 4 (1999): 817–839.

——. "When the Buddha Sued Viṣṇu." In *Constituting Communities: Theravada Traditions in South and Southeast Asia*, edited by John Holt, Jacob N. Kinnard, and Jonathon Walters, 83–106. Albany: State University of New York Press, 2003.

Kinsley, David. *Tantric Visions of the Divine Feminine: The Ten Mahāvidyās*. California: The University of California Press, 1997.

Kister, M. J. "Sanctity Joint and Divided: On Holy Places in the Islamic Tradition." *Jerusalem Studies in Arabic and Islam* 20 (1996): 18–65.

Kletter, Raz. *Just Past? The Making of Israel Archaeology*. London: Equinox Publishing Ltd, 2006.

Klostermaier, Klaus. "Hindu Views of Buddhism." In *Canadian Contributions to Buddhist Studies*, edited by R. Amore, 60–82. Waterloo: Wilfred Laurie University Press, 1979.

Knott, Kim. *The Location Of Religion: A Spatial Analysis*. Sheffield: Equinox, 2005.

Kofsky, Arieh, and Guy G. Stroumsa, eds. *Sharing the Sacred: Religious Contacts and Conflicts in the Holy Land, First-Fifteenth Centuries, CE*. Jerusalem: Yad Izhak Ben Zvi, 1998.

Koppedrayer, K. I. "The Interweave of Place, Space, and Biographical Discourse at a South Indian Religious Centre." In *Pilgrims, Patrons, and Places: Localizing Sanctity in Asian Religions*, edited by Phyllis Granoff and Koichi Shinohara, 279–296. Toronto: UBC Press, 2003.

Kostova, Rossina, Kazimir Popkonstantinov, and Tom Higham. "Relics of the Baptist: Scientific research planned for finds excavated in Sozopol, Bulgaria in 2010 (Radiocarbon Dating, DNA testing)." Paper presented at "Saint John the Baptist and His Cults" colloquium held at St. John's College, Oxford, June 24, 2001.

Lamotte, Étienne. "La légende du Buddha." *Revue de l'histoire des religions* 134 (1948): 37–71.

Landes, Richard. *Relics, Apocalypse, and the Deceits of History: Ademar of Chabannes, 989–1034*. Cambridge: President and Fellows of Harvard College, 1995.

Lane, Belden C. *Landscapes of the Sacred: Geography and Narrative in American Spirituality*. Baltimore: Johns Hopkins University Press, 2001.

Langeiesche, William. *American Ground: Unbuilding the World Trade Center*. New York: North Point Press, 2002.

Law, B. C. "'Cetiya' in the Buddhist Literature." In *Studia Indo-Iranica: Ehrengabe für Wilhelm Geiger*, edited by Walther Wüst, 42–48. Leipzig: Harrasowitz, 1931.

Lefebvre, Henri. *The Production of Space*. Translated by D. Nicholson-Smith. Oxford: Basil Blackwell, 1991.

Legge, James. *A Record of Buddhistic Kingdoms, Being an Account by the Chinese Monk Fa-Hien of his Travels in India and Ceylon (A.D. 399–414) in Search of the Buddhist Books of Discipline*. Oxford: Clarendon Press, 1886.

Leoshko, Janice, ed. *Bodhgaya: Site of Enlightenment*. Bombay: Marg Publications, 1988.
——. "On the Construction of a Buddhist Pilgrimage Site." *Art History* 19, no. 4 (1996): 573–597.
——. *Sacred Traces: British Explorations of Buddhism in South Asia*. Surrey, UK: Ashgate, 2003.
Lévi-Strauss, Claude. *Introduction to the work of Marcel Mauss*. Translated by Felicity Baker. London: Routledge, 1987.
Lincoln, Bruce. *Holy Terrors: Thinking about Religion after September 11*. Chicago: University of Chicago Press, 2003.
Linenthal, Edward T. *Sacred Ground: Americans and Their Battlefields*. Urbana: University of Illinois Press, 1991.
Linge, George. "Ensuring the Full Freedom of Religion on Public Lands: Devils Tower and the Protection of Indian Sacred Sites." *Boston College Environmental Affairs Law Review* 27, no. 2 (2000): 307–338.
Losty, Jeremiah P. "The Mahabodhi Temple Before its Restoration." In *Aksyayanivi: Essays Presented to Dr. Debala Mitra in Admiration of Her Scholarly Contributions*, edited by G. Bhattacharya, 335–357. New Delhi: Sri Satguru, 1991.
Low, Setha. "The Memorialization of September 11: Dominant and Local Discourses on the Rebuilding of the World Trade Center Site." *American Ethnologist* 31, no. 3 (2004): 326–339.
Lubell, Sam. "Reflecting Absence Chosen as World Trade Center Memorial." *Architectural Record* 192, no. 2 (2004): 21–21.
Ludden, David, ed. *Contesting the Nation: Religion, Community, and the Politics of Democracy in India*. Philadelphia: University of Pennsylvania Press, 1996.
——. "Orientalist Empiricism: Transformations of Colonial Knowledge." In *Orientalism and the Postcolonial Predicament: Perspectives on South Asia*, edited by Carol A. Breckinridge and Peter van der Veer, 250–278. Philadelphia: University of Pennsylvania Press, 1993.
——. *Reading Subaltern Studies: Critical History, Contested Meaning and the Globalization of South Asia*. London: Anthem South Asian Studies, 2002.
Mahābharata: Text as Constituted in Its Critical Edition. Vol. I. Poona: Bhandarkar Oriental Research Institute, 1971.
Mahabodhi Journal: Diamond Jubilee Souvenir. 1891–1951. Calcutta: Mahabodhi Society, 1952.
Malalgoda, Kitsiri. *Buddhism in Sinhalese Society: 1750–1900*. Berkeley: University of California Press, 1976.
Malandra, Geri H. "The Mahabodhi Temple." In *Bodhgayā: The Site of Enlightenment*, edited by Janice Leoshko, 10–28. Bombay: Marg, 1988.
Malpas, J. E. *Place and Experience: A Philosophical Topography*. Cambridge: Cambridge University Press, 1999.
Manhart, Christian. "The Afghan Cultural Heritage Crisis: UNESCO's Response to the Destruction of Statues in Afghanistan." *American Journal of Archaeology* 105, no. 3 (2001): 387–388.

Marcus, George. "Imagining the Whole: Ethnography's Contemporary Efforts to Situate Itself." *Critique of Anthropology* 9, no. 3 (189): 7–30.
Markham, R. A. "How on Earth Could Places Become Holy? Origins of the Christian Idea of Holy Places." *Journal of Early Christian Studies* 2, no. 3 (1994): 257–272.
Marranci, Gabriele. "Multiculturalism, Islam and the Clash of Civilisations Theory: Rethinking Islamophobia." *Culture and Religion* 5, no. 1 (2004): 105–117.
Marshall, Peter, ed. *The British Discovery of Hinduism in the Eighteenth Century.* Cambridge: Cambridge University Press, 1970.
Martin, Rena. "Native Connection to Place: Policies and Play." *American Indian Quarterly* 25, no. 1 (2001): 35–41.
Masuzawa, Tomoko. *In Search of Dreamtime: The Quest of the Origin of Religion.* Chicago: University of Chicago Press, 1993.
McAvoy, Leo. "American Indians, Place Meanings and the Old/New West." *Journal of Leisure Research* 34, no. 4 (2002): 383–396.
McMahan, David. *The Making of Buddhist Modernism.* New York: Oxford University Press, 2008.
Meri, Josef. *The Cult of Saints among Muslims and Jews in Medieval Syria.* Oxford: Oxford University Press, 2002.
——. "Relics of Piety and Power in Medieval Islam," *Past & Present* 206, no. 5 (2010): 97–120.
Metcalf, Thomas. *Ideologies of the Raj: The New Cambridge History of India* 3, no. 4. Cambridge: Cambridge University Press, 1994.
Miller, Barbara Stoler, ed. *The Powers of Art: Patronage in Indian Culture.* Delhi: Oxford University Press, 1992.
Miller, Bruce G. *"Culture as Cultural Defense: An American Indian Sacred Site in Court." American Indian Quarterly* 22, nos. 1/2 (1998): 83–97.
Misitelli, Jean. "World Heritage, Between Universalism and Globalization." *International Journal of Cultural Property* 11, no. 2 (2002): 323–336.
Mitchell, W. J. T. "Holy Landscape: Israel, Palestine, and the American Wilderness." *Critical Inquiry* 26, no. 2 (2000): 193–223.
——. *What Do Pictures Want? The Lives and Loves of Images.* Chicago: University of Chicago Press, 2005.
Mitchell, W. J. T., ed. *Landscape and Power.* Chicago: University of Chicago Press, 2002.
Mitra, Rajendralala. *Buddha Gaya: The Great Buddhist Temple, Hermitage of Sakya Muni.* Calcutta: Bengal Secretariat Press, 1878.
Mitter, Partha. *Much Maligned Monsters: A History of European Reactions to Indian Art.* Chicago: University of Chicago Press, 1992.
Morinis, E. Alan. *Pilgrimage in the Hindu Tradition: A Case Study of West Bengal.* Delhi: Oxford University Press, 1984.
Morinis, E. Alan, ed. *Sacred Journeys: The Anthropology of Pilgrimage.* Westport, CT: Greenwood Press, 1992.

Mus, Paul. "The Iconography of an Aniconic Art." *RES* 14 (1987): 5–28.

Musitelli, Jean. "World Heritage, Between Universalism and Globalization." *International Journal of Cultural Property* 11, no. 2 (2002): 323–336.

Muthiah, S., ed. *Where the Buddha Walked*. Madras: T. T. Maps and Publications, 1990.

Nakash, Yithak. *The Shi'is of Iraq*. Princeton, NJ: Princeton University Press, 1994.

——. "The Visitation of the Shrines of the Imams and the Shi'i Mutjahids in the Early Twentieth Century." *Studia Islamica* 81, no. 1 (1995): 153–164.

Ñāṇamoli, Bhikkhu, trans. *The Dispeller of Delusion (Sammohavinodanī)*. Part I. London: Pali Text Society, 1987.

Nandy, Ashis, Shikha Trivedy, Shail Mayaram, and Achyut Yagnik. *Creating a Nationality: The Ramjanmabhumi Movement and Fear of the Self*. Delhi: Oxford University Press, 1995.

Nasr, S. H. "Ithna Ashariyah." *Encyclopedia of Religion*, edited by Lindsay Jones. Detroit, MI: Macmillan, 2005.

Nasr, Vali. *The Shia Revival: How Conflicts Within Islam Will Shape the Future*. London: Norton, 2006.

Nietzsche, Friedrich. *Untimely Meditations*. Cambridge: Cambridge University Press, 1997.

Nobel, Philip. *Sixteen Acres: Architecture and the Outrageous Struggle for the Future of Ground Zero*. New York: Metropolitan Books, 2005.

Norman, K. R. *Pāli-Literature, Including the Canonical Literature in Prakrit and Sanskrit of All the Hinayāna Schools of Buddhism*. Wiesbaden: Otto Harrassowitz, 1983.

Nugteren, Albertina. "Ritual Around the Bodhi-Tree in Bodhgaya." In *Pluralism and Identity: Studies in Ritual Behaviour*, edited by J. Platvoet and K. van der Toorn, 145–166. Leiden: E. J. Brill, 1995

Obeyesekere, Gananath. "Personal Identity and Cultural Crisis: The Case of Anagarika Dharmapala." In *The Biographical Process: Studies in the History and Psychology of Religion*, edited by F. Reynolds and D. Capps, 221–252. The Hague: Mouton and Company, 1976.

O'Flaherty, Wendy, trans. *The Rig Veda*. New York: Penguin, 1981.

Okakura, Kakuzo. *The Awakening of Japan*. New York: The Century Co., 1904.

——. *The Ideals of the East, with Special Reference to the Art of Japan*. New York: Dutton, 1903.

Olcott, Henry Steel. "The First Leaf of the Theosophical Society." *The Theosophist* 12, no. 2 (1890): XX–XX.

Olmsted, Frederick Law. Introduction to "The Yosemite Valley and the Mariposa Big Trees, a Preliminary Report (1865)," by Laura Wood Roper. *Landscape Architecture* (October 1952).

Orsi, Robert A. *Between Heaven and Earth: The Religious Worlds People Make and the Scholars Who Study Them*. Princeton, NJ: Princeton University Press, 2005.

Owens, Bruce McCoy. "Monumentality, Identity, and the State: Local Practice, World Heritage, and Heterotopia at Swayambhu, Nepa." *Anthropological Quarterly* 75, no. 2 (2002): 269–316.

Pandey, Gyanendra. *"In Defense of the Fragment: Writing about Hindu-Muslim Riots in India Today." Representations* 37 (1992): 27–55.

Pandey, Gyanendra, ed. *Hindus and Others: The Question of Identity in India Today*. New Delhi: Viking Penguin, 1993.

Panikkar, K. N., ed. *The Concerned Indian's Guide to Communalism*. New Delhi: Viking, New Delhi, 1990.

Paranavitana, S. *The God of Adam's Peak*. Ascona, Artibus Asiae Supplementum XVIII (Artibus Asiae Publishers, 1958): 11–22.

Parker, Patricia L. "Guidelines for Evaluation and Document Traditional Cultural Properties." U.S. Department of the Interior, National Park Service, 1990.

Parry, Jonathan. *Death in Banaras*. Cambridge: Cambridge University Press, 1995.

Paul, Debjani. "Antiquity of the Visnupada at Gaya: Tradition and Archaeology." *East and West* 35, nos. 1–3 (1985): 103–141.

Pelletier, Stephen C. *The Iran-Iraq War: Chaos in a Vacuum*. New York: Praeger, 1992.

Pennington, Brian. *Was Hinduism Invented? Britons, Indians, and Colonial Construction of Religion*. Oxford: Oxford University Press, 2005.

Peterson, Merril D., and Robert C. Vaughan, eds. *The Virginia Statute for Religious Freedom*. Cambridge: Cambridge University Press, 1990.

Pew Forum on Religion and Public Life. "U.S. Religious Landscape Survey." 2008. Accessed November 11, 2011. http://religions.pewforum.org/.

Phillips, Martin. *Contested Worlds: An Introduction to Human Geography*. Handts, England: Ashgate, 2005.

Pinault, David. *Horse of Karbala: Muslim Devotional Life in India*. New York: Palgrave, 2001.

Pinch, William R. "Soldier Monks and Militant Sadhus." In *Contesting the Nation: Religion, Community, and the Politics of Democracy in India*, edited by David Ludden, 140–161. Philadelphia: University of Pennsylvania Press, 1996.

Pratimālakṣaṇam. Calcutta: Calcutta University Press, 1933.

Preston, James J. "Spiritual Magnetism: An Organizing Principle for the Study of Pilgrimage." In *Sacred Journeys: The Anthropology of Pilgrimage*, edited by Alan Morinis, 31–46. Westport, CT: Greenwood Press, 1992.

Price, Nicole. "Tourism and the Bighorn Medicine Wheel: How Multiple Use Does Not Work for Sacred Land Sites." In *Sacred Sties, Sacred Places*, edited by David L. Carmichael, Jane Hubert, Brian Reeves, and Audhild Schanche, 257–264. London: Routledge, 1994.

Price, Sally. *Primitive Art in Civilized Places*. Chicago: University of Chicago Press, 1989.

Prothero, Stephan. *The White Buddhist: The Asian Odyssey of Henry Steel Olcott*. Bloomington: Indiana University Press, 1996.

Rahula, Walpola. *History of Buddhism in Ceylon: The Anuradhapura Period, 3rd Century BC–10th Century AC*. 2d ed. Colombo: Gunasena, 1966.

Rao, T. A. Gopinatha. *Elements of Hindu Iconography*. 2 vols. Madras: Law Printing House, 1914–1916.

Raven-Hart, Rowland. *Where the Buddha Trod: A Buddhist Pilgrimage*. Colombo: Lake House, 1966.

Reeves, Brian O. K. "Vision Quest Sites in Southern Alberta and Northern Montana." In *Kunaitupil: Coming Together on Native Sacred Sites*, edited by Brian O. K. Reeves and Margaret A. Kennedy, 162–178. Calgary: The Archaeological Society of Alberta, 1993.

Reeves, Brian O. K., and Margaret A. Kennedy, eds. *Kunaitupil: Coming Together on Native Sacred Sites*. Calgary: The Archaeological Society of Alberta, 1993.

Relph, Edward. *Place and Placeness*. London: Pion, 1976.

Ricker, Di Mari. "Courts Soul-Search in Religious Law Claims." *Student Law* 26 (1997–98): 22–27.

Robinson, Rowena, and Sathianathan Clark. *Religious Conversion in India: Modes, Motivations, and Meanings*. Oxford: Oxford University Press, 2007.

Rodman, Margaret. "Empowering Place: Multilocality and Multivocality." *American Anthropologist* 94, no. 3 (1992): 640–656.

Roerich, George, trans. *Biography of Dharmasvāmin: A Tibetan Monk Pilgrim*. Patna: K. P. Jayaswal Research Institute, 1959.

Ross-Bryant, Lynn. "Sacred Sites: Nature and Nation in U.S. National Parks." *Religion and American Culture* 15, no. 1 (2005): 31–62.

Roy, Beth. *Some Trouble with Cows: Making Sense of Social Conflict*. Berkeley: University of California Press, 1994.

Roy, P. K. "Coming Storm." *Frontline* (October 13–36, 1990): 26–29.

Sack, Robert. *Homo Geographicus*. Baltimore: Johns Hopkins University Press, 1997.

San Miguel, Gear L. "How Is Devils Tower a Sacred Site to American Indians?" 1994. Accessed April 12, 2012. http://www.nps.gov/deto/historycultur/sacred-site.htm.

Sarkar, Sumit. "Hindutva and the Question of Conversions." In *The Concerned Indian's Guide to Communalism*, edited by K. N. Pannikkar, 73–106. New Delhi: Viking, New Delhi, 1990.

Sayyid, Salman, and Abdulkaroom Vakil, eds. *Rethinking Islamophobia*. New York: Columbia University Press, 2010.

Schama, Simon. *Landscape and Memory*. New York: Random House, 1995.

Schopen, Gregory. "An Old Inscription from Amarāvatī and the Cult of the Local Monastic Dead in Indian Buddhist Monasteries." *Journal of the International Association of Buddhist Studies* 14.2 (1991): 281–329.

——. "Archaeology and the Protestant Presuppositions in the Study of Indian Buddhism." *History of Religions* 31 (1991): 1–23.

——. "The Buddha as an Owner of Property and Permanent Resident in Medieval Indian Monasteries." *Journal of Indian Philosophy* 18 (1990): 181–217.

——. "Burial 'Ad Sanctos' and the Physical Presence of the Buddha in Early Indian Buddhism." *Religion* 17 (1987): 193–225.

——. "On the Buddha and his Bones." *Journal of Indian Philosophy* 108, no. 4 (1990): 181–217.

——. "Relic." In *Critical Terms for Religious Studies*, edited by Mark C. Taylor, 256–268. Chicago: University of Chicago Press, 1998.

——. "The Phrase *sa pṛthivīpradeśaś caityabhūto bhavet* in the Vajracchedikā: Notes on the Cult of the Book in Mahāyāna." *Indo-Iranian Journal* 17 (1975): 147–81.

Scott, Jamie, and Paul Simpson-Housley, eds. *Sacred Places and Profane Spaces: Essays in the Geographics of Judaism, Christianity, and Islam*. Westport, CT: Greenwood Press, 1991.

Sells, Michael. *The Bridge Betrayed: Religion and Genocide in Bosnia*. Berkeley: University of California Press, 1998.

Sen, Amartya. *Identity and Violence: The Illusion of Destiny*. New York: Norton, 2006.

Seshyadri, H. V., ed. *RSS: A Vision in Action*. Bangalore: Sahitya Sindhu Prakashana, 1988.

Shafi, Sophia. "Muslim Monsters from Prophet Muhammad to Bin Laden: Stereotypical Images of the Muslim Male." PhD diss., Iliff School of Theology and the University of Denver, 2010.

Sheldrake, Philip. *Spaces for the Sacred: Place, Memory, and Identity*. Baltimore: Johns Hopkins University Press, 2001.

Shepherd, Robert. "UNESCO and the Politics of Cultural Heritage in Tibet." *Journal of Contemporary Asia* 36, no. 2 (2006): 243–257.

Sherman, Daniel, and Terry Nardin, eds. *Terror, Culture, Politics: Rethinking 9/11*. Bloomington: Indiana University Press, 2006.

Shields, Rob. *Places on the Margin: Alternative Geographies of Modernity*. London: Routledge, 1991.

Shinohara, Koichi. "The Story of the Buddha's Begging Bowl: Imagining a Biography and Sacred Places." In *Pilgrims, Patrons, and Places: Localizing Sancitity in Asian Religions*, edited by Phyllis Granoff and Koichi Shinohara, 68–107. Toronto: UBC Press, 2003.

Shyrock, Andrew, ed. *Islamophobia/Islamofilia: Beyond the Politics of Enemy and Friend*. Bloomington: Indiana University, 2010.

Simpson, David. *9/11: The Culture of Commemoration*. Chicago: University of Chicago Press, 2006.

Simpson, Moira G. *Making Representations: Museums in the Post-Colonial Era*. London: Routledge, 1996.

Sing, Bahadur, and Rai Ram Anugrhraha Narain. *A Brief History of Bodh Gayā Math, District Gayā*. Calcutta: Bengal Secretariat Press, 1893.

Smith, Jonathan Z. "The Bare Facts of Ritual." *History of Religions* 20 (1980): 112–127.

——. "Differential Equations: On Constructing the Other." In *Relating Religion: Essays in the Study of Religion*, 230–251. Chicago: University of Chicago Press, 2004.

——. *Map Is Not Territory: Studies in the History of Religions*. Chicago: University of Chicago Press, 1978.

——. *To Take Place: Toward Theory in Ritual*. Chicago: University of Chicago Press, 1987.

Snellgrove, David, ed. *The Image of the Buddha*. Paris: UNESCO, 1978.

Soifer, Aviam. "The Fullness of Time." In *Religion and the Law: Obligation of Citizenship and Demands of Faith*, edited by Nancy Rosenblum, 245–179. Princeton, NJ: Princeton University Press, 2000.

Soja, Edward W. *Postmodern Geographies: The Reassertion of Space in Critical Social Theory*. London: Verso, 1989.

——. *Thirdspace: Journeys to Los Angeles and Other Real-and-Imagined Places*. Oxford: Blackwell, 1996.

Sondhi, M. L., and Apratim Mukarji, editors. *The Black Book of Gujarat*. Delhi: Manak Publications, 2002.

Sosis, Richard. *"Why Sacred Lands Are Not Indivisible: The Cognitive Foundations of Sacralising Land." Journal of Terrorism Research* 2, no. 1 (2011): 17–44.

Spooner, Brian. "The Function of Religion in Persian Society." *Iran* 1 (1963): 83–96.

Sturken, Marita. *Tourists of History: Memory, Kitsch, and Consumerism from Oklahoma City to Ground Zero*. Durham, NC: Duke University Press, 2007.

Suagee, Dean B. "Tribal Voices in Historic Preservation: Sacred Landscapes, Cross-Cultural Bridges, and Common Ground." *Vermont Law Review* 21 (1996):145–224.

Swearer, Donald K. "Hypostatizing the Buddha: Buddhist Image Consecration in Northern Thailand." *History of Religions* 34 (1995): 263–280.

Tachiki, Satoko. "Okakura Kakuzo (1862–1913) and Boston Brahmins." PhD diss., University of Michigan, 1986.

Tambiah, Stanley J. *Leveling Crowds: Ethnonationalist Conflicts and Collective Violence in South Asia*. Berkeley: University of California Press, 1996.

Thakur, Vijay Kumar. "Evolution of Gayā as a Religious Complex: An Historical Note." In *Pilgrimage Studies: Text and Context*, edited by D. P. Dubey, 172–191. Allahabad: Society of Pilgrimage Studies, 1990.

Thomas, J. T. "Climbing Ban Upheld at Devils Tower." *High Country News*. 27 April 1998.

Tilley, Christopher. "Introduction: Identity, Place, Landscape and Heritage." *Journal of Material Culture* 11, nos. 1/2 (2006): 7–32.

Tilly, Charles. "Contentious Conversation." *Social Research* 65, no. 3 (1998): 491–510.

Todorov, Tzvetan. "Tribunals, Apologies, Reparations, and the Search for Justine: In Search of Lost Crime." *The New Republic* (January 2001): 9–10.

Tomasky, Michael. "Battleground Zero." *The New York Review of Books*. May 1, 2003. Accessed October 19, 2011. http://www.nybooks.com/articles/archives/2003/may/01/battleground-zero/

Trainor, Kevin. *Relics, Ritual, And Representation in Buddhism: Rematerializing the Sri Lankan Theravada Tradition*. Cambridge: Cambridge University Press, 1997.

Trenckner, V., ed. *The Majjhima Nikāya*. Vol. I. London: Pali Text Society, 1888.

Trevithick, Alan. *The Revival of Buddhist Pilgrimage at Bodh Gaya (1811–1949): Anagarika Dharmapala and the Mahabodhi Temple*. Delhi: Motilala Banarsidass, 2006.

Trompf, Garry. *In Search of Origins*. New Delhi: Sterling, 1990.

Tuan, Yi-Fu. *Topophilia: A Study of Environmental Perception, Attitudes, and Values*. Englewood Cliffs, NJ: Prentice Hall, 1974.

Turner, Victor. *Dramas, Fields, and Metaphors: Symbolic Action in Human Society*. Ithaca: Cornell University Press, 1974.

——. *The Forest of Symbols: Aspects of Ndembu Ritual*. Ithaca, NY: Cornell University Press, 1967.

——. *Process, Performance, and Pilgrimage: A Study in Comparative Symbology*. New Delhi: Concept, 1979.

——. *The Ritual Process*. Ithaca, NY: Cornell University Press, 1969.

——. "Variations on a Theme of Liminality." In *Secular Ritual*, edited by Sally Moore, 27–41. Leiden: van Gorcum, 1978.

Turner, Victor, and Edith Turner. *Image and Pilgrimage in Christian Culture*. New York: Columbia University Press, 1978.

Unmack, Fred. "Equality Under the First Amendment: Protecting Native American Religious Practices on Public Lands." *Public Land Law Review* 8 (1987): 307–339.

Vaidya, P. L., ed. *Lalitavistara*. Buddhist Sanskrit Texts 1. Dharbhanga: Mithila Insititute, 1958.

Van der Veer, Peter. *Religious Nationalism: Hindus and Muslims in India*. Berkeley: University of California Press, 1994.

Van Gelder, Geert Jan. "A Flood of Bubbling Blood and a Talking Head: John the Baptist in the Islamic Sources." Paper presented at "Saint John the Baptist and His Cults" colloquium held at St. John's College, Oxford, June 24, 2001.

Van Gennep, Arnold. *The Rites of Passage*. Translated by Monika B. Vizedom and Gabrielle L. Caffee. Chicago: University of Chicago Press, 1960.

Van Passen, C. *The Classical Tradition of Geography*. Groningen: J. B. Wolters, 1976.

Varadarajan, Siddharth. *Gujarat, the Making of a Tragedy*. London and Delhi: Penguin Books, 2002.

Vidyarthi, L. P. *The Sacred Complex in Hindu Gaya*. Bombay: Asia Publishing House, 1961.

Vogel, J. Ph. "The Earliest Sanskrit Inscriptions in Java." In *Publications van den Oudheidkundigen Dienst in Nederlandsch-Indie I: Uitgegeven door het Koninklijk Bataviaasch Genootschap van Kunsten en Vetenschappen* (1925): 17.

Waghorne, Joanne Punzo. "Dressing the Body of God: South Indian Bronze Sculpture in its Temple Setting." *Asian Art* 3 (1992): 9–34.

Waghorne, Joanne Punzo, and Norman Cutler, eds. *Gods of Flesh/Gods of Stone: The Embodiment of Divinity in India*. Chambersburg: Anima Books, 1985.

Walker, Bethany. "Commemorating the Sacred Spaces of the Past: The Mamluks and the Umayyad Mosque at Damascus." *Near Eastern Archaeology* 67, no. 1 (2004): 26–39.

Walleser, M., and H. Kopf, eds. *Monarathapūranī: Buddhaghosa's Commentary on the Anguttara Nikāya*. Vol. 1. London: The Pali Text Society, 1924.

Watkins, Joe. "Place-meant," *American Indian Quarterly* 25, no. 1 (2001): 41–45.

Weber, Paul J., ed. *Equal Separation: Understanding the Religion Clauses of the First Amendment*. New York: Greenwood Press, 1990.

Weaver, Jace, ed. *Defending Mother Earth: Native American Perspectives on Environmental Justice*. Maryknoll, NY: Orbis, 1996.

Welch, Michael. *Scapegoats of September 11th: Hate Crimes and State Crimes in the War on Terror*. Piscataway, NJ: Rutgers University Press, 2006.

Westen, Peter. "The Empty Idea of Equality." *Harvard Law Review* 95, no. 3 (1982): 537–596.

Wickremeratne, L. A. "Religion, Nationalism and Social Change in Ceylon, 1865–85." *Journal of the Royal Asiatic Society* 2 (1969): 123–150.

Williams, David C., and Susan H. Williams. "Volitionalism and Religious Liberty." *Cornell Law Review* 76 (1991): 769.

Winslow, Anastasia P. "Sacred Standards: Honoring the Establishment Clause in Protecting Native American Sacred Sites." *Arizona Law Review* 38 (1996): 1291–1343.

Winter, Jay. *Sites of Memory, Sites of Mourning: The Great War in European Cultural History*. Cambridge: Cambridge University Press, 1995.

Witte, John. "The Essential Rights and Liberties of Religion in the American Constitutional Experiment." *Notre Dame Law Review* 71 (1996).

Wolpert, Stanley. *A New History of India*. New York: Oxford University Press, 1977.

Wondolleck, Julia. "Incorporating Hard-to-Define Values into Public Lands Decision Making: a Conflict Management Perspective." In *Nature and the Human Spirit: Toward an Expanded Land Management Ethic*, edited by B. L. Driver et al., chapter 23. State College, PA: Venture Publishing, 1996.

Woodward, F. L., translator. *Udāna: Verses of Uplif and Itivuttaka: As It Was Said*. London: Pali Text Society, 1935.

Wright, Brooks. *Interpreter of Buddhism to the West: Sir Edwin Arnold*. New York: Bookman Associates, 1957.

Yaeger, Patricia. "Rubble as Archive, or 9/11 as Dust, Debris, and Bodily Vanishing." In *Trauma at Home: After 9/11*, edited by Judith Greenberg, 187–194. Lincoln: University of Nebraska Press, 2003.

Zelliot, Eleanor. *From Untouchable to Dalit: Essays on the Ambedkar Movement*. New Delhi: Manohar, 2001.

Zellmer, Sandra B. "Sustaining Geographies of Hope: Cultural Resources on Public Lands." *University of Colorado Law Review* 73 (2002): 413–519.

Zizek, Slovaj. *Welcome to the Desert of the Real!* London: Verso, 2002.

Index

45 Park Place, 40–41. *See also* Burlington Coat Factory
absence
  and Ground Zero, 33–35, 39, 55
  footprints as marker of, 57, 61, 64
Adam's Peak (also Śrī Pāda), 77
Advani, L.K., 18–19
agency, 15, 23–25, 101
  in Turners' work, 23–25
Aghaie, Kamran Scot, 147, 228
AIRFA (American Indian Religious Freedom Act), 181
Ambedkar, A.K., xii
Ambedkar Buddhists, xii, 136–139, 141
American Society for Muslim Advancement, 41
Amitābha, 109–111
aniconism thesis, 61
anti-structure, 9, 22
Antiquities Act, 173, 182
Appadurai, Arjun, 143, 174, 192
Arad, Michael, 33–35
Archaeological Survey of India, 99, 121–22, 173, 186, 189, 205n.8
Arnold, Sir Edwin, xvi, 13, 82–83, 85–89, 91, 95–99, 101–103, 105, 108, 122, 136, 218n.74
Asher, Frederick, 59, 104
Ashkelon, 145–146, 148–149, 154–155
Ashura, 159, 165–166, 168
Atlas Shrugged, website, 40, 47
Ayodhya, xvi, xix, 6–7, 9, 13–22, 26–28, 30–31, 46, 54, 59, 80–81, 133, 137–138, 147, 150, 160
  and pilgrimage, 14
  as fluid, 6, 59
  as symbol, 7
  as synechdoche, 14
  and Turners, 14
  history of, 15
  yātrās, 21
avatāra (also avatar), 74
  Buddha as, 93, 101–103, 106–108, 110, 139
  Rāma, 16

Babar, 7, 15
Babri Masjid, 15–16, 19, 49, 150, 197n.44
  destruction of, 21–22, 24, 47
Bajrang Dal, 18–19, 198n.69
  and Turner, 24
Baksh, Hossain, 84–85
Bamiyan, destruction of Buddhas, 143–144, 155
  and UNESCO, 144, 192
  rebuilding, 229n.27
Bareau, André, 65, 207n.22
Basso, Keith, 178
Bayley, Sir Charles Stuart, 130–131

Bear Lodge 173, 175, 188. *See also* Devil's Tower *and* Mato Tipila
  legal case, 172–73, 177
  Multiple Use Association, 177
Behari, Bepin, 107–108
Bender, Barbara, ix
Bhabha, Homi, 5, 189
Bhaktin, Mikhail, 59, 68
Bhardwaj, Surinder, 158
BJP (Bharata Janata Parishad), 18–21, 25
Bloomberg, Michael, 43
blurring. *See also* fluidity, hybridity, *and* multivalence
  of Buddha image's identity, xiv, 74
  and relics, 61
  conversion of, 78–79
  of footprints' iconography, 56–57, 70–77, 103
  of origins, 67–68
  of religious identities, xiv, xix, 4–5, 155
Bodhgayā, ix, xii, 67–68, 70, 72, 81–144, 174, 175, 188–190, 206. *See also* Arnold, Edwin *and* Dharmapala, Anagarika
  and colonialism, 81–84
  as Jerusalem, 89
  as living a temple, 118
  as Mecca, 89
  as Secondspace, xvi
  as tourist site, 121, 126–129
  as a World Heritage Site, 118–144
  court case, 106–112
  early restoration of, 130–134
  footprints at, 70–79
  Hindu presence at, 87–88, 92–93, 95, 98–101, 105–109
  relation to Gayā, 68–69
body, relics as, 61–64
borders, 5, 188–189
Bourdieu, Pierre, xvii, 2, 24, 32, 50, 52, 164
Bourdillon, James, 94–95
Boyarin, Daniel, 5, 188
Braudel, Fernand, 187
bricoleur, xvii
Brown, Peter, 157, 159,
British East India Company, 86
Buber, Martin, 9–10, 12
Buchanan, Francis, 86–88, 95, 130, 132, 134
Buddha, the, 56–79
  as an *avatāra*, 93, 101–103, 106–108, 110, 139
  at Rajgīr, ix–x
  and Vaśiṣṭha, 30–32
  blurred identity of, xiv
Buddha image, 81–82, 84–85, 92–95, 97–98, 100, 102–112. *See also* footprints of, relics of, *and* Bamiyan
  veneration by Hindus, xi, xiv, xiv, xix 60, 114, 122, 136, 139
Buddhaghosa, 63
Buddhism, orientalist depictions of, 60, 84, 88–89, 94–102, 133–134
  relationship to Hinduism, xix, 60, 90, 93–102, 108, 114, 133, 139
Burlington Coat Factory, 33, 40–41, 52
Bush, George W., 53, 164
Butler, Judith, 46, 52, 55, 95
Byrne, Denis, 133, 135
Bynum, Caroline Walker, 12–13

caitya, 65–66, 75
cakra, motif on footprints 73–74
Casey, Edward, 156
Cathedral of St. John, 150
cathedral, Yosemite as, 170
cetiya, 65–66
Chidester, David, 2–3, 188
classification, and colonialism, 58. *See also* taxonomy
  and the sacred, 178
  of footprints, 64–67, 74

of images, 212n.68
of relics, 64, 74
climbing ban, 176, 184, 235, 257
Cohen, Erik, 223n.26
Cohn, Bernard, 58, 127
Collins, Richard B., 180
colonialism, 58, 60, 76, 81, 84, 88, 119, 127–28, 133–34, 141, 172. *See also* Archaeological Survey of India, Bodhgayā, Buddhism, classification, *and* taxonomy
communitas, 6–14, 17–20, 22, 24–25, 83, 114, 159, 162–163
forms of, 10–11, 14
Community Board no. 1, 42, 54
comparison, xvii–xviii, 49, 67, 88, 100, 144, 188
comparative religion, xi, 188
Comstock, Richard, 51
conservation, 124–125, 128, 133–135. *See also* preservation *and* restoration
Conservation Plan, for Bodhgayā, 122–123
contentious repertoires, 32
conversion, 4–5, 60, 67, 78, 100
Cordoba House, 40–42, 47, 54. *See also* Park51
Cresswell, Tim, 174
Curzon, Viceroy Lord, 94

D'Oyly, Charles, 89–90
Dabashi, Hamid, 160, 163–165
Dakṣa, 28–29
Dalit, xii, 4, 115, 137–138, 190
Dalmia, Vasudha, 83
Damascus, Great Mosque of, xix, 145–154, 158. *See also* Umayyad Mosque
Danell, William, 89
Dasein, 163, 175
Davis, Richard, 17, 59, 104–105, 197n.44, 205n.8
Deloria, Vine Jr., 175, 181–183
Derrida, Jaques, 35, 152, 155, 172
Development Plan, for Bodhgayā, 122, 127, 129, 140
Devils Tower, 138, 173–179, 182, 184–186, 188, 190. *See also* Mato Tipila
Dharmapala, Anagarika, 84–85, 87, 89–96, 98–114, 131, 135–138
relationship with Henry Steele Olcott, 85, 90–93, 112
difference, xvii–xviii, 7–8, 21, 23, 114, 167
Diller, Elizabeth, 35
Doṇa, 63
Doniger, Wendy, xvii
Doyle, Tara, 138
Dubuisson, Daniel, 180
Durkheim, Émile, 2–3, 12, 21, 23–24, 50, 53–54, 169, 178–179, 191
dust, 36–37, 39, 41

Eade, John, 174
effervescence, 24
Edney, Matthew 132
ekamata yajña, 16
El-Gamal, Sharif, 41–42
Elgin, Lord 109, 219n.102
Eliade, Mircea, 2–3, 161, 167
erasure, 35, 62, 150, 152, 155–156, 172
Errington, Shelly, 142–143
Establishment Clause, 176, 185, 191
exceptionalism, 38
externalization, 22–23

Faxian, x, 77, 121, 130, 210n.45
FCMP (Final Climbing Management Plan), 176–177
fences, 187–89, 191
Firstpace, xvi, 190
Fixico, Donald, 179
footprint,
blurred identities of, 28, 56–57, 67–68, 73–78, 81, 103, 190

footprint (*Cont.*)
of the Buddha, 61–67, 72
at Ground Zero, 33–36, 38
of Viṣṇu, 70–71
Foucault, Michel, xvi, 46, 129, 132, 135, 143, 171–172, 189
Fowle, Bruce, 36
Flood, Finbarr Barry, 150, 227n.86
fluidity, xiii, xiv, 4–6, 9, 32, 50, 52, 56–57, 59–60, 65, 68, 76–77, 104–105, 118–119, 125, 128, 135, 146, 164, 167. *See also* blurring, hybridity, *and* multivalence
Fresh Kills landfill, 36–37, 41
Freud, Sigmund, 22–23
Friedland, Roger, 3
Frost, Robert, 187–188, 191

Gayā, xii, 57, 68–72, 75–78, 97, 100, 106, 109, 132, 210–211n.53, 211n.55
Gayāmahātmya, 71
Gayāsura, 71
Geller, Pamela, 47
Gingrich, Newt, 48, 53, 202n.43
Girard, René, 31, 199n 78
Giris, 82, 87, 99, 106–107, 109–110, 132. *See also* Bodhgayā, Hindu presence at
Gonda, Jan, 102, 219
Great Mosque of Damascus, xix, 146–154, 172. *See also* Damascus
great tradition, 11
Griffin, Rayanne, 179
Ground Zero, xvi, xix, 25–26, 31–40, 44, 46–55, 57, 59, 162, 191, 204n.67. *See also* Park51
Ground Zero Mosque, 26, 31, 48, 53. *See also* Park51 *and* Cordoba House

habitus, 24, 32, 50, 52, 164, 231n.64
Hansen, Thomas Blom, 20–22
Hanuman, 15–16, 19
Harvey, David, 169, 186
Hassner, Ron, 167, 231n.81
Haugeland, John, 163
head
of Husayn, xix, 145–149
of John the Baptist, xix, 145, 147–154
Hecht, Richard D., 3
Heidegger, Martin, xvi, 35, 162–164, 175, 178, 186. See also *Dasein*
Herzfeld, Michael, 138
heterotopia, 129, 150
Hindutva, 15, 21–22, 24, 139
Holmwood, Herbert, 110–111
Hornborg, Alf, 179
Human Geography, 162
Huntington, Samuel, 46
Husayn (also Hossein), 145–149, 154, 158–161, 164–166
Huyssen, Andreas, 30, 78, 150, 154–155
hybridity, xiii, 5, 188–191. *See also* blurring, fluidity, *and* multivalence
Hyder, Syed Akbar, 156, 161

I-Thou, 9–10
ICOMOS (International Council on Monuments and Sites), 119
identity, xiii–xiv, xvi, 2–10, 15, 19, 21, 32, 46, 82, 84, 95, 103, 114, 138, 147, 149, 155, 160, 163–164, 166–167, 170, 178, 186, 189–190, 196n.20, 199n.78. *See also* fluidity, hybridity, *and* pilgrimage
of images, 56–61, 68, 73, 76–79, 104–105, 110, 138 (*see also* footprints)
of places, 26, 30, 81, 106, 170, 175
Iran-Iraq war, 162, 165
Israel, destruction of mosques, 154–155
Israeli West Bank Barrier, 188, 191

Jailas, 69
janmabhūmi (also *janmabhoomi*), 16, 18

Jerusalem, 3, 7, 27, 49, 81, 152–154, 157–158, 166
Bodhgayā as, xvi, 87, 89, 91, 97
John the Baptist, xix, 145, 147–150, 152–154

Kakar, Sudhir, 13, 22–23, 54, 199n.78
Karbala, xvi, 12, 147–149, 155–156, 158–168. *See also* Ashura
fluidity of, 164, 167–168
campaign, 165
complex, 160, 163, 165
karsevak, 20, 198–199n.69
Kertzer, David, 23, 199
Khan, Daisy, 41–42, 49
Kister, David, 158
Klostermaier, Klaus, 102, 219
Kufa, 146, 151, 158

Lakota, 173, 177
Lal, Nanda Kishore, 106, 113
Laloo, Yadav, 137
LaVerdier, Julian, 35
Lazio, Rick, 40, 43
Lefebrve, Henri, xv, xvi, xviii, 195n.9
Leoshko, Janice, 89, 216–217n.38
Lévi-Strauss, Claude, xvii, 3, 195
liminality, 6–7, 9, 12–14, 21, 24, 83, 114
Linenthal, Edward T., 2–3
liṅgam, 60, 78, 99–100, 122–123, 206n.8. See also *stūpa*, as *liṅgam*
little tradition, 11
living temple, 118, 124, 126, 132, 138, 140–141
LMDC (Lower Manhattan Development Corporation), 34, 38, 205
lok śākti, 19
Lough Derg, 11, 162
Low, Setha, 40
Lower Manhattan, xvi, 31, 33–34, 37–43, 52. *See also* LMDC
Ludden, David, 15, 225n.50
ludic, 7, 14, 20

Macpherson, George, 108–110, 220n.119
Macpherson, William, 110–111
Mahabodhi Society, 107, 113
Mahābodhi Temple (also Mahābodhi Vihāra), xii, 76, 82, 84–85, 94, 105–108, 114, 117, 119, 124, 131–32, 136–139, 190. See *also* Arnold, Sir Edwin, Bodhgayā, Dharmapala, Anagarika, *and* WHS
as a WHS, 117–119, 122–129, 135, 137–142
Hindu presence at, 76, 87–89, 92–93, 97–99, 106–112, 133
management of, 112, 115, 117, 119, 121–122, 136, 138–140
models of, 131–132, 134
restoration of, 86, 100–101, 130–131
Mahant, 16, 82, 85, 88, 92–94, 98–100, 106–113, 130–131, 137
Mahāparinibānnasuta, 62–63, 66, 121
Marcus, George, 2
Markham, Robert, 157–158
martyrdom, 11–12, 19–20, 146, 148, 159, 163
Mashad, 159, 161
Masjid Al-Farah, 52
Masjid Manhattan, 52
math, 82, 87, 99, 215n.19. *See also* Bodhgayā, Hindu presence at *and* Mahābodhi, Hindu presence at
Mather, Stephen, 170
Mato Tipila, xvi, xix, 81, 172–173, 175, 177–180, 182, 185–186. *See also* Devils Tower
Memorial Quadrant, 38, 49
messiness, ix, xiii, xvi, xvii, 2–3, 27, 136, 173, 191
Miller, Bruce G., 180, 182–184
Mitra, Rajendralala, 67–68, 70, 73–75, 87–88, 90, 100–103, 105, 107, 130–131, 134, 141, 210n.48, 220n.106
monumental heterogeneity, 136

Morinis, Alan, 30
mosque, xix, 7, 15–16, 20–22, 26, 31, 41–43, 47–49, 51, 53–54, 146–155, 158, 168, 172, 190, 202, 204, 228–229, 238, 245, 258
Mountain States Legal Foundation, 177
Müller, Friedrich Max, 89
multivalence, 57, 68, 76–77, 103, 105. *See also* blurring, fluidity, *and* hybridity
mūrti, xix, 71, 107–108, 212n.68
museums, effect on images, 57–58, 73, 75, 77, 118–119, 135, 142, 144, 205n.4, 205–206n.8, 221, 223, 226n.64
Myoda, Paul, 35

Najaf, 148, 159–161
Nakash, Yitzhak, 159
Nandy, Ashis, 20, 25
Nasr, S.H., 157
Nasr, Vali, 159
National Parks, 169–172, 176, 179, 184, 189–190
National Register of Historic Places, 173, 182
Native Americans
  absence in National Parks, 171–172
  conception of Devils Tower, 173–177, 179–180, 185–186, 191
  conception of the sacred, 180–186
Ndembu, 8, 13
Nehru, Jawarhalal, 16, 82
NPS (National Park Service), 176, 179

Okakura, Kakuzo, 111–112
Olcott, Henry Steele, 85–93, 113, 219n.101
Olmstead, Frederick Law, 170, 177
Omar, Mullah Mohammad, 143
Organic Act of 1916, 171, 184
Orientalism, 4, 81–82, 84–85, 89–95, 99–102, 107, 115, 129, 133, 140–141, 225n.50
origins, obsession with, 4, 60, 67–68, 70–72, 76–77, 88–89, 210n.50, 216n.33
Orsi, Robert, ix, 191
Other, conception of the, 4, 10, 22, 31, 43, 46–47, 52, 55, 81, 84, 88–89, 94, 144, 188, 199n.78, 204n.74
Otto, Rudolph, 3, 81–82,
Owens, Bruce Owens, 134, 140
ownership, 32, 106–107, 109, 120–121, 142, 175, 181, 186

pāda. *See* footprints
palimpsest, 30–31, 78, 134, 156
panopticon, 171
panoramic view, 171, 177
Park51, 31, 33, 41–43, 46–49, 51–55, 80–81, 118, 133, 138, 191. *See also* Cordoba House, Ground Zero, Ground Zero Mosque, Khan, Daisy, *and* Rauf, Imam Feisal Abdul
Pataki, George, 34–37, 43, 48–49, 51
Paul, Debjani, 67, 70, 73
Pelletier, Stephen, 165
Petefish, Andy, 177, 184–185, 190
picturesque, 89, 132, 171, 224n.38
Pilgrimage
  Arnold, Edwin, xvi, 97
  Buddhist, x, 66, 86, 91, 103, 115, 130 (*see also* Bodhgayā *and* Mahābodhi Temple)
  Christian, 153, 156–157
  contested, 7, 15,
  Ground Zero as, 51
  Hindu, xi, xiii, 15–18, 132 (*see also* Karbala)
  and identity, 4
  Karbala, 148, 155–162
  Muslim attitudes toward, 149, 157–158
  non-Hajj, 157–158
  Rāma's bricks, 7, 17

and tourism, 126, 194n.5
Turners on, 1, 6–11, 19, 21, 23, 25, 83, 162
Porto, 142
Prasad, Rajendra, 115
prayer bundles, 173, 176
preservation, 102, 117–119, 140–144, 170–171, 173, 179, 182–184, 187–92. *See also* conservation *and* restoration
Preston, James, 194n.5
Pryor, Stefan, 38
pūjā, xiv, xix, 64, 101, 78, 99–101, 115. See also *Rām śīla pūjā*

Rām śīla pūjā, 17–18, 21
Rāma (also Rām), 7, 15–18
Rāmayāna, 16, 19
ratra, 18
Rath Yātrā, 18–19
Rauf, Imam Feisal Abdul, 41–42, 49, 52, 54, 191
Reflecting Absence, 33
relic
Buddhist conceptions of, 61–67, 207n.22, 209n.30, 210 n.45 (*see also* footprint)
Head of Husayn as, 147, 149
Muslim attitude toward, 145, 158
Native American artifacts as, 172
John the Baptist, of, 152–154
markers of absence, 35
spread of Christianity, 154–158
Umayyad use of, 152, 154
Relph, Edward, 162
restoration, 136, 138, 140. *See also* conservation *and* preservation
of Bamiyan Buddhas, 143
of Bodhgayā, 86–88, 91–92, 95, 119, 121–126, 130–136, 138, 140, 142–143
and UNESCO, 119–123, 142–143
Ṛg Veda, 70–72
Ricoeur, Paul 55
ritual, xiii, 10–13, 18, 22–25, 29, 37, 56–59, 67–69, 70–73, 75, 78, 85, 88–89, 94, 98, 102, 104, 106, 110, 116, 123–124, 126–127, 137, 139, 147, 159–161, 164–168, 173, 175–176, 178, 185–186, 190, 197n.38, 199n.78, 219n.62
rock climbers, 172–177, 179, 184–185, 190–191. *See also* climbing ban
Roosevelt, Theodore, 173, 179
Ross-Bryant, Lynn, 170–171, 189–190
Roy, Sanjit, 115
RSS (Rashtriya Swayamsevak Sangh), 21, 196n.20, 198–199n.69

Saccabandha, 64–65
sacred
Bodhgayā as, 80, 87, 91, 93, 97–98, 129, 133, 139
as construct, 2–3, 6, 25–26, 27, 32, 55, 129, 142, 154, 186, 188, 191
definition of, xviii, 2–3, 50–52, 142, 161, 167, 175, 178–186, 191–192, 194n.5
emplacement of, 157–158
Devils Tower as, 175–179, 188
Durkheim's conception of, 50, 54, 178–179 (*see also* Durkheim, Émile)
National Parks as, 170, 171–173, 190
Native American conceptions of, 173–175, 177–186, 191
and otherness, 46, 48–50, 52
and ritual, 168
Tārapīṭh as, 29–30, 32
time, 157
Ground Zero as, 27, 33–34, 36, 38, 51–55
śākta pīṭha, 28–32
śākti, 28–30
Sallnow, Michael, 174
sanātana dharma, 114
sandals, of Rāma, 21

Sasai, Bhadant Nagarjun Surai, 138–139
Satī, 28–30, 32
Schama, Simon, 170
Schopen, Gregory, 61, 66, 89
Secondspace, xvi, 190
Sen, Amartya, 82
September 11, xvi, 27, 40, 45–46, 52–53
shadow of Ground Zero, 38–39, 50–51, 55
Shah of Iran, 164, 166
Shariati, Ali, 164
Shī'a (also Shī'i), xvi, 145–149, 155, 157–168
Shields, Rob, xviii, 27, 164, 231n.64
Silverstein, Larry, 37
Simpson, David, 35
SIOA (Stop Islamization of America), 47–48
Śiva (also Siva), xi, 28–32, 71, 77–78, 100, 114, 122. See also *liṅgam*
Smith, Jonathan Z., xvii–xviii, 2, 13, 37, 154, 156–157, 166–167, 192
Soja, Edward, xv–xviii
sous rature, 35, 152. *See also* erasure
Snellgrove, David, 61
spatialisation, 164, 231n.64
Spencer, Robert, 42, 47
Spooner, Brian, 166
śraddhā (also shraddha), 87–88, 97
Śrī Pāda (also Adam's Peak), 77
Stietencron, Heinrich von, 83
strategy, 143, 180
stūpa (also stupa), 64–66, 75, 78, 99, 127, 129, 135–136
  as *liṅgam*, 60, 78, 99–100, 122–123, 206n.8
Sturken, Marita, 33–36, 39
Sun Dance, 173
Sunni, 15, 147–149, 157–158, 166
Swayambhu, 140, 228n.88

Tagore, Rabindanath, 112, 114
Taliban, 143–144, 155, 192, 227–28n.87, 229n.27
Tārā, 28–32
Tārāpiṭh, 28–32
taxonomy, 58, 60, 76, 99, 128, 132. *See also* classification *and* colonialism
Temple Act, 226
Temple Mount, 3, 49
Temple of Jupiter, 150
Thirdspace, xv–xviii, 190, 193–194
Tilley, Christopher, 199
Tilly, Charles, 1, 25, 32–33, 194, 199n.81
Todorov, Tzvetan, 123
tomb, xiii, 32
  of Husayn, 161, 165
  of Imams, 158–159, 161
  of John the Baptist, 153–154
topophilia, 162
tourism, xii, 116, 120–121, 126–129, 142, 223n.26
Trainor, Kevin, 63–64
Trevithick, Alan, 112
Tuan, Yi-Fu, 162
Turner, Edith and Victor, 1, 4, 6–14, 19–25, 32, 83, 114, 194–197, 199–200, 214
Twin Towers, 28, 34–35, 37, 52, 57

Umayyad
  Dynasty, 146, 151–152, 154, 172
  Mosque. *See* Great Mosque of Damascus
UNESCO (United Nations Education, Science, and Culture Organization), 117–121, 124, 126, 128, 138–144, 171, 174–175, 186, 189, 192, 222n.3, 227n.87, 229. *See also* conservation, preservation, *and* restoration
United Flight 175, 40

Vaiṣṇava, xi–xiii, 57, 61, 68, 73–78, 85, 99, 102, 106–108, 216. *See also* Bodhgayā, Hindu presence at, Buddha image, veneration by Hindus, *and* footprint

van der Leeuw, Gerardus, 3
van Gennep, Arnold, 13–14
Vaśiṣṭha, 29–30
VHP (Vishva Hindu Parishad), 16–21, 25
Viṣṇu, xiv, xix, 28–30, 82, 101, 102–103, 107, 219n.93. *See also* Vaiṣṇava
  footprint of, 56–57, 67–78, 81, 190, 211n.57 (*see also* footprint, blurred identities)
  images of, 60, 94, 100, 106–108, 110, 122 (*see also* Buddha image, veneration by Hindus)
Vivekananda, Swami, 112
Vulture's Peak, x–xii, xiv, xix, 104

Wahhabis, 160
WHS (World Heritage Site), 117–129, 131–132, 136–144. *See also* UNESCO
Williams, Mark, 43
Winter, Jay, 34
World Trade Center, 27, 31, 35, 37, 39–41, 43–44, 46, 48, 52, 54–55, 142, 160, 201. *See also* Ground Zero

Yaeger, Patricia, 36
yātrā, 18–19, 21, 198
Yazid, 146–147, 164–165

Zizek, Slovoj, 202